Bicycle for the Mind

E.B Cohen

First edition, 2026

Contents

Bicycle for the Mind

A History of the Personal Computer Revolution

E.B Cohen

First edition, 2026.

This is a work of popular history. It rests on the public record of the personal-computer age — the machines themselves and the magazines that announced them, the patents and product manuals, the corporate histories and antitrust filings, the oral histories collected by the Computer History Museum, and the reporting and book-length accounts of those who covered this industry as it happened, among them Paul Freiberger and Michael Swaine, Steven Levy, Michael Hiltzik, Robert X. Cringely, and Walter Isaacson. It does not invent events or put words into mouths that the record does not support. Where a figure is disputed, where a familiar story turns out to be a myth, or where the evidence simply runs out, the text says so plainly.

For everyone who ever typed a first command into a blinking cursor — and wondered what the machine would do next.

> "What a computer is to me is the most remarkable tool that we have ever come up with. It's the equivalent of a bicycle for our minds." — Steve Jobs

> "The best way to predict the future is to invent it." — Alan Kay, Xerox PARC

> "Never trust a computer you can't throw out a window." — a hobbyist's proverb from the early years

A Note on Names, Numbers, and Memory

The people in this book did not know, while they were living it, that they were making history. That is worth holding onto, because hindsight flattens everything into inevitability. In 1975 it was entirely reasonable to believe that computers would always be the property of governments and large corporations, that no ordinary person would ever need one, and that the men and women soldering circuit boards in garages and hotel ballrooms were harmless hobbyists chasing a toy. The story told here is dramatic precisely because, for a long time, the smart money was on the other side.

A word about numbers. Much of this story is well documented — machines were reviewed, sales were reported, lawsuits produced sworn testimony — but some of the most interesting quantities are slippery. Early companies rose and collapsed too fast for careful accounting; unit-sales claims were often marketing; and the private fortunes made and lost were frequently guessed at. Where this book gives such figures, they are the best available estimates, and are named as estimates.

A word about memory. Many of the founding stories of the personal computer — the garage, the visit to Xerox, the deal that made Microsoft — have been told so often, and so lovingly, that they have hardened into legend. Legends are usually built on truth, but they smooth away the accidents, the rival claims, and the people who were written out. This book tries, where it can, to restore some of that texture: to note that the famous garage was for a while a bedroom, that the men who invented the future at Xerox mostly watched others get rich from it, and that for every celebrated founder there were engineers, spouses, and rivals whose names history mislaid.

Finally, a word about the word *revolution*. It is overused, and this book uses it deliberately. In the space of a single human lifetime, the computer went from a room-sized machine tended by specialists to an object more numerous than the human race, carried in the pockets of billions. Power over information — over calculation, communication, creation, and memory itself — passed from institutions to individuals. Whatever else it was, that was a revolution. This is the story of how it happened, and of the odd, brilliant, quarrelsome, and visionary people who, mostly without meaning to, changed the world by trying to build a computer small enough to call their own.

Chapter 1: The Machine in the Basement

In the spring of 1946, in a cramped, unair-conditioned room on the ground floor of the Moore School of Electrical Engineering at the University of Pennsylvania, a machine the size of a modest house hummed and clicked and glowed. It was called ENIAC—the Electronic Numerical Integrator and Computer—and it filled a space roughly thirty feet by fifty, its forty black steel cabinets, each nine feet tall, arranged in a great U along the walls. Inside those cabinets glowed nearly eighteen thousand vacuum tubes, each a small orange filament of light, alongside some seventy thousand resistors, ten thousand capacitors, six thousand switches, and fifteen hundred relays, all stitched together by an estimated five million hand-soldered joints. The whole assembly weighed thirty tons and drew about a hundred and sixty kilowatts of electricity—enough that a persistent Philadelphia legend held that the lights of West Philadelphia dimmed whenever the machine was switched on. The story is almost certainly apocryphal, the electrical grid being rather more robust than the tale allows, but that such a rumor could take hold and endure tells you something true about how the machine loomed in the public imagination. When ENIAC ran, banks of tiny neon lamps blinked across its face like the lights of a distant city, and the young women who operated it—mathematicians who had been recruited during the war and were called, without irony, "computers" themselves—moved among the cabinets with clipboards and cable diagrams, plugging and unplugging heavy black wires to tell the machine what to do.

There was nothing personal about it. ENIAC had been built in secret for the U.S. Army to calculate artillery firing tables, the dense sheets of numbers a gunner needed to know how high and far a shell would travel under a given set of conditions—accounting for the weight of the projectile, the powder charge, the wind, the air temperature, even the curvature and rotation of the earth over a long flight. A skilled human with a mechanical desk calculator might take twenty hours to work out a single trajectory, and a single firing table demanded thousands of them; ENIAC could compute one trajectory in about thirty seconds, faster than the shell itself would take to reach its target. That was the promise of electronic computing, and it was staggering. But the machine belonged wholly to the institution that owned it. To reprogram ENIAC for a new problem was not a matter of typing but of physically rewiring the thing—rerouting cables, resetting three thousand switches by hand—a labor that could take days, and its every waking hour was accounted for by the government that had paid roughly half a million wartime dollars to build it. A citizen off the street could no more use ENIAC than he could commandeer a battleship.

The six women who first made ENIAC compute have only lately been restored to the story, and their experience captures how alien this new kind of work was. When the machine neared completion, the Army chose them—Kay McNulty, Betty Jean Jennings, Betty Snyder, Marlyn Wescoff, Fran Bilas, and Ruth Lichterman—from among the roughly one hundred human "computers" already grinding out trajectories by hand. There were no programming languages, no manuals, no compilers; the very concept of software did not yet exist. The women taught themselves the machine from its wiring diagrams, learning by trial and error how to break a differential equation down into steps a bank of electronics could perform, then translating those steps into a physical choreography of plugged cables and dialed switches. It was intellectually ferocious work, and it was largely invisible. When the Army unveiled ENIAC to the press on February 15, 1946, in a triumphant demonstration that put the machine on the front pages, the programmers who had made the demonstration run were not introduced, not photographed as principals, not named. Some of them appeared in publicity pictures and were assumed by later viewers to be models posed for decoration. Only in the 1990s, when historians revisited the records for the machine's fiftieth anniversary, did their contribution come fully to light. It is a fitting emblem for an age in which the machine was celebrated and the people bent to its service were treated as interchangeable parts.

It is often said that ENIAC was the world's first digital computer and that, like the machines on your desk today, it thought in the binary ones and zeros of modern electronics. In fact ENIAC did neither thing so cleanly. It was not the first electronic digital computer—Britain's wartime Colossus machines, kept secret for decades, and John Atanasoff's earlier experimental device at Iowa State both have claims that predate it—and, more surprisingly, ENIAC did not work in binary at all. It counted in ordinary decimal, storing each digit from zero to nine in a ring of ten vacuum tubes, so that the machine's guts mirrored the ten fingers of the human hand rather than the abstract two-state logic that would later define computing. This made ENIAC in some ways closer to a colossal electronic adding machine than to its successors. The clean binary architecture we now take for granted came slightly later, and understanding that ENIAC reasoned in tens rather than twos is a useful reminder that the "obvious" foundations of computing were anything but obvious to the people inventing them.

The vacuum tubes themselves were the machine's glory and its curse. A vacuum tube is essentially a light bulb pressed into service as a switch: a glass envelope with the air pumped out, a filament that glows, and electrodes that let a small voltage control a larger flow of current, turning it on or off thousands of times a second with no moving parts. Multiply that by eighteen thousand and you have the fastest calculating engine on earth—and also a device statistically doomed to break. A tube has a lifespan, and with so many of them a few were bound to fail every day, each failure halting the machine and sending technicians hunting through the cabinets for the single dead bulb among thousands. Skeptics had predicted ENIAC would be useless, unable to run for more than a few minutes before something blew. The chief engineer, J. Presper Eckert, beat the problem with a stroke of practical genius: he ran the tubes at far below their rated power, gentle enough that they lasted, and he insisted the machine never be switched off, since the thermal shock of heating and cooling killed more tubes than steady operation ever did. Under this regime ENIAC eventually achieved stretches of days between failures—remarkable reliability for a machine its critics had written off, though even so it stood idle a good part of the time in its early years.

This was the world into which the idea of a personal computer would eventually be born, and to understand how radical that idea was, one must first understand how thoroughly the machine of the mid-twentieth century was the opposite of personal. The computers that followed ENIAC in the 1950s were commercial descendants of the same lineage, and they were enormous, expensive, and jealously guarded. When the International Business Machines Corporation—IBM, already a titan of punched-card tabulating machines—entered the electronic computer business, it built room-filling behemoths like the IBM 701 in 1952 and the later 700 and 7000 series, machines leased for tens of thousands of dollars a month to corporations, insurance companies, universities, and government agencies. A single such installation might cost more than a fleet of automobiles. These were capital assets, and they were treated accordingly.

The physical setting reinforced the sense of remove. A mainframe lived in a special room—raised floors to hide the thick cabling, heavy air-conditioning to fight the heat, sometimes glass walls so that visitors could admire the spinning tape reels without breathing on the equipment. Around the machine there grew up a kind of priesthood. The operators wore white lab coats, partly for cleanliness and partly, one suspects, for the authority the uniform conferred. They alone were permitted to touch the computer. An ordinary programmer or scientist who wanted a calculation performed did not sit down at the machine; that would have been unthinkable, like a parishioner wandering up to perform his own sacrament. Instead he wrote out his program by hand, then transferred it, one line at a time, onto stiff rectangular cards by punching patterns of holes into them with a keypunch machine. A single program might fill a deck of hundreds or thousands of cards, and woe to the person who dropped one—the sequence, once scrambled, could take hours to sort back into order. Experienced hands learned to draw a diagonal stripe across the top of a full deck with a marker, so that a dropped stack could at least be roughly reassembled by lining the stripe back up, a small human trick against a very human catastrophe.

The programmer carried his precious deck to a submission window and handed it across to an operator, as one might hand a prescription to a pharmacist. Then he waited. The computer worked in what was called batch processing: it took in one job at a time, in a queue, chewing through each in turn and printing the results on wide fan-folded paper. If the programmer was lucky, he might get his printout back in a few hours. If the computing center was busy, or if the job was scheduled for an overnight run, he might not learn the outcome until the next morning. And here was the cruelest part of the arrangement. If he had made a single mistake—a misplaced comma, a wrong card, a typo in a variable name—the machine would halt, the run would fail, and the printout would tell him only that something had gone wrong. He would fix the error, punch a new card, resubmit the deck, and wait again. A task that a later generation would perform in seconds could stretch across days of submission and waiting, the human mind held perpetually at arm's length from the machine that was supposed to serve it. It is a discipline hard to imagine now, when a mistyped line of code is corrected and rerun in the same breath, but for a generation of scientists it was simply what thinking with a computer felt like: slow, formal, and mediated by a wall of specialists.

The turning point of the middle era came in April 1964, when IBM bet the company on a bold and expensive gamble called the System/360. The name promised coverage of a full circle of needs, and the idea was genuinely revolutionary in its own right: instead of building incompatible machines for different customers, IBM would offer a whole family of computers, from small to large, that all spoke the same language and ran the same software. A business could buy a modest model and, as it grew, upgrade to a larger one without throwing away its programs. The System/360 was one of the great industrial undertakings of the age, costing IBM some five billion dollars to develop—more, adjusted for inflation, than the Manhattan Project—and it nearly broke the firm in the process. It succeeded so completely that it defined corporate computing for a generation and made IBM synonymous with the computer itself. Yet for all its brilliance, the System/360 was still a mainframe—a machine for institutions, tended by specialists, sitting behind glass in a climate-controlled room.

Even in this cathedral age, though, two heresies were quietly taking root that would eventually crack the whole edifice open. The first was time-sharing. Researchers at MIT and elsewhere had grown impatient with the tyranny of batch processing and asked a simple, subversive question: what if a single powerful computer could switch its attention so rapidly among many users that each of them felt, at his own terminal, as though he had the whole machine to himself? By the early 1960s, working systems demonstrated exactly that. A user sat at a teletype or a screen, typed a command, and received a response within seconds—an intimacy with the computer that batch processing had never allowed. Time-sharing did not put a machine on anyone's desk, but it planted a seductive idea: that a person might have a direct, conversational relationship with a computer, thinking alongside it rather than mailing requests to a distant altar.

The second heresy was smallness. In 1965 a scrappy company from Massachusetts called Digital Equipment Corporation, founded by an MIT-trained engineer named Ken Olsen, introduced the PDP-8. It was not a mainframe and did not pretend to be one. It cost around eighteen thousand dollars—a fraction of the price of an IBM installation—and it was compact enough to sit on a bench or roll around on a cart, small enough that a single laboratory or a small business could own one outright rather than renting a slice of something larger. DEC called it a minicomputer, and it sold by the tens of thousands. For the first time, a computer could belong to a department, a research group, even a determined individual. The machine was climbing out of the basement.

You can still feel ENIAC's shadow in the pocket you carry. The phone in your hand runs on the very binary logic ENIAC lacked, packs the work of those eighteen thousand tubes into transistors far too small to see, and answers you in the same breath you ask—the exact conversational intimacy the mainframe priesthood forbade. Every time you correct a typo and it simply fixes itself, with no deck to repunch and no overnight wait, you are enjoying the precise freedom that the scientists of 1946 could only dream of. The distance between their world and ours is the story this book sets out to tell.

The dream of a truly personal computer, however, would

not begin with an engineer at all, but with a wartime administrator sitting down after the war to imagine a machine that could hold the whole of a person's memory in its head.

Chapter 2: As We May Think

In July 1945, as the war in the Pacific ground toward its violent conclusion, readers of The Atlantic Monthly opened their magazines to find an essay by a man who had spent the previous six years commanding the largest scientific enterprise in American history. Vannevar Bush was no dreamy futurist. A gruff, pipe-smoking engineer from Massachusetts, he had built analog calculating machines at MIT in the 1930s—including a room-sized mechanical marvel called the Differential Analyzer that solved equations with spinning shafts and gears—and during the war he had served as director of the Office of Scientific Research and Development, the agency that marshaled some six thousand American scientists and oversaw everything from radar to the proximity fuze to the Manhattan Project itself. He was, in a real sense, the man who had organized American science for total war, and he had the ear of two presidents. And now, with victory in sight, he was turning his mind to a different question—one that had less to do with weapons than with the burden that all this new knowledge would place upon the human mind. His essay was titled "As We May Think," and it would echo for the rest of the century.

The timing was deliberate and freighted with feeling. Bush had watched the machinery of science he built be turned toward destruction, and the essay carries an undertone of a man hoping to point that machinery somewhere better. When the piece was reprinted two months later, in an abridged and lavishly illustrated form, it did not appear in some obscure technical journal but in Life, the most popular magazine in America, its pages reaching millions of ordinary households between photo spreads of the war's end. Artists were commissioned to draw Bush's imagined devices—a strange desk with glowing screens, a scientist wearing a camera on his brow—so that a machinist in Ohio or a schoolteacher in Georgia could see the future sketched out in the same weekly that carried the news of the atomic bomb. Few technical essays in history have ever been placed before so vast an audience, and that accident of publication would matter enormously, because among those millions of readers, as we shall see, was a young man who would carry the essay's vision to San Francisco two decades later.

Bush's worry was simple and, in retrospect, prophetic. The world's store of recorded knowledge was growing faster than any person could hope to follow. "There is a growing mountain of research," he wrote, and the investigator was "staggered by the findings and conclusions of thousands of other workers—conclusions which he cannot find time to grasp, much less to remember." Whole discoveries lay buried and forgotten in the avalanche of publication, not because they were wrong but because no one could locate them again. He offered a haunting example: the work of the Austrian monk Gregor Mendel, who founded the science of genetics, had lain unread and unappreciated for a generation simply because the handful of people capable of grasping it never happened upon it. The problem, Bush argued, was not that people were failing to think, but that the tools for storing and retrieving what they thought were hopelessly primitive. Libraries organized their holdings alphabetically and numerically, by rigid categories, when the human mind did nothing of the kind. The mind, he observed, "operates by association." It leaps from one idea to the next along a web of connections, "in accordance with some intricate web of trails carried by the cells of the brain." Why, he asked, should our machines not work the same way?

From that question Bush conjured a device. He called it the Memex, a compression of "memory" and "index," and he described it in loving, concrete detail even though he knew the technology to build it did not yet exist. The Memex, as he imagined it, would be a desk—an ordinary-looking piece of office furniture with slanting translucent screens set into its top, a keyboard, and sets of buttons and levers. Inside, on spools of microfilm, would rest the whole of a person's books, records, letters, and notes, compressed so tightly that, as Bush calculated with an engineer's relish, a man might store the entire contents of a great research library in a corner of his desk and, filling it at a furious pace, take hundreds of years to run out of room. A user could summon any document to the screen in an instant. But the true magic of the Memex lay in what Bush called associative indexing: the ability to link any two items together, so that tapping a button would carry the reader from one document directly to another he had connected to it. A researcher could build "trails" of linked materials—a chain of articles, images, and personal annotations on, say, the history of the bow and arrow—and save that trail, name it, share it, or return to it years later. Whole professions, Bush imagined, would grow up around the making of trails: "trail blazers," he called them, who found their joy in establishing useful paths through the common record. "Wholly new forms of encyclopedias will appear," he wrote, "ready-made with a mesh of associative trails running through them." It is worth walking through exactly how Bush imagined this working, because the mechanism is what makes the foresight so uncanny. To join two documents, the Memex user would call both to the twin screens, then tap a key; the machine would print a shared code number in the margin of each, and thereafter tapping that code on one document would instantly spin the microfilm to the other, in either direction. Build up a chain of such links and you had a trail; and because the codes were stored on the film alongside the documents, a whole trail could be copied and passed to a friend, who could drop it into his own Memex and follow your path through the record. Strip away the film and the levers and describe only the behavior—click a marked word, jump to the linked page, share the path with others—and you have described the web browser with almost no translation required. He was imagining, in the summer of 1945, on spinning reels of film, something very close to the hyperlink, the personal database, and the crowd-built encyclopedia all at once.

The essay ranged further still into territory that now reads like prophecy. Bush foresaw dry photography that developed itself without chemicals, machines that could take dictation and turn speech into text, and calculators that reasoned through logic rather than mere arithmetic. In one memorable passage he described a hands-free camera for the researcher of the future: "The camera hound of the future," he wrote, "wears on his forehead a lump a little larger than a walnut," snapping pictures of whatever he looks at—an image that anyone who has strapped on a wearable camera or narrated a video with a phone raised to eye level will recognize with a start. He got the details wrong almost every time; he bet on microfilm and mechanical levers when the future lay in electronics and magnetic storage. But he got the shape of the thing uncannily right.

It is often said that Vannevar Bush invented hypertext, or even that he anticipated the internet whole. That claim needs a careful correction. The Memex was never built, and Bush never intended it to be a computer at all—it contained no electronics, no logic, no programming, only microfilm, photocells, and clever mechanical linkages, an electromechanical dream from a man who had spent his life among gears. The word "hypertext" would not be coined until 1965, by a young visionary named Ted Nelson, who quoted Bush's essay at length in doing so. What Bush actually contributed was not a machine but a reorientation, and that turned out to be the more valuable gift. For decades the computer—still barely born—had been conceived as an engine of calculation, a device for institutions to crunch numbers at scale: firing tables, census counts, payrolls, ballistics. Bush imagined something entirely different. He imagined a machine in the service of one person's thinking, a tool that would not replace human judgment but amplify it, that would follow the associative leaps of an individual mind and help that mind reach further than it could alone. The essay lodged itself in the imaginations of the people who would go on to invent the real thing, and nearly every one of the field's pioneers would later name it as a formative influence.

The essay's afterlife proved richer than its author could have guessed, and richer than his own convictions would have allowed. Bush, for all his imagination, remained at heart a man of the analog age; he was skeptical of the digital electronic computers then being born, distrusted their reliability, and kept faith with spinning film and mechanical linkages long after the tide had turned against them. He was, in a sense, the wrong prophet for his own prophecy. Yet the vision outran the man. Ted Nelson would quote "As We May Think" at length when he coined the word "hypertext" two decades on; Douglas Engelbart would trace the seed of his life's work to reading it in a Red Cross library; and half a century after its publication, when a young British engineer named Tim Berners-Lee sat down to explain the origins of the World Wide Web, he named Vannevar Bush's essay among its ancestors. Few pieces of writing have ever been wrong about so many particulars and right about so much that mattered.

The dream lay dormant, more or less, through the 1950s—the decade of the mainframe and the batch queue, when computing marched off in exactly the institutional direction Bush had not intended. Then, in 1960, a psychologist turned computer scientist named Joseph Carl Robnett Licklider picked up the thread and pulled it forward. Everyone called him Lick. He was warm and gregarious where

Bush had been gruff, a man who studied the human mind for a living and had become fascinated, almost obsessed, by how badly humans and computers communicated. Licklider had made a careful study of his own working life, keeping track of how he actually spent his hours, and discovered, to his dismay, that something like eighty-five percent of the time he spent "thinking" was actually spent on clerical drudgery—finding information, plotting data on graph paper, getting into a position to make a decision rather than actually making it. A computer, he realized, could take on precisely that drudgery, freeing the human mind for the genuine thinking only it could do.

He set down this vision in 1960 in a paper with a title that captured the whole idea: "Man-Computer Symbiosis." The word symbiosis was chosen with care. Licklider was not predicting that machines would think for us, and he was not, like some of his contemporaries, worried that machines would soon think better than us. He imagined instead a partnership, a living together of two very different kinds of intelligence, each doing what it did best. "The hope," he wrote, "is that, in not too many years, human brains and computing machines will be coupled together very tightly, and that the resulting partnership will think as no human brain has ever thought and process data in a way not approached by the information-handling machines we know today." Man would set the goals, formulate the questions, supply the intuition; the computer would handle the routine work, the storage, the calculation, the searching. For that partnership to work, the human and the machine would have to interact in real time—conversationally, immediately—which was one reason Licklider became an early and passionate champion of time-sharing over the batch queue. He even sketched the machinery of the coupling in surprising detail, imagining desk-side consoles, screens that could draw as well as print, and something very like speech recognition, a generation before any of it was practical.

Then came the stroke of fortune that made Licklider more than a theorist. In 1962 he was hired to run a new office within the Pentagon's Advanced Research Projects Agency, ARPA, the organization the United States had created in a panic after the Soviet launch of Sputnik. Licklider was given command of its computing research and a budget that, by the standards of the field, was enormous. And he spent it not on weapons but on his vision. He funneled money to the best computing minds at MIT, at Stanford, at Berkeley, at Carnegie Mellon and the University of Utah—an informal fraternity he addressed, in a half-joking 1963 memo, as the "Members and Affiliates of the Intergalactic Computer Network." He funded time-sharing systems, research into computer graphics, artificial intelligence, and the human-machine interface. He did not dictate results; he found brilliant people who shared his conviction that the computer should serve the individual mind, and he set them free. In doing so he seeded nearly every laboratory that would matter to the coming revolution, including, before long, the machinery of a computer network that would grow into the internet. That playful memo about an intergalactic network is now regarded by many historians as a founding document of the connected world.

You meet Bush's Memex every time you open a web browser. The blue underlined link that carries you from one page to a related one is his associative trail made real; your browser's history and bookmarks are the personal trails he imagined a "trail blazer" laying down; and a collaboratively built encyclopedia that anyone can consult in seconds is precisely the "new form of encyclopedia, ready-made with a mesh of associative trails" he described on the page. He got the medium wrong and the spirit exactly right—which is perhaps the highest compliment one can pay a prophet of technology.

Among the millions who read "As We May Think" was a young Navy radar technician stationed in the Philippines at the war's end, killing time in a Red Cross library while he waited for a ship home. He pulled a copy of Life off the shelf, read Bush's essay, and never quite forgot it. His name was Douglas Engelbart, and he believed a computer could augment the human intellect itself—and he was about to prove it, in a single astonishing afternoon, before a stunned audience in San Francisco.

Chapter 3: The Mother of All Demos

On the afternoon of December 9, 1968, some two thousand computer professionals filed into the Civic Auditorium in San Francisco for a session of the Fall Joint Computer Conference. They expected the usual fare: a man at a lectern, a slide projector, an hour of technical talk about some incremental advance in hardware or programming. What they got instead would be remembered, decades later, as "the Mother of All Demos"—ninety minutes that contained, in embryo, nearly the entire future of personal computing. At the center of the stage sat a mild, precise engineer named Douglas Engelbart, forty-three years old, wearing a short-sleeved white shirt and a headset microphone. In front of him was a curious three-part console: a keyboard, a five-key device for his left hand, and, for his right hand, a small wooden block with a button on top and a wire trailing from its rear end like a tail. His colleagues had taken to calling it a mouse.

Behind Engelbart hung a projection screen twenty-two feet wide. On it appeared not slides but the live image of his computer display, mixed with a video feed of his own face and hands, so that the audience could watch him work and watch what the machine did at the same time. This alone was a technical feat of considerable daring—the images were being relayed by two microwave links from Engelbart's laboratory in Menlo Park, some thirty miles away, and projected onto the big screen through a borrowed video projector originally built for the aerospace industry. Pulling it off required leased telephone lines, a pair of specially built modems, rented microwave dishes on the roof, and a small army of engineers coordinating it all. And here is a detail that delights anyone who knows what came next: one of the men operating the cameras and mixing the video that day was Stewart Brand, the countercultural impresario behind the Whole Earth Catalog—so that the buttoned-down world of federally funded engineering and the barefoot world of the Bay Area counterculture were, quite literally, running the same show. But the audience quickly stopped noticing the medium, because they could not stop staring at the message. Engelbart began to type, and words appeared on the screen. He moved the mouse, and a marker—he called it a "bug"—slid across the display, and with it he selected words, moved them, copied them, deleted them. He organized a shopping list into categories and then, with a few motions, collapsed and expanded it into an outline that could be viewed at different levels of detail. He linked one document to another so that a click carried him instantly from a reference to the thing it referenced. He was demonstrating, all at once and for the first time in public, the computer mouse, on-screen windows, hypertext linking, real-time text editing, outline processing, and a graphical, interactive relationship with a machine that responded to a person the instant he acted.

Then it grew stranger still. Engelbart brought a colleague onto the shared screen—a man named Bill Paxton, sitting back at the lab in Menlo Park—and the two of them edited the same document together, in real time, each able to see the other's cursor moving across the text, their two voices carried over a live audio link while a small video window showed Paxton's face in the corner of the display. To an audience in 1968, accustomed to submitting decks of punch cards and waiting overnight for a printout, this was scarcely believable. Engelbart and his partner were videoconferencing and collaborating on a networked document, thirty miles apart, in an era when most of the people in the room had never so much as touched a computer directly. When it was over, the audience gave Engelbart a standing ovation. One observer later said he felt as though he had watched a man conduct thirty-five miles of "unforgiving technology" like an orchestra, and that everything simply worked, which itself bordered on the miraculous.

The left hand deserves a word of its own, because it points to the road not taken. Beside the keyboard sat that five-key device, which Engelbart called a chord keyset, and it worked rather like the keys of a piano: instead of striking one lettered key per character, the user pressed several keys at once in combination, each pattern of fingers standing for a different letter, much as pressing three notes together sounds a chord. With five keys a trained hand could, in principle, enter any letter of the alphabet without ever leaving the keyset, freeing the other hand to stay on the mouse. It was ingenious, and a devoted few swore by it, but it demanded weeks of practice to master, and there Engelbart's whole philosophy collided with the appetites of the coming market. He genuinely believed that people should be willing to train hard to wield a powerful tool, the way a musician trains for an instrument; the world, it turned out, wanted tools that asked nothing of it. The mouse, which any child could grasp in seconds, conquered the planet. The chord keyset, which promised more power at the price of real effort, vanished almost without a trace—a small casualty of the same preference for ease over mastery that would shadow Engelbart for the rest of his career.

The demonstration had not sprung from nowhere. Engelbart had been nursing his vision for the better part of two decades, ever since a moment of clarity in 1950. Newly engaged and suddenly confronting the question of what he wanted to do with his life, he had reasoned his way to a conclusion that would consume the rest of it. The world's problems, he decided, were growing more complex and more urgent at a frightening rate, while humanity's collective ability to deal with them was not keeping pace. If he could find a way to raise that collective ability—to make groups of people smarter and more capable when facing hard problems—he would be doing the most useful work he could imagine. And it occurred to him, drawing partly on a wartime memory of Vannevar Bush's "As We May Think," which he had read as a young radar technician in the Philippines, that a computer might be the instrument to do it. Not a computer that thought for people, but one that boosted their power to think, to organize, to collaborate. He called this project the augmentation of human intellect, and it became his life's cause.

For years almost no one took him seriously. The idea of a person sitting at a screen, interacting moment to moment with a computer, ran against every assumption of the batch-processing age; colleagues told him it was impractical, even faintly ridiculous, and one skeptical review of his early proposal complained that he seemed to want to build a "framework" for thinking rather than any concrete device. But Engelbart was stubborn, and eventually he found patrons. Money from ARPA—the office that J.C.R. Licklider had built and that carried forward Licklider's own conviction that computers should augment the individual mind—and from NASA allowed Engelbart to establish his own laboratory at the Stanford Research Institute, which he named the Augmentation Research Center. There, through the 1960s, he and a devoted team of young engineers built a system they called NLS, for oN-Line System, and it was NLS that the audience in San Francisco saw performing that December afternoon.

The mouse itself Engelbart had conceived years earlier, in 1964, jotting the idea into a notebook during a computer-graphics conference when his mind wandered from the speaker to the problem of how a person might point at things on a screen. His lead engineer, Bill English, took the sketch and built the first working model: a carved block of pine with two perpendicular metal wheels underneath that measured motion in two directions as the box was pushed across a desktop. Engelbart's team tested it in careful experiments against light pens, joysticks, and a knee-operated lever, timing how quickly and accurately users could point with each, and the humble wooden mouse simply won. There is a charming uncertainty at the heart of its origin. Asked years later who had actually named the device, Engelbart could only shrug: "No one can remember. It just looked like a mouse with a tail, and we all called it that." The cord, in the first prototype, trailed out the front, under the user's wrist; someone soon had the sense to flip it to the back, and the mouse assumed the shape it has kept ever since. When English filed the patent in 1967, the word "mouse" appears nowhere in it—the invention was solemnly christened the "X-Y Position Indicator for a Display System."

It is often said that Engelbart grew rich and famous as the man who invented the mouse. In fact the opposite is closer to the truth, and the reality is one of the quiet injustices of this history. The Stanford Research Institute, which owned the patent, eventually licensed it to Apple for a reported sum of around forty thousand dollars—a single modest payment for what would become one of the most ubiquitous objects on earth. Engelbart himself, as an employee, received no royalties at all, and the patent expired in 1987, just as the mouse was becoming a fixture on tens of millions of desks. He would later note, without much bitterness, that he never earned a cent from the invention that made his name. And in any case he found the world's fixation on the mouse faintly disappointing, because to him it was the least of what he had shown that day. The mouse was a means; the end was augmenting the collective human intellect, and it was the end that mattered.

And yet, for all its dazzle, the demonstration did not ignite the revolution one might have expected. In the years that followed, Engelbart's influence proved deep but strangely indirect, and his personal fortunes turned difficult. His grand ambition—not merely to invent tools but to teach people to work in radically new ways, to co-evolve with their machines toward higher collective intelligence—was harder to sell than the tools themselves. NLS was powerful but complex; the five-key handset and the layered commands demanded real training, and the world wanted computers that were easy, not computers that made you smarter through effort. Funding tightened. Many of his most talented researchers drifted away, some of them lured, in the early 1970s, to a gleaming new laboratory that the Xerox Corporation had established just a few miles away in Palo Alto—the Palo Alto Research Center, where they would take Engelbart's ideas about mice and screens and windows and refine them into something the wider world could actually use. Bill English himself, the man who built the first mouse, was among those who left for Xerox, carrying the idea with him and building a cleaner version there with a rolling ball inside in place of the two wheels. Engelbart, the man who had shown the future to two thousand people in a single afternoon, watched much of his vision walk out the door to be realized by others, and for a long stretch he was, if not forgotten, then badly underappreciated.

It is worth pausing on the phrase by which the demonstration is now universally known, because it too testifies to how long the world took to catch up with Engelbart. Nobody called it "the Mother of All Demos" in 1968; the name was bestowed a quarter century later, in the early 1990s, by the technology journalist Steven Levy, who was reaching back to a bit of Gulf War slang—Saddam Hussein had promised "the mother of all battles"—to convey just how thoroughly Engelbart's ninety minutes had contained every demo that would ever follow. The grainy black-and-white film of that afternoon survived, and it has since become something close to a sacred text among the people who design our software, studied frame by frame for the ideas packed into it. What almost none of them absorbed, then or now, was the thing Engelbart cared about most. The gadgets were never the point. He called his method "bootstrapping": the notion that a group of people, armed with better tools and willing to learn genuinely new ways of working, could lift their own collective intelligence, then use that raised intelligence to build still better tools, in a spiral without end. The world happily took his mouse and his windows and left the harder, humbler dream of collective betterment lying on the auditorium floor.

That is one of the recurring ironies of this history: the people who see furthest are rarely the ones who arrive first. Engelbart had demonstrated, in 1968, ideas that would not reach ordinary desks for fifteen or twenty years, and he had done it with a machine that filled a laboratory and cost a fortune, tended by a team of specialists—a long way still from anything a person could own. His demo was a vision of the destination, glimpsed from a great distance, before the road to it had been built. Recognition came only late in his life; not until 1997, nearly thirty years after the demonstration, did he receive the Turing Award, computing's highest honor, and with it the belated acknowledgment that the strange console he had operated that December afternoon had contained the seeds of nearly everything that followed.

You live inside the world Engelbart sketched that day more completely than almost anyone in that auditorium could have imagined. Every video call in which faces float in little windows while a shared document scrolls beneath them; every time two people in different cities type into the same file and watch each other's cursors dart across the screen; every link you click, every word you drag from one place to another, every outline you expand and collapse—all of it was on that twenty-two-foot screen in 1968, running on a machine the size of a room, thirty miles from the man operating it. What took a laboratory and a microwave relay and a small army of engineers to stage once, for ninety astonishing minutes, now sits idle in your pocket, waiting.

But even as Engelbart labored inside his institute, a very different current was rising outside the laboratories—a scruffy, idealistic movement of hobbyists and dreamers and countercultural rebels who believed, with almost religious fervor, that computing power should be torn from the hands of the priesthood and given to the people.

Chapter 4: Bicycles for the Mind

In the fall of 1968, a few months before Douglas Engelbart took the stage in San Francisco, a large-format newsprint publication appeared in the head shops and communes and back-to-the-land bookstores of Northern California. It was called the Whole Earth Catalog, and its cover bore a photograph of the entire planet, blue and cloud-wrapped, floating alone in the black of space—an image that had become possible only because the space program had begun sending cameras far enough out to look back. The catalog's founder, a lanky Stanford-trained biologist and former Army paratrooper named Stewart Brand, had lobbied NASA for exactly such a photograph, selling buttons on the Berkeley campus that asked, "Why haven't we seen a photograph of the whole Earth yet?" He believed the image would change how people thought about themselves, and he built a publication around the idea that ordinary individuals, armed with the right tools and information, could take charge of their own lives without waiting for governments or corporations to do it for them. The catalog's motto, printed inside, read: "We are as gods and might as well get good at it." Its purpose, Brand wrote, was to provide "access to tools." It was no fringe pamphlet, either; in 1972 the Whole Earth Catalog won the National Book Award, the first catalog ever to do so, an astonishing honor for a countercultural how-to guide that sat somewhere between a hardware store, a reading list, and a manifesto.

This was the improbable soil in which the idea of the personal computer would take root. On its face, nothing could seem further apart than the counterculture of the late 1960s—with its distrust of institutions, its communes, its psychedelics and protest marches—and the computer, which in the popular imagination of the era was the very emblem of cold, dehumanizing, institutional power. Students at Berkeley had famously pinned their protest to the IBM punch card, that stiff rectangle stamped with the warning "do not fold, spindle, or mutilate," which seemed to reduce a human being to a number processed by an uncaring machine; some wore the cards around their necks or burned them in imitation of draft cards. The computer belonged to the military, to the corporation, to the Establishment. To love it was to love Big Brother. When the student leader Mario Savio stood on the steps of Sproul Hall during Berkeley's Free Speech Movement in 1964 and cried that there comes a time when "you've got to put your bodies upon the gears and upon the wheels" of the machine to make it stop, the machine he meant was partly a metaphor for the university and the state—but the imagery of grinding, dehumanizing mechanism was drawn straight from the age of the computer, and everyone in the crowd understood it. It is often said, on the strength of such images, that the counterculture was simply anti-technology, a movement of Luddites in tie-dye who wanted to unplug the modern world and go back to the land. In fact the truth was subtler and more interesting. Brand and those around him drew a sharp distinction between technology that centralized power in distant institutions and technology that returned power to the individual—between the mainframe humming behind glass and the well-chosen hand tool, the geodesic dome, the small machine you could understand and control yourself. They were not against tools; they were passionately for the right ones. And in a twist that still surprises people, a strand of that movement came to see the computer not as the enemy but as the ultimate tool of personal liberation—if only it could be pried loose from the institutions that hoarded it.

The bridge between these two worlds ran through a particular corner of the San Francisco Bay Area, where Stanford's laboratories and the emerging electronics industry of the peninsula sat cheek by jowl with the utopian ferment of Berkeley and Haight-Ashbury. Many of the young engineers and programmers of the region were themselves products of the counterculture; they had marched, they had experimented, they read the Whole Earth Catalog, and they saw no contradiction in believing both that the system was broken and that the right technology could help fix it. Brand himself made the connection explicit, and he had been present at the creation in more ways than one—he was among the crew operating the cameras at Engelbart's great demonstration in December of that same year. In 1972 he wrote a now-famous article for Rolling Stone, one of the first pieces of mainstream journalism to treat computer culture with fascination rather than dread, describing the young hackers he had watched playing a game called Spacewar deep into the night on the machines at Stanford's artificial intelligence lab. "Ready or not," he declared, "computers are coming to the people." He saw in these obsessive young programmers not servants of the machine but its liberators, and he predicted, with startling accuracy, that the computer would follow the same path the transistor radio had—from expensive institutional curiosity to cheap personal possession. The same technology that had served the Pentagon might, in the right hands, become an instrument of individual freedom.

Others were already trying to make that happen in the most literal way. In 1972, in Menlo Park, a former engineer and educator named Bob Albrecht helped found an organization with a deliberately populist name: the People's Computer Company. It was a nod to Big Brother and the Holding Company, Janis Joplin's band, and it captured the movement's insurgent spirit. Albrecht was an evangelist who hauled a teletype terminal around to schools to let children play with a computer, taught them the friendly BASIC language, and threw dinners where he served wine and Greek dancing alongside programming lessons. The People's Computer Company published a scrappy newsletter, ran a storefront where anyone could walk in and use a computer terminal or play games for a small fee, and preached the gospel that computing should be fun, accessible, and available to everyone—especially to children and ordinary people, not just to credentialed specialists in white coats. Its very first newsletter, in October 1972, carried a hand-drawn cover with a slogan that became something of a manifesto: "Computers are mostly used against people instead of for people; used to control people instead of to free them; time to change all that—we need a People's Computer Company." Here the batch-processing priesthood of the previous decades was being challenged not by a rival corporation but by a band of Bay Area idealists who wanted to hand the machine directly to the crowd.

The most concrete experiment of all in handing the machine to the crowd appeared in Berkeley in the summer of 1973, when a group that included an engineer named Lee Felsenstein set a battered teletype terminal inside a plywood box next to the bulletin board at Leopold's Records, a student record store. It was called Community Memory, and it was the first time ordinary members of the public could walk up to a computer terminal and simply use it. The terminal was wired over a slow telephone link to a time-shared mainframe across the bay in San Francisco, and anyone who wandered in—no login, no fee, no credential—could type a message, tag it with keywords, and read what strangers had left behind. People posted poetry, looked for chess partners and rides and bandmates, argued, joked, and invented an anonymous trickster persona who held forth on philosophy. It was, in every meaningful sense, the first public online community, a social network built a decade before the personal computer and forty years before the phrase existed, and it grew directly out of the conviction that computing was a public good that belonged in a record store, not behind glass in a corporate basement.

No one carried the banner of computer liberation more flamboyantly than a mercurial, self-taught visionary named Ted Nelson. The son of a film director and a Broadway and film actress, Nelson was brilliant, restless, and constitutionally unable to fit into any institution that would have him; he would later say, with some pride, that he had a mind that jumped so fast it could never abide a straight line. He had been thinking since the early 1960s about a grand system for linking all of the world's writing together through what he called, coining the word himself in 1965, "hypertext"—text that branched and connected in nonlinear ways, allowing a reader to follow associative trails through a vast web of documents. It was, in spirit, a direct descendant of Vannevar Bush's Memex, which Nelson quoted at length, and he dreamed of building it into a universal library he called Project Xanadu. Xanadu became one of the great might-have-beens of computing—a system so ambitious and so endlessly revised that it never really shipped; one technology magazine would eventually dub it "the longest-running vaporware story in the history of the computer industry." It is a caution worth remembering: the man who gave us the word for the links that stitch the modern web together spent decades unable to build the thing he had imagined.

But Nelson's most immediate contribution came not from the system he could never quite finish but from a book he wrote and self-published in 1974, the year before the first personal computer kit went on sale. Directly inspired by the sprawling, do-it-yourself format of Brand's Whole Earth Catalog, he printed it himself, laid out in a chaotic collage of hand-scrawled notes, cartoons, and dense typographic ranting, and he bound it so that it could be read from either end. One side was titled Computer Lib, its cover showing a raised fist; flip it over and the other side was Dream Machines. It is often reckoned the first book ever written about the personal computer, and it appeared before there was quite such a thing to write about.

Computer Lib opened with a battle cry that summed up the whole movement: "You can and must understand computers NOW." Nelson raged against the mystification of computing, against the notion that the machines were the private property of a technical elite who used jargon and glass walls to keep ordinary people out. He gave the racket a name—"cybercrud," his word for the intentional nonsense that computer people told everyone else to keep them intimidated and dependent—and his rallying cry was "Down with Cybercrud." Computers, he insisted, were simple in principle and belonged to everyone; the priesthood was a fraud, and the sooner people realized it, the sooner they could seize the technology for their own purposes. The book had no publisher, no marketing, and an anti-authoritarian design that made it nearly unreadable in places, and yet it passed from hand to hand among the hobbyists and dreamers of the coming revolution like a piece of samizdat, and many of the people who would go on to build the personal computer industry later described it as the book that lit the fuse. It gave a name and a philosophy to a feeling that was already in the air: that computing power was a form of power, and that power should belong to the people.

There is a metaphor, coined a little later, that captures the essence of what these dreamers were reaching for. Steve Jobs would one day describe reading, as a boy, an article in Scientific American that measured the efficiency of locomotion across the animal kingdom—how much energy different creatures spent to travel a given distance. The condor came out on top; the human being, walking, was unimpressive, somewhere down the middle of the list, far less efficient than many animals. But a human being on a bicycle blew the condor away, vaulting to the very top and becoming the most efficient traveling thing on the planet. The lesson stayed with Jobs for the rest of his life. The computer, he said, was "the equivalent of a bicycle for our minds"—not a replacement for human thought but an amplifier of it, a simple machine that let a person travel intellectual distances they could never manage on foot. That image, of technology as a humble tool that multiplies the reach of an ordinary individual, was exactly the dream that Brand and Albrecht and Nelson were chasing in the early 1970s, years before the machine to fulfill it existed. They had the philosophy, the fervor, and the slogans. What they still lacked was a computer cheap and small enough for a single person to own.

The spirit of that moment did not stay locked in the 1970s. When the Whole Earth Catalog published its final regular edition in 1974, Brand printed on the back cover a photograph of a country road at dawn with a farewell caption: "Stay hungry. Stay foolish." Three decades later, a middle-aged Steve Jobs, addressing the graduating class of Stanford University in a commencement speech now watched by tens of millions online, told them that those words had been the parting message of a publication he had revered in his youth—"Stewart and his team put out several issues of the Whole Earth Catalog," he said, "and then when it had run its course, they put out a final issue"—and he passed the benediction along to a new generation. If you have ever seen that speech, or worn out the phrase on a poster or a graduation card, you have met the counterculture of Brand and Nelson directly, its faith that the right tools in ordinary hands can remake a life carried forward, word for word, into our own century.

Making the tool itself possible would require a revolution of a different kind altogether—one that had been quietly unfolding for two decades in the laboratories of the electronics industry, where scientists had learned to conjure switches and circuits out of little more than purified sand and controlled bolts of electricity.

Chapter 5: Sand and Lightning

Two days before Christmas in 1947, in a laboratory in Murray Hill, New Jersey, a small group gathered around an ugly little contraption on a workbench and watched a needle jump. The device was a tangle of gold foil, a chip of germanium, and a plastic wedge, held together with wax and a bent paper clip, and it looked like nothing at all—certainly not like the seed of the modern world. But when a faint electrical signal was fed into it, a much larger signal came out the other side, and a voice spoken into a microphone at the input came out the loudspeaker noticeably louder. The little assembly had amplified electricity. Walter Brattain, the experimentalist whose deft hands had built the thing, and John Bardeen, the quiet theoretical genius who understood why it worked, had made the first working transistor a week earlier, on December 16, and now they were showing it to the laboratory's brass. They worked at Bell Telephone Laboratories, the research arm of the American telephone monopoly, and Bell's interest was intensely practical: the phone network ran on millions of vacuum tubes and electromechanical relays, and both were bulky, hot, power-hungry, and prone to failure. Something small and durable that could switch and amplify a signal would be worth a fortune to a company that had to maintain a nation's worth of them.

The device did not even have a name yet, and the way it got one is a small delight of the story. For half a year Bell's engineers called it clumsy things—the "semiconductor triode," the "surface states amplifier"—until a ballot was circulated around the laboratory in the spring of 1948 inviting the staff to vote on a proper name. The winning coinage came from an electrical engineer named John R. Pierce, who wrote science fiction on the side under a pseudonym and had a writer's ear for a good word. He fused "transconductance," a measure of the device's amplifying action, with "resistor," the kind of component it was, and proposed "transistor." It won the vote, and the name it beat—and the fact that the most important electronic device of the century was christened by committee ballot, thanks to a moonlighting science-fiction author—is the kind of humble accident that runs all through this history.

It is often said that William Shockley invented the transistor, and his name is indeed forever attached to it—he shared the 1956 Nobel Prize with Bardeen and Brattain, and he would loom over the rest of this book. But Shockley was not in the room on the day the first one worked. He had set the research program in motion and supervised it, yet the crucial breakthrough was made by his two subordinates while he was elsewhere, and he learned of their triumph secondhand. By his own later admission he felt a stab of something close to envy at being left on the sidelines of his own project, and over the Christmas holidays, working largely alone and in secret in a hotel room in Chicago, he devised a superior and more manufacturable design of his own: the junction transistor, a sandwich of semiconductor layers that could be produced as a solid, rugged block rather than a fragile assembly of foil and paper clips. Shockley's rivalrous, wounded pride thus produced the version of the transistor that industry could actually mass-produce—a reminder that the neat phrase "Shockley invented the transistor" flattens a messier and more human truth, in which the decisive first device was built by other hands and the famous man raced to catch up with his own laboratory.

To grasp why the transistor mattered so enormously, one has only to remember ENIAC, glowing in its Philadelphia room with eighteen thousand vacuum tubes, each a small glass bulb that burned hot, drew power, and failed with dispiriting regularity, so that operators were forever hunting down the one dead tube among thousands that had brought the whole machine to a halt. The vacuum tube was the switch and amplifier on which all early electronics depended, and its limitations set a hard ceiling on how complex, how small, and how reliable a machine could ever become. The transistor did everything the vacuum tube did—switching current on and off, amplifying weak signals—but it was a sliver of solid material with no glass, no vacuum, no glowing filament to burn out. It could be made tiny. It sipped power instead of gulping it. It ran cool, switched fast, and, once manufacturers learned to make it well, lasted essentially forever. It was, quite simply, the invention that made everything else in this book possible.

It is worth pausing to understand, in plain terms, what a transistor actually does, because the whole of the digital world rests on so simple a trick. Imagine a garden hose with a foot pedal pressing on it. A small effort on the pedal can stop or start a powerful flow of water, so that a weak action controls a strong one. A transistor is an electrical version of that pedal, with no moving parts: a small voltage applied to one terminal controls a much larger current flowing between two others, either amplifying a faint signal into a strong one or, used as a switch, snapping the current fully on or fully off. That on-or-off, the presence or absence of current, is the physical embodiment of the binary one and zero. String transistors together so that the output of one flips the switch of the next, and you can build circuits that add, compare, remember, and decide. A computer, for all its apparent magic, is in the end nothing but many millions of these tiny switches, flicking one another on and off billions of times a second. The genius of the age lay not in any single grand machine but in learning to make that one humble switch smaller, cheaper, and more numerous without end.

The transistor's power came from a peculiar class of materials called semiconductors—substances that were neither good conductors of electricity like copper nor good insulators like glass, but something in between, and whose electrical behavior could be precisely controlled by introducing tiny, carefully measured impurities, a process called doping. Add a trace of one element and the material carries current one way; add a trace of another and it carries it the other; join the two and you have a device that lets current pass in one direction but not the reverse. The first transistors were made of germanium, but the material that would come to define the age was its cousin, silicon—the second most abundant element in the Earth's crust after oxygen, making up more than a quarter of it by weight, and the principal ingredient of ordinary sand. Silicon was harder to purify and work with than germanium, but it tolerated heat far better and formed a beautifully stable insulating layer of oxide on its surface when heated in air, a property that would prove crucial for manufacturing. The whole of the coming revolution would be built, almost unbelievably, on refined sand and controlled pulses of electricity—on the taming of a common mineral to channel lightning in patterns of astonishing precision. When people later spoke of Silicon Valley, they were naming the industry after the very stuff of the beach.

Bell Labs announced the transistor to the public at a press conference in New York on the last day of June 1948, and the world, tellingly, shrugged. The great newspapers gave it only a few paragraphs; the New York Times buried the news near the bottom of a radio column, well after an item about a soap-opera schedule. Almost no one grasped that a tiny sliver of germanium on a laboratory bench would, within a single lifetime, remake industry, warfare, communication, and daily life more thoroughly than almost any invention in human history. The device was simply too small, too quiet, and too strange for its significance to register.

For a decade, though, the transistor solved one problem only to expose another. Engineers could now build circuits from thousands of tiny, reliable transistors instead of fragile tubes—but each transistor, each resistor, each capacitor was still a separate component that had to be manufactured individually and then wired to its neighbors by hand, joint by soldered joint. As designers dreamed of ever more complex circuits, they ran headlong into what the industry came to call, with real anxiety, "the tyranny of numbers." A sophisticated machine might require tens of thousands of components and hundreds of thousands of hand-soldered connections, and every one of those joints was a chance for error and a point of failure. It was becoming physically impossible to build the circuits that theory said were possible, not because the parts did not exist but because no one could assemble them reliably. The transistor had shattered the ceiling of the vacuum tube age only to reveal a new one just above it.

The escape came, as such things often do, from two men working independently and arriving at the same essential insight within months of one another. In the summer of 1958, a newly hired engineer at Texas Instruments named Jack Kilby found himself alone in the lab; too junior to have earned the company's mass summer vacation, he had the run of the place and time to think. His idea was radical in its simplicity. What if all the components of a circuit—the transistors, the resistors, the capacitors, and the wires between them—were made not separately but together, all at once, out of a single piece of semiconductor material? On September 12, 1958, he demonstrated a crude but working version: a sliver of germanium, glued to a glass slide and trailing a few fine wires, with the elements of a complete circuit formed into one monolithic block. When his supervisors applied power, a clean sine wave rolled across the oscilloscope screen. It was the first integrated circuit. A few months later, in early 1959, at Fairchild Semiconductor in California—a company founded by a group of talented young men who had fled Shockley's tyrannical management—an engineer named Robert Noyce independently conceived the same idea and improved upon it in a decisive way. Noyce's version was built on silicon, and it used that stable oxide layer to lay down flat metal connections directly on the chip's surface, so that the components and their wiring could be printed together in a single planar process. Noyce's approach was the more practical and manufacturable of the two, and it became the template for essentially every chip that followed. Both men are rightly honored as co-inventors of the integrated circuit, and the courts and the industry, after years of patent dispute, effectively divided the credit between them. When the Nobel Prize in Physics at last recognized the achievement in 2000, it went to Kilby alone—not by way of judgment, but because Noyce had died a decade earlier, and the prize is never awarded posthumously.

The consequences of putting an entire circuit onto a single chip were almost too large to comprehend at first, but one man saw them coming with uncanny clarity. In 1965 Gordon Moore, a chemist who had been one of Noyce's co-founders at Fairchild, was asked to write a short article for the trade magazine Electronics predicting the future of his field. Looking at the mere handful of data points then available—the number of components that engineers had managed to cram onto a single chip in each of the preceding years—Moore noticed a pattern: the number was roughly doubling every year. He projected the trend boldly forward and predicted that this doubling would continue for at least a decade, yielding chips of a complexity that seemed, at the time, like science fiction—he illustrated the article with a cartoon of a department-store counter selling "handy home computers" to baffled shoppers, a joke in 1965 and a prophecy in hindsight. The observation, which he refined a decade later to a doubling roughly every two years, came to be known as Moore's Law, and it would hold with eerie fidelity for half a century, becoming both a description of the industry and a self-fulfilling prophecy that drove it, as every company raced to keep pace with the line on Moore's graph. Each doubling meant chips that were smaller, faster, cheaper, and more powerful than the last, on a relentless exponential march. The implication was staggering: computing power that had once filled a room would, in a matter of years, shrink to fit in a hand, and its cost would fall toward the trivial.

You can measure how faithfully that prophecy was kept by reaching into your pocket. The processor in a modern smartphone holds on the order of tens of billions of transistors, each one a switch far smaller than a single virus, etched into a flake of silicon smaller than a fingernail—more individual switches on that one chip than there were seconds in all of recorded human history before the transistor was invented. The frail assembly of foil and germanium that Brattain and Bardeen coaxed to life two days before Christmas in 1947 has multiplied into a number so vast it defeats the imagination, and it all still rests on the same trick: a tiny switch made of purified sand, flicking on and off, on and off, faster than thought.

In 1968 Moore and Noyce left Fairchild to start a company of their own, dedicated to pushing this shrinking as far and as fast as it would go; they called it Intel, a contraction of "integrated electronics." Within three years, one of Intel's engineers would take the logic of the integrated circuit to its ultimate conclusion, gathering the entire calculating brain of a computer onto a single chip of silicon smaller than a fingernail—and in that moment, the machine that had once lived in a basement, tended by a priesthood, would finally become small enough and cheap enough for a single person to own.

Chapter 6: The Traitors of Fairchild

On a September morning in 1957, eight young men walked into the offices of Shockley Semiconductor Laboratory in Mountain View, California, and, in effect, resigned from the future their boss had promised them. They were chemists and physicists and engineers, most of them still in their twenties, and they had come west because of one name. William Shockley had won a share of the Nobel Prize for co-inventing the transistor at Bell Labs, and when he left the East Coast to start his own company in the apricot orchards south of San Francisco, he had recruited some of the brightest technical minds in America to join him. Now those minds were leaving. Shockley, brilliant as he was, had turned out to be an impossible man to work for—paranoid, abusive, prone to posting employees' salaries on the wall for all to compare and once demanding that his staff submit to lie-detector tests over a trivial cut on a secretary's finger that he suspected, absurdly, to be sabotage. He had also made a disastrous technical bet, steering the company away from the silicon transistors his young researchers wanted to build and toward an exotic four-layer device of his own that never found a market. The eight had tried, quietly, to go over his head to the company's financier, hoping Shockley might be eased upstairs into some harmless advisory role. When that failed, they decided to leave together, reasoning that eight men walking out as one could accomplish what no single resignation could.

Shockley called them "the traitorous eight," and the label stuck, though history would render its verdict very differently. It is worth naming them, because between them they would help father an entire industry: Julius Blank, Victor Grinich, Jean Hoerni, Eugene Kleiner, Jay Last, Sheldon Roberts, and, at the intellectual center of the group, Gordon Moore and Robert Noyce. Noyce, the son of an Iowa minister, was a physicist with an easy charisma and a reckless streak—he had once, as a college student, stolen and slaughtered a neighbor's pig for a dormitory luau and narrowly escaped expulsion. He combined genuine scientific depth with the manner of a natural leader, the kind of man others instinctively followed. Moore, quieter and more precise, was a chemist from the Bay Area with a gift for seeing patterns others missed and a temperament as steady as Noyce's was magnetic. Together they became the gravitational core around which the breakaway group organized itself.

The eight had a technology in mind but no company to build it in, and here the story bends toward the peculiar financial machinery that would come to define the region. A young investment banker named Arthur Rock, working in New York and holding a fresh Harvard MBA, took an interest in their predicament. The conventional wisdom of the day held that respectable financing did not flow to a band of employees who had just quit en masse; a group of technical men owning and running their own firm was nearly unheard of. Rock worked through a list of some three dozen established companies looking for one willing to bankroll the defectors, and was turned down by all of them, before he found his backer in Sherman Fairchild—an inventor, playboy, and industrialist who happened, through inherited stock, to be the largest single shareholder in IBM. Fairchild Camera and Instrument agreed to put up a loan of around a million and a half dollars, with an option to buy the venture outright later, and so in September 1957 Fairchild Semiconductor was born. The founding had a ceremonial flourish that has passed into legend: lacking any formal contract at first, the eight men and their two financiers are said to have sealed their partnership by each signing ten crisp new one-dollar bills, so that ten signed banknotes served as the improvised articles of a company that would change the world.

Their mandate was to make transistors out of silicon rather than the germanium that then dominated the market. Silicon was the harder material to work with, but it was abundant—it was, after all, the stuff of ordinary sand—and it tolerated heat far better than germanium did. The bet paid off almost immediately. Fairchild landed a contract to supply transistors for the guidance computer of the Minuteman missile, and the Cold War's appetite for miniaturized electronics became the young company's first great customer. But the invention that mattered most was still to come, and it emerged from a problem that everyone in the industry could see but no one could solve: the wiring, the "tyranny of numbers," the impossibility of hand-soldering ever more components into ever more complex circuits.

The decisive breakthrough is often credited wholesale to Noyce, and he deserves much of the honor, but the quiet hinge on which it turned belonged to one of the less famous of the eight. Jean Hoerni, a Swiss-born physicist with doctorates from both Cambridge and Geneva, devised in 1959 a manufacturing technique he called the planar process: instead of building transistors up in fragile ridges on the surface of the silicon, he diffused them down into a flat wafer and sealed the whole thing under a protective, insulating layer of silicon oxide, leaving a smooth and durable plane. It was Hoerni's flat, sealed surface that made Noyce's leap possible, for on such a surface one could simply print thin metal connecting lines directly onto the chip, wiring an entire circuit together photographically in a single step. Noyce saw that possibility and seized it, conceiving the monolithic integrated circuit built on silicon; but it rested on Hoerni's planar foundation, and the two inventions together—one celebrated, one half-forgotten—are what actually broke the tyranny of numbers. A Texas Instruments engineer named Jack Kilby had demonstrated a rival version of the integrated circuit a few months earlier, and Kilby and Noyce are today jointly credited as its co-inventors; but it was the Fairchild approach, printable and mass-producible, that pointed the way to everything that followed.

It is easy to forget how nearly the integrated circuit failed to catch on, and who rescued it. When Fairchild and Texas Instruments first offered their chips, established engineers were skeptical, even scornful; a single integrated circuit cost far more than the handful of separate transistors it replaced, and old hands distrusted the idea of buying a sealed block they could not repair or modify. What saved the chip was the Cold War and the Space Race. The military wanted the guidance computer for its Minuteman II missile to be small and reliable, and NASA wanted the Apollo Guidance Computer, the machine that would steer astronauts to the Moon, to be lighter and more dependable than anything built from discrete parts—and both were willing to pay almost any price to get it. For a stretch in the mid-1960s these two programs together bought the overwhelming majority of all the integrated circuits produced in the United States. That guaranteed demand let the manufacturers pour money into their factories, refine their methods, and ramp up volume, and as volume climbed the price per chip collapsed—from tens or hundreds of dollars apiece to just a few dollars within a few years. The government's appetite for miniature electronics, in other words, paid to build the learning curve down which the entire consumer revolution would later coast. The chip that would one day cost pennies was first made affordable on the taxpayer's dime.

Fairchild grew explosively, and in growing it did something its founders scarcely intended: it seeded an entire industry. The place had a culture unlike the buttoned-down East Coast electronics firms—open, informal, meritocratic, impatient with hierarchy. Engineers wore short sleeves, argued in the hallways, and believed that a good idea from a junior researcher deserved to win over a bad one from a manager. But Fairchild the parent company, back on the East Coast, siphoned the semiconductor division's profits into unrelated ventures and doled out stock options stingily, and talented people began to notice that they could grow far richer by leaving to start their own firms. They left in waves, founding company after company, until the region was thick with businesses whose founders could trace their lineage back to that one building in Mountain View. The offspring became known as the "Fairchildren," and there were dozens of them; by one later count, of the roughly ninety semiconductor firms operating in the area a generation on, the great majority could draw a direct line of descent back to Fairchild. Eugene Kleiner, one of the original eight, would go on to co-found Kleiner Perkins, the venture firm that later staked Amazon and Google—so that the habit of technical people leaving to build something new, financed by people who understood their work, became the region's very metabolism.

It is worth pausing on that word "traitors," because the framing tells its own story. In the corporate morality of the 1950s, to quit your employer as a group and take your talents elsewhere was something close to disloyalty, and Shockley's bitter label carried real sting at the time. History has inverted the judgment completely. What looked like treachery was in fact the founding act of a new kind of economy, one in which ideas and the people who carried them, rather than factories or patents locked in a corporate vault, were the real capital—and in which the natural and honorable thing to do with a good idea your employer would not pursue was to walk out the door and build it yourself. The region did not yet have its famous name. It would arrive in January 1971, when a trade journalist named Don Hoefler ran a series of articles in Electronic News under the headline "Silicon Valley, USA," borrowing a phrase a friend had suggested, and the label for the stretch of orchard land between San Jose and San Francisco stuck for good.

By 1968, even Noyce and Moore had grown restless. The parent corporation had passed Noyce over for its top job, and the pair could feel the place calcifying, its inventiveness draining into the same corporate sludge they had fled Shockley to escape. That summer they walked out to start again. Moore later said the decision was less about a grand plan than a simple desire to get back to the excitement of building something small and new. They turned once more to Arthur Rock, who by now had moved west and helped pioneer a new kind of financing built on backing brilliant people rather than proven products—the beginnings of modern venture capital. This time there was no list of three dozen rejections; Rock, who believed in the two men without reservation, raised the entire two and a half million dollars in a matter of days, largely on the strength of a short letter and his own reputation, and put in a good deal of his own money besides. The new company was briefly called NM Electronics, for Noyce and Moore, before they settled on a contraction of "integrated electronics": Intel.

They brought with them a third man who would prove as essential as either founder. Andrew Grove—born András Gróf in Budapest, a Jewish refugee who had survived the Nazi occupation as a child, then fled Hungary on foot after the Soviet crackdown of 1956 and arrived in America nearly deaf in one ear and barely speaking English—had run the labs at Fairchild and possessed a discipline the two founders lacked. If Noyce was the visionary and Moore the deep thinker, Grove was the operator, the man who turned ideas into shipped products and loose collegiality into a functioning company. His management style could be ferocious, and he would later title one of his books, only half in jest, "Only the Paranoid Survive." But it was Grove who would eventually build Intel into an industrial powerhouse. The three of them together—the charismatic physicist, the pattern-seeing chemist, and the exacting refugee—formed one of the most consequential partnerships in the history of American business.

Noyce, in particular, grew into something more than a founder; he became the presiding spirit of the whole region, so influential and so widely beloved that he was known, only half in jest, as "the Mayor of Silicon Valley." He set the informal, open, no-reserved-parking, first-name culture that the valley's companies would imitate for generations, and he made a deliberate practice of mentoring the young entrepreneurs coming up behind him. Among his protégés was a brash young man named Steve Jobs, who would seek Noyce out for advice and dinner and long motorcycle-shop conversations, and who later called him one of his heroes—"a national treasure," Jobs said of him. When Jobs and his generation built their own companies in Noyce's image, they were extending a lineage that ran straight back through Intel and Fairchild to eight men and ten signed dollar bills. Others of the original eight and their many recruits spread the pattern further still: Fairchild alumni went on to help found National Semiconductor, Advanced Micro Devices, and dozens of other firms, until the entire valley was, in a real sense, one enormous family tree with a single Mountain View building at its root.

Something of that founding moment reaches you every time you read of two engineers quitting a giant to launch a startup in a garage, every time a venture capitalist writes a check on the strength of a founder's vision rather than a finished product. That entire pattern—the mobility of talent, the money that chases people instead of proven goods, the honorable defection—was invented, in its modern form, by eight men walking out of a bad boss's office and the banker who believed in them. What had begun as an act Shockley branded treason had, in just over a decade, produced the integrated circuit, the venture-capital model, and the freewheeling engineering culture that would define a stretch of orchard land soon to be renamed after its principal product. The human network was in place, the money had learned how to flow, and the silicon was ready. What Intel needed now was a way to see where all of it was heading—a way to turn a decade of doubling and shrinking into something like a prophecy.

That prophecy already existed, in an article Gordon Moore had published three years earlier, and it would come to be known as a law.

Chapter 7: A Law About the Future

In the spring of 1965, an editor at Electronics magazine asked Gordon Moore to write something about the future of semiconductor components for the publication's thirty-fifth anniversary issue. Moore was then still at Fairchild, running its research and development, and he was not by nature a man given to grand pronouncements. He was a chemist who liked data. But he had been keeping track of something on the graph paper in his lab, and when he sat down to write, he decided to plot it out and see where the line pointed. What he found, and what he published in the April 19 issue under the unglamorous title "Cramming More Components onto Integrated Circuits," was one of the most quietly influential observations of the twentieth century.

The idea was simple enough that Moore could state it in a sentence, though its consequences would take decades to unfold. He had noticed that the number of components engineers could economically fit onto a single integrated circuit had been roughly doubling every year since the technology's birth. A chip that held a single transistor in 1959 held about fifty by 1965, and the trend showed no sign of slowing. Moore drew his line forward and made a prediction that, at the time, verged on the absurd: that this doubling would continue for at least another decade, so that by 1975 a single chip might hold some sixty-five thousand components. And he did not stop at the numbers. In a passage that reads today like a small act of prophecy, he wrote that integrated circuits would lead to "such wonders as home computers—or at least terminals connected to a central computer—automatic controls for automobiles, and personal portable communications equipment." In 1965, when a computer filled a room and cost as much as a house, and a telephone was a heavy object bolted to the wall by the phone company, this was very nearly science fiction—and yet he named the home computer, the car computer, and the mobile phone, the three machines that would define the half century to come, in a single throwaway sentence in a trade journal.

It was, in truth, a modest piece of technical journalism, and Moore had only four or five data points to work from. He was extrapolating from the thinnest of evidence, drawing a straight line on semilogarithmic paper and trusting that the future would stay obligingly on the line. There was no physical law compelling transistors to shrink on schedule, no equation in nature that said components must double at any particular rate. What Moore had spotted was not a law of physics at all but a law of economics and engineering effort—a pattern in how well and how fast a young industry was learning to do its work. He did not even call it a law, and he was faintly embarrassed by the eventual grandeur of the name. That honor came later, around 1970, when a Caltech professor and friend named Carver Mead began referring to "Moore's Law," and the phrase proved far too catchy to dislodge.

It is often said that Moore's Law predicts computing power will double every eighteen months. Moore himself never said any such thing. His original 1965 figure was a doubling every year; when he revisited the data a decade later, in 1975, he revised it to a doubling roughly every two years, which is the canonical version. The famous "eighteen months" was a later blending, generally credited to an Intel executive named David House, who folded in the fact that the transistors were also getting faster, not merely more numerous, and concluded that raw computing performance would double about every year and a half. The precise interval mattered less than the astonishing fact that the trend held at all, year after year, decade after decade, as engineers found ever more ingenious ways to etch smaller and smaller features onto silicon.

To feel why a doubling that continues without stopping is so disorienting, it helps to recall an old legend about the inventor of chess. Offered any reward he wished by a delighted king, the inventor asked only for grains of wheat on a chessboard: one grain on the first square, two on the second, four on the third, and so on, doubling for each of the sixty-four squares. The king, thinking the request charmingly modest, agreed—and discovered too late that the total came to more wheat than had been grown in the history of the world, a heap that would bury the kingdom. The early squares are humble and unremarkable; the explosion all happens at the far end of the board, where each single step doubles everything that came before it. Moore's Law put the semiconductor industry on that chessboard and kept it marching, one square at a time, for more than fifty squares. The human mind, built to reason in straight lines, simply cannot feel what waits in the later squares until it arrives there and finds the sky darkened with grain.

The sheer scale of what the law compounded into is difficult to hold in the mind even with the fable in hand. Consider the two endpoints. In 1971, Intel would ship its first microprocessor, a chip called the 4004 that contained roughly twenty-three hundred transistors, each of them a marvel of miniaturization by the standards of the day. A modern processor of the twenty-first century would contain well over a hundred billion transistors on a comparable sliver of silicon. That is not a doubling or a tripling but a multiplication by tens of millions, achieved not in a single leap but through the patient, relentless accumulation of one doubling atop another, generation after generation. Had the automobile improved at a comparable rate, a car would travel faster than the speed of light and cost less than a cup of coffee. The comparison is a cliché of the industry precisely because no ordinary human intuition can grasp the arithmetic of sustained exponential growth.

It helps, too, to understand how the doubling was actually achieved, because the method is more elegant than the arithmetic suggests. Chips are not assembled but printed. The circuit pattern is drawn at enormous size, then shrunk and projected through lenses onto a wafer of silicon coated in a light-sensitive film, in a photographic process called photolithography—essentially the same trick as making a print from a negative, but in reverse and at unimaginably fine scale. To double the number of transistors on a chip, engineers did not need to invent a new kind of transistor; they mainly needed to sharpen the focus of that projection, printing the same patterns a little smaller each time. Sharper lenses, shorter wavelengths of light, cleaner chemistry—each improvement let them shrink the features and pack in more switches on the same sliver of silicon. And because a smaller transistor is also a faster and a thriftier one, each shrink delivered three gifts at once: more transistors, quicker switching, and lower power, all from the same square of sand. This is why the consequences compounded so ferociously. The cost side is the part that still beggars belief. In the early 1960s a single transistor might cost on the order of a dollar; today a dollar buys well over a billion of them. No commodity in the history of commerce—not grain, not steel, not light, not any manufactured thing—has ever fallen so far in price, so fast, for so long. Robert Noyce himself once put the acceleration plainly: in 1959 his invention made it possible to put a single circuit on a chip; by 1964 you had to fit ten just to stay in the game; six years after that, a thousand.

What began as an observation slowly hardened into something stranger and more powerful: a prophecy that made itself come true. Because everyone in the industry believed the doubling would continue, everyone planned for it. Chip designers laid out products for capabilities that did not yet exist, confident the manufacturing would catch up on schedule. Equipment makers built the next generation of fabrication tools to hit the targets the law implied. Executives set research budgets and product roadmaps by it. Competitors raced one another to stay on the curve, knowing that to fall behind was to die. The prediction became a coordinating mechanism for an entire global industry, a shared clock by which thousands of companies synchronized their most expensive bets—so that the semiconductor industry may be the only one in history to have run for half a century on a schedule it set for itself by reading a magazine article. Moore had described a trend; in describing it, he had helped will its continuation. It is one of the rare cases in which a forecast, simply by being widely believed, altered the behavior of everyone who might have proven it wrong.

The article itself became, in time, an object of veneration bordering on the comic. Original copies of that April 1965 issue of Electronics grew so scarce and so coveted that in 2005, when the prediction turned forty, Intel publicly offered ten thousand dollars for a clean copy. The winning issue turned up in the attic of an engineer in England, who had kept his old trade magazines for decades and beat the rush to the mailbox; and around the same time, librarians reported that would-be treasure hunters had begun quietly razoring the Moore article out of bound library volumes, so that a modest 1965 essay on chip manufacturing became the target of petty theft in reading rooms. Few pieces of technical writing have ever been so literally worth stealing.

Moore himself remained modest about the whole affair to the end of his long life. He had, he liked to point out, gotten the details wrong more than once and had been as surprised as anyone that the trend endured; he never imagined, he admitted, that the industry would keep the pace for fifty years. He never patented the idea, never claimed it was inevitable, and repeatedly warned that it would eventually run into the hard walls of physics—that transistors could not shrink below the size of atoms, that heat and quantum effects would someday impose a limit no cleverness could evade. For decades those predicted limits kept receding just out of reach, defeated by yet another engineering breakthrough. Moore lived to see the company he co-founded become one of the largest on earth and the industry he helped create wire itself into nearly all of modern life, and he lived a very long time, from 1929 until his death in 2023 at the age of ninety-four, giving away much of the fortune the law had helped him earn.

You feel the aftershocks of Moore's Law every time a three-year-old phone begins to lag, every time last year's marvel becomes this year's bargain-bin castoff, every time a device that would once have filled a warehouse turns up as a free giveaway in a cereal box or a birthday card that plays a song. The relentless cheapening of computation, the sense that electronics grow obsolete almost as fast as we can buy them, the quiet expectation that next year's machine will be better and cheaper than this year's—all of it is the lived experience of the curve Moore first sketched from five dots on a piece of graph paper. In recent years engineers have argued, with some justice, that the classic doubling is finally slowing, that the fable's board is running out of squares. But the world it built is the one we now inhabit, and there is no leaving it.

The law also has a subtler legacy hidden inside every gadget you own, one born of the moment the free ride began to end. For roughly forty years, each new generation of smaller transistors was not only more numerous but individually faster, so that chips simply ran at higher and higher speeds—the clock rate climbing from the 4004's fraction of a megahertz into the gigahertz—and software grew quicker without programmers lifting a finger. Around the middle of the 2000s that particular bargain broke down: the transistors kept shrinking, but pushing a single processor ever faster began to generate more heat than any chip could shed, and the steady climb in clock speed stalled. The industry's answer was to stop making one processor faster and start putting several side by side on the same chip, dividing the work among them. That is why the phone in your pocket and the laptop on your desk are advertised as "quad-core" or "octa-core"—not one brain running ever faster, but several brains laboring in parallel, a direct architectural consequence of Moore's Law bending against the limits of physics. The relentless doubling did not so much stop as change its shape, and the multicore chip is the fingerprint it left on the machines of our own moment.

There is a temptation, looking back, to treat Moore's Law as the whole story—to imagine that the personal computer arrived simply because transistors kept getting cheaper and more plentiful until, at some threshold, a computer small enough and affordable enough for one person became inevitable. That version contains a truth. Without the relentless doubling, none of what followed would have been possible; the raw material of the revolution was cheap, abundant computation, and the law is the reason it became cheap and abundant. But laws do not build machines. Somebody still had to look at all those transistors crammed onto a chip and imagine what to do with them—had to see, in a slab of etched silicon, not just more components but a different kind of thing entirely.

At Intel, that leap of imagination was about to happen, prompted by an unlikely source: a Japanese company that wanted nothing more than a better desktop calculator.

Chapter 8: A Computer on a Chip

In the summer of 1969, a delegation of engineers from a Japanese calculator company called Busicom arrived at Intel's young offices in Santa Clara carrying a stack of blueprints and a large ambition. Intel was barely a year old and still made its living selling memory chips, but Busicom wanted something more: a set of custom integrated circuits for a new line of desktop calculators, printing machines meant to sit on the desks of accountants and shopkeepers. The Japanese engineers had designed the logic themselves, and their plan called for roughly a dozen specialized chips, each hard-wired to perform one particular task—one for the keyboard, one for the printer, one for the display, and so on. It was a sensible design by the conventions of the day. It was also, to the eyes of one Intel engineer, needlessly, almost painfully complicated.

That engineer was Marcian "Ted" Hoff, a soft-spoken researcher whom Intel had hired as its twelfth employee and assigned, more or less, to figure out what to make of interesting problems. Hoff studied the Busicom design and grew uneasy. The proposed chips were so complex and so specialized that they seemed to defeat the whole economic logic of Intel's business, which depended on making a few standardized products in enormous volume. Each custom chip would have to be designed from scratch, used only in this one calculator, and then discarded when the calculator was obsolete. There had to be a better way, and Hoff, who had spent time around the general-purpose minicomputers then coming into use—in particular the elegant, spare little PDP-8 from Digital Equipment Corporation—began to think about the problem from the opposite direction. What if, instead of building a dozen chips that each did one fixed thing, Intel built a single chip that could do anything: a small, simple, general-purpose central processing unit that would perform whatever task a program told it to?

The insight was deceptively radical. A calculator, in Hoff's conception, did not need custom hardware for every function. It needed a modest processor, some memory to hold instructions, and a program stored in that memory telling the processor what to do. Change the program and you could change what the chip did without touching the silicon at all. This was, in miniature, the same stored-program idea that had animated the great room-sized computers of the previous two decades—the notion, traceable back to the mathematician John von Neumann and the pioneers of the 1940s, that a computer's instructions could live in its memory as just another kind of data, so that the same physical machine could become a thousand different machines depending on what you loaded into it. No one, though, had yet dared to compress the beating heart of a computer—its arithmetic, its logic, its control—onto a single sliver of silicon small enough to hold between two fingers. Hoff sketched an architecture built around such a chip, and Intel's management, including Robert Noyce, gave him room to pursue it, though the company's primary obligation remained delivering something Busicom could actually sell. Noyce, ever the encourager, is said to have told Hoff to keep exploring the idea on the side even as the official calculator project ground forward.

An idea, however elegant, is not a working chip, and here the project stalled. Hoff had conceived the architecture, and a colleague named Stanley Mazor helped refine it, but neither man was a specialist in the difficult art of translating a logical design into the physical reality of transistors laid out on silicon. For months the concept languished, more promise than product. Busicom, meanwhile, was waiting, growing impatient, and had sent one of its own engineers, Masatoshi Shima, across the Pacific to help see the work through. When Shima arrived at Intel in the spring of 1970 expecting to find a nearly finished design, he was dismayed—by his own later account, appalled—to discover that little more than the concept existed on paper. The project needed someone who could actually build the thing.

That someone arrived in April 1970. Federico Faggin was an Italian physicist and engineer, newly hired from Fairchild, where he had done pioneering work on a manufacturing technique called silicon-gate technology. In the older way of making chips, the tiny gates that switched each transistor were made of metal, laid down in a separate step that had to be aligned by hand under a microscope, wasting space and slowing the transistors down. Faggin's silicon-gate method used the silicon itself to form the gates, so that the transistors could be packed more tightly, switch faster, and be positioned far more precisely. It was, as it happened, precisely the technique the ambitious new chip would require, and Faggin was one of the few people in the world who had mastered it. He took over the project on practically his first day and found himself in a desperate race, working punishing hours, sometimes sleeping little, to turn Hoff's architecture into a design that could actually be manufactured, inventing along the way the layout methods that would let so much circuitry fit into so little space. Shima, the Busicom engineer, stayed on and threw himself into the work beside Faggin, and the two men pushed through months of intense labor, checking and rechecking by hand the intricate patterns that would be photographically shrunk and etched onto the silicon. When the first fully functional chips came back from fabrication in the small hours of an early 1971 morning and Faggin tested them alone through the night, they worked—

and he drove home at dawn and woke his wife to tell her he had just built something that would change the world.

The result was the Intel 4004, and it was a small miracle of density. Onto a chip no larger than a fingernail, Faggin had crammed roughly twenty-three hundred transistors—the whole central processor of a computer, its ability to add and subtract and follow instructions, reduced to a single component. It was a four-bit processor, meaning it handled information in the smallest of gulps, four binary digits at a time, and by any raw measure it was feeble, ticking along at a clock speed of some seven hundred and forty thousand cycles a second and managing perhaps sixty thousand operations in that time—a rate a room-sized mainframe of the era would have found laughable. And yet Intel liked to point out a comparison that captured the wonder of it: this fleck of silicon smaller than a postage stamp had roughly the computing muscle of ENIAC itself, the thirty-ton, eighteen-thousand-tube colossus that had glowed and sweated in its Philadelphia room a quarter century before. The machine that had filled a basement now fit under a fingertip. Faggin, proud of what he had made and wanting to leave a private signature on it, etched his initials—a tiny "F.F."—into the corner of the chip's design, so that every one of the millions of 4004s ever manufactured carried, invisibly, the mark of the man who built it.

Intel introduced the 4004 to the public in November 1971 with an advertisement in a trade newspaper that announced, with more accuracy than the world yet appreciated, "a new era of integrated electronics." It is often told as a tale of visionary corporate daring, a company boldly setting out to put a computer on a chip. The truth is more accidental and more human. The microprocessor was not born of a grand plan to democratize computing; it was born as a cost-cutting shortcut to fill a calculator order from a Japanese client, pursued on the margins by an engineer who simply found the original design too clumsy to bear. Intel's leadership was, for a long while, genuinely unsure that the thing had much of a future beyond calculators, and the company nearly let the whole opportunity slip away.

For the commercial story very nearly did go sideways. Busicom had paid for the development and initially held exclusive rights to the chip, and had Intel honored that arrangement, the microprocessor might have remained locked inside a line of Japanese adding machines. But Busicom fell into financial difficulty and came back asking for a lower price. Hoff and Noyce spotted their chance: Intel would grant the discount, they proposed, in exchange for the right to sell the microprocessor to anyone else, for any purpose other than calculators. Busicom, needing the savings and seeing little value in rights to a chip it thought of as merely its calculator's brain, agreed, and Intel bought back the freedom to sell the 4004 to the world for a reported sixty thousand dollars. It was one of the great bargains in the history of technology—sixty thousand dollars for the commercial rights to the microprocessor—and Busicom, which would fade and vanish within a few years, surely came to regret it.

There is a tangle of legitimate claims about who invented the microprocessor first, and honesty requires acknowledging them. Other engineers were pursuing similar ideas at the same moment. Texas Instruments would soon have a competing single-chip design, and, most tantalizingly, a young engineer named Ray Holt had designed a remarkably sophisticated processor chip set for the flight computer of the Navy's F-14 Tomcat fighter—work that may well have produced functioning microprocessor silicon before the 4004, but that was classified by the military and kept secret for decades, unsold and unseen. What is not in dispute is that the 4004 was the first microprocessor offered for sale on the open market, the first that ordinary companies could simply order from a catalog and design into their own products. Hoff had supplied the concept, Mazor the architectural refinement, Shima the calculator expertise and relentless drive, and Faggin the implementation that made it real. It was a genuinely collaborative invention, and its parentage would be argued over for years afterward, with more than a little bitterness about who deserved the lion's share of the credit. History has tried, belatedly, to share it out fairly: in 2009 the United States awarded its National Medal of Technology jointly to Hoff, Mazor, and Faggin for the invention of the microprocessor, and Faggin, whose silicon-gate craftsmanship had turned an architecture on paper into a working chip, would later receive further honors of his own. Shima, too, is now remembered among the microprocessor's fathers, his contribution rescued from the footnotes where it long languished. But the machine itself settled the deeper question beyond dispute: a computer's mind could be manufactured like any other commodity, by the thousand, and stamped out on silicon.

Once the chip was free to be sold to all comers, engineers everywhere quickly grasped what Intel's own executives had been slow to see—that a cheap, programmable processor could be the brain of almost anything. Not just a calculator but a cash register, a traffic light, a gas pump, a scale, an elevator, a laboratory instrument, a pinball machine. Orders began to arrive from directions no one had predicted, and Intel discovered, to its own mild astonishment, that it might be in a far larger business than the one it had thought it was in. This is where you meet the 4004's descendants today, and it is not mainly in the computer on your desk. It is in the several dozen tiny processors humming inside an ordinary car, in the chip that runs your microwave and the one in your washing machine, in your key fob and your thermostat and the little brain inside a greeting card that plays a tune when you open it. Far more microprocessors are manufactured each year for these invisible, humble jobs than for anything we would recognize as a computer—tens of billions of them—each a distant grandchild of the modest chip Faggin built to satisfy a calculator company. The world quietly filled up with computers long before most people noticed they owned even one.

Even before the 4004 reached the market, a second and more

capable chip was taking shape at Intel, and its origins reveal how little anyone yet understood the thing they were building. A Texas firm called Computer Terminal Corporation, maker of a sleek programmable terminal called the Datapoint 2200, had come to Intel wanting its multi-chip processor design shrunk onto a single piece of silicon. Intel obliged, producing a chip it would sell as the 8008—an eight-bit processor, twice the appetite of the 4004, able to swallow information in bytes rather than four-bit nibbles. But Computer Terminal Corporation, when it saw the result, judged the chip too slow and too demanding of supporting parts for its terminal, and walked away, leaving Intel free to sell the design to whoever wanted it. So for the second time in as many years, a customer handed Intel the future and declined to keep it: first Busicom with the 4004, now a terminal company with the 8008. The instruction set that Computer Terminal Corporation had specified for its terminal, and that Intel cast into silicon almost as an afterthought, would echo forward through Intel's next chip and, eventually, into the processors of the IBM PC and nearly every personal computer that followed—a lineage begun by a company that thought it was merely ordering a part.

The 4004 itself was too weak to run a real computer of its own; four bits at a time could drive a calculator or a traffic signal but not much more. Faggin, for his part, would soon leave Intel to found his own company, Zilog, and design a more powerful chip that would help ignite the coming boom. Yet the principle had been proven, and Intel now understood, however dimly, that it might be in a different business than the one it had set out to enter. The next step was clear enough to those with eyes to see it: build a processor powerful enough that someone might reasonably wrap an entire computer around it—and put the machine, at last, into the hands of a single person.

Chapter 9: The 8080

In April 1974, Intel placed the 8080 microprocessor on sale, and though almost no one outside a narrow world of engineers noticed at the time, the machine that would ignite the personal computer revolution had just been born. It did not look like a revolution. It was a rectangle of black plastic barely two inches long, forty metal legs protruding from its sides like a mechanical centipede, a chip meant to be soldered onto circuit boards inside industrial equipment. But inside that unremarkable package sat something the 4004 had only gestured toward: a processor genuinely powerful and flexible enough that a person could build a real computer around it. Intel priced it at three hundred and sixty dollars, a figure the company's own salesmen chose in part as a wink at IBM, whose famous System/360 mainframes had made those three digits shorthand for serious computing. The joke carried an unspoken boast. Here, for the price of a nice television set, was a scrap of silicon that Intel believed could stand in the lineage of the room-sized machines that had until then belonged only to governments and corporations.

The road from the 4004 to the 8080 ran through an intermediate step, and that step was the 8008. Even as Faggin's team was finishing the four-bit calculator chip, another customer had come to Intel with a different need. A Texas company called Computer Terminal Corporation, later known as Datapoint, wanted a chip to run a "smart" terminal, and it wanted one that handled data eight bits at a time rather than four—enough to represent a full character of text, a letter or a digit, in a single gulp. Intel took on the work, and in 1972 it released the result as the 8008, the world's first eight-bit microprocessor. Like the 4004, it emerged from a collaboration in which Ted Hoff and Stanley Mazor shaped the architecture and Federico Faggin drove the physical design, with the customer's requirements setting the terms. There is a delicious irony buried in the 8008's origin, and it is one of the most consequential rejections in the history of technology: Computer Terminal Corporation, having commissioned the chip, ultimately decided it was too slow for their terminal and walked away, leaving Intel holding a general-purpose processor it had never meant to build. Intel, uncertain what else to do with it, simply put the orphaned chip in its catalog and sold it to anyone who wanted one. The 8008 was more capable than the 4004, but it was still awkward and slow, hemmed in by design compromises and by the limits of the manufacturing of its day. It hinted at what an eight-bit processor could be without quite delivering it.

The 8080 delivered it. Faggin had been agitating for a successor that would fix the 8008's flaws, and in November 1972 Intel hired the man who would help him build it: Masatoshi Shima, the brilliant Japanese engineer who had come from Busicom and had worked shoulder to shoulder with Faggin on the logic of the original 4004. Together they set about building a processor that would be, by the standards of 1974, genuinely formidable. The design was finished on the ninth of August, 1973; the first working silicon came back from the fabrication line in January 1974; and by that spring the chip was on the market. Fabricated with an improved manufacturing process, the 8080 ran many times faster than its predecessor, could address far more memory, and offered programmers a richer and more sensible set of instructions to work with. Where the 8008 had crawled along at something under a megahertz, the 8080 hummed at two million cycles a second and could grind through several hundred thousand instructions in the time it took to blink. Where the 8008 had been a cramped and grudging little chip, the 8080 was expansive. It could reach sixty-four thousand bytes of memory, a quantity that seemed almost luxurious. For the first time, a single inexpensive chip contained enough raw capability that a clever engineer could imagine surrounding it with memory and input and output and calling the result a computer.

The improvements sound abstract in the recounting, but each one loosened a shackle that had bound the 8008, and it is worth pausing to see, concretely, what those shackles were. Consider the business of reaching into memory. A processor stores its program and its data in memory chips arranged like an immense street of numbered mailboxes, and to fetch or deposit a byte it must first name the address—shout out the house number—of the box it wants. The number of addresses a chip can name is set by the width of its address bus, the bundle of wires that carries those house numbers. The 8080 had sixteen such wires, and sixteen binary digits can count from zero to sixty-five thousand five hundred and thirty-five, which is why the chip could reach exactly sixty-four kilobytes and not a byte more. The 8008 had only fourteen address lines and could name a mere sixteen thousand boxes, a ceiling that made ambitious programs impossible. Then there was the matter of doorways. The 8008 had been squeezed into an eighteen-pin package, far too few metal legs to give every signal its own path, so it was forced to shuffle addresses and data back and forth through a single narrow doorway, one crowded handful at a time. The 8080 spread its signals across forty pins and moved information in and out with far less contortion. Faggin, Shima, and Mazor also made a shrewd architectural choice, giving the chip's internal registers—its handful of tiny, lightning-fast scratchpads—specialized roles and letting them pair up to hold sixteen-bit numbers, which let the same limited budget of transistors do considerably more work. There were only some forty-five hundred transistors on the whole device, a number a modern processor exceeds many billions of times over, and every one of them had to earn its place.

It helps, too, to be concrete about what "eight-bit" actually meant, because the phrase is thrown around as if everyone knows. A bit is a single one-or-zero, the smallest possible scrap of information; string eight of them together and you have a byte, which can take any of two hundred and fifty-six distinct patterns—enough to stand for any letter of the alphabet, any digit, any punctuation mark, with room to spare. The 4004 had handled its world four bits at a time, in nibbles too small to hold a single character; the 8080 grabbed a full byte in one motion, which is why it could shuffle text, run richer programs, and generally behave less like a calculator and more like a computer. When you read that a processor is "eight-bit" or "sixty-four-bit," this is all the number is telling you: how big a bite of information the chip swallows in one gulp. The jump from four to eight, modest as it sounds, was the difference between a machine that could juggle numbers and one that could handle language.

Two further refinements mattered enormously and are easy to overlook. The first was chemical. The 8008 had been built in an older silicon-gate technique called PMOS; the 8080 switched to a faster variant called NMOS, and the change did more than boost speed. It made the chip compatible with the ordinary TTL logic chips that engineers already had piled on their workbenches, so the 8080 could be wired directly into the world of existing components without a translator sitting between them. The second refinement was subtler and, for the future of the whole industry, perhaps the most important of all: the 8080 inherited and extended the basic instruction set of the 8008. The modest body of software already written for the earlier chip could be carried forward and made to run on the new one. It seems a small housekeeping virtue. It was in fact the first significant instance of backward compatibility, the principle that new machines should honor the software of old ones, and it would go on to shape the entire computer industry and to make and unmake fortunes for the next half century.

Someone at Intel described the 8080 as an engine looking for a vehicle, and the phrase captured the situation exactly. Intel had built a superb little power plant, but the company still thought of itself as a supplier of components to other manufacturers—makers of cash registers and scales and machine-tool controllers and traffic-light timers—and it had scarcely any conception that its chip might sit at the center of a machine an individual would own. This is worth stating plainly, because it corrects a myth that has grown comfortable with age. It is often said that Intel invented the microprocessor in order to launch the personal computer. In fact Intel did nothing of the kind, and would have laughed at the suggestion. The engine existed before anyone had designed the automobile to put it in, and the men who ran Intel spent the crucial year of 1974 selling the 8080 to industrial buyers and looking no further. Their own market forecasts imagined embedded controllers, not a machine on a hobbyist's kitchen table. The vision would have to come from outside.

Intel was not alone in the field for long, and the arrival of rivals would matter enormously to the story about to unfold, because competition drove prices down and choices up. The most immediate challenger came from Motorola, an established electronics giant that in 1974 introduced its own eight-bit processor, the 6800. It was an elegant design, admired by many engineers for the cleanness of its architecture, and it gave Intel its first serious competitor in the microprocessor business. But the more consequential rivals were still gathering, and several of them would spring, fittingly, from Intel's own ranks and from the restless, defection-prone culture that Fairchild had bred a generation earlier.

The pattern of talented engineers walking out to start something better, so central to the birth of Silicon Valley, now repeated itself in the world of microprocessors. A group of engineers from Motorola, frustrated that their company would not pursue a cheaper chip, left to join a small firm called MOS Technology, where they designed a processor called the 6502. It was functionally similar to Motorola's 6800 but dramatically cheaper—when it was unveiled at a trade show in 1975 it sold for twenty-five dollars, a price so far below the going rate that engineers walking the aisles assumed it must be a hoax or a stripped-down toy—and that low price would soon make it the beating heart of some of the most important early personal computers, machines from Apple and Commodore and Atari. Meanwhile Federico Faggin himself, the man who had turned Hoff's concept into the 4004 and then built the 8080, grew frustrated at Intel, where he felt the individuals who actually created the chips went unrecognized, and did what so many valley engineers before him had done: he left. In 1974 he co-founded a company called Zilog, and there, reunited with Shima, he set out to design a processor that would run every program written for the 8080 but do it faster, on a single voltage supply, with a friendlier set of surrounding parts. The chip they produced, the Z80, would become one of the most widely used microprocessors of its era. The children of Fairchild were now begetting children of their own.

That lineage is not a museum piece; you very likely carry its descendants in your pocket and on your desk. The instruction set that Faggin and Shima and Mazor sketched for the 8080 was carried forward, extended and re-extended, into Intel's 8086 in 1978, and from there into the chips that ran the original IBM PC and every Windows machine since. The processor humming inside a modern laptop, for all its billions of transistors and its dozens of parallel cores, still answers, at its deepest level, to commands whose grammar was laid down for that forty-legged chip in 1974—a startling act of continuity, as if today's skyscrapers were still built to fit doorframes measured out in a medieval workshop. The Z80, for its part, went on to run everything from early arcade machines to the Texas Instruments graphing calculators that a generation of students smuggled into math class, and a close cousin of it kept the beat inside Nintendo's original Game Boy. When a teenager in 1999 played Tetris on a bus, a great-grandchild of the Altair's engine was doing the counting.

The 8080 also called forth, almost immediately, the first true operating system for small computers, and that too belongs to its legacy. A softspoken former naval officer and computer scientist named Gary Kildall, moonlighting as a consultant to Intel, wrote in 1974 a compact program he called CP/M—Control Program for Microcomputers—that let an 8080-based machine store and retrieve files on a floppy disk and manage the running of other programs. Before CP/M, every hobbyist computer was an island, its software written for its own peculiar hardware; CP/M offered a common floor that thousands of different machines could stand on, so that a program written once could run on any of them. It became the dominant operating system of the late 1970s, and its significance for what came later is hard to overstate. When IBM went looking for an operating system for its forthcoming personal computer at the end of the decade, it first knocked on Kildall's door, and the system it eventually bought instead—the one that made Microsoft's fortune and was christened MS-DOS—was closely modeled on the way CP/M worked. The lineage of the software on a modern computer, in other words, reaches back to the 8080 just as surely as the lineage of its silicon does.

But all of that lay just ahead. In the final months of 1974, the 8080 sat in Intel's catalog, a marvel of engineering waiting for a purpose its makers had not imagined, while the men who ran the company kept selling it to industrial customers and looking no further. The vision would have to come from someone unencumbered by Intel's assumptions about what computers were for and who they were for. It would come, improbably, from a struggling little electronics outfit in Albuquerque, New Mexico, run by a man who sold model-rocket kits and calculator parts by mail and who was, at that moment, desperate enough to bet his failing company on the wild notion that hobbyists might want a computer of their very own.

That company was called MITS, and the machine it was

about to build around the Intel 8080 would be named the Altair 8800.

Chapter 10: A Company in the Desert

On a flat stretch of Albuquerque, in a strip of low commercial buildings baking under the New Mexico sun, there sat in the early 1970s a storefront that had once been a restaurant. The Enchanted Sandwich Shop was gone; in its place, wedged between a laundromat and a massage parlor, was a small electronics company with a name far grander than its premises: Micro Instrumentation and Telemetry Systems. Inside, past cheap paneling and secondhand desks, engineers bent over circuit boards while a tall, heavyset man with a booming voice moved among them like a force of weather. Ed Roberts was thirty, a former Air Force officer with a degree in electrical engineering and an appetite for risk that alarmed everyone who lent him money. He stood six feet four and carried close to three hundred pounds, and when he was certain about something—which was nearly always—he was almost impossible to argue with. He believed, against most of the available evidence, that his little company in the desert was about to change the world. He turned out to be right, though not in any way he could have predicted, and the being-right nearly bankrupted him first.

Roberts had founded MITS in 1969 with a handful of partners, all of them tied in one way or another to the electronics work being done at nearby Kirtland Air Force Base, where Roberts had been stationed in the laser division of the Weapons Laboratory. The original idea was almost quaint. Model-rocket hobbyists—of whom there were surprisingly many, launching small solid-fuel rockets into the enormous New Mexico sky—wanted to know how high their rockets flew and how they behaved in flight. MITS proposed to sell them telemetry: tiny transmitters and light-flashing instruments that a rocket could carry aloft to report back on its own journey. It was a charming business and a small one. The rocketry market was never going to make anyone rich, and the partners drifted away, leaving Roberts increasingly in command of a company chasing whatever the electronics hobby world would buy.

What the hobby world wanted, in the early 1970s, was calculators. The pocket calculator had arrived as one of the first consumer miracles of the integrated-circuit age, and companies large and small rushed to sell them. MITS pivoted hard. Roberts designed calculator kits—bags of parts that an ambitious hobbyist could solder together into a working machine, sold through the mail and advertised in the back pages of electronics magazines. For a while it worked spectacularly. Orders poured into the little storefront; MITS grew to more than a hundred employees; Roberts hired, expanded, borrowed. The four-function calculator that a hobbyist could build on a kitchen table was, in its way, a marvel, and it made MITS briefly a real presence in the calculator trade.

The flagship of this brief golden age was a calculator kit called the MITS 816, and its success gives a sense of how quickly Roberts's fortunes could swing. He had persuaded a skeptical banker to keep extending credit on the strength of his certainty, a pattern that would repeat itself throughout the company's life; Roberts was a man who could talk a lender into one more loan when the ledgers said otherwise, and his sheer conviction became a kind of collateral. For a season the calculator kits justified that faith, moving in numbers that briefly made MITS a name in the hobby press. But the very thing that made a calculator cheap to build—the ever-falling price of the integrated circuits at its heart—was a knife that cut both ways, because the same falling prices that let a small company sell a kit also let a giant sell a finished product for less than the kit's parts.

Then the giants moved in. Texas Instruments, which manufactured the very chips that companies like MITS depended on, began selling finished calculators directly to consumers—and at prices below what MITS paid for the components alone. It was a classic squeeze, the kind that has crushed countless small manufacturers before and since, and it was merciless. The bottom fell out of the calculator market almost overnight. By 1974 MITS was drowning. The company carried roughly a quarter of a million dollars in debt—an enormous sum for so small an operation—and Roberts, by his own later accounts, was staring at ruin. He had bet the company on calculators, and larger players had simply reached down and taken the game away.

A more cautious man would have folded, paid what he could, and gone looking for a salaried job. Roberts did the opposite. Cornered, deeply in debt, running a company most of his creditors expected to disappear, he decided to gamble everything one more time—on an idea that nearly everyone he described it to considered either impossible or pointless. He would build a computer. Not a calculator, not an instrument, but an actual general-purpose digital computer, small enough and cheap enough that an ordinary electronics hobbyist could own one. In an era when a computer meant a refrigerator-sized machine costing tens of thousands of dollars, tended by professionals in air-conditioned rooms, the notion that a lone enthusiast might want one—let alone afford one—struck sober observers as absurd. Roberts thought otherwise. The hobbyists who had bought his rocket telemetry and his calculator kits were, he believed, exactly the people who would kill to own a computer of their own, if only someone would build them one they could pay for.

The technical door had just been opened by a company four hundred miles to the west. In 1971 Intel had produced the 4004, the first commercial microprocessor—an entire central processing unit etched onto a single sliver of silicon. By 1974 Intel had followed with the 8080, a far more capable eight-bit processor that was, for the first time, powerful enough to serve as the brain of a real, if modest, computer. It was the 8080 that made Roberts's gamble conceivable, and the arithmetic of that gamble turned on a single shrewd negotiation. Intel listed the 8080 at three hundred and sixty dollars in small quantities, a price that would have made a sub-four-hundred-dollar computer flatly impossible—the chip alone would have eaten the entire budget. But Roberts, bargaining as a manufacturer promising to buy in volume, talked Intel into selling him the processors for around seventy-five dollars apiece. That one deal is what made the whole proposition work. Take a seventy-five-dollar brain, add a power supply and a metal case and a bag of cheaper supporting chips bought at scale, sell the result as a kit the customer assembles himself, and suddenly the fantastical price on the eventual magazine cover was not a fantasy at all but a spreadsheet that balanced.

Around that single chip Roberts set out to design a complete computer, and the design that emerged was spartan in the extreme, deliberately so. Every dollar of cost had to come out somewhere. There would be no keyboard, no screen, no printer—none of the things a modern person pictures when imagining a computer. The machine was essentially a metal box holding a power supply, the 8080 processor, a small amount of memory, and a row of toggle switches and blinking lights on the front panel through which a determined user could laboriously enter and read programs in raw binary. It was, to the uninitiated, almost comically austere: a box of switches that lit up. But to Roberts, and to the hobbyists he was betting on, it was something close to sacred. It was a computer—a real, programmable, general-purpose computer—and it would belong to whoever built it.

Roberts was not, it turned out, quite the only person dreaming this dream, and the rivalry that spurred his machine into print is one of the stranger accidents of the story. A few months earlier, in July 1974, the competing hobbyist magazine *Radio-Electronics* had put on its cover a build-it-yourself computer called the Mark-8, designed by a Virginia Tech graduate student in chemistry named Jonathan Titus and based on Intel's older, weaker 8008 chip. The Mark-8 was a genuine microcomputer kit, and it sold to hobbyists as a five-dollar booklet of instructions plus a set of circuit boards, and it landed with enough of a splash to alarm the editors of *Popular Electronics,* who did not care to be scooped by their archrival on so exciting a frontier. It was precisely this competitive sting that sent Les Solomon hunting for a computer project of his own—something better than the Mark-8, something with the more capable 8080 at its heart. In one of history's quiet ironies, Titus had actually offered his design to *Popular Electronics* first, and been turned down; the magazine's rejection of the Mark-8 and its subsequent scramble to answer *Radio-Electronics* is a large part of why the Altair, and not some 8008-based also-ran, became the machine that lit the fuse. Roberts arrived, in other words, at the exact moment a national magazine was desperate for what he was building.

To sell the machine to the world, Roberts needed two things he did not have: a national audience and a name. The audience he found in New York, at the offices of the hobbyist bible *Popular Electronics,* whose technical editor Les Solomon had been hunting for exactly such a project. The name has hardened, like so much of this story, into legend, and it deserves to be flagged as such. The version most often repeated holds that the machine was christened after a star in *Star Trek.* Solomon himself, speaking to the audience at the first Altair Computer Convention in March 1976, said the credit belonged to his twelve-year-old daughter Lauren, who was watching an episode one evening and remarked, "Why don't you call it Altair—that's where the Enterprise is going tonight." The episode was almost certainly "Amok Time," the only installment of the original series that sends the crew toward the star Altair. It is a lovely story, and it may even be true, but it is worth noting that Solomon told it years after the fact and that other participants remembered it differently; one account credits a magazine editor named John McVeigh, who is said to have suggested "Altair" simply because the machine was a stellar performer and the name had a suitably cosmic ring. The polished *Star Trek* version, in other words, is best treated as a pleasant probability rather than settled fact. What is certain is the result: the machine acquired a name that sounded like the future, the Altair 8800.

One detail of the *Popular Electronics* arrangement deserves to be better known, because it upends the usual picture of the journalist and his subject. The cover article that introduced the Altair to the world was not written by a staff reporter at all; it was written, in large part, by Ed Roberts himself, together with his engineer Bill Yates. The two men in Albuquerque drafted the very piece that would present their machine to four hundred thousand readers as an objective breakthrough, an arrangement that would raise eyebrows in any modern newsroom but that suited everyone involved: the magazine got the sensational project it craved, and MITS got to describe its own creation in the most glowing possible terms. Roberts, in other words, did not merely build the Altair and its economics; he helped author the myth of it, shaping the words that would send the checks flooding toward his door. It was salesmanship of a very high order from a man who, whatever his troubles with a soldering budget, understood better than almost anyone that a product is also a story.

There remained the small matter of showing the thing to the world, and here the desert company's luck ran characteristically ragged. In October 1974 Roberts and his head engineer, Bill Yates, finished the first working prototype and crated it up for shipment to New York, entrusting it to the Railway Express Agency for the long haul east. The machine never arrived. The Railway Express Agency, an old and failing freight company, was in the throes of a labor strike and would collapse entirely within months, and somewhere in that chaos the only finished Altair in existence simply vanished. It was never recovered. The most important prototype in the history of personal computing had been lost by a dying delivery service, and it has never turned up since—no museum holds it, no collector has ever produced it. The entire remaining hopes of a small, indebted company in the New Mexico desert, and, though no one yet knew it, the future of a whole industry that did not yet exist, disappeared into a shipping company's death throes.

Roberts had bet everything, and now the object of the bet was gone. There was no time and no money to build another before the magazine's deadline. What happened next—the improvised solution that put an empty box on the most famous cover in computing history, and the deluge of mail that followed—would decide whether MITS lived or died. It is worth pausing, before that deluge, to notice where all of this was happening. Not in California, not in Boston, but in a converted sandwich shop in Albuquerque, a city with no particular claim to technological fame. And yet that unlikely address would soon draw two young men from a thousand miles away to write software for the Altair, and the little company they founded there to do it would be called Micro-Soft. The desert had, almost by accident, become the birthplace of an industry—a reminder that revolutions rarely begin where the maps say they should.

But that lay ahead. First there was a magazine cover to save, and a machine that no longer existed to photograph.

Chapter 11: The Cover That Started Everything

On newsstands across America in the last days of December 1974, the January 1975 issue of *Popular Electronics* appeared with a photograph that would become one of the most consequential magazine covers of the twentieth century. The issue had been registered with the copyright office on the twenty-ninth of November and reached the racks around the nineteenth of December, in the crowded shopping days before Christmas, so that the machine that would launch an industry arrived, fittingly, as a kind of gift. The image showed a rectangular metal box, deep blue with a brushed-aluminum front panel, studded with two neat rows of toggle switches and a scatter of small indicator lamps. Beside it ran the promise that made grown hobbyists' hearts race: "PROJECT BREAKTHROUGH! World's First Minicomputer Kit to Rival Commercial Models." And in smaller type, the detail that turned excitement into action—the machine, the Altair 8800, could be had as a kit for three hundred and ninety-seven dollars, or fully assembled for six hundred and twenty-one. A real computer, the cover declared, for the price of a decent stereo. Men who had spent their lives assuming that owning a computer was as fantastical as owning a jet fighter stood in drugstores and hobby shops and read the words again to be sure.

The word "minicomputer," it should be said, was a small and telling piece of salesmanship. The Altair was not a minicomputer at all; a minicomputer in 1974 meant a machine like Digital Equipment's PDP-11, a cabinet-sized workhorse costing many thousands of dollars that hummed away in laboratories and businesses. The Altair was something genuinely new for which the ordinary reader had no word—a microcomputer, built around a single microprocessor chip—but "microcomputer" would have meant nothing to a newsstand browser, whereas "minicomputer" borrowed the prestige of the real thing. The cover, in other words, dressed the future in the respectable clothes of the present. It was a forgivable sleight of hand, and it worked.

The man most responsible for putting that box on that cover was Les Solomon, the magazine's technical editor, a former adventurer and a shrewd judge of what would set his readers alight. *Popular Electronics* was, in the 1970s, the bible of the American electronics hobbyist—a monthly gospel of build-it-yourself projects, from ham radios to burglar alarms, read by a devoted congregation of engineers, tinkerers, students, and dreamers. Solomon understood that his readers did not merely want to read about technology; they wanted to hold a soldering iron and make it themselves. He had been looking for a genuine computer project, something that would electrify the hobby, and when Ed Roberts pitched him a complete, affordable, buildable computer from a struggling company in New Mexico, Solomon recognized the story of a lifetime. He championed the Altair inside the magazine and gave it the cover, and in doing so he lit a fuse that neither he nor Roberts could have measured.

There was, however, a complication that the gorgeous cover photograph quietly concealed. The prototype MITS shipped to New York for the photo shoot never arrived; it was lost in the collapse of the Railway Express Agency, the freight company that had been carrying it east. So the blue box gleaming on the most famous cover in personal-computer history was not the real machine at all. Solomon and his staff, working from an earlier batch of photographs and with a deadline bearing down, dressed up an empty mockup—a case with a front panel of switches and lamps and essentially nothing behind them—and photographed that. The most influential computer image ever printed was, in the strictest sense, a picture of a machine that could not compute. Nor did the deception end at the cover: the production Altairs that MITS eventually shipped had a completely different internal circuit-board layout from the lost prototype the article described. The real Altairs would work—thousands upon thousands of them would soon be humming on hobbyists' workbenches—but the one that launched the revolution was a promise wearing the face of a product.

For the reader who sent away his money, what arrived was a lesson in just how bare a "real computer" could be. The Altair came, in its kit form, as a heavy carton of parts: a metal case, a power supply, a backplane, a bag of integrated circuits and resistors and capacitors, and pages of instructions. The buyer had to build it—hours of careful soldering, with real risk that a single cold joint or reversed component would leave the machine dead. And when at last it was assembled and switched on, the Altair did, from a modern vantage, essentially nothing that looked like computing. It had no keyboard. It had no screen. It had no way to store a program when the power went off. What it had was that front panel—the rows of switches and lights that had gleamed on the cover—and through them, and only them, the human being communicated with the machine.

To use the Altair in its original form was an act of monkish discipline, and it is worth walking through a single concrete example to feel just how far the personal computer had to travel. Suppose you wanted the machine merely to add two small numbers. You would first have to know the numeric codes that the 8080 understood for "load this number," "add this number," and "stop," and you would have to look them up in a manual and translate them into their eight-on-or-off binary digits. Then you would set the eight data switches on the front panel to spell out the first instruction, ones up and zeros down, and flip the deposit switch to lodge that byte in memory. Then the next byte. Then the next. A program to add two numbers and hold the answer might run to a dozen such bytes, each entered by hand, and a single switch left in the wrong position anywhere in the sequence would produce silence or nonsense. When you finally ran it, the machine answered not on a screen but by lighting a row of lamps in the pattern of the binary result, which you then had to translate back into a number in your head. Hobbyists nonetheless devised whole games this way; one famous early program, "Kill the Bit," made a single point of light race around the lamps while the player stabbed at switches to catch it. The base kit shipped, moreover, with a mere two hundred and fifty-six bytes of memory—not kilobytes, not megabytes, but two hundred and fifty-six individual bytes, an amount so small it could barely hold a sentence. And yet hobbyists wept over it, because it was theirs, and because for the first time the thing sitting on the bench was genuinely, undeniably a computer.

It is worth dwelling for a moment on the sheer reach of that single issue, because the cover did its work not on a handful of insiders but on a vast and dispersed congregation. *Popular Electronics* went out to something like four hundred thousand subscribers and newsstand buyers, and the Altair cover reached, among that multitude, very nearly every person who would matter to the coming revolution. In Cambridge, Massachusetts, a Honeywell programmer named Paul Allen spotted it at a kiosk and sprinted to show his friend Bill Gates. In the San Francisco Bay Area, the same issue helped inspire the hobbyists who would within weeks convene the first meeting of the Homebrew Computer Club. All across the country, in basements and spare bedrooms and garages, engineers and teenagers and retirees read the same three digits—three hundred and ninety-seven dollars—and felt the same jolt of disbelief and desire. Few magazine covers in history can claim to have detonated so precisely on so much latent talent at once; it was less a publication than a starting gun, and thousands of people heard it fire in the same week.

For the buyer determined to escape the tyranny of the front panel, the natural next step was a used Teletype, and the detail illuminates just how improvised early personal computing really was. The favored device was the ASR-33, a hulking electromechanical Teletype originally built for sending messages over telegraph and telex lines, which could be wired to the Altair through an add-on interface card so that a user could finally type commands on a keyboard and read the machine's replies printed on a roll of paper. These machines were noisy, oil-stained industrial relics, often bought secondhand for a few hundred dollars—frequently more than the computer itself—and they clattered like a hail of typewriters. But paired with an Altair and, soon, with a language to run on it, the Teletype turned the blinking box into something a person could actually converse with, and the awkward marriage of a 1963 telegraph machine to a 1975 microcomputer was, for many hobbyists, the moment their Altair stopped being a curiosity and became a tool.

What kept the Altair from being merely a clever dead end—a toy that blinked and did nothing more—was a decision Roberts and his engineers made about how the machine was built inside. Rather than solder every component onto one fixed board, they designed the Altair around a row of connector slots wired together by a shared set of electrical lines, a common pathway along which every part of the machine could send and receive signals. This shared pathway was a bus, and the Altair's version of it, with its roughly one hundred electrical contacts, would come to be known as the S-100 bus. Here it is worth correcting a flattering misconception. It is often said that Roberts engineered this open, expandable bus as a farsighted act of design, a deliberate gift to the tinkerers who would build upon it. In fact the origin was far more humble and largely accidental: MITS reached for a cheap and readily available hundred-pin edge connector—the kind used in other equipment—and simply wired the raw signals of the 8080 out to its pins, many of them without much thought for elegance or for future standardization. Several of those signals were poorly defined, and the design would give later engineers no end of grief. The bus became an industry standard not because it was well engineered but because it was there first and everyone copied it; only in 1976 did other companies gather to formalize it and give it the neutral name S-100, precisely so they would not have to advertise a competitor's product every time they mentioned it.

Yet accidental or not, that openness would prove to be the machine's deepest legacy, more important in the long run than its processor or its price. Roberts had built the Altair to save his company, and he assumed MITS would supply the add-on boards its customers needed. But the empty slots did not care who filled them. Almost immediately, small companies and lone engineers began designing S-100 cards of their own—memory boards, interface boards, boards to connect the Altair to a teletype so a user could finally type instead of flipping switches. A single machine had, by publishing its own internal wiring to the world, created the seed of an entire ecosystem. The personal computer would grow up not as a sealed appliance but as an open platform, a thing others could build upon, and much of what made the coming revolution a revolution—the swarm of small companies, the culture of tinkering and improvement—traces back to those hundred humble contacts.

You live inside that decision still. Every time you slot a graphics card into a desktop tower, plug a device into a USB port, or add a peripheral that a company other than your computer's maker designed and sold, you are enjoying the inheritance of the Altair's open bus—the principle that a computer should be a platform others can extend, not a sealed box. The app stores and plug-in marketplaces of the present are the same idea grown to planetary scale: an open set of slots, and a swarm of strangers rushing to fill them with things the original maker never imagined. The hundred crude contacts on the back of a blue box in Albuquerque were the first faint sketch of that world.

For all its austerity, the machine inspired a devotion that is hard to convey to anyone who has only known computers as sealed appliances. Most buyers chose the kit over the pricier assembled version, not merely to save money but because building it themselves was the point—the hours of soldering were an initiation, and the first time a freshly assembled Altair blinked its lights in an ordered pattern rather than dead silence, its builder had earned a small, real victory over the machine. Owners wrote to one another comparing notes, formed local groups to help each other track down faults, and treated the successful boot of a home computer as an event worth celebrating. The very name carried a whiff of aspiration: "8800" was chosen to echo the Intel 8080 at its heart while sounding weightier, more like the model number of some serious piece of laboratory equipment than a hobbyist's toy. That, in the end, is what the cover had promised and what the kit delivered—not a useful tool, not yet, but membership in something, the right to say that a real computer sat on your bench and answered to you.

None of this, in December 1974, was visible to Ed Roberts, who was mainly praying that enough readers would send money to keep his creditors at bay. He and his lender had done the arithmetic and concluded that if the Altair sold a few hundred units over the coming year, MITS might just survive. It was a modest, defensive hope, the calculation of a man trying not to drown. What actually happened in the weeks after that blue box hit the newsstands overwhelmed every projection anyone at MITS had dared to make.

The mailbags began to arrive in Albuquerque, and they did not stop.

Chapter 12: The Flood

In the second week of 1975, an employee at the little MITS storefront in Albuquerque carried the day's incoming mail to a desk and began to open it, and something was clearly wrong—or clearly wonderful, depending on how one felt about being buried alive. The envelopes held checks. Not a trickle of checks but a torrent, hundreds of them, from hobbyists across the country who had read the *Popular Electronics* cover and mailed away their money for a computer that, in many cases, MITS had not yet figured out how to manufacture in quantity. Within days the company that had been staring at bankruptcy was holding more orders than it could count, from people willing to pay in advance and wait weeks or months for the privilege of soldering together a box of switches. Ed Roberts had gambled that a few hundred Americans might want a computer of their own. He had radically, gloriously underestimated his fellow citizens.

To measure just how badly he had underestimated them, one need only compare his hopes with the reality. Roberts and his banker had studied the numbers and concluded that MITS would break even if it could sell two hundred Altairs over the whole of the coming year; the loan that kept the company alive was extended on roughly that expectation. Within the first three months, the backlog stood at four thousand orders. The first full month after the cover appeared, February 1975, brought something on the order of a thousand of them—five times the entire year's sales Roberts had prayed for—and the flood did not recede. By the end of spring the company had shipped roughly twenty-five hundred machines and still could not keep pace; by August more than five thousand Altairs had gone out the door. These figures, like most numbers from the era's fast-rising and chaotic little firms, are best treated as good estimates rather than audited totals; MITS was not, in those months, a company with the leisure to reconcile its ledgers. But the shape of the thing is unmistakable. A near-dead company in a converted sandwich shop had become the improbable center of a national phenomenon.

To grasp what this did to MITS as a physical operation, it helps to picture the storefront in January and then again in October of the same year. In January the company employed fewer than twenty people, a scrappy band who knew one another's coffee orders. By October it had grown to around ninety—a fourfold-and-more expansion in ten months, achieved on the fly, with new hires soldering and packing and answering phones almost before their desks arrived. The building strained at the seams. Inventory piled up; half-built machines waited on scarce parts; the phones rang without pause with customers demanding to know where their computers were. MITS was living the entrepreneur's most dangerous dream, the one that kills as many companies as failure does: too much success, arriving too fast, for an organization built to handle a fraction of it.

The strain showed in the machines themselves. Rushed into production, assembled from parts sourced under pressure, the Altair was, by the honest testimony of the people who built and bought it, a temperamental beast. Kits arrived with missing pieces or faulty components. Power supplies ran hot. And the memory boards MITS shipped to expand the machine beyond its meager base earned a reputation for unreliability that would haunt the company. The trouble is worth understanding, because it explains the opening that others would rush through. MITS's expansion board used what is called dynamic memory, a kind of storage that holds each bit as a tiny electrical charge in a microscopic capacitor. The catch with dynamic memory is that these charges leak away within a fraction of a second, like water seeping out of thousands of tiny buckets, so the circuitry must race around constantly topping each one up—refreshing it—before the bit fades to nothing. MITS's refresh scheme was poorly designed and easily disturbed, so the boards would quietly lose the very data a hobbyist had spent an evening laboriously toggling in. Building an Altair that actually worked could require not only skill with a soldering iron but persistence bordering on stubbornness. And still they came, because the alternative was owning no computer at all, and to the people mailing checks to New Mexico that was no alternative worth considering.

For every headache the Altair caused, it also created an opportunity—and this is where the flood of orders began to shape something larger than a single company's fortunes. The Altair's open bus, those hundred electrical contacts waiting in empty slots, meant that its very shortcomings were invitations to entrepreneurs. MITS could not build reliable memory boards fast enough, or well enough? Then someone else would. Two engineers named Bob Marsh and Gary Ingram, working out of a Berkeley garage, designed a memory board that used static memory—a costlier but far more dependable design that did not need the fussy constant refreshing—and it plugged straight into the Altair's slots and simply worked. Their company, Processor Technology, was born of MITS's flaws and would soon become one of the best known of the add-on makers, eventually building a celebrated computer of its own. But it was one among many. Small firms sprang up almost overnight to sell what MITS could not: better memory, interface cards to connect the Altair to teletypes and, later, to keyboards and screens, cassette-tape systems for storing programs, boards for every purpose a hobbyist could imagine. A cottage industry was condensing out of the air around a single product, and it was doing so with startling speed. What is striking, in hindsight, is how much of that industry was built by people scratching their own itch: a hobbyist who could not get a MITS memory board to hold its data would design a better one, discover that thousands of other owners had the same complaint, and find himself, almost by accident, running a company. The Altair's very unreliability, in this sense, was a gift to the ecosystem, because every flaw was a market waiting to be served.

Before long the imitation climbed from add-on cards to whole computers, and the most successful challenger is a machine many people have seen without knowing it. A California company called IMS Associates, run by a businessman named Bill Millard, looked at the Altair's flaws and its open bus and built a sturdier, better-engineered machine of its own that plugged into the very same S-100 slots and ran the very same software. Released late in 1975, the IMSAI 8080 is generally reckoned the first "clone" in personal-computer history—a product that borrowed a rival's architecture wholesale and did the job more reliably—and it sold on the order of seventeen to twenty thousand units, comfortably outselling many of its contemporaries. If the IMSAI's boxy blue face looks oddly familiar, it is because a fictional teenager used one to nearly start a nuclear war: the computer that David Lightman hunches over in the 1983 film *WarGames*, dialing into a military supercomputer from his bedroom, is an IMSAI 8080, and for a generation of moviegoers it became the very image of what a home computer was. Other Homebrew-adjacent firms filled in the rest of the ecosystem. Cromemco, founded by two Stanford men, Harry Garland and Roger Melen, sold a board called the Dazzler that could throw crude color graphics onto a television screen, giving the hobbyist's austere machine its first splashes of color; Processor Technology, having conquered the memory problem, went on to build the Sol-20, among the first of these machines to arrive as a finished unit with a keyboard built right in, pointing toward the appliance-like computers still a couple of years away.

This swarm of small suppliers marked something genuinely new in the world: the birth of a hobbyist market, a commercial ecosystem organized around a personal computer. Before the Altair there had been no such thing, because there had been no personal computer for a market to organize around. Now there was a product, a growing installed base of thousands of owners hungry for anything that would make their machines more capable, and a rising tide of little companies eager to sell it to them. The print world moved with startling speed to serve this new tribe. In September 1975, only months after the flood began, a magazine called *Byte* appeared, devoted entirely to the microcomputer and its owners, and it swelled within a few years into a fat monthly volume as thick as a phone book, stuffed with technical articles and page after page of advertisements from the hundreds of little companies now selling boards, kits, and programs. Where *Popular Electronics* had treated the computer as one hobby project among many, *Byte* treated it as a world unto itself, and its arrival signaled that the microcomputer had graduated from a novelty into a subculture large enough to sustain its own press. Advertisements for add-on boards began to fill the back pages of the electronics magazines, right beside the MITS ads. Newsletters appeared, and one of the most influential of them came from inside MITS itself: a young marketing man named David Bunnell, who wrote the company's documentation and launched a customer newsletter called *Computer Notes*, sensed before almost anyone that this new machine would need its own press. Bunnell would go on to found a string of magazines—*PC Magazine, PC World, Macworld*—that defined technology journalism for a generation, so that the sprawling world of tech media you scroll through today, the reviews and the launch-day coverage and the endless commentary, traces a direct line back to a mimeographed hobbyist newsletter stapled together in Albuquerque. The word *microcomputer* moved from novelty to common currency. An industry was assembling itself, piece by piece, board by board, out of the enthusiasm of people who had until a few months earlier had no idea they were an industry at all.

To reach the hobbyists scattered across a continent, MITS did something that now seems charmingly of its moment: it put the computer on the road. In the summer of 1975 the company outfitted a motor home as a traveling showroom—the famous "MITS Mobile," a blue-and-white van that rolled from city to city with Altairs aboard, holding seminars in hotel conference rooms where curious enthusiasts could see the machine run, ask questions, and place their orders in person. Hundreds turned out at each stop, and the caravan became a kind of revival meeting for a faith that had until recently had no churches. It was at one of these stops, near Palo Alto, that a pre-release paper tape of Altair BASIC was spirited away and copied—the spark of the piracy fight still to come—so that the very tour meant to sell the machine also, unintentionally, seeded the free-sharing culture that would soon enrage its software authors. The MITS Mobile is a small, vivid emblem of the whole moment: a computer company reduced to barnstorming the country in a van, because the market it had created was so new that no one yet knew any other way to reach it.

It is worth pausing on who these buyers were, because they were not, for the most part, chasing any practical application, and here a common assumption deserves correcting. It is often said, in tidy retrospect, that the Altair's runaway success proved there had been pent-up demand for practical home computing all along—that Americans had been waiting to balance their checkbooks and organize their recipes on a machine of their own. In fact almost none of the early buyers had any such use in mind, and the Altair in its raw form could not have served them if they had; it could barely be persuaded to add two numbers and blink out the answer. What the buyers wanted was the machine itself—the fact of possession, the intoxicating knowledge that a real computer sat on the workbench and answered to them alone. They joined clubs, traded tips, formed correspondence networks, and pooled their ingenuity, and in doing so they became the first citizens of a new culture. The personal computer was, at its birth, less a tool than an object of devotion, and the flood of orders into Albuquerque was the first great census of the faithful.

That devotion had its high liturgy, too. In March 1976, MITS and Bunnell staged the World Altair Computer Convention, the first conference ever held for owners of personal computers, and hundreds of hobbyists made the pilgrimage to Albuquerque to meet one another in the flesh, compare machines, and hear Ed Roberts speak. It was, in its way, the ancestor of every packed technology keynote and sold-out fan convention that has followed—grown men traveling across a continent to celebrate a product they loved. And yet MITS's own moment in the sun would prove astonishingly brief. The chaos never fully resolved, the competitors multiplied, and within two years Roberts would sell the company to a larger firm called Pertec, pocket a few million dollars, and walk away from computing altogether. In one of the stranger second acts in the industry's history, the man who built the first successful personal computer moved to rural Georgia, took up farming, and then went back to school to become a small-town medical doctor, spending the rest of his life tending patients who mostly had no idea what he had once set in motion.

Ed Roberts had set out to save his company and had instead, without quite intending to, called an industry into being. But an industry needs more than hardware. A box of switches and lights, however beloved, was a machine without a voice—it needed a language, some way for a human to tell it what to do in something other than raw, hand-toggled binary. And in Cambridge, Massachusetts, that same *Popular Electronics* cover had just been spotted by two young men who thought they knew exactly how to give the Altair a tongue.

Chapter 13: Two Kids and a Language

On a cold morning in the winter of 1974 into 1975, Paul Allen was crossing Harvard Square in Cambridge, Massachusetts, when he stopped at a kiosk and saw the cover. There, on the January issue of *Popular Electronics,* sat the blue box with its rows of switches—the Altair 8800, a real computer for under four hundred dollars. Allen, twenty-one and working as a programmer for Honeywell nearby, bought the magazine and hurried across the freezing street to Currier House, where his friend Bill Gates, nineteen and a Harvard sophomore, was living. The two had known each other since their teens at the Lakeside School in Seattle, where they had shared a consuming, slightly illicit obsession with computers in an age when almost no teenager had touched one—sneaking after hours onto time-shared machines, once getting themselves banned from a company's computer for exploiting bugs in its accounting system. Allen slapped the magazine down and told Gates, in effect, that it was happening—the thing they had always talked about, the moment when computers got small and cheap enough for ordinary people, was happening right now, and if they did not move immediately they would miss it. Gates read the cover and agreed. Their shared fear, often repeated in later years, was as simple as it was galvanizing: that the revolution was going to happen without them.

What the Altair conspicuously lacked, the two young men understood at once, was a way for a human being to actually program it without the torture of the front-panel switches. It needed a language—a high-level programming language in which a person could write instructions in something resembling English and arithmetic, rather than hand-entering binary a byte at a time. The obvious candidate was BASIC, the Beginner's All-purpose Symbolic Instruction Code, a teaching language developed a decade earlier at Dartmouth that was clear, friendly, and beloved by the very sort of enthusiast now buying Altairs. To feel the difference such a language makes, imagine wanting the machine to print a greeting five times. Through the front panel, that meant looking up opcodes and toggling dozens of bytes by hand; in BASIC it meant typing a couple of short lines a child could read, and letting the interpreter do the translating into the machine's binary tongue. If someone could write a version of BASIC that ran on the Altair's Intel 8080 processor, in the machine's cruelly small memory, then the box of switches would become something a person could genuinely command. Gates and Allen resolved that they would be that someone—before anyone else thought of it, and before they had any real idea whether they could pull it off.

There was one enormous, almost comic problem: they did not have an Altair. Neither of them had ever seen one, touched one, or run a single instruction on an 8080. The machine existed for them only as a photograph and a set of technical specifications. Before writing a line of code they placed a now-famous phone call to Ed Roberts in Albuquerque, claiming—with the airy confidence of the very young—that they had a BASIC nearly finished and asking whether MITS would be interested. This was, to put it charitably, an exaggeration; they had written nothing at all. Roberts, who had reportedly fielded similar boasts from others, was noncommittal but willing to see a demonstration, and a date was set for the spring of 1975. That was enough. Gates and Allen now had a deadline for software that did not exist, for a machine they had never used, in a race whose other runners they could not see.

The way they solved the machine-they-did-not-have problem was not conjured from nothing; it grew, remarkably, out of an earlier failure, and the connection is worth telling because it corrects the tidy legend of two prodigies inventing everything from scratch. A few years before, still teenagers, Gates and Allen had started a little venture called Traf-O-Data, whose premise was to read the paper tapes produced by the rubber traffic-counting hoses stretched across roads, tally the cars, and sell tidy reports to city traffic departments. To crunch the data they had a machine built around Intel's earlier 8008 chip, and because that hardware was often unfinished, Allen had written a program on a big PDP-10 mainframe that imitated the 8008—a simulator that let the mainframe pretend, instruction by instruction, to be the little chip. Traf-O-Data itself was a flop; in a famously mortifying episode, when the partners finally demonstrated their traffic machine to Seattle officials, the hardware refused to work at all, and only Allen's frantic improvising saved any dignity. But that emulator turned out to be one of the most valuable failures in business history. Confronted now with the need to develop for an 8080 they did not possess, Allen simply took his old 8008 simulator, studied the Altair's programming manual, and rewrote it to imitate the newer chip instead. The big time-shared computer in Harvard's Aiken Computation Laboratory would now pretend, byte by byte, to be an Altair that sat a thousand miles away and that they had never laid eyes on.

It is worth lingering on that Traf-O-Data misadventure, because it is the sort of formative failure the tidy legends leave out. The little company had three partners—Gates, Allen, and a third friend named Paul Gilbert, who actually built the traffic-counting hardware—and it never made real money; over its life it took in a few thousand dollars and mostly frustrated its founders. The mortifying demonstration became family lore precisely because it went so wrong: the machine that had performed flawlessly on Allen's mainframe emulator sputtered and died when the real hardware was wheeled in front of paying officials, and it fell, by one account, to Gates's own mother to help smooth things over. Had Traf-O-Data succeeded as a business, the two might have stayed in the traffic-data trade and never written a line of Altair BASIC. Instead it failed in just the right way, teaching Allen the exact skill—simulating one computer on another—that would let two young men in Massachusetts write software for a machine sold out of a storefront in New Mexico. The whole edifice of Microsoft, one could say, rests on a traffic-counting company that couldn't count traffic.

Gates, meanwhile, threw himself into writing the BASIC interpreter itself, targeting this simulated processor and agonizing over every byte, because the Altair's memory was so brutally small that the entire language had to fit in a space most programmers would have considered laughably inadequate. The finished interpreter—complete with its own routines for reading input, printing output, and editing lines—had to squeeze into four kilobytes, roughly four thousand bytes, less storage than a single small photograph on a modern phone consumes, less than the text of a couple of pages of this book. Into that keyhole Gates fit an entire working programming language. They were joined by a third contributor, Monte Davidoff, a fellow Harvard student who overheard them fretting about mathematics and volunteered to write the floating-point routines that let the language handle fractions and very large numbers. For roughly two months the work consumed them. Gates in particular vanished into it, coding in marathon stretches, sleeping at his terminal, subsisting on the fumes of obsession, chasing the language down into the machine one economical instruction at a time—all of it aimed at a computer that, to them, was still nothing but a simulation running on borrowed mainframe time that Harvard's administrators, when they later noticed, were distinctly unhappy about, though no written rule quite covered what the students had done.

The moment of truth came when Allen flew to Albuquerque to demonstrate the software on a real Altair for the first time. He carried the finished program on a roll of punched paper tape—the fragile physical medium on which the interpreter was stored, a ribbon of holes that a reader could feed into the machine. The stakes could hardly have been higher, and the confidence hardly more misplaced, for their code had never once run on actual hardware; it had only ever run on Allen's imitation of the hardware. On final approach into the Albuquerque airport, Allen realized with a jolt that they had forgotten something essential: they had never written a bootstrap loader—the small preliminary program, entered by hand through the front-panel switches, that the Altair needed in order to read the paper tape in the first place. Without it the machine would have no way to ingest their masterpiece at all. Working in raw 8080 machine code, on a notepad, from memory and first principles, Allen scribbled out the loader before the plane touched down. At the MITS office, with Roberts watching, Allen toggled in his hand-written loader, fed in the paper tape, and waited while the teletype clattered. The Altair printed a prompt asking how much memory the system had. Allen answered, typed a short command, and the machine responded correctly. Their BASIC, written for a computer they had never seen, worked—barely, on the first genuine try, in front of the one man whose opinion could make or break them. Allen later confessed that he was as astonished as anyone; there had been no reason to expect that thousands of lines of untested code, aimed at simulated hardware, would spring to life on the real thing at the first attempt.

The borrowed mainframe on which all this had been built would later cause Gates a measure of trouble worth noting, because it complicates the heroic version of the tale. The PDP-10 in Harvard's Aiken Computation Laboratory was funded in part by the Defense Department's research arm, and it was not obviously meant for two undergraduates to develop a commercial product on—Allen was not even a Harvard student, which made his heavy use of the machine harder to justify. When administrators looked into the unusual volume of computer time being consumed, the episode raised pointed questions about a student using a federally funded academic machine to build a business. No formal ruling ever quite settled the matter—there was, conveniently, no written policy that plainly forbade what they had done—but the affair lends a certain irony to Gates's later, famous fury over other people using his software without paying, given that his own first product had been born on computer time he had not exactly bought.

Roberts was sold. MITS agreed to license the BASIC and distribute it with the Altair, and Allen soon took a job at MITS in Albuquerque as its director of software, while Gates traveled back and forth from Cambridge, taking a leave from Harvard that quietly hardened, over the next two years, into a permanent departure. To hold the enterprise they were building, the two needed a name for their partnership, and on the fourth of April, 1975, in Albuquerque, they formally established one that fused the two words at the center of everything they were doing: microcomputer software. They called it "Micro-Soft," hyphen and all in the earliest days, before the punctuation quietly fell away and the name settled into the single word the world would come to know. Here it is worth dispelling a piece of folklore: Microsoft is popularly imagined to have been born in a Seattle garage, in the manner of so many origin myths, but there was no garage and it was not Seattle. The company was founded in a dusty New Mexico desert town, in a rented office in the orbit of Ed Roberts's improbable machine, by two men barely out of their teens who had bet everything on the conviction that the future of computing lay not in the hardware but in the code that made it sing.

The deal that made it all real also quietly established a principle the industry had never needed before. When MITS agreed to distribute Altair BASIC, Gates and Allen did not sell the program outright; they licensed it, collecting a royalty on copies while keeping ownership of the code itself, and—crucially—they retained the right to license the same BASIC to other computer makers. This was a radical inversion of how the business had always worked. In the mainframe world, software came bundled with the machine, an afterthought thrown in by the hardware maker; the notion that the software might be the valuable thing, the asset a separate company owned and licensed to whoever built the hardware, was close to unheard of. Gates, still a teenager, grasped it with startling clarity, and the insight—that value was migrating from the metal to the code—would prove more important than any single program he ever wrote. The original paper tape of that first Altair BASIC, incidentally, survives; a roll of it now rests in the collection of the Computer History Museum, a fragile ribbon of punched holes that happens to be one of the founding documents of the world's largest software company.

That bet is one you cash in every day without thinking about it. The language they squeezed into four kilobytes became the seed of Microsoft's entire fortune, and versions of Microsoft BASIC would soon be burned into the memory of the Apple II, the Commodore 64, the TRS-80, and countless other machines, so that a whole generation of children first learned that they could command a computer by typing `PRINT` and `GOTO` into a home machine—their first taste of the strange power of making a machine obey. The very idea that software is a thing worth building a company around, that the programs matter as much as the metal, begins here, with two kids, a language, and a roll of paper tape. Altair BASIC transformed the machine from a blinking curiosity into something a person could truly program.

But it also created a problem that would soon detonate into one of the defining conflicts of the entire personal-computer age—a clash over a question no one had quite had to answer before: when a program can be copied perfectly and endlessly for free, does anyone actually own it? That question was about to be posed, furiously and publicly, in an open letter that a very angry young Bill Gates was preparing to write.

Chapter 14: An Open Letter

In February 1976, subscribers to the newsletter of the Homebrew Computer Club and readers of several other hobbyist publications opened their mail to find a letter that read less like a business communication than a howl of outrage. It was dated the third of February, addressed "An Open Letter to Hobbyists," and signed by William Henry Gates III, General Partner, Micro-Soft. The twenty-year-old author did not bother with pleasantries. He accused the very community that had embraced his software—the enthusiasts trading Altair BASIC hand to hand across the country—of theft, plain and simple. "As the majority of hobbyists must be aware," he wrote, "most of you steal your software. Hardware must be paid for, but software is something to share. Who cares if the people who worked on it get paid?" The words landed like a thrown gauntlet in a culture that had, until that moment, regarded the free swapping of programs not as a crime but as a virtue, even a duty. With one letter, Gates opened a wound that has never entirely healed and named, for the first time and in the sharpest possible terms, the conflict at the heart of the software business that did not yet exist.

To understand why Gates was so angry, one has to understand how his BASIC had escaped into the wild, and the story has an irony he may not have fully appreciated. In June of 1975, MITS had sent a promotional caravan it called the MITS Mobile touring the country to show off the Altair, and at a stop near Palo Alto—a demonstration that drew many Homebrew members—a roll of the pre-release Altair BASIC paper tape was, by the most repeated account, quietly lifted from the floor. It found its way to a Homebrew regular named Dan Sokol, who had access to a tape-duplicating machine, and Sokol ran off dozens of copies. At the next meeting he arrived with a cardboard box full of them and handed them out for free, on the club's understood condition: that whoever took one would make more copies and pass them along. Within weeks the interpreter Gates, Paul Allen, and Monte Davidoff had labored over for months was circulating across the country without a cent flowing back to its authors. To the hobbyists doing the copying, this was simply how the community worked and how good software spread. To Gates, who had counted the hours poured into every byte and expected a royalty on each copy, it was straightforward stealing—and it stung all the more that his product had been set loose, in effect, by MITS's own marketing tour.

His argument, stripped of its heat, was coherent and, in its way, prophetic. Writing good software, Gates insisted, was hard work—real work, requiring enormous investment of time and skill. He reckoned that the value of the computer time alone that had gone into developing the language exceeded forty thousand dollars, and he pointed out, with some bitterness, that once the royalties, the manual, the tape, and the overhead were tallied, Altair BASIC had been for its authors a break-even proposition at best; by his estimate, fewer than one in ten of the people running his BASIC had actually paid for it. If hobbyists expected quality software to exist at all, someone had to be willing to write it, and no one would write it for a living if the fruits of that labor were simply taken. "The thing you do do is prevent good software from being written," he told the copiers. "Who can afford to do professional work for nothing? What hobbyist can put three man-years into programming, finding all the bugs, documenting his product, and distribute it for free?" It was a challenge and a prediction rolled into one: that a world in which software was free to copy would be a world in which good software went unwritten, because the people capable of writing it would go do something that paid.

At the root of the quarrel lay a genuinely new fact about the world, one worth pausing over because it is easy to take for granted now. A program is not like a chair or a radio or a book. When Dan Sokol ran off his copies, each duplicate tape was a perfect, bit-for-bit twin of the original, indistinguishable from it, produced at almost no cost and taking nothing away from the person who had held the tape before. Photocopy a novel and the copy is grainy, bound clumsily, plainly inferior; duplicate a program and the copy is the thing itself, flawless and complete. Software was the first commodity in history that could be reproduced infinitely and perfectly for essentially nothing, and that single strange property is what made the old rules of ownership fit it so awkwardly. Gates was insisting that this magical copyability should not exempt software from being paid for; the hobbyists felt, just as strongly, that a thing which could be shared at no cost to anyone almost demanded to be shared.

The community he was scolding held, then, with equal conviction, a nearly opposite view—and it is only fair to give that view its full weight, because it was not the mere self-serving rationalization Gates implied. The hobbyist ethic had grown out of a genuine and generous tradition, one that ran back through the university computing labs and the early hacker culture, in which information was meant to be shared and improved upon by the whole community rather than locked away for private gain. To these enthusiasts, to withhold a program, or to demand payment each time it was reproduced, felt like an artificial scarcity imposed on something that wanted by its nature to be free. They had built their fragile new world on mutual aid—trading tips, boards, and programs freely—and many of them saw Gates not as a wronged craftsman but as an interloper trying to fence in a commons. Some also noted, not without justice, that Gates and Allen had themselves developed their BASIC on Harvard's mainframe, using expensive computer time they had not exactly paid full freight for, and found the young man's lecture on the sanctity of paying for what one uses a touch rich.

Here a common simplification deserves correcting. It is often said that the hobbyists were simply pirates helping themselves to a finished commercial product, as one might shoplift a radio. But in early 1976 there was scarcely a commercial software industry to steal from. Software was normally given away with the hardware, or written by the buyer, or swapped among friends; the notion of software as a standalone product with a price on it was still faint and strange. Gates's letter, in other words, was not really a defense of an established norm. It was an attempt to invent one—to declare into being a rule that did not yet exist, and to shame a community into accepting it. That is precisely why the letter matters so much, and why it is fair to call it the birth cry of the commercial software industry. Before it, software was largely an afterthought. Gates's letter, for all its youthful stridency, planted a flag on the idea that software was property, that its makers deserved to be paid, and that taking it without paying was theft. That proposition, so contested in 1976, would within a few years become the foundation of one of the largest industries the world had ever seen—an industry in which the same Bill Gates would grow richer than the founders of any hardware company he once envied.

MITS, for its part, had already tried to fight the copying with pricing, and the scheme it devised throws the whole quarrel into sharp relief. The company sold Altair BASIC for around five hundred dollars if you bought it on its own—a deliberately punishing sum—but for a small fraction of that, on the order of a hundred and fifty dollars or less, if you also bought a MITS Altair and one of its memory boards.

The logic was transparent: make the software cheap for honest customers who bought the hardware, and dear for anyone who had acquired an Altair, or a clone, without paying MITS for the metal. It was an early, awkward stab at the problem every software seller would wrestle with forever after—how to charge for something that costs almost nothing to copy—and it satisfied no one. Hobbyists who felt gouged by the five-hundred-dollar sticker were only more inclined to duplicate a tape that a friend had bought cheap, which is more or less exactly what happened, and which is what set Gates to writing in the first place.

The reaction to the letter was, predictably, ferocious, and it can be measured with unusual precision. Gates received something on the order of three to four hundred letters in response, and by his own account only five or six of them contained any payment; the overwhelming majority were furious, denouncing him at club meetings and in newsletters as arrogant, as greedy, as a young man who fundamentally misunderstood the spirit of the movement he was trying to profit from. Yet the letter also worked, in a subtler sense than winning the argument. It forced the question into the open and made the hobbyists confront, for the first time, that the thing they were building had commercial stakes—that the friendly world of free-flowing paper tapes was going to have to reckon with money, ownership, and the professionals who would soon flood in. The age of innocence, in which a computer was purely a hobbyist's toy and its software a gift freely given, was ending, and Gates had been rude enough to announce it out loud.

The hobbyists did not merely fume; some of them answered Gates in the most pointed way imaginable, by building exactly the thing his letter claimed could not exist—good software written for free. Even before the Open Letter appeared, a Stanford lecturer named Dennis Allison and the volunteers around a Menlo Park nonprofit called the People's Computer Company had begun designing a stripped-down, wholly free version of the language called Tiny BA-

SIC, small enough to run on the same tiny machines, and they published its inner workings openly for anyone to type in, improve, and pass along. The newsletter they created to spread it grew into a legendary magazine, *Dr. Dobb's Journal*, whose very first issues carried Tiny BASIC out to the world at no charge. Its editor, Jim Warren, made the rebuttal explicit, writing that there was "a viable alternative to the problems raised by Bill Gates in his irate letter"—namely, software so freely shared that no one needed to steal it, because no one needed to buy it. Here, in embryo, was the whole future argument between proprietary and free software, playing out within months of Gates's letter: on one side a company insisting code was property, on the other a community proving that code could be a gift, each camp building the world it believed in.

Gates, for his part, did not let the matter drop. A few months later he published a shorter follow-up, sometimes called his "Second and Final Letter," walking back none of his central claim even as he acknowledged the storm his first note had raised. And the piracy he complained of never really stopped; it merely became a permanent feature of the software business, one that companies would spend the next half century fighting with copy protection, license keys, activation servers, and lawsuits. The industry's eventual answer was less a victory than a truce: software would be sold not as an object you owned but as a license you were granted, the fine print that still governs nearly every program you use.

The argument he started that February has never really ended; you take a side in it, usually without noticing, several times a day. Every time you click "I agree" to a license before installing an app, every anti-piracy warning, every subscription that lets you use software you never truly own, is the direct descendant of Gates's insistence that code is property to be paid for. And every time you use a web browser built on open code, or run the free operating system that quietly powers most of the world's servers and every Android phone, you are living inside the hobbyists' opposite conviction—that software shared freely and improved by many hands can be a public good. The free-software and open-source movements that flowered in the decades after, giving the world Linux and countless tools that anyone may copy and study, were in a real sense the hobbyist ethic vindicated, growing up alongside the commercial industry Gates called into being rather than being extinguished by it. Both sides of that garage-era argument, remarkably, won.

There is a final irony that only the passage of decades could supply. The furious young man who insisted in 1976 that no one had a right to give away the fruits of others' labor would, half a century on, be remembered as much for giving away a fortune as for building one—devoting the back half of his life to a foundation that spends billions to fight disease and poverty, much of it, in a sense, returning to the world the value he once fought so hard to fence in. Historians marking the letter's fiftieth anniversary have noted the strangeness of it: that the founding document of proprietary software was written by a man who would become one of history's great philanthropists, and that the hobbyists he scolded for their generosity would live to see their ethic of sharing become, in the open-source movement, one of the most productive forces in the modern economy. Both the letter and the community it attacked, in other words, aged into something more complicated and more humane than the shouting match of 1976 could have predicted.

But that hobbyist age, even in its twilight, had a beating heart—a room where the ethic of sharing that so infuriated Gates had been forged, and where the future of the personal computer was being argued out week by week among a crowd of tinkerers, one of whom was quietly building a machine that would change everything.

Chapter 15: The Homebrew Computer Club

On the rainy evening of March 5, 1975, some thirty men crowded into a two-car garage on a quiet street in Menlo Park, California, and sat on folding chairs and upturned crates amid the tools and clutter, waiting to see who else had come. The garage belonged to Gordon French, an engineer who had cleared space in it for the occasion, and the gathering had been called by French together with Fred Moore, a gentle, idealistic activist and computer enthusiast who had done much of the organizing. On a workbench, as if presiding over the proceedings, sat one of the very first Altair 8800s to reach the San Francisco Bay Area—a review machine that MITS had shipped to a local outfit called the People's Computer Company—and it was the object, more than any other, that had drawn these strangers out into the rain. They went around the room introducing themselves and describing what they were interested in and what they hoped to build, and by the time the evening ended, something had been set in motion that would help define the next decade of the personal computer. They would come to call themselves the Homebrew Computer Club.

The men in that garage were, in the main, exactly the

hobbyists this history has been tracking: engineers and technicians from the electronics firms thickening along the peninsula south of San Francisco, students, tinkerers, a few dreamers with more enthusiasm than credentials. What united them was a hunger that had until very recently seemed almost embarrassing to admit—the desire to own and understand a computer, to hold in their own hands the kind of machine that had always belonged to corporations and universities and the government. The Altair on the bench proved that the dream was no longer fantasy, and it gave the assembled tinkerers a common object to gather around, dissect, complain about, and improve. And complain they quickly did, which corrects a tidy assumption people often make about that first meeting. It is easy to imagine the club forming to worship the Altair as a triumph; in fact the members almost immediately grew impatient with the machine's crudeness and limits, and Homebrew became less a fan club for the Altair than a workshop devoted to building something better than it—to routing around MITS entirely. Fred Moore, in particular, carried into the room a conviction that would shape the club's whole character: that these people should pool their knowledge freely, that the way to advance was to share what you knew and what you built rather than hoard it. That ethic—generous, communal, faintly utopian—became the club's animating spirit, and it was formalized within days when Moore began editing a mimeographed newsletter, the first issue of which appeared on March 15, 1975, carrying members' discoveries out to a readership far larger than any garage could hold.

Nothing captured the strange magic of those early meetings better than a demonstration given by a member named Steve Dompier, and it is worth telling in full because it shows how much wonder these people found in machines that could, on paper, do almost nothing. Dompier owned one of the first Altairs in the region, and while running a program on it one day he noticed that a nearby transistor radio began emitting bursts of noise in time with the machine's calculations. A lesser tinkerer would have cursed the interference and moved the radio. Dompier recognized an instrument. What was happening was that the Altair's processor, switching its circuits on and off hundreds of thousands of times a second, threw off faint radio waves as a byproduct—electromagnetic leakage that the AM radio picked up as buzzing. By carefully arranging loops in his program to run at particular speeds, Dompier discovered he could control the pitch of that buzz, turning the computer's accidental radio static into chosen musical notes. He spent weeks toggling in the program by hand, and at a Homebrew meeting he set an ordinary radio beside his Altair and let the machine play, of all things, the Beatles' "The Fool on the Hill," followed by "Daisy Bell." The room, packed with hardened engineers, erupted. A computer with no speaker, no sound hardware of any kind, not so much as a way to display a letter on a screen, had just performed music by weaponizing its own electrical noise—and the hobbyists went wild, because they understood exactly how improbable and how clever it was.

The sharing ethic that so defined Homebrew did not spring from nowhere on that rainy night; it was inherited from a small Bay Area subculture that had been insisting for years that computers ought to belong to the people. A few miles away, in Menlo Park, an organization with the wonderfully countercultural name of the People's Computer Company had since 1972 been run by a former textbook author named Bob Albrecht, who evangelized for putting computing—especially the friendly BASIC language—into the hands of ordinary citizens and schoolchildren, and it was to Albrecht's group that MITS had sent one of its first review Altairs. Lee Felsenstein, before he ever picked up the Homebrew microphone, had helped build something even more radical: a 1973 project called Community Memory, which wired a battered teletype terminal into a record store in Berkeley and let anyone off the street type messages into a shared computer—arguably the first public computerized bulletin board, a social network assembled from surplus parts a full generation before the internet. Homebrew, in other words, was the confluence of two streams: the hardware hackers who wanted to own a machine, and the idealists who believed a machine could knit a community together. That fusion is what gave the club its peculiar double character, at once a swap meet for circuit boards and a congregation for a mild technological utopianism.

The Homebrew Computer Club quickly outgrew Gordon French's garage, moving to larger and larger venues and eventually settling for much of its life into an auditorium at the Stanford Linear Accelerator Center, where hundreds would attend. The format that emerged was pure to the club's spirit and became legendary among those who lived it. Meetings opened with a "mapping" or random-access period in which anyone could stand up and share news, ask a question, describe a problem, or announce a breakthrough; this rolling, freewheeling exchange of information was the heart of the thing. Afterward members would spill out into a "swap" of sorts, trading parts, schematics, tips, and programs—the free exchange of software that would so enrage Bill Gates was, at Homebrew, simply how things were done. There were no dues to speak of at first, no hierarchy that mattered, no gatekeeping. If you had something to teach, you taught it; if you needed help, you asked, and the room answered. It was less a club in the buttoned-down sense than a recurring town meeting of a nascent civilization.

And what a civilization it turned out to be, though no one in the room could have known it at the time. The roster of people who passed through the Homebrew Computer Club in its heyday reads, in retrospect, like a founders' list for an entire industry. Adam Osborne, who would go on to build one of the first portable computers, was a fixture and wrote a widely read column. Lee Felsenstein, an engineer with a countercultural streak who had cut his teeth on a pioneering public computer-terminal project called Community Memory, served as the club's master of ceremonies for years and would later design the influential Osborne 1. George Morrow, Harry Garland, Roger Melen, and a host of others who founded early microcomputer companies moved through its meetings. Something on the order of two dozen companies are said to have been founded by people who met or were inspired at Homebrew. It is tempting to call it a startup incubator before anyone had coined the term, but the comparison flatters modern incubators more than it does Homebrew, and it misses the point. The club had no program, no funding, no plan to launch anyone into business; it offered nothing but folding chairs, a microphone, and the free exchange of information. That such riches poured out of so unstructured a thing is precisely its lesson—that the deepest engine of the coming revolution was not capital or strategy but a community of obsessives freely teaching one another.

More than a talking shop, the club became the debut stage on which the coming industry first showed itself, and the roll call of premieres is remarkable. It was at Homebrew, not in any boardroom or press event, that Steve Wozniak first passed around the hand-built board that would become the Apple I, handing out photocopied schematics in the pure spirit of the room. Processor Technology's Sol, Cromemco's color-graphics boards, and a parade of memory cards and interfaces made their first appearances before this audience of merciless experts, who would praise a clever design and pitilessly diagnose a bad one within the same breath. The club's mimeographed newsletter, meanwhile, carried the week's discoveries far beyond the auditorium, so that a schematic demonstrated on a Wednesday night in Palo Alto might be soldered up in a bedroom in Ohio a fortnight later. In this way a single room of a few hundred people functioned as the nervous system of a national movement, its ideas propagating outward at the speed of the postal service, and much of what the world would soon call the personal-computer industry was, for a season, simply whatever the members of Homebrew happened to be excited about that month.

Presiding over much of this, and giving the club its distinctive voice, was Lee Felsenstein at the microphone and the steady undercurrent of Fred Moore's sharing ethic beneath it. Moore himself, it should be said, was in some ways an unlikely father of a computer club—a pacifist and antiwar activist more interested in what these machines might do for ordinary people and communities than in the technical thrill of the hardware. He kept the early membership lists by hand, believing that connecting people was the whole point, that a computer was valuable chiefly for what it let human beings do together. The club he helped start would run for more than a decade, holding meetings from that first rainy night in March 1975 until it finally wound down in December 1986, by which time the world it had helped create had grown so large and so commercial that a garage-born club of hobbyists no longer had the same reason to exist. In its span, Homebrew served as the town hall of the microcomputer revolution on the West Coast—the place where the loose, brilliant, argumentative energy of the movement gathered itself into something with direction. Its living descendants are everywhere the moment you look: the hackerspaces and maker fairs where strangers still gather to build, the open-source projects in which programmers scattered across the planet improve one another's code for free, the local user groups and repair collectives—all of them running, whether they know it or not, on the same conviction that lit up that garage, that knowledge shared multiplies rather than divides.

There is a poignancy to how the story ended for the club's gentle founder. Fred Moore, who had cared less about the machines than about the people they might bring together, drifted away from computing as the movement he had helped start turned into an industry worth billions, returning to the activism that was his first love; he was killed in a car accident in 1997, having grown steadily more estranged from the commercial juggernaut his little garage meeting had helped unleash. That tension—between the sharing, communal spirit of the founders and the vast fortunes the technology would soon generate—runs like a fault line through the whole history of the personal computer, and it was already visible at Homebrew. The same free exchange of programs that the members practiced as a matter of principle was, at that very moment, driving a young software author named Bill Gates to distraction, and the friendly anarchy of the club would within a few short years give way to a world of proprietary products, non-disclosure agreements, and the guarded secrecy of companies worth more than nations. Homebrew was, in a sense, the last innocent moment of the revolution, when the future could still be passed around a room on a sheet of photocopied schematics and everyone assumed that was simply how it should be.

For all the future notables in the room, the club's most consequential regular was a shy, brilliant young engineer from the nearby town of Sunnyvale who rarely spoke up at the microphone but soaked in everything he saw. Steve Wozniak had attended from that first rainy meeting—a friend, Allen Baum, had handed him a flyer—and what he saw there lit a fire in him. He would later describe it as a genuine eureka moment, saying plainly that the Homebrew Computer Club was the inspiration for what he did next: that seeing the Altair and hearing the members talk about owning their own computers made him resolve to design a machine of his own, cheaper and more elegant than anything on that workbench, to prove to the people at Homebrew that an affordable computer was possible. Wozniak was a virtuoso of circuit design, capable of doing with a handful of chips what others needed dozens to accomplish, and he possessed the pure, joyful engineer's instinct to give away what he made. When he finally built his computer—the machine that would be unveiled, tellingly, not to the press but to the club, on a Homebrew evening the following year—his first impulse was entirely in the Homebrew spirit: he wanted to hand out the schematics freely, so that anyone in the room could build one too.

He had a friend, though—a persuasive, intense young man

he had known since their teens, a fellow tinkerer with far grander and more commercial ambitions than Wozniak's own—who had a very different idea about what the two of them should do with such a machine.

Chapter 16: The Wizard and the Salesman

Sometime in 1971, in a garage in the flatlands of Sunnyvale, California, a lanky twenty-year-old with a soldering iron bent over a small metal box no larger than a paperback, tracing wires with the concentration of a watchmaker. His name was Stephen Wozniak, and the device he was building was, technically, a felony. It was a blue box—an electronic tone generator that mimicked the precise multi-frequency signals the telephone company used to route long-distance calls—and when it worked, it would let its owner place calls anywhere on Earth for free, riding the phone network like a stowaway. Woz, as everyone called him, had first read about such contraptions in an *Esquire* article titled "Secrets of the Little Blue Box," published in October of that year, and the notion that a handful of transistors could fool the vast, humming, coast-to-coast machinery of the Bell System struck him as almost unbearably beautiful. The trick at the heart of it was startlingly simple once you understood it: the phone network signaled to itself using audible tones, and a single pure note at exactly twenty-six hundred cycles per second, blown into a long-distance line, would fool the system into thinking the line was idle and hand the caller the keys to the whole switching network. Woz built a version that used purely digital circuitry, cleaner and more reliable than the analog boxes the phone "phreaks" had been passing around, and when at last it emitted the right cascade of tones and a distant line clicked open, he felt the particular joy that would define his life: the joy of making a clever thing work.

The blue box was not only an engineering exercise; it was an invitation to mischief, and one prank in particular has passed into legend because Wozniak himself has told it many times. Using his box, Woz once dialed his way through the international network to the Vatican in the small hours of the morning, and, in a thick accent, announced that he was Henry Kissinger—then the American secretary of state—calling to speak urgently with the Pope. The bewildered Vatican operator, taking him seriously, said the pontiff was sleeping but that a bishop would be roused to come to the phone; only when someone senior finally checked with the real Kissinger's people did the ruse collapse. It is a small story, but it captures the spirit of the thing: for Woz the point was never money or malice but the sheer delight of proving that a homemade circuit could reach across the planet and knock on the door of the Holy See.

Standing beside him, watching, calculating, was a sixteen-year-old high schooler named Steven Jobs. He did not fully understand the circuitry—few did the way Woz did—but he understood something Woz had not yet considered. This wonderful, forbidden little box could be sold. The two of them fell into an easy partnership, driving up and down the Peninsula and through the college dormitories peddling blue boxes for around a hundred and fifty dollars apiece; by their own later accounts they moved on the order of two hundred of them before the danger and the hassle ended the trade. It was a small, faintly criminal, entirely thrilling venture, and it revealed in miniature the pattern of everything that would follow. Wozniak was the engineer, the one who could conjure elegance out of silicon and wire. Jobs was the one who saw that elegance had a price tag, an audience, a future. Years later Jobs would say plainly that if not for the blue boxes, there would have been no Apple. He believed it, and there was truth in it.

The blue-box trade was never entirely safe, and one night it nearly ended in disaster in a way that foreshadowed the partnership's whole dynamic. Selling their boxes in a pizza parlor, the two were once robbed at gunpoint of one of the devices; on another occasion, stopped by police in a parking lot with a box in hand, a quick-thinking Wozniak passed it off as a musical synthesizer, and the officers, turning the mysterious gadget over in the dark, let them go. That either of them kept at so risky a hustle says something about them both—Woz for the pure engineering thrill of a machine that could outwit the phone company, Jobs for the intoxicating proof that a clever object could be turned into cash. The template of their later company was already fully formed in these teenage capers: one man who built the impossible thing because building it was joy, and one who understood that the thing could change the world only if someone had the nerve to sell it.

That template—the brilliant, unworldly maker paired with the driven, persuasive seller—has become so central to the mythology of technology that we now reach for it reflexively, casting nearly every startup as a hacker and a hustler, a Woz and a Jobs. The pattern was not invented in that Sunnyvale garage, but it was stamped so indelibly onto the culture there that it became the template every venture capitalist would later look for, the story every founding duo would be measured against. When people today speak of a company needing both a "technical cofounder" and a visionary front man, they are, whether they know it or not, retelling the story of two young men and a box of tones.

They had met a year or two earlier through a mutual friend, Bill Fernandez, in the same Silicon Valley suburbs where their fathers worked and their childhoods overlapped. On the surface they could hardly have seemed less alike. Wozniak, five years older, was shy, sweetly guileless, a compulsive prankster whose idea of rebellion was a rigged television jammer or an elaborate joke, and whose deepest desire was simply to design the most beautiful circuits he could imagine and show them to his friends. He had no interest in money for its own sake and a positive discomfort with confrontation. Jobs was his opposite in almost every register: intense, mercurial, barefoot and often unwashed in those years, a seeker who dabbled in fruitarian diets and Eastern mysticism, who would drop out of Reed College after a single semester yet keep auditing a calligraphy class that would one day shape the typography of an entire industry, and who possessed, even as a teenager, a frightening capacity to bend other people to his vision through sheer force of will. Colleagues would later call it his reality distortion field. Yet the two shared a bedrock of common ground—a love of electronics, a Bob Dylan obsession, a taste for pranks, and a conviction, still inchoate, that technology was not merely a business but a kind of counterculture, a way of putting power into the hands of ordinary people.

Their paths diverged and rejoined through the early seventies. Wozniak, after a restless stint at the University of Colorado and De Anza College, landed the job of his dreams in 1973 at Hewlett-Packard, designing calculators in the company that was, to a young Bay Area engineer, holy ground. HP was everything a decent employer should be: humane, meritocratic, run by two revered founders who wandered the labs and knew their engineers by name. Woz loved it there, and he assumed he would stay forever—a loyalty that would soon lead him to do something that reveals the gulf between the two friends. Jobs, meanwhile, drifted through Reed, through a spiritual pilgrimage to India, and into a job at the video-game company Atari, where his abrasiveness so grated on the daytime staff that he was shifted to the night shift. In one of the era's more revealing episodes, Atari offered a bounty—one hundred dollars for every chip a designer could eliminate—to whoever could streamline a new game called Breakout. Jobs, who could not have designed the circuit himself, enlisted Wozniak, who threw himself at the problem over four sleepless nights and produced a design of such radical economy that it stripped the chip count to the bone. The catch was that Woz's minimalism made the prototype almost impossible for Atari to manufacture, but the ingenuity was undeniable. Jobs told Woz that Atari had paid a bonus of just seven hundred dollars and handed him half, three hundred and fifty. The real bonus had been five thousand. Wozniak did not learn the truth for a decade, and when he did he wept—less over the money than over the deception by a friend. The story sits uneasily against the partnership's mythology, but it is well attested, and it says something true about both men that they built an empire together anyway.

Breakout mattered for more than the betrayal it exposed, because the design lodged in Wozniak's mind and would resurface in the machine that made him famous. "A lot of features of the Apple II went in because I had designed Breakout for Atari," he said later. "I had designed it in hardware. I wanted to write it in software now." The color graphics, the paddle controls, the built-in sound, even the impulse to fold a game's worth of capability into a general-purpose computer—all of it traced back to those four nights at Atari. It is a useful corrective to a widespread assumption. People often picture the two Steves as interchangeable co-inventors, or imagine Jobs as the technical brain of the pair. In fact the engineering was Wozniak's alone; Jobs, by his own admission, could not design a working circuit. What Jobs supplied was something Woz conspicuously lacked—the certainty that these clever creations were not merely toys to be shown off to friends but products the world would pay for, and the ferocious will to make that happen.

What drew them back into orbit in the spring of 1975 was a room full of like-minded obsessives gathering in Menlo Park. The Altair 8800 had appeared on the cover of *Popular Electronics* that January, and its arrival had electrified the hobbyists of the Bay Area. On March 5, 1975, thirty-odd enthusiasts crowded into the garage of an out-of-work engineer named Gordon French to pass around one of the first Altairs and talk about what these new microprocessor kits might become. They called themselves the Homebrew Computer Club, and within weeks the meetings had outgrown the garage and moved to an auditorium at the Stanford Linear Accelerator Center, where as many as several hundred people would eventually assemble. The club's presiding spirit was a passionate community organizer named Lee Felsenstein, who ran the meetings with a wooden pointer and a gift for herding anarchic genius, and the club's ethos was pure countercultural idealism: information wanted to be shared, schematics wanted to be copied, and the microcomputer was a tool of liberation to be spread as widely as possible. Members swapped chips, tips, and designs freely, in a spirit closer to a barn-raising than a marketplace.

Wozniak attended that first meeting—Allen Baum, an old friend, had brought him a flyer—and though he was too shy to say much, he came home transformed. Here were his people, and here was a problem worthy of his gifts. The Altair, for all the excitement it generated, was a forbidding thing: you programmed it by flipping switches on the front panel and read its answers off a row of blinking lights. To Wozniak, who had spent years dreaming of owning a computer of his own but could never afford one, the future was obvious. A computer should not speak in switches and lights. It should connect to a typewriter keyboard for input and to an ordinary television set for output, so that a person could type a command and watch letters appear on a screen, the way the great time-sharing terminals worked but on a machine a single human could own. That instinct—to lean on a television the buyer already had rather than an expensive dedicated display—was the quiet stroke of genius that would make his design radically cheaper than anything else on that workbench, and it is an instinct you honor every time you plug a computer into a monitor or a laptop lights up its own screen; the marriage of keyboard, processor, and glowing display that everyone now takes for granted was, in 1975, a novel bet.

There remained the question of a brain, and here Wozniak's frugality made the difference between a dream and a buildable thing. The obvious processors were out of reach for a hobbyist: Intel's 8080 and Motorola's elegant 6800 each cost well over a hundred and fifty dollars, more than Woz could justify spending. Then, late in 1975, the engineers at MOS Technology put their 6502 chip on sale for twenty-five dollars—a price so low it changed his arithmetic overnight. Because the 6502 was closely modeled on Motorola's 6800, Wozniak could adapt the design he had already been sketching, and suddenly the whole machine became affordable. Every Homebrew meeting now sent him back to his workbench at HP by day and his kitchen table by night, wiring toward a machine that would let a person and a computer finally sit down together as equals. In keeping with the club's ethic, his instinct was to give the design away for free. And in keeping with his loyalty to Hewlett-Packard, he first offered the whole invention to his employer—an act of corporate good faith that is easy to forget in the mythology. HP, seeing no market for a hobbyist's home computer, turned him down. It would not be the last time a giant failed to recognize the future taking shape in a spare room.

By the summer of 1975 Wozniak was deep into a design that would become the first product of a company that did not yet exist, and Jobs was watching, already wondering what it might be worth.

Chapter 17: The Apple I

On the night of June 29, 1975, in a cluttered apartment bedroom, Stephen Wozniak typed a few characters on a keyboard he had wired to a jumble of chips on a board, and letters appeared, glowing, on the screen of a television set. It was, he would later say, the most satisfying moment of his life. No one before had built a small, affordable computer that a person could operate this simply—type on a keyboard, read the result on a video display—and Woz had done it essentially alone, at his kitchen table and his HP workbench, out of parts he could get his hands on and a design of astonishing economy. That single working demonstration, a character echoed from keyboard to screen, was the seed of everything Apple would become. He remembered the exact texture of the moment: it was the first time in history, as far as he knew, that anyone had typed a character on a keyboard and watched it appear instantly on a screen in front of them on a machine they owned. The engineers who ran the great mainframes had teletypes and terminals, but those were tethered to million-dollar machines in air-conditioned rooms. This one sat on a table, and it belonged to him.

The machine that grew from it over the following months would come to be called the Apple I, and its genius lay in its parsimony. Wozniak was a virtuoso of doing more with less, of shaving a chip here and a wire there until a circuit achieved a kind of crystalline minimalism, and the Apple I was his masterwork in that vein. He built it around a microprocessor almost no one else in Homebrew was using. The glamorous choices of the day were Intel's 8080 and the Motorola 6800, but both cost in the neighborhood of a hundred and seventy-five dollars, a sum a hobbyist engineer on an HP salary could scarcely justify. Then, in the fall of 1975, a small Pennsylvania firm called MOS Technology began selling a chip called the 6502 for around twenty-five dollars—a fraction of the price, and, to Wozniak's delight, a capable processor besides. He and his friend Allen Baum bought the 6502 over a table at a conference in San Francisco, and Woz built his computer around it, hand-writing a version of the BASIC programming language to run on it so that ordinary people could actually tell the machine what to do. That detail is worth pausing on, because it captures the audacity of the man: Wozniak had never taken a formal course in writing a programming language, had never even seen the source code of another BASIC, and simply reasoned out how one ought to work from first principles, sketching it on paper and translating it by hand into the numerical codes the 6502 understood. The Apple I was, at its heart, a single circuit board that married that cheap processor to a keyboard interface and a television-terminal circuit, doing away with the front-panel switches and blinking lights that made the Altair such a chore.

Even so, the Apple I demanded a certain devotion from its owner. When you switched it on, it woke into a tiny built-in program called the Monitor—not a screen, in this sense, but a bare-bones supervisor that let you inspect and change the machine's memory a byte at a time. To do anything useful you first had to load Wozniak's BASIC, and in the early days that meant buying a separate little accessory Woz designed, the Apple Cassette Interface, which sold for around seventy-five dollars and let the machine read programs off an ordinary audio cassette player. You would press play on the recorder, listen to the shrieking modem-like tones of the data, and hope the transfer completed without error before you could begin to type a program of your own. It was fussy and it was fragile, and it was still a revelation, because for the first time the whole cycle—load, type, run, see the answer on a screen—happened at a desk, on a machine a person owned outright.

It is worth being concrete about what that meant to use, because the leap is easy to underestimate from the far side of half a century of screens. To operate an Altair, the machine that had electrified the hobbyist world only a year earlier, you flipped a row of toggle switches on the front panel to enter each instruction in binary, one byte at a time, then pressed a button to load it into memory, and read your answer off a row of little red lights. Entering even a short program could take the better part of an hour of switch-flipping, and a single mistake meant starting over. Wozniak's insight was to treat the television and the typewriter keyboard—two things a hobbyist might already own or scrounge—as the natural windows into the machine. You typed a command; the machine answered in glowing green characters. The Apple I still expected you to talk to it in a spare, cryptic dialect, and it woke up knowing nothing but a bare monitor program until you loaded BASIC from a cassette tape, a process that could itself be maddening. But the fundamental grammar of the thing—keyboard in, screen out—was the grammar every personal computer would speak thereafter.

None of this arrived from nowhere. Wozniak had been building computers, in a sense, since boyhood, sketching logic diagrams for machines he had no parts to construct and redrawing them obsessively to use fewer chips, treating the reduction of a design to its barest essentials as a private sport. As a teenager he had built, with his friend Bill Fernandez, a little machine they dubbed the "Cream Soda Computer" for the beverage they drank while assembling it, and though it was primitive it taught him the discipline he would carry into the Apple I. By 1975 he was an engineer at Hewlett-Packard designing calculators—a job he genuinely loved—and his evenings and weekends belonged to the Homebrew Computer Club, a gathering of Bay Area enthusiasts who met to swap chips, schematics, and enthusiasm in the wake of the Altair's debut. It was in that room, among people who believed almost as a matter of faith that computing power ought to be wrested from corporations and handed to individuals, that Wozniak found both his audience and his purpose. The Apple I was, in a real sense, a Homebrew machine: designed to be shown off at a Homebrew meeting, admired by Homebrew members, and copied freely by anyone in the club who cared to build one.

True to the ethos of the Homebrew Computer Club, Wozniak's first instinct was not to sell his creation but to give it away. He brought the design to the club's meetings and demonstrated it proudly, and he passed out photocopies of his schematics to anyone who wanted them, free of charge. This was simply how things were done among the hobbyists: you shared what you knew, you helped the next person build a better machine, and the reward was the admiration of your peers and the advance of the whole community. Woz wanted nothing more than to be the clever fellow who had figured out how to put a computer on a keyboard and a TV, and to show his friends how he'd done it. He would happily have remained an HP engineer forever, handing out schematics as a hobby. Indeed, dutiful to a fault, he offered the design to Hewlett-Packard first, believing that anything he invented on the company's time morally belonged to them—and by his own account HP declined it not once but on five separate occasions, unable to see a market for a small computer aimed at ordinary people. Only after HP formally released any claim to it did Wozniak feel free to pursue it himself. It is one of the great might-have-beens of the industry: the personal computer revolution was offered, gratis, to one of the most respected engineering firms in the world, and politely turned down.

Steve Jobs saw the same demonstrations and drew an entirely different conclusion. Where Woz saw a gift to the community, Jobs saw a product. He grasped that most of the people marveling at the Apple I would never actually build one; the world of the Homebrew Club was small, and even within it, the labor of gathering the right chips and soldering them correctly onto a home-etched board defeated many an enthusiast. What if, Jobs proposed, they sold the thing already assembled—not a bare kit and a bag of parts, but a finished, working printed circuit board that a buyer needed only to add a keyboard, a power supply, and a television to use? It was a modest idea by later standards, and the Apple I would still arrive as a naked board with no case, no keyboard, and no monitor. But it was a decisive conceptual shift. Jobs was proposing to take Wozniak's freely shared design and turn it into a business, and after some persuasion the two agreed to try.

The turning point came in the summer of 1976, and it walked through the door of a computer store. Paul Terrell was a shrewd early retailer who had opened one of the first computer shops in the country, the Byte Shop, on El Camino Real in Mountain View. Jobs, never shy about a cold approach, went to see him—by one telling, still in his sandals, with the fervent intensity that either repelled people or reeled them in—and pitched the Apple I. Terrell was interested, but not in what Jobs was offering. He did not want bare boards that his customers would still have to solder and populate with parts. He wanted machines his customers could actually use. And so Terrell made an offer that would change the history of computing: he would buy fifty fully assembled and tested Apple I boards, at about five hundred dollars apiece, for a total on the order of twenty-five thousand dollars, cash on delivery. It was, for two young men with no company and no capital, a staggering sum—the first real order either of them had ever received, and proof that Jobs's instinct had been right. Wozniak would later pay Terrell the highest compliment he could think of, calling him the "fourth founder" of Apple, for it was Terrell's insistence on finished machines, and his willingness to buy them, that transformed a garage curiosity into an actual business with an actual customer.

There was, however, a catch that revealed how thin the ground beneath them was. Terrell wanted assembled boards, and assembling fifty of them meant buying components in bulk—hundreds of chips, sockets, connectors, and circuit boards—which meant money the partners did not have. Jobs, undaunted, talked a parts distributor into extending them thirty days of credit on the strength of the Byte Shop's purchase order, betting that they could build and deliver the boards, collect Terrell's cash, and pay their suppliers before the note came due. It was a high-wire act of the kind that would recur throughout Apple's early years, a business run at the very edge of its means, held aloft by Jobs's nerve and Wozniak's ability to make the machines actually work.

The Apple I was never a mass-market triumph. In all, only around two hundred were ever made, and they sold at the memorably whimsical price of $666.66. It is often assumed there was something deliberately mischievous, even satanic, in that string of sixes, and the coincidence has fed a small mythology over the decades—but the truth is far more prosaic. Wozniak simply liked repeating digits; he found numbers like 666 or 777 easy to type and pleasing to look at, and it happened to sit at a comfortable one-third markup over the roughly five-hundred-dollar wholesale figure. There was, he has patiently explained many times since, no diabolical intent whatever, and he was rather bemused to discover that anyone read one into it. The machine had no case; buyers often mounted the board in a wooden box or a briefcase. It required the user to supply a keyboard, a display, and a transformer. By any ordinary measure it was a hobbyist's curiosity, and today the surviving examples are among the most coveted artifacts in all of computing. Part of the reason so few survive is a deliberate act of corporate housekeeping that collectors now regard with a kind of horror. Once the

Apple II arrived and made the Apple I obsolete overnight, the company found itself burdened with supporting a machine only Wozniak really understood, and it hit upon a tidy solution: it offered Apple I owners generous trade-in credit toward the shiny new Apple II, coaxing the old boards back in. But rather than resell or refurbish the returned units, Apple simply destroyed them. Jobs, ever impatient with yesterday's news, wanted the first machine gone, and so a substantial fraction of the roughly two hundred boards ever built were knowingly scrapped by the very company that had made them—which is precisely why, of that original run, the whereabouts of only sixty to eighty are known today. Fewer than seventy are reliably documented as surviving, and a working, well-provenanced Apple I can now command sums well into the hundreds of thousands of dollars at auction—one changed hands for nearly a million—which means the little board that a customer once carried home for six hundred and sixty-six dollars is, gram for gram, among the most valuable pieces of consumer electronics ever built. If you have ever stood before a glass case in a computer museum and looked at a bare green circuit board with a few dozen chips soldered to it, wondering why it was treated like a Vermeer, this is why: you were looking at the first product of the company that taught the world to switch on a computer and simply use it.

But its true significance was not commercial. The Apple I proved three things at once: that Wozniak could design a computer people wanted, that Jobs could sell it, and that the two of them together could deliver on a real order to a real customer. What they lacked, in the summer of 1976, was a company. To fill that fifty-board order and everything that might follow, the two Steves needed to make themselves official, and on the first day of April they would do exactly that.

Chapter 18: Founding Apple

On April 1, 1976—April Fools' Day, a coincidence none of them seems to have intended as a joke—three men signed a partnership agreement to found a company they called Apple Computer. Two of them were the young men already known to this story: Stephen Wozniak, twenty-five, the shy engineering wizard still drawing a paycheck from Hewlett-Packard, and Steven Jobs, twenty-one, the barefoot visionary who had talked the Byte Shop into a fifty-board order. The third was a figure history has treated as a footnote, though he deserves better: Ronald Wayne, a forty-one-year-old Atari draftsman and engineer whom Jobs admired for his steadiness and his experience in the ways of business. Jobs had met Wayne at Atari, where the older man's air of unflappable competence and his willingness to hold forth on philosophy, economics, and the mechanics of running a company made a deep impression on the intense young employee. Jobs brought Wayne in precisely because he was the grown-up in the room—a man who had already run a small company of his own, who knew how partnerships worked, and who could mediate between Jobs's impetuousness and Wozniak's caution. Wayne himself, with dry humor, later described his role as "the adult in the room." On paper the ownership split reflected these roles: Jobs and Wozniak took forty-five percent each, and Wayne the remaining ten, his stake meant to give him a tie-breaking vote should the two Steves ever deadlock. It was Wayne who drafted the original partnership document, in prose so ornately formal that it reads today like something from another century; Wayne who drew the company's first logo—an intricate pen-and-ink rendering of Isaac Newton seated beneath his apple tree, a stray fruit poised in the branches above his head, with a ribbon of Wordsworth wound around the border; and Wayne who wrote the Apple I's manual.

The name itself has been the subject of more speculation than perhaps any brand in the industry, and the truth appears to be pleasingly mundane. By Jobs's own later account, he had recently returned from working at an apple orchard, an experience tied to one of his fruitarian phases, and he simply liked the word: it was fun, it was approachable, it was unintimidating, and—not least—it would come alphabetically ahead of Atari, his former employer, in the phone book and in any list of exhibitors. He floated it to Wozniak as they drove down the highway from the airport, half-suggesting they think of something better, and setting themselves a deadline; if neither could come up with a name they liked more by the end of the day, Apple it would be. Neither of them ever did. In an industry that named its products with cold strings of numbers and acronyms—the 8080, the PDP-8, the KIM-1—the choice of a warm, ordinary piece of fruit was quietly radical, a hint that this company intended its machines for human beings rather than institutions. There is a persistent legend that the name was a homage to the mathematician Alan Turing, who is said to have died beside a poisoned apple, or a nod to the Beatles' Apple Records; Jobs, asked about such theories over the years, gently waved them away. The truth was simpler and more human than any of the myths: he liked apples, he had been eating a fruitarian diet and working the orchard, the word made him happy, and it beat Atari in the alphabet. Sometimes a name is only a name, chosen by a hungry young man who thought it sounded friendly. The now-famous logo of a rainbow apple with a bite out of it lay some years in the future; for the moment the brand was that fussy Victorian engraving of Newton, so detailed that when shrunk to fit on a product it became an illegible smudge—which was rather the point at which Jobs's design instincts and Wayne's would part ways.

To fund the venture, the founders sold what they had. Jobs sold his Volkswagen Microbus, and Wozniak sold his prized Hewlett-Packard 65 programmable calculator, a beloved and expensive instrument that had cost him hundreds of dollars, and between the two sales they raised something in the neighborhood of thirteen hundred dollars of working capital—enough, barely, to begin buying the parts to fill Paul Terrell's order. The VW, in a small comic footnote, soon broke down on its new owner, and Jobs had to chip in for repairs. It was a shoestring operation in the most literal sense, capitalized by the sale of a used van and a pocket calculator, and it depended entirely on the thirty-day credit Jobs had wrangled from a parts supplier against the Byte Shop's purchase order. There was no cushion, no investor, no line of credit at a bank—only a bet that the boards could be built and delivered and paid for in the narrow window before the bills came due.

Ronald Wayne, watching all this, grew uneasy, and it is here that his story turns from footnote to legend. He was older than the two Steves, he had modest assets worth protecting—a house, a bank account, the accumulated ballast of a middle-aged life—and he had been burned before by a business failure in the slot-machine trade that had collapsed and left him personally responsible for its debts. That old wound had taught him a lesson he could not unlearn. In a partnership, unlike a corporation, each partner is personally liable for the whole of the company's obligations—and Wayne understood, with a clarity the young men perhaps lacked, that if the undercapitalized, credit-dependent Apple collapsed under the weight of that parts order, the creditors could come after him, because he was the only partner with anything worth seizing. Jobs and Wozniak, he reasoned, were young and penniless and had nothing to lose; he had everything. He worried too, he later admitted, that he might spend the next twenty years of his life shuffling papers in a documentation department, and that the whole enterprise, driven by Jobs's boundless and frankly alarming nerve, might simply be the sort of runaway train he had ridden to ruin once already.

And so, less than two weeks after signing the founding document, on April 12, 1976, Ronald Wayne walked into the county office and formally withdrew from the partnership, selling his ten percent stake back to Jobs and Wozniak. He was paid eight hundred dollars for relinquishing his share, with a further fifteen hundred dollars some months later to formally release any future claim against the newly incorporated company—by most accounts bringing his total to around twenty-three hundred dollars. That ten percent, had he held it, would today be worth hundreds of billions of dollars, a figure so vast it strains comprehension, and Wayne's decision has become the most famous act of self-protective caution in the history of American business, the parable every startup founder invokes as a warning. Yet Wayne, for the whole of his long life—he lived into his nineties, in a modest home in Nevada, selling stamps and rare coins and the occasional signed document to make ends meet—insisted with remarkable equanimity that he had made the right choice for the man he was at the time. "I made the best decision based on the information available at the time," he would say, and he steadfastly refused to spend his old age drowning in regret over a fortune he could not, being who he was, ever have stayed to earn. There is a certain dignity in that refusal, and it is worth remembering that the roller-coaster years ahead—the crushing hours, the brinkmanship, the near-collapses—might genuinely have broken a cautious man of forty-one. Wayne knew himself, and chose peace over the vertigo of a ride he did not want to take.

The story has one last, exquisitely painful footnote. Wayne kept, for years, his copy of the original three-page partnership agreement he had drafted—the founding document of Apple—and eventually, needing money, he sold it in the mid-1990s for a few hundred dollars. In 2011, that same contract came up at auction and sold to a collector for roughly 1.6 million dollars. It is a number that captures the whole tragicomedy of Ronald Wayne in miniature: the man who walked away from a fortune could not even hold on to the piece of paper on which the fortune was founded, and it too went to someone else for a sum that would have kept him comfortable for the rest of his days. And yet, asked about it, Wayne only shrugged. He had, he maintained, spent his life doing work he found interesting, owed no one anything, and slept soundly. There are worse epitaphs.

With Wayne gone and the order to fill, the two remaining founders set to work in the place that has since passed into legend: the garage of the Jobs family home at 2066 Crist Drive in Los Altos, where Steve had grown up under the roof of his adoptive parents, Paul and Clara Jobs. Paul, a machinist with a gift for craftsmanship who had taught his son to care about how things were made—to finish the back of a cabinet as beautifully as the front, even where no one would ever look—cleared space for the young company, and the garage became Apple's mythic birthplace, the humble origin every great enterprise seems required to claim. But honesty compels a correction to the myth, and Wozniak himself has been the first and most insistent to make it. The garage was never really where the work happened. It had no proper workbench at first, no soldering station, no real room; it was, in Woz's blunt recollection, "a bit of a myth"—a symbol we cling to more than a fact. The actual labor—the assembling and testing of the Apple I boards, the burn-in and debugging—took place largely inside the house, in the bedrooms and at the kitchen table and on any flat surface that could hold a stack of circuit boards. One bedroom held the finished boards; a burn-in operation, running the machines for hours to shake out the ones that would fail early, occupied a corner; and around the kitchen table a small crew of family and friends—including Jobs's sister Patty and a friend named Elizabeth Holmes—sat pressing chips into sockets by hand, an assembly line of exactly the sort of people you would expect to find in a suburban kitchen on a weeknight. That the myth of the garage persists so stubbornly says something about how badly we want our revolutions to begin in humble, tangible places—a single symbolic room, a door left open, a young man bent over a soldering iron in the half-light. The Jobs house was humble enough to satisfy the legend; the geography has simply drifted a few dozen feet, from the kitchen where the soldering iron actually smoked to the garage that photographs better.

The garage, for its part, has had the last word on the myth. Whatever the historians and even Wozniak say about where the soldering actually happened, the house at 2066 Crist Drive was in 2013 designated a historic property by the Los Altos Historical Commission, its garage enshrined precisely as the birthplace of Apple—proof that a good origin story, once it takes root, is nearly impossible to uproot with mere facts. Pilgrims still drive slowly past it. The company that sells the most valuable brand on earth traces its lineage, officially and unofficially, to a suburban carport where, by the honest account of one of its founders, comparatively little of the founding actually occurred.

Whatever the precise room, the work got done. Here the story brushes against another common misconception—that Apple was born flush with a big customer's money. In fact the terms were harrowing: Terrell had promised cash on delivery, not a penny before, and the Byte Shop had a reputation among suppliers for being slow to pay its bills, so the entire enterprise rested on the assumption that a customer with shaky credit would hand over the money the moment the boards arrived. When Jobs delivered the finished boards, Terrell was reportedly a little taken aback—he had perhaps imagined something more finished, in a case—but he paid, the supplier was settled before the thirty days ran out, and Apple Computer had survived its first order and turned its first real money. It was a partnership of two now, not three, run out of a suburban tract house, undercapitalized and improvisational, with a founder who could sell anything and a founder who could build anything. What they had built and sold so far was a hobbyist's board with no case and no keyboard—a thing for the initiated. But Wozniak, even as the Apple I shipped, was already imagining something far more ambitious: not a bare board for tinkerers, but a finished, friendly machine that an ordinary person might carry home and simply switch on.

The partnership would not stay a partnership for long. Within months the ambitions of the second machine would demand more money and more structure than two young men and a suburban kitchen could supply, and early in January 1977 Apple Computer would be formally incorporated, with the retired chip-marketing executive Mike Markkula putting up the capital and the credibility the enterprise lacked. It was Markkula, too, who would issue Wozniak an ultimatum that reveals how close the whole story came to ending before it began: Woz, still devoted to Hewlett-Packard and reluctant to gamble a secure engineering career on a fruit-named startup, at first refused to leave HP and join Apple full-time, and had to be talked into it by friends and family who saw, as he did not yet, that the thing he had built at his kitchen table was about to become his life's work. He relented. The shy engineer who had only wanted to hand out schematics became, almost against his own inclination, the technical heart of a real corporation.

That machine, when it arrived the following year, would transform Apple from a garage partnership into a genuine company—and the personal computer from a curiosity into an appliance.

Chapter 19: The Apple II

On the morning of April 16, 1977, in the vast, fluorescent-lit halls of the Brooks Hall convention center in San Francisco, a small booth belonging to a company almost no one had heard of drew a crowd it had no business drawing. The occasion was the first West Coast Computer Faire, the largest gathering the young personal-computer industry had yet staged, and Apple Computer—flush with a recent infusion of cash and determined to look bigger than it was—had spent lavishly on a professional booth right at the entrance, complete with a backlit acrylic sign bearing a new logo, having deliberately elbowed its way to prime position so that anyone walking in would meet Apple first. Behind the counter sat the machine that would justify all the theatrics: the Apple II, housed not in a raw metal chassis or a hobbyist's wooden box but in a sleek, honey-beige plastic case with a gently sloping keyboard, looking less like a piece of laboratory equipment than like something you might find in a well-appointed den. On its screen, in color, danced a demonstration program that painted the words and images in hues no other machine at the Faire could produce. People stopped, stared, and asked when they could buy one. There is a small irony worth savoring: for all Apple's showmanship, the machines on the booth were among only a handful actually built, and Jobs had fretted over whether the plastic cases—still bubbling with cosmetic flaws from a rushed molding job—would look finished enough to fool the crowds. They did.

The Apple II was, in its engineering, another Wozniak tour de force, and in several respects it was even more radical than the Apple I. At its heart again beat the inexpensive MOS Technology 6502, the twenty-five-dollar processor that had made the first machine possible. But Woz had wrapped it in a set of innovations that were, by the standards of 1977, close to miraculous. Chief among them was color. Here Wozniak's genius took a form that even other engineers found almost uncanny, because he generated color not with dedicated color-generating hardware, as any textbook would have prescribed, but by exploiting a defect. American color television worked by a fussy standard called NTSC, and Woz realized that if he timed his black-and-white dots to line up with the color subcarrier of a television signal, the set's own circuitry would be fooled into painting them in color—an effect engineers call "artifact color," a happy accident harnessed on purpose. It let him conjure a full palette out of a handful of cheap chips, and it was so counterintuitive that colleagues who examined the design afterward could scarcely believe it worked at all. He gave the machine high-resolution and low-resolution graphics modes and sound, so that from the very start the Apple II could display vivid images and play games, capabilities that would prove central to its appeal. And he built into its read-only memory a version of the BASIC language he had written himself, known as Integer BASIC, so that the instant a buyer switched the machine on it was ready to be programmed—no tapes to load, no cartridges to insert, just a blinking prompt inviting the user to begin. When Wozniak described the machine to the world in the May 1977 issue of *Byte* magazine, he opened with a sentence that reads now like a manifesto for the whole coming age: "To me, a personal computer should be small, reliable, convenient to use, and inexpensive."

Perhaps Wozniak's most consequential decision was one of openness, and it produced one of the most important arguments in the company's history. He designed the Apple II with eight expansion slots along the back of its main board—connectors into which a user or an outside company could plug additional circuit boards to add capabilities the original designers had never imagined: memory, printers, disk drives, modems, controllers of every kind. Jobs, ever the advocate of a clean, closed, controlled product, argued for fewer slots, perhaps two, wanting the machine to be a sealed appliance that did what Apple intended and nothing more. Wozniak, who remembered the joy of tinkering and who knew from his years at Hewlett-Packard that engineers would always dream up something to plug into a spare slot, insisted on eight, and he prevailed. It proved a decision of almost incalculable importance. Those slots turned the Apple II into a platform—an open frontier that a whole ecosystem of third-party hardware and software makers would rush to settle. When, a couple of years later, a spreadsheet called VisiCalc appeared and businesses needed a way to store their data, it was into one of those slots that Apple's own floppy-disk controller went, and the machine that Woz had left deliberately unfinished became, in the hands of strangers, something none of its makers had foreseen. The settling of that frontier, more than any single feature, is what let the machine endure for well over a decade.

There was one more piece of Wozniak wizardry, and it arrived a year after the machine itself, in the form of the Disk II floppy-disk drive. In the early days the Apple II stored programs on cassette tape, a slow and maddeningly unreliable business in which a program might take minutes to load and fail as often as not. Over the Christmas break of 1977, Jobs told Wozniak that Apple needed a disk drive to be taken seriously, and pointed him at the annual Consumer Electronics Show in January as a deadline. Existing floppy-drive controllers were dense thickets of chips; Wozniak, studying the problem afresh, threw out the conventional approach and devised a controller of astonishing economy, offloading much of the work onto clever software and timing so that his design used only a handful of chips where others used dozens. He and a colleague, Randy Wigginton, worked around the clock and had a working drive demonstrated at the show within roughly two weeks. Engineers who examined the Disk II regarded it, like the color circuitry, as a small miracle of minimalism, and it mattered enormously: a fast, affordable, reliable floppy drive was exactly what a business tool needed, and when VisiCalc arrived the following year it was the Disk II that gave people somewhere sensible to keep their spreadsheets. Wozniak himself later called it the finest piece of engineering he ever did.

If Wozniak supplied the circuitry, a small cast of others supplied the things that turned a brilliant design into a finished product. The elegant case owed its lines to a designer named Jerry Manock, whom Jobs commissioned to make the machine look approachable rather than technical, with soft corners and a warm color chosen to blend into a home. The power supply—an unglamorous but critical component—came from Rod Holt, a seasoned engineer and self-described socialist whom Jobs recruited with characteristic persistence; Holt designed for the Apple II a switching power supply, a comparatively novel and difficult approach that ran cooler and lighter than the heavy, heat-belching linear transformers other computers relied upon, and that let the machine run silently, without the whirring cooling fan that Jobs despised as noisy and inelegant. Holt's fan-less design became one of the machine's quiet signatures. The documentation, so often an afterthought in an industry that spoke only in schematics, fell in large part to Jef Raskin, a thoughtful advocate of simplicity who would later conceive the project that became the Macintosh; the Apple II's chief reference manual bore the disarming title *Byte Into an Apple*, and it was written on the principle that a person who had never seen a computer should be able to sit down and understand it. Together these contributions embodied a philosophy Jobs was already articulating: that the whole experience of the product mattered, from the color on the screen to the shape of the case to the sentences in the manual.

But a beautiful machine is not the same thing as a company, and by late 1976 Apple's ambitions had outrun its shoestring finances. To manufacture the Apple II in quantity, to market it, to build an actual business, the two Steves needed real capital and real management—and here entered the third indispensable figure of Apple's founding era. A. C. "Mike" Markkula was a young man who had already retired, at thirty-three, having made a small fortune in stock options as a marketing manager at the chip makers Fairchild and Intel. In the fall of 1976 he was persuaded to drive out to the Jobs garage, half-expecting to waste an afternoon, and what he saw convinced him that this was not a hobby but the leading edge of an industry about to explode. Early in 1977 Markkula agreed to invest, personally putting in around ninety thousand dollars and securing a bank line of credit that brought the young company's available capital toward a quarter of a million dollars, and he did something arguably more valuable still: he sat down and wrote a business plan, projecting—to the disbelief of nearly everyone, including himself on a cautious day—that Apple would grow into a five-hundred-million-dollar company and join the Fortune 500 within a few years. He became the third partner and effectively the adult supervision the company needed, recruiting an experienced semiconductor executive, Michael Scott, as the first president, and lending the enterprise the credibility that let it be formally incorporated as Apple Computer, Inc., in January 1977.

Markkula understood something else, something the hobbyists never grasped: that in a market where the machines themselves were becoming comprehensible only to specialists, image and reputation would decide who won. He brought in Regis McKenna, the most influential marketing and public-relations man in Silicon Valley, whose firm crafted Apple's early advertising and public presence. It was McKenna's shop that helped give the company its friendly rainbow-striped apple—retiring Ron Wayne's ornate Newton engraving for a simple, colorful, bitten piece of fruit whose stripes, not incidentally, advertised the very color graphics that set the Apple II apart—and that placed the Apple II in the pages of consumer magazines rather than only hobbyist newsletters. Markkula distilled his own philosophy into a one-page memo he titled "The Apple Marketing Philosophy," built on three words: empathy, meaning a real understanding of the customer's feelings; focus, meaning the discipline to do a few things well and ignore the rest; and impute, his coinage for the idea that people judge a product by the signals it sends, so that even the packaging and the manuals must whisper quality. These were not the instincts of a garage of hobbyists. They were the instincts of a consumer-products company, and they would define Apple for decades.

The Apple II went on sale on June 10, 1977, at a starting price of around thirteen hundred dollars, and it was, quite simply, the machine that made the company. It is often said that the Apple II conquered the market from the moment it appeared, but the truth is more gradual and more interesting: for its first year and more it sold respectably rather than spectacularly, outnumbered in the wider market by the cheaper TRS-80, and its transformation into a genuine phenomenon came only when the arrival of an affordable floppy-disk drive in 1978 and the killer spreadsheet in 1979 gave people a reason they could not refuse. But once that reason arrived, the Apple II's open architecture and polish carried it to heights nothing else could match. Over the years that followed it would sell in the millions—some five to six million across its long life—spawn an entire industry of software and peripherals, and carry Apple, exactly as Markkula had predicted, onto the Fortune 500 and, on December 12, 1980, into a triumphant public stock offering. That offering was itself a landmark: it was the most oversubscribed initial public offering since Ford Motor Company had gone public in 1956, it sold out within minutes, and by the end of the day it had created more millionaires in a single stroke than any event in history to that point—something like three hundred of them, from Wozniak and Jobs down to early employees who had taken stock instead of salary and clerks who had bought a few shares on a hunch. Wozniak, characteristically, would later give and sell shares to employees he felt the offering had shortchanged. In four and a half years the two young men who had sold a van and a calculator to buy parts had built a company worth well over a billion dollars. If you have ever used a computer that boots up ready to run, that you expand by plugging in a card or a peripheral, that comes wrapped in packaging designed to feel like a gift rather than a component, you are living inside choices first bundled together in that beige box: Wozniak's engineering, Jobs's obsession with the whole experience, Holt's silent power supply, Raskin's human manuals, Markkula's money and plan, McKenna's marketing—all of it converging to transform a two-man partnership into a corporation.

The machine's longevity is itself a kind of monument to Wozniak's design. The Apple II—stylized in its early advertising with the bracket-and-slash flourish "Apple][" —was not a product that flared and vanished. In one form or another, through the Apple II Plus, the IIe, the IIc, and the IIGS, the basic architecture Woz laid down in 1977 stayed in production and on sale until 1993, an astonishing sixteen-year run in an industry that usually measures a product's life in months. Long after the Macintosh had become the face of Apple, it was the humble, endlessly expandable Apple II that quietly paid the company's bills, its sales to homes and above all to schools throwing off the profits that funded Apple's more glamorous adventures. Wozniak had built not merely a computer but a platform durable enough to outlast the decade that made it.

Yet Apple was not alone in seeing the opportunity of 1977, and in that same season two very different companies—one a maker of calculators, the other a chain of electronics stores—were readying machines of their own that would turn a hobbyist's dream into a national phenomenon.

Chapter 20: The PET and the Trash-80

In January 1977, on the crowded floor of the Consumer Electronics Show in Chicago, amid the din of stereo systems and video games and every gadget the electronics industry could dream up, a stout machine with a chunky calculator-style keyboard and a small built-in screen sat glowing on the Commodore booth. It was called the PET—the Personal Electronic Transactor, an acronym cheerfully reverse-engineered to ride the era's craze for pet rocks—and it looked, to the crowds who gathered around it, less like a computer than like some strange new species of appliance. Unlike the Altair and its kin, the PET was all one piece: a nine-inch cathode-ray tube in a trapezoidal metal housing, a flat chiclet keyboard, and a cassette-tape recorder for storage, all fused into a single wedge of sheet metal, so that a buyer needed only to plug it into the wall and switch it on. There was nothing to assemble, no television to hook up, no separate anything. It was, in the most literal sense, a personal computer you could carry home and use, and it announced that the age of the ready-made machine had arrived.

The intelligence inside the PET traced back to a soft-spoken engineer named Chuck Peddle, whose fingerprints were all over the personal-computer revolution though his name remained little known outside it. Peddle had been the driving force behind the very chip that made cheap computing possible—the MOS Technology 6502, the same twenty-five-dollar microprocessor at the heart of both Apple machines. He had designed it, along with a small team, precisely to be radically cheaper than the Intel and Motorola processors of the day, which sold for around a hundred and seventy-five dollars apiece; the story goes that when Peddle's group first offered the 6502 for sale at a trade show, buyers were so suspicious of the low price that the team kept a jar stuffed with cash on the table simply to prove the chips were real and for sale. To show the world what the 6502 could do, Peddle's team had already built the KIM-1, a bare single-board computer that became a cult favorite among hobbyists and, not incidentally, planted in Peddle's mind the idea of a complete, finished machine. When Commodore, a scrappy calculator and electronics firm, acquired the struggling MOS Technology in 1976, it acquired Peddle and his chip together, and Peddle promptly set about persuading his new bosses to let him build a real computer around his own creation. He was given roughly six months to have something ready for the January show, and the result was the PET, designed at a sprint and running a version of BASIC licensed from a small, hungry software company run by two young men named Bill Gates and Paul Allen.

Commodore's acquisition of MOS Technology gave it a weapon none of its rivals possessed, and it is central to understanding everything Tramiel would do next. Apple and Radio Shack had to buy their microprocessors from outside suppliers, paying whatever the market charged; Commodore, having swallowed the very company that fabricated the 6502, owned its own chip factory. It could make the brains of its computers at cost, which meant that in any price war Tramiel could keep cutting long after competitors who bought their chips had bled dry. This vertical integration—owning the whole chain from silicon to finished machine—was Tramiel's true edge, and it was why "business is war" was not mere bluster in his mouth. He had the ammunition to outlast almost anyone, and over the coming years he would use it to devastating effect, dropping prices to levels that drove one rival after another out of the home-computer trade.

That licensing deal deserves a moment, because it became one of the quiet turning points of the industry and, for one party, a lasting regret. Where Apple and Radio Shack would pay Microsoft for BASIC on terms that scaled with sales, Commodore, in the person of the famously tight-fisted Jack Tramiel, negotiated a single flat fee—by most accounts around twenty-five thousand dollars—for the right to put Microsoft BASIC on as many machines as Commodore could ever build. Since Commodore would eventually ship its computers by the tens of millions, it was, from Microsoft's side, a spectacularly bad bargain, and one that Gates is said to have rued for years afterward. From Commodore's side it was pure Tramiel: pay once, own it forever, and never let a supplier take a cut of your volume.

The man who owned Commodore and drove it forward was one of the most formidable and least sentimental characters in the industry: Jack Tramiel, born Jacek Trzmiel in Łódź, Poland, a survivor of the Auschwitz concentration camp who had been liberated by American soldiers, come to the United States with nothing, and used a small loan to build first a typewriter-repair shop and then a calculator empire. He lived by a creed he repeated like a mantra—"business is war"—and those who dealt with him learned that he meant it literally. Tramiel had watched the calculator market, which had made his fortune, get devoured by Japanese and Texas Instruments price-cutting, and he was grimly determined that computers would be his revenge. His philosophy was volume and price: build machines "for the masses, not the classes," undercut everyone, and win on the sheer number of units out the door. The PET embodied that creed. It was cheap, self-contained, and defiantly unglamorous. Its most notorious feature was its keyboard: to keep the whole machine sealed and rugged, Commodore had given it a flat "chiclet" keypad with small, closely spaced keys like a pocket calculator's, a layout that touch typists loathed and reviewers mocked, and which Commodore was eventually forced to replace with a proper full-travel keyboard on later models. There was trouble with the name, too, once the machine crossed the Atlantic. In Europe, the Dutch electronics giant Philips held a competing trademark on "PET," and so Commodore was obliged to rebrand the machine there under the initials of its parent company, selling it as the CBM series—Commodore Business Machines—so that the very same computer went by two different names on two different continents. Despite the awkward keyboard and the naming muddle, and though production delays meant the machines demonstrated at that January show did not actually reach buyers in real numbers until October, the PET established Commodore as one of the three companies that would define personal computing in 1977—and it planted the seed of a price war Tramiel would wage without mercy for years. That war would culminate, at the decade's turn, in the Commodore VIC-20 and the Commodore 64, machines so cheap and so widely sold that the 64 alone would become, by many reckonings, the best-selling single computer model of all time.

While Commodore approached the market as a calculator maker chasing volume, an entirely different kind of company came at it from an entirely different direction. Tandy Corporation was the parent of Radio Shack, and Radio Shack was not a technology company in the Silicon Valley sense at all—it was a vast, humble chain of small electronics stores, thousands of them, scattered across strip malls and main streets in nearly every town in America, selling batteries and stereo cables and citizens-band radios and hobbyist components to ordinary consumers. It was precisely this that made Radio Shack's entry so significant. When it decided to sell a computer, it possessed something neither Apple nor Commodore could dream of: a retail distribution network already in place, staffed and stocked, within driving distance of virtually every household in the country. There is a nice irony here, too: Chuck Peddle had earlier carried his PET concept to Radio Shack, hoping the chain would sell it for him, and been turned away—so the retailer that could have sold the Commodore machine instead resolved to build its own.

The machine Radio Shack introduced, on August 3, 1977, at a press conference in New York, was the TRS-80—Tandy Radio Shack, built around the Zilog Z80 microprocessor. The project had begun almost as a lark, championed inside the company by a Tandy buyer named Don French and an engineer named Steve Leininger, whom French had personally recruited out of the Silicon Valley hobbyist scene—Leininger, in fact, had worked at a computer store and haunted the very clubs where the Apple I and its cousins first appeared. The two men had to argue their way past a skeptical corporate leadership that could not quite believe ordinary people would want a computer at all. Where Apple had chosen the 6502, the TRS-80 used the Z80, a capable and popular chip of the era, and where the Apple II wooed buyers with color and sleek design, the TRS-80 wooed them with price and availability. It sold, in its basic configuration with a keyboard, a monitor, and a cassette recorder, for $599.95—a genuinely mass-market figure, hundreds of dollars less than an Apple II—and it could be bought, seen, and carried out the door at the same store where a customer already went for transistors and speaker wire.

The most telling detail of the whole enterprise is how little Radio Shack's own leadership believed in it. The company's management was so convinced the machine would flop that, by a story often repeated, the initial production run was set at around three thousand units—roughly the number of Radio Shack stores—on the theory that if no customer ever bought one, each store could at least use its unsold computer to keep its own books, so that nothing would be truly wasted. That caution proved almost comically misplaced. Word of the machine spread, and the orders poured in faster than anyone had dared to imagine; within the first month or so the company had taken on the order of ten thousand orders, and demand only climbed from there, overwhelming Radio Shack's expectations and revealing an appetite for personal computers far larger than the industry had grasped.

The TRS-80 was, admittedly, a plain machine. Its display showed only black-and-white text and blocky graphics; its early keyboards were prone to a "keybounce" that made a single tap register as several characters; and its cost-cut, radio-frequency-noisy construction—it was known to spray electrical interference across nearby televisions and radios—earned it a mocking nickname that stuck for the rest of its days: the "Trash-80." Enthusiasts of the more elegant Apple II wore the joke as a badge of superiority, and the name has followed the machine into the history books. That noisiness was more than a punchline, too; the Model I threw off so much radio-frequency interference that when the Federal Communications Commission tightened its rules on electronic emissions, the machine could not be made to comply, and Radio Shack was compelled to discontinue the original TRS-80 rather than rework it, replacing it with the better-shielded Model III. The very trait that earned the machine its nickname helped, in the end, to kill it. But the nickname missed the point entirely. For hundreds of thousands of Americans, the Trash-80 was the first computer they ever owned, the first they ever programmed, the first that ever sat on a kitchen table or a bedroom desk—and it was theirs precisely because it was cheap and because it was sold everywhere, at a counter they already knew, by a clerk they could ask for help. Radio Shack would go on to sell the machine and its successors by the hundreds of thousands, and for a time Tandy was among the largest sellers of personal computers on Earth, moving more units in those first years than Apple itself. Whatever it lacked in polish, the Trash-80 delivered on the promise that mattered most: a real computer, affordable, and available around the corner. A generation of programmers, engineers, and entrepreneurs cut their teeth on its blocky screen, and if you have ever bought a computer off a shelf at an ordinary store rather than from a specialist—if you have ever treated a computer as just another thing to pick up on an errand—you are the heir of what Radio Shack proved in 1977. The very idea that a computer belongs on the shelves of a general store, beside the batteries and the headphones, priced and packaged for an impulse as much as a considered purchase, was close to unthinkable before Tandy demonstrated it. Every big-box electronics aisle and every online storefront that sells computers like any other consumer good descends, in a straight line, from that skeptical decision to stock roughly three thousand machines on the theory that the stores could at least use them to keep their own books.

Both machines, for all their differences, quickly grew software libraries and communities that would have astonished their makers. The TRS-80 became a favorite of small-business bookkeepers and of a young generation of programmers; an entire cottage industry of games and utilities sprang up around it, including the pioneering text-adventure games of a programmer named Scott Adams, who squeezed entire interactive worlds into a handful of kilobytes and sold them by mail order. The PET, meanwhile, carried a hidden signature of the software rivalry to come. Bill Gates, wary that Commodore's flat-fee purchase of Microsoft BASIC gave the company his code forever, had his team bury a small trap in it: type a particular obscure command and the machine would flash the word "MICROSOFT" on the screen, an Easter egg planted so that if a competitor ever stole the code, Microsoft could prove authorship. It sat there, undiscovered by ordinary users for years, a tiny act of corporate self-defense hidden inside one of the era's most popular computers.

By the late summer of 1977, then, three machines had reached the market from three companies that could hardly have been more different—a fruit-named Silicon Valley startup with a beautiful color machine, a calculator empire run by a survivor who thought business was war, and a chain of neighborhood electronics stores with a distribution network no one could match. Each had cracked the mass market in its own way, and together they would come to be remembered by a single, almost biblical name.

Chapter 21: The Trinity

By the close of 1977, a curious thing had happened to the American living room. In a growing number of them, on a desk in a spare bedroom or a corner of the kitchen, there now sat a machine that a decade earlier would have lived behind glass in a climate-controlled room tended by men in white coats. It might have been a honey-colored Apple II glowing with color graphics, or a wedge-shaped Commodore PET with its cassette deck built in, or a plain gray TRS-80 bought at the neighborhood Radio Shack for under six hundred dollars. Whichever it was, it belonged to an ordinary person—a hobbyist, a schoolteacher, a small-business owner, a curious teenager—who had switched it on and begun, haltingly, to learn what it could do. The computer had come home, and it had done so not through a single machine or a single visionary but through three of them at once, arriving within months of one another in a single extraordinary year.

That the three machines came to be grouped together was, at first, an accident of timing, but the grouping would eventually acquire a name of near-mythic weight. The enthusiast publication *Byte* magazine is generally credited with looking back and christening the Apple II, the Commodore PET, and the TRS-80 the "1977 Trinity"—the three computers that, together, marked the moment the personal computer stopped being a kit for solder-wielding hobbyists and became a finished product for the general public. It is worth pausing on a small myth here, because it is instructive: the phrase is so widely attributed to a specific *Byte* article that it is often quoted as gospel, yet researchers combing the magazine's digital archives have struggled to find the exact issue in which it supposedly first appeared, which suggests the term crystallized gradually, in hindsight, rather than springing fully formed from one editor's pen. And like all such tidy formulations it flattens a messier reality; there had been other machines, other pioneers, and 1977 had no clean boundaries. But the phrase stuck because it captured something true. In the space of a few months, three real companies had shipped three real, self-contained, ready-to-use computers to a national market, and nothing about computing was ever quite the same again.

What made the Trinity so revealing was how utterly unalike its three members were—not merely as machines but as businesses, as philosophies, as answers to the question of what a personal computer was even for. Apple came at the problem as a designer's company, founded by two young men in a Silicon Valley suburb and steered by a marketing man's conviction that image and elegance and the whole experience of a product were what mattered; its Apple II wooed the buyer with color, with sound, with a case that looked at home in a den, and with an open architecture of expansion slots that invited a whole industry to build upon it. Commodore came at it as a calculator maker chasing volume, driven by Jack Tramiel's merciless creed of price and mass production, its PET built around the very 6502 chip that Chuck Peddle had designed to be cheap enough to change the world. And Tandy came at it as a retailer, its plain, affordable TRS-80 riding into millions of American homes not on the strength of its specifications but on the strength of the thousands of Radio Shack storefronts that stood within driving distance of nearly every household in the country. A fruit-named startup, a calculator empire, and a chain of electronics shops: three roads to the same destination, each proving in its own way that there was a mass market for a machine the experts had insisted no ordinary person would ever want.

The technical family resemblances beneath the differences were themselves telling. Two of the three—the Apple II and the PET—ran on the same MOS Technology 6502, the twenty-five-dollar processor that had done more than any marketing campaign to bring computers within reach of ordinary wallets, while the TRS-80 ran on the competing Zilog Z80, a chip designed, as it happened, by former Intel engineers who had struck out on their own. All three offered a version of the BASIC programming language, most of it traceable to the tiny software firm of Bill Gates and Paul Allen, so that a buyer could begin writing programs the moment the machine warmed up—though, in a distinction that mattered more than it seemed, the Apple II and TRS-80 shipped at first with versions that handled only whole numbers, while Commodore's licensed Microsoft BASIC could juggle decimals, a small superiority Commodore had bought outright for a flat fee. All three fused a microprocessor, a keyboard, a display, and some form of storage into something a non-specialist could actually operate. That shared reliance on BASIC is easy to pass over, but it quietly shaped a generation. Because all three machines woke into a version of the language and invited their owners to program, the first thing millions of people ever did with a computer was write, however clumsily, a few lines of code of their own. A child could type a short program to print a name across the screen forever, or to ask a riddle and check the answer, and in doing so absorb, without a lesson, the fundamental idea that a computer is a thing you instruct rather than merely operate. Whole careers in software began with a listing copied out of a magazine on a Trinity machine, and the tiny company that supplied most of that BASIC—the partnership of Bill Gates and Paul Allen, then a scrappy outfit of a few young programmers—would ride the language into every corner of the industry and become, within a decade, the most powerful software company on earth. The Trinity did not just sell hardware; it taught a generation to think in code, and it launched the firm that would dominate the age to come.

They were, in other words, variations on a common theme that the industry had only just learned to play: take the cheap microprocessor that had appeared at the start of the decade, wrap it in a friendly package, price it for a household rather than a corporation, and sell it to the public. Each of the three did this differently, and each found its own audience, but together they established the template for everything that would follow—and, indeed, for the device you likely carry in your pocket today, which is still, at bottom, a processor married to a keyboard and a screen and a store of memory, sold ready to switch on.

There is a small but revealing quarrel buried in the very name, and it is worth airing, because it shows how history tidies itself. To call these three the "Trinity" is to imply that they and they alone opened the age of the ready-made home computer, and that is not quite fair to the machines the label leaves out. There were other contenders in that fertile season—the Sol-20 from Processor Technology, a handsome walnut-trimmed machine beloved of hobbyists; the various single-board and kit computers still pouring out of the post-Altair boom; a scattering of European and Japanese efforts just beginning to stir. What set the three apart was not that they were first but that they were fully assembled, sold to the general public through real retail channels, and backed by companies with the will and means to make thousands of them. The Trinity is less a statement about invention than about arrival: these were the machines that carried the personal computer across the threshold from the workshop into the ordinary home, and the tidiness of the number three—so satisfying, so quotable—has done the rest.

Nowhere did that arrival matter more than in the schools, a chapter of the story that the raw sales figures understate. Apple, guided by Markkula's marketing instincts and a shrewd donation program, pushed hard to place the Apple II in American classrooms, reasoning that a child who learned to compute on an Apple would want an Apple at home and would grow into an adult who bought one. The bet paid off spectacularly. For the better part of a decade the Apple II was the machine on which a whole generation of American schoolchildren first met a computer—first typed a BASIC program, first guided a wagon train across the plains in the educational game *The Oregon Trail*, first watched a cursor blink and understood, dimly, that the thing was waiting for them. Commodore and Radio Shack fought for the same ground, and the classroom became one of the fiercest battlefields of the price war, but it was Apple that most deeply wove itself into the memory of a generation. If you are of a certain age and the words "You have died of dysentery" produce a pang of recognition, you met the Trinity in a school computer lab, and it shaped how you think about machines to this day.

The numbers told the story of a genuine phenomenon, and they also correct a lingering assumption about which machine "won." It is easy to suppose, given Apple's later dominance, that the Apple II ran away with the era from the start. In fact, through the late 1970s the TRS-80 was the best-selling of the three by a wide margin, carried by Radio Shack's unmatched reach; Apple's own revenues, meanwhile, tell the story of a rocket only just beginning to climb, rising from around seven hundred and seventy-five thousand dollars in fiscal 1977 to roughly a hundred and eighteen million within three years. The PET, for its part, would sell something on the order of two hundred thousand units over its life and launch Commodore into a computing business that would soon put machines into homes by the millions and touch off price wars that reshaped the entire market. The revolution that Ed Roberts had glimpsed with the Altair, that the Homebrew hobbyists had dreamed of over their swapped chips and photocopied schematics, that Wozniak had wired at his kitchen table and Jobs had willed into a company—that revolution had, in 1977, gone mainstream.

The later fates of the three companies traced arcs as different as their origins. Commodore, wielding Tramiel's ruthless economics, would spend the early 1980s slashing prices until it had driven a good many rivals—including, eventually, the makers of the very PET's competitors—out of the home-computer business entirely, before corporate infighting and Tramiel's own departure sent it into a long decline that ended in bankruptcy. Radio Shack, having ridden its store network to early dominance, found that same network becoming a liability when computing moved on to standards it did not control, and Tandy gradually retreated from the machines it had once led the world in selling. Apple alone, of the three, would survive into the twenty-first century as a computer company, and only after a near-death experience of its own in the 1990s. It is a sobering reminder that being present at the creation guarantees nothing; two of the three founders of the home-computer age did not live, as companies, to see it mature.

And yet, for all their color and cleverness and mass appeal, these machines still faced a stubborn question, one that would decide whether they became lasting tools or passing fads. A computer, however friendly, is only as useful as what it can be made to do, and in 1977 the honest answer for most buyers was: not very much yet. You could program it in BASIC if you had the patience and inclination; you could play games; you could store recipes or balance a checkbook in ways that were often more trouble than doing them by hand. There is a poignant, half-remembered truth about those first years, which is that a great many of the machines sold in the flush of enthusiasm ended up switched off in closets, their owners having run out of things to do with them once the novelty of typing a few BASIC programs had faded. The hardware revolution had put a capable machine on the desk of anyone who wanted one. But the machine sat there waiting for a reason to be indispensable—waiting, that is, for software compelling enough that a person would buy the computer simply in order to run it. The industry did not yet have a word for such a program, but it would soon:

the killer application, the piece of software so valuable that it justified the entire purchase.

It is worth pausing to feel what those first years were actually like for the ordinary buyer, because the frustration is the thing the glossy retrospectives leave out. You brought your Apple II or PET or TRS-80 home, unpacked it, plugged it in, and were met—after the initial thrill—by a blinking prompt and a profound silence about what to do next. If you wanted the machine to do anything, you generally had to program it yourself, in BASIC, typing line after line copied laboriously out of a hobbyist magazine, any single mistyped character enough to make the whole thing fail. You stored your work on cassette tape, which was slow and treacherous and lost your program as often as it saved it. For the technically inclined this was pure joy, a puzzle box that rewarded patience. For everyone else it was a handsome, expensive paperweight, and a great many of the machines sold in the first flush of the Trinity ended up gathering dust once the novelty wore thin. The revolution had produced the hardware; it had not yet produced a reason for a normal person to keep the machine switched on.

That word, and the program that gave rise to it, was about to arrive in the form of a humble grid of numbers that would let an ordinary businessperson do in seconds what had once taken a weekend of pencil, paper, and eraser—and it would change everything.

Chapter 22: The Visible Calculator

In the spring of 1978, a twenty-six-year-old graduate student named Dan Bricklin sat in a lecture hall at Harvard Business School, watching a professor at the blackboard erase and rewrite a grid of numbers. The professor was working through a production-planning problem, the kind of exercise that filled the case-method curriculum, and he had drawn a matrix of rows and columns on the board in chalk. When a student pointed out an error in one of the early figures, the professor sighed, wiped away not just the wrong number but the entire cascade of calculations that depended on it, and began the tedious business of recomputing each cell by hand. Bricklin, who had already spent years writing software at Digital Equipment Corporation—where he had worked on one of the first computerized typesetting systems—before deciding that an MBA might round out his engineering, watched the chalk dust settle and felt a small, specific irritation take root. He had done exactly this kind of work himself, filling accounting worksheets with pencil, and he knew the misery of it: change one assumption at the top of the sheet and you had to walk the consequences down through every subtotal, erasing and rewriting, hoping you had not missed a dependent figure buried three columns over.

The financial spreadsheet was ancient by 1978, a paper artifact that bookkeepers had ruled by hand for generations, a grid of rows and columns onto which businesses projected their futures. What made it powerful was also what made it agonizing. Every cell might depend on other cells, so a single revised number could ripple through hundreds of hand calculations, and any recalculation invited fresh arithmetic errors. Bricklin, daydreaming through the lecture, began to imagine a machine that would do the walking for you. He has often described the specific image that came to him: he pictured, borrowing a metaphor from the fighter planes he had read about, a kind of heads-up display for numbers, an electronic blackboard and electronic chalk on which you could type values and formulas and watch the whole grid recompute itself instantly whenever any figure changed. He imagined even being able to use a mouse—a device almost no one had heard of—to point at the cells, though the hardware of the day would force him to settle for the arrow keys. He called the idea, in his own head, a visible calculator, a tool that would let you see the numbers and the relationships between them at the same time, and would never make you recompute anything by hand again.

He was hardly the first person to dream of automating a ledger, and honest history must note that others had circled the idea. Programs for financial modeling ran on mainframes and timesharing systems, and a Berkeley accounting professor named Richard Mattessich had described computerized budget spreadsheets, in principle, as early as the early 1960s. What Bricklin conceived was different in a way that turned out to matter enormously: an interactive, visual, personal tool that a single person could sit in front of and manipulate directly, watching the grid respond in real time, on a machine that cost a few thousand dollars and sat on a desk. That combination—not the abstract concept of a spreadsheet, which was old, but its embodiment in a cheap, responsive, personal machine—was the true invention.

Bricklin sketched his idea and even wrote a crude demonstration over a weekend in the BASIC language on a borrowed Apple II, a program that could scroll a small grid of numbers around the screen. It was primitive—it could barely do more than move a highlighted box from cell to cell—but it was enough to convince him the thing could work. He needed a real programmer to build it properly, someone who could wring performance out of the tiny, slow microprocessors of the day, and he knew exactly whom to ask. Bob Frankston was an old friend from MIT, a brilliant and famously nocturnal software engineer who thought in terms of systems and elegance, and who could write the tight assembly-language code that a consumer machine with only a few thousand bytes of memory would demand. The two men had known each other since their undergraduate years, and their temperaments meshed: Bricklin the designer with a clear vision of what the user should experience, Frankston the implementer who could make it real inside the cruel constraints of 1970s hardware.

The building of it was a grind of exactly the unglamorous sort that legends omit. Frankston, working on a rented Multics timesharing computer reached over a phone line, did his coding in the small hours largely because the machine's time was billed by the hour and the rates dropped after midnight—so the first spreadsheet was written, in part, to save money on the very kind of computing it was about to make obsolete. He labored to fit the whole program into a space so cramped that every byte was contested, hand-optimizing the arithmetic and the screen-handling to squeeze an interactive engine onto a machine with a whisper of memory. There is a nice human detail in how thoroughly the pair underestimated their creation: Bricklin has recalled that they worried, seriously, about how they would ever sell enough copies to make back their costs, and set their early sales hopes at figures they would later blow past in a matter of weeks. Neither man imagined he was building the program that would launch an industry; they thought they were building a useful tool for people like the classmates and professors they knew.

They set up shop, more or less, in an attic. Frankston did much of the coding on a rented timesharing system in the dead of night, when computer time was cheaper and the machine less crowded, working through the small hours in an attic room of a house in Arlington, Massachusetts. To sell the thing they would need a business, and here entered a third figure, Dan Fylstra, another Harvard Business School product who had founded a fledgling software venture called Personal Software out of his apartment. Fylstra had an Apple, some marketing instinct, and a willingness to publish and distribute software at a time when almost no one knew what a software company was supposed to look like; he lent Bricklin the very Apple II on which the prototype was built. Bricklin and Frankston formed a company they called Software Arts to develop the program; Fylstra's Personal Software, later renamed VisiCorp, would publish and sell it. The arrangement was a handshake into the unknown, because there was no established industry, no shelf in any store, no category on any form for what they were about to make.

The program that emerged they named VisiCalc, a compression of "visible calculator," and it was a marvel of disciplined engineering. Frankston crammed an entire interactive spreadsheet engine into roughly twenty-five kilobytes of code, small enough to run on a stock Apple II with as little as thirty-two kilobytes of memory—a feat of compression that later programmers, accustomed to software measured in the millions of bytes, regard with something like awe. It presented the user with a grid of lettered columns and numbered rows, a movable cursor, and a line where you entered your formulas. You could type a number into a cell, or a formula that referred to other cells by their coordinates—instructing cell C10, say, to hold the sum of everything in column C above it—and the moment you changed anything, the entire sheet recalculated and redisplayed itself. What had taken the Harvard professor a chalk-dusted quarter hour now happened faster than the eye could follow. The idea of the visible calculator, the thing Bricklin had glimpsed staring at a blackboard, was suddenly sitting on a desk, alive and responsive, doing in an instant what generations of clerks had done with pencils and erasers and enormous patience.

VisiCalc was released on October 17, 1979, priced initially around one hundred dollars, and at first almost no one understood what they were looking at. It was not a game, not a programming language, not a word processor. Salespeople in the handful of computer stores that existed struggled to explain it, and reviewers reached for analogies that did not quite fit. Yet the people who did understand it—the accountants and analysts and small-business owners who had spent their working lives inside those paper grids—reacted with something close to disbelief. They would sit down at a demonstration, change a single number at the top of a projection, and watch a year's worth of figures rearrange themselves instantly, and their expressions would change as they realized what it meant. Bricklin liked to recount how people would look at the screen, look back at him, and ask, warily, whether it was really doing what they thought it was doing—and when he said yes, they did not want to buy the program so much as the whole computer that ran it. He would tell, too, of demonstrating the program to accountants who had spent decades ruling ledgers by hand, and watching a kind of vertigo cross their faces as they grasped that the drudgery which had defined their working lives had just been rendered obsolete in a single afternoon—part exhilaration, part something close to grief for all the wasted hours. That doubled reaction, wonder shadowed by the sense of a world ending, is the truest measure of how radical the thing was.

Here lies one of the great and instructive injustices of the story, and a widely held misconception worth correcting. It is often assumed that the inventors of the spreadsheet, having produced the most important business program of the age, must have grown fabulously rich and locked their creation behind an ironclad patent. In fact Bricklin could not patent VisiCalc at all: under the law of the late 1970s, software was generally held to be an unpatentable abstraction, a mere set of mathematical steps, and the courts had not yet opened the door they later would. So the single most influential idea in personal-computer software was left essentially unprotected, free for anyone to imitate—and imitated it swiftly was. Within a few years a torrent of rivals appeared, most consequentially Lotus 1-2-3, which ran faster on the new IBM PC and buried VisiCalc so thoroughly that the pioneer was gone as a product by the mid-1980s. VisiCalc sold on the order of seven hundred thousand copies in its brief heyday, a staggering figure for the time, and made its creators a comfortable but modest sum—nothing remotely proportional to the industry it launched. Bricklin has borne this with characteristic grace, observing that he got to invent the spreadsheet, which was reward enough, and that the lack of a patent may well have helped the whole category flourish faster than it otherwise would have.

The program had its limits, of course, and they are worth naming because they measure how far we have come. Bricklin and Frankston's first VisiCalc offered a grid of only sixty-three columns and two hundred and fifty-four rows—a fraction of the millions of cells a modern spreadsheet spreads before you—and it had to solve, for the first time in a consumer product, a genuinely thorny puzzle that users never saw: in what order should the machine recalculate the cells so that no formula was computed before the values it depended upon? Get that wrong and a sheet would show stale or nonsensical answers. Their solution was imperfect—early versions simply swept through the grid column by column, which could trip up certain chains of dependencies—but it worked well enough for the budgets and forecasts real people built, and later spreadsheets would refine it into the "natural order" recalculation we now take entirely for granted. Every one of those quiet engineering decisions became a convention that hundreds of millions of people would inherit without ever knowing a choice had been made.

And flourish it did, in a way that reaches directly into your own life. Every time you open a spreadsheet today—every Microsoft Excel budget, every Google Sheets shared with a colleague across the world, every grid of cells that recalculates the instant you change a figure—you are using the direct descendant of the thing Bricklin sketched over a weekend and Frankston squeezed into an attic's worth of code. The lettered columns and numbered rows, the formula that points at other cells, the miracle of watching a hundred numbers update at a keystroke: all of it was there, essentially complete, in that first twenty-five kilobytes.

Dan Bricklin, for his part, made peace with his strange place in history and went on to a long and productive career in software, founding other companies and remaining, into his seventies, a thoughtful elder statesman of the industry, generous with his memories and free of rancor. He is universally credited now as the father of the electronic spreadsheet, honored with awards and enshrined in the halls of computing, and his original hand-built prototype and the story of that Harvard lecture hall are preserved in museums. He has often observed, with the equanimity of a man who understands exactly what he did and did not get, that being remembered as the person who invented the spreadsheet is its own kind of fortune, and not one that any latecomer with a faster program could ever take away. The money went elsewhere; the idea, and the credit for it, stayed with him.

That was the astonishing thing, the detail that would soon reshape an entire industry. The machine had become secondary to the program. Bricklin had set out to build a better calculator and had instead built the first piece of software so useful that people would purchase an entire computer simply to run it, and the consequences of that inversion were about to remake how the world thought about what a personal computer was actually for.

Chapter 23: The Killer App

Somewhere in a computer store in 1980, a customer walked up to the counter and asked for an Apple II, and when the salesman began to describe the machine's memory and its expansion slots and its color graphics, the customer cut him off. He did not care about any of that. He wanted the computer, he said, because he wanted to run VisiCalc. This scene, or something very like it, repeated itself in shop after shop across the United States over the following months, and it marked the arrival of a phenomenon that the young industry did not yet have a word for. People were not buying a computer and then looking for something to do with it. They were buying a specific program and treating the computer as a necessary accessory, the way one might buy a record and, only incidentally, need a turntable to play it. The most striking evidence of the inversion is a figure that still astonishes: by some contemporary accounts, more than a quarter of all Apple IIs sold in 1979 were bought expressly to run VisiCalc, and dealers told of customers who already owned another computer altogether and simply added a two-thousand-dollar Apple II to their order on the spot, once they had seen the spreadsheet do its trick, because VisiCalc ran on the Apple and not on the machine they owned.

The term that eventually attached itself to this phenomenon

was "killer application," or killer app, meaning a piece of software so compelling that it single-handedly drives the sale of the hardware it runs on. It is worth correcting a small and common misconception here, because it reveals how legends form. The phrase is so bound up with VisiCalc that people often assume it was coined in 1979 to describe it; in fact the expression did not come into circulation until the late 1980s, and VisiCalc earned the title retroactively, crowned the first killer app by a generation of writers looking back on how the personal computer had grown up. The word was invented later, but the thing it named was born in those Apple II demonstrations, and VisiCalc was, by universal consent, the original and for a long time the definitive example. The concept it crystallized has become one of the most powerful ideas in all of technology strategy. Ever since, the makers of platforms—computers, phones, game consoles, operating systems—have understood that their fortunes rest not only on the elegance of their hardware but on whether some irresistible piece of software chooses to call their machine home. Whole billion-dollar empires have risen and fallen on the presence or absence of a single killer app, and the executives who chase them are, whether they know it or not, chasing a lesson first taught by two young men and a spreadsheet in the autumn of 1979.

The numbers told the story with brutal clarity. VisiCalc had been written for the Apple II, and for roughly a year it ran on no other machine, which meant that anyone who wanted the miracle spreadsheet had to buy Apple's computer to get it. Steve Jobs never forgot the debt; he acknowledged in later years how much VisiCalc had done for Apple, and the timing could not have been more decisive. The Apple II had been a clever machine looking for a serious purpose, beloved of hobbyists but hardly a fixture of American business, and VisiCalc handed it exactly that purpose overnight. Over its lifetime the program sold more than seven hundred thousand copies in its first six years, with total sales eventually approaching a million—staggering figures for an era when the entire installed base of personal computers was measured in the hundreds of thousands and the very idea of a software bestseller had not yet been imagined. Software Arts, the company Bricklin and Frankston had incorporated on the second day of January 1979 to build the thing, found itself riding a wave no one had known was coming.

Word of the program spread partly through an unlikely evangelist. Benjamin Rosen was a securities analyst at the investment bank Morgan Stanley who wrote a widely read newsletter on the electronics industry, and when he encountered VisiCalc he grasped its significance faster than almost anyone and championed it in print to an audience of investors and executives who trusted his judgment. Rosen's enthusiasm helped carry news of the spreadsheet out of the narrow hobbyist press and into the offices of people with money and influence, and it is a measure of how completely he understood what he was seeing that he would soon leave Wall Street to become a venture capitalist—backing, among other ventures, both the Compaq computer company and the software firm that would ultimately dethrone VisiCalc itself. The prophet of the first spreadsheet financed the machine and the program that buried it.

What VisiCalc really did was change the answer to a question that had dogged the personal computer since its birth: what is it good for? Through the middle 1970s the honest answer had been that a personal computer was good for learning about computers, for playing games, for the pleasure of tinkering, and for a scattering of hobbyist projects that impressed other hobbyists. It was a toy—a marvelous and educational toy, but a toy—and serious businesses regarded the machines with the polite skepticism reserved for expensive novelties. VisiCalc demolished that perception. Here at last was a reason for a businessperson to spend two or three thousand dollars, a tool that paid for itself in the hours it saved and the analyses it made possible. An accountant could model a budget in an afternoon that would have taken a week by hand. A manager could ask "what if" questions—raise the price of a product five percent, and watch the projected profit for every month of the coming year rearrange itself instantly—and could do it privately, at a desk, without booking time on the company mainframe or waiting days for the data-processing department to run the numbers and hand them back. That last point mattered more than it might seem. For decades, access to serious computation had been rationed and gatekept, the property of a priesthood of programmers in a locked room. VisiCalc put a small piece of that power directly into the hands of the person who actually needed the answer, and there was no going back. The change ran deeper than any single office, reaching into the very culture of business. Before the spreadsheet, financial projection had been a laborious, semiannual ritual, a set of numbers ground out by hand and then left largely untouched because revising them was too painful. The instant recalculating grid made projection cheap, and what is cheap gets done constantly. Managers began to run their businesses by scenario, testing assumptions the way a scientist tests hypotheses, and a whole vocabulary of "what-if" and "run the numbers" entered the language of the workplace. Business schools reorganized their teaching around the tool; the leveraged-buyout artists and deal-makers of the 1980s built their audacious financial models on descendants of VisiCalc, modeling debt and cash flow at a speed that would have been unthinkable a decade earlier. Some scholars have argued, plausibly, that the spreadsheet did as much to reshape American finance as any deregulation or tax change of the era, precisely because it let ambitious people imagine and test far more elaborate financial structures than a pencil ever could. The personal computer, almost overnight, stopped being a hobbyist's plaything and became a business machine, and the transformation flowed not from any change in the hardware but from a single brilliant program.

For a few golden years the men who had built VisiCalc rode the wave. Software Arts developed and refined the program, while VisiCorp—the renamed Personal Software—published and marketed it and built a small empire of related products around it, all bearing the "Visi" prefix. Money poured in. VisiCalc was ported to other machines, including, eventually, the IBM PC. The two Dans and Bob Frankston became, within the small world of the software business, something like celebrities, the inventors of the tool that had legitimized an entire industry. And then, with the cruel symmetry that so often attends first movers, it all came apart, and the unraveling carried a lesson that would echo through the history of technology.

The first and most consequential failure was one of foresight rather than execution. Bricklin and Frankston never obtained a patent on the electronic spreadsheet, because in the late 1970s the law generally regarded software as an unpatentable abstraction and their attorneys saw little point in trying. Bricklin has spoken about it since with rueful candor, allowing that a patent on the recalculating spreadsheet might have changed the fortunes of everyone who ever built one—while also gently noting that its absence may have let the whole category bloom faster. Either way, the idea was free for the taking, and taken it was. Competitors studied VisiCalc, learned from its limitations, and set out to build something better and faster, most fatefully a program called Lotus 1-2-3, engineered specifically for the new IBM PC. Lotus was quicker, could draw charts, and arrived precisely as corporate America was standardizing on IBM's machine; it did to VisiCalc exactly what VisiCalc had done to the empty afternoon of the early personal computer, and it did it without mercy.

The second failure was internal and self-inflicted, and it is a textbook case of a company destroying itself from within at the worst possible moment. The relationship between Software Arts, which owned the program, and VisiCorp, which held the exclusive license to sell it, curdled into a bitter dispute over royalties, deadlines, and control. In the autumn of 1983 VisiCorp sued Software Arts for some sixty million dollars, alleging that Software Arts had dragged its feet on new versions; Software Arts countersued, charging that

VisiCorp had stopped promoting VisiCalc in order to push a fancy program of its own called Visi-On. The legal war consumed money, attention, and above all time—the one resource a technology company can never recover—and it distracted both firms precisely when Lotus was eating their lunch. When the suit finally settled in September 1984, VisiCorp paid Software Arts half a million dollars and handed over the VisiCalc trademark, but the victory was hollow: the market had moved on. VisiCorp faded and was gone within a few years of its greatest triumph, and Software Arts collapsed soon after, its remnants sold, fittingly and painfully, to Lotus. The company that had published the most important program of its era did not survive to see the decade out.

The cruelest twist of all is bound up in the man who inherited the throne. Mitch Kapor had orbited the VisiCalc world from early on: he wrote two companion programs, VisiPlot and VisiTrend, that produced graphs and statistical analyses to accompany the spreadsheet, and he sold the rights to them for a sum in the neighborhood of a million dollars. With that money—money that flowed, in effect, out of the VisiCalc ecosystem—Kapor founded Lotus Development Corporation and built Lotus 1-2-3, the very program that would render VisiCalc obsolete. Rosen, the newsletter prophet, helped fund him. So the fortune generated by the first spreadsheet capitalized the second, which destroyed the first: a nearly perfect closed loop of creative destruction, the kind of thing that happens so often in the technology business that it has come to seem almost like a law of nature. The pioneers clear the ground; the settlers take the land.

There is a particular poignancy in the fate of VisiCalc, and Bricklin himself has always told the story without bitterness, treating it as a case study rather than a grievance. He had built something genuinely new, a tool that changed how a generation of people worked and that proved, for the first time, that software could be the whole point of owning a computer. He had watched it sell nearly a million copies and reshape an industry. And he had watched the rewards flow, in the end, not to the inventors but to those who came after—the fast followers who patented nothing but copied everything and arrived with better products at a better moment. It is a pattern you can still see at work whenever a single application sells a whole platform: the game that moves a console, the chat app that decides which phone a country carries, the one piece of software people simply must have and will buy whatever machine it demands. Every one of those moments is a descendant of the day a customer walked into a computer store and asked not for a computer but for VisiCalc. The visible calculator had made the personal computer matter, and in doing so it had opened a door through which its own successors would come charging.

The pattern VisiCalc established would repeat almost immediately, and on a far grander stage. When IBM entered the personal-computer market in 1981 with a machine that would define business computing for a generation, it too needed a reason for corporations to buy it, and it found one in a spreadsheet: Lotus 1-2-3, which did for the IBM PC precisely what VisiCalc had done for the Apple II, selling the hardware on the strength of the software until the two became inseparable in the mind of every purchasing manager in America. The killer app had become a recognized force of nature, a thing hardware makers now prayed for and courted, because the lesson of VisiCalc was unmistakable: whoever controlled the software people could not live without controlled the market, no matter whose name was stamped on the box. It was a lesson Microsoft, watching closely, would learn better than anyone.

The spreadsheet had proven that a single program could sell a machine, and now a rival waited in the wings, built for the business computer that IBM was about to unleash, ready to inherit everything VisiCalc had won.

Chapter 24: Words on a Screen

In an office in the late 1970s, a secretary sat before a machine that looked like a television set married to a typewriter, its screen glowing with green letters, and performed an act that would have seemed like sorcery to anyone raised on carbon paper. She had typed a two-page letter, noticed a mistake in the opening paragraph, and instead of rolling a fresh sheet into a typewriter and beginning the whole page again, she moved a cursor back to the offending word, deleted it, typed a correction, and watched the text below reflow to close the gap. Then she pressed a key and the machine printed a clean, perfect copy. The machine was a Wang word processor, and in offices across the country such devices were quietly abolishing one of the great daily miseries of white-collar work: the tyranny of the typewriter, on which every error meant retyping and every revision meant starting over.

An Wang, the brilliant Chinese-born engineer whose company bore his name, had built Wang Laboratories into a powerhouse on the strength of these dedicated word-processing systems, purpose-built machines that did one thing, handled text, and did it superbly. Through the late 1970s the Wang systems dominated the corporate office, and for a while it seemed that word processing would remain the province of specialized hardware—expensive terminals wired to central processors, sold to businesses by the roomful. But the same revolution that VisiCalc had announced in the world of numbers was about to arrive in the world of words, and it would arrive not as a better machine but as software: a program that could turn any general-purpose personal computer into a word processor as capable as Wang's dedicated iron, at a fraction of the cost. The very idea that a business would buy a single-purpose machine for writing memos would come to seem, within a few years, as quaint as keeping a room full of typists.

The program that led that revolution was WordStar, and its origins lay with a former MITS and IBM marketing man named Seymour Rubinstein, who in September 1978 founded a small software company called MicroPro International. Rubinstein understood markets, and he sensed that the personal computers then running the CP/M operating system—the eight-bit business machines gathering in small offices—needed a serious word-processing program to justify themselves. To build it he turned to a gifted and prolific programmer named Rob Barnaby. Here it is worth pausing to correct the tidy legend, which holds that Barnaby simply sat down and conjured a full word processor out of nothing in a heroic burst. The truth is more interesting: Barnaby had already written for MicroPro a bare-bones text editor called WordMaster, and WordStar grew out of that earlier program, enhanced and extended with the on-screen formatting features that made it revolutionary. Barnaby was indeed the sole author of that early code, thousands of lines of tight Intel assembly language squeezed into the cramped memory of a CP/M machine, and Rubinstein supplied the market vision and the feature list drawn from watching what real users needed. MicroPro began selling the renamed WordStar in June 1979, priced at four hundred and ninety-five dollars, with the printed manual costing another forty. It was not cheap. It did not need to be.

What made WordStar genuinely radical was a phrase that sounds unremarkable today but was close to miraculous then: "what you see is what you get." On a Wang and on most rivals, formatting was a matter of embedded codes and guesswork; on WordStar, the text on the glowing screen was arranged more or less as it would appear on the printed page, so a writer could see the shape of a paragraph as it took form. WordStar was not, however, easy in the way later programs would be. Personal computers of its era had no mouse, and their keyboards often lacked the arrow keys and function keys that would later be taken for granted, so WordStar controlled everything through combinations of the control key and letter keys. To move the cursor up, down, left, or right, a user pressed the control key together with E, X, S, and D—a diamond-shaped cluster on the left of the keyboard that a touch typist could reach without ever looking down. To delete, to scroll, to save, to format, one memorized a whole lexicon of these control-key incantations. It sounds forbidding, and to a newcomer it was, but the design hid a genuine virtue: an experienced WordStar user never lifted his hands from the home row, never reached for a distant key or a mouse that did not exist, and could edit text at something approaching the speed of thought. A generation of writers and secretaries and lawyers learned that diamond by heart, and many of them mourned it for decades afterward.

WordStar also gathered around itself a small ecosystem of companion programs that extended what a writer could do, and these deserve mention because they prefigured features we now take for granted. There was MailMerge, which let a user marry a form letter to a list of names and addresses and print a personalized copy for each—the direct ancestor of every "mail merge" that has plagued and blessed office workers since. And there was SpellStar, an add-on spelling checker that would comb a document against a dictionary and flag words it did not recognize, a novelty in an age when catching a typo still generally meant reading every line yourself. Bundled together, WordStar and its satellites turned a bare CP/M business computer into a genuine writing workstation.

The single greatest stroke of distribution, though, came from outside MicroPro entirely. In 1981 a former book publisher named Adam Osborne launched the Osborne 1, one of the first portable computers—a hefty, sewing-machine-sized box with a tiny five-inch screen that a person could, with some effort, actually carry—and he sold it on a radical premise: the machine came with a whole suite of software already included in the price, software that would have cost more than the computer itself if bought separately. Chief among the bundled programs was WordStar. Overnight, every Osborne buyer became a WordStar user, and the portable's runaway early success poured the word processor into tens of thousands of hands that might never have sought it out. It was one of the first great demonstrations that bundling software with hardware could build a user base faster than any advertisement, a lesson the industry would return to again and again.

The market responded quickly. MicroPro advertised that five thousand people had bought WordStar in its first eight months, and the momentum only built from there; by May 1983 *Byte* magazine could call WordStar "without a doubt the best-known and probably the most widely used personal computer word-processing program." For several years it was simply the standard, the word processor that came to mind when anyone said the words, running on the CP/M machines that dominated small-business computing before the IBM era. Its dominance bred a certain complacency, and when the personal-computer world lurched toward new hardware and the IBM PC's operating system, WordStar's failure to adapt quickly enough opened a fatal gap. Into that gap stepped a rival from, of all places, Orem, Utah—a program called WordPerfect, built by a company that grew out of work by Alan Ashton and Bruce Bastian. WordPerfect took a different design philosophy, leaning on the row of function keys along the keyboard, each key and combination mapped to a command, with a plastic template that fit over the keys to remind users what did what. It offered a meticulous approach to formatting and a famous "reveal codes" function that let a user peel back the document and see the hidden instructions shaping it. Through the 1980s WordPerfect steadily overtook WordStar and became, in its turn, the dominant word processor of the business world, its blue screen and white text a fixture of law offices and secretarial pools—until the next great shift, the arrival of graphical interfaces and Microsoft Word, would eventually unseat it too.

The rise of the software word processor also spelled a slow doom for the dedicated machines that had come before. An Wang's company, which had built an empire on hardware that did nothing but process words, found its market evaporating as ordinary personal computers, running programs like WordStar and later WordPerfect and Word, matched and then surpassed the specialized terminals at a fraction of the cost. Why buy a machine that could only write letters when the machine on the next desk could write letters, keep the books with a spreadsheet, and run a hundred other programs besides? Wang Laboratories, once one of the most valuable technology companies in America, declined through the 1980s and filed for bankruptcy in 1992, a casualty of the very flexibility that made the general-purpose personal computer irresistible. WordPerfect, for its part, built ferocious loyalty in part through a legendary customer-service operation—for years the company offered free telephone support, staffed by real people who would patiently talk a baffled secretary or lawyer through whatever had gone wrong, a level of hand-holding that bound offices to the product until the arrival of Microsoft Word for Windows swept the whole landscape aside.

Yet WordStar never entirely died, and its afterlife furnishes one of the most charming footnotes in the history of software. Decades after the program had vanished from store shelves, the novelist George R. R. Martin—author of the sprawling saga that became *Game of Thrones*—revealed that he writes his books on a DOS computer running WordStar 4.0, a program older than many of his readers. He keeps that machine deliberately disconnected from the internet, a fortress against distraction and, as he put it, against the spell-checkers and autocorrect features of modern software that presume to know that he really meant "the" when he wrote a made-up name. WordStar, he said, does everything he needs and nothing he does not want. It is a striking testament that the control-key diamond and the plain green screen could still satisfy one of the most successful storytellers of the age, forty years on. Nor is Martin alone in his loyalty. The WordStar control-key layout—that diamond of cursor motions and its lexicon of commands—so thoroughly imprinted itself on the writers who learned it that it never entirely died. To this day several modern text editors and programming tools quietly offer a "WordStar mode," a set of keyboard shortcuts that reproduces the old diamond, so that a programmer born decades after MicroPro folded can, if he wishes, still move his cursor with the same finger-memory a 1979 secretary used. It is one of those ghostly persistences that haunt the history of technology: the hardware is gone, the company is gone, the operating system is gone, and yet the muscle memory of a few keystrokes lives on in software written in a century the original programmers never imagined.

The deeper story, though, was never the horse race between one program and another but the change these programs worked on the act of writing itself. For the entire prior history of the typewriter, text had been physical and unforgiving. Words committed to paper stayed there; revision meant retyping, and the labor of retyping imposed a quiet conservatism on writers, a reluctance to tinker, to rearrange, to cut a paragraph and try it somewhere else, because every change carried a cost measured in fresh sheets and lost hours. The screen dissolved that cost. Text became fluid, provisional, endlessly malleable. A writer could draft badly on purpose, knowing everything could be fixed later; could move a block of prose from the end of a document to the beginning with a few keystrokes; could try three versions of a sentence and keep the best. Whole paragraphs could be summoned, banished, and resurrected without a trace. The psychology of composition shifted, and not everyone welcomed it; some writers argued then, and argue still, that the ease of endless revision produced flabbier, less considered prose, and that the discipline of the typewriter had virtues the screen destroyed. Martin's isolated DOS machine is, in its way, a vote for the old rigor. But the tide was irresistible.

Offices felt the change first and most dramatically. The typing pool—that institution of the twentieth-century workplace where rows of clerks, almost always women, retyped drafts marked up by executives—began its long decline, because a document no longer had to be retyped from scratch to incorporate an edit. Legal work, dependent on the endless revision of contracts and briefs, was transformed. And authorship itself migrated to the screen, slowly at first and then all at once, as novelists and journalists who had sworn by their typewriters discovered that they could not go back. Writing had become, for the first time in the history of the written word, an act performed against glowing glass rather than pressed into paper, and there was no returning to the old way. The change reached even the most stubborn craftsmen of the sentence. Newspaper rooms that had clattered with typewriters for a century fell silent within a few years as reporters moved to terminals and screens; publishers who had received typed manuscripts for generations began to accept, and then to require, files stored on disk. A few celebrated holdouts clung to their typewriters and made a point of it, but they became curiosities, and each passing year thinned their ranks. The screen had not merely made writing easier; it had made a particular relationship with words—provisional, revisable, weightless—the default condition of everyone who wrote for a living. Every document you draft today, reflowing as you cut and paste and revise without a thought, is the grandchild of that green-lettered diamond of control keys—and, in a quieter sense, of the secretary who first watched her text close a gap and knew the typewriter's reign was ending.

Yet all of these programs, WordStar first among them, ran on top of something invisible—a layer of software that stood between the application and the machine and made the whole business-computing world of the era possible—and that hidden foundation had a name and an inventor of its own.

Chapter 25: CP/M and the First Standard

In the early 1970s, in Pacific Grove on California's Monterey Peninsula, a young computer scientist named Gary Kildall was teaching at the Naval Postgraduate School and moonlighting as a consultant for a chip company down in Silicon Valley called Intel. Intel had produced a small, cheap microprocessor, and Kildall, fascinated by the little chips, took his pay partly in hardware and began writing software for them in his spare time, often at the kitchen table or in a back room, tinkering the way the best of his generation tinkered. Before he ever wrote an operating system, he had already given the microprocessor something it badly needed: a real programming language. In 1973 he created PL/M, the first high-level language written for a microprocessor, so that programmers building on Intel's chips would not have to hand-code every instruction in raw machine numbers. To make that language genuinely useful, though, he needed a way to store and retrieve programs and data, and the storage that had arrived was a bulky eight-inch floppy disk drive from Memorex. So he set out to write a program that could manage the flow of information between a microprocessor and a floppy drive, a small piece of software that would sit in charge of the machine and orchestrate its parts. He called it CP/M, for Control Program for Microcomputers, and in writing it he created something the world had not seen before: an operating system for personal computers.

The birth of that program was far less tidy than its later importance would suggest. Kildall wrote the software itself in a matter of weeks, but when he tried to build the electronic hardware to shuttle data between the processor and the drive, the circuitry simply refused to work, and CP/M sat idle, a finished set of instructions with no way to reach the disk. The breakthrough came only when a friend and gifted hardware engineer named John Torode built a working controller. Late one afternoon in the fall of 1974, in a backyard workshop in Pacific Grove, the two men loaded CP/M from a strip of punched paper tape onto a diskette, told the machine to start itself from the disk, and watched a single character appear on the screen: an asterisk, the program's prompt, blinking patiently, waiting for a command. It was one of those small, unwitnessed moments on which enormous things turn. An operating system had just booted a microcomputer from a disk for the first time, and almost no one on earth knew or cared.

An operating system is the layer of software that manages a computer's fundamental resources, its memory, its storage, its input and output, and provides a stable set of services on which application programs can run. This is worth stating plainly, because a stubborn misconception surrounds CP/M: that Kildall invented the operating system as such, conjuring the very idea from nothing. He did not. Mainframes and minicomputers had run sophisticated operating systems for years, some of them vast and powerful. What the new microcomputers lacked was not the concept but any usable, standard version of it. The machines being cobbled together by hobbyists and small firms largely had no operating system at all; each was its own island, and software written for one would not run on another. Kildall's real achievement was to take an idea from the world of big computers and shrink it to fit a chip that cost a few hundred dollars, and then to make it a common tongue. CP/M gave the eight-bit microcomputers built around the Intel 8080 and the compatible Zilog Z80 processors a shared foundation, a predictable environment in which a program like the word processor WordStar or a business accounting package could expect to find its files, read the keyboard, and write to the screen and the printer in the same way from one machine to the next. Kildall and his wife, Dorothy McEwen, who ran the business side with formidable competence, founded a company to sell it. They first called it Intergalactic Digital Research and soon, more soberly, Digital Research, Incorporated, operating out of a staid Victorian house at 801 Lighthouse Avenue in Pacific Grove that they gradually converted into a bustling software headquarters.

The genius of CP/M, the thing that made it a standard rather than merely one more program tied to one more machine, lay in an architectural decision of quiet brilliance, and it did not arrive all at once. In the earliest versions the machine-specific code was tangled together with the rest, and porting CP/M to a new computer meant painful surgery. Working with a programmer named Glen Ewing, Kildall pulled all of the machine-specific communication out into a single small module he called the BIOS, the Basic Input Output System, which handled the intimate details of talking to a particular computer's physical devices. The hardware of early microcomputers was gloriously inconsistent; every manufacturer wired its disk drives and serial ports and memory differently, so that software speaking directly to one company's hardware would be baffled by another's. Above the BIOS sat the rest of CP/M, identical everywhere, indifferent to the hardware beneath because it spoke only to the BIOS and let the BIOS worry about the wiring. To bring CP/M to a new computer, a manufacturer had only to write or adapt the small BIOS for that machine, and instantly the entire universe of CP/M software would run on it. That word, BIOS, would echo through the rest of this book and into the machine on your desk today; it was Gary Kildall who coined it. The abstraction he built around it, separating the portable from the machine-specific, was one of the foundational ideas of practical computing, and it let CP/M spread across a bewildering variety of hardware from dozens of makers.

Underneath, CP/M was really three programs stacked one atop another, and it helps to picture them to see why the design was so clever. At the bottom sat the BIOS, the only part that knew the particular machine. Above it sat the BDOS, the Basic Disk Operating System, which kept track of files and directories and offered programs a tidy menu of services—open this file, read that record, print this character—without caring what hardware ultimately carried them out. And at the top sat the CCP, the Console Command Processor, the part that put the A> prompt on the screen and interpreted what the user typed. When a word processor asked to save a document, it spoke to the BDOS in a language identical on every CP/M machine; the BDOS then turned to the BIOS, which alone knew how to nudge this specific disk drive into writing this specific sector. A manufacturer bringing out a new computer replaced only the bottom layer and inherited the other two unchanged. That layered separation of concerns is now taught as a first principle of software design, and it is the reason a program written for one CP/M machine in 1979 could run, untouched, on a hundred others.

To sit at a CP/M machine was to meet an idiom that has never really gone away. When the system booted, it presented a prompt like A>, in which the letter named the currently selected disk drive, so that a second drive was B and a hard disk, when such things arrived, was often C. A user typed DIR to see a directory of files, PIP to copy them from one place to another, and the name of any program to run it; the operating system would fetch that program from the disk, load it into a region of memory called the Transient Program Area, and hand it the machine. Files carried short names of up to eight characters followed by a three-letter type, so that a letter to the bank might live as LETTER.TXT and a program as WS.COM. None of this is a museum piece. Open a command window in Windows today and you will still find drive letters, still type DIR to list files, still see the ghost of the eight-plus-three filename, because Microsoft's DOS was deliberately built to look and behave like CP/M, and Windows inherited the conventions from DOS. The A> prompt that flickered to life in a Pacific Grove backyard is, in a real sense, still running under the surface of a billion computers.

And spread it did. Through the late 1970s and into the early 1980s, CP/M became the dominant operating system for serious eight-bit business microcomputers, the common tongue of the industry. Companies building machines around the Z80 processor adopted it; software houses wrote their programs to run under it, knowing that CP/M compatibility meant access to a large and growing market rather than a single machine's small one. A businessperson could buy a computer from one manufacturer and a word processor from another and a spreadsheet from a third, and reasonably expect them all to work together, because they all rested on the same operating system. This was the ecosystem, the network of interoperable hardware and software, that WordStar and the spreadsheets and countless business programs inhabited. For a period of several crucial years, if you were running a small business on a microcomputer, you were almost certainly running CP/M, and the name Digital Research carried the kind of weight in the industry that few software companies had ever known.

Nothing captured the power of that ecosystem better than a squat, ugly, luggable machine that appeared in the spring of 1981. The Osborne 1, dreamed up by a former computer-book publisher named Adam Osborne and designed by the Homebrew veteran Lee Felsenstein, weighed nearly twenty-five pounds, folded into the shape of a sewing machine, and had a screen barely five inches across. It cost seventeen hundred and ninety-five dollars, and its genius was pure salesmanship married to the CP/M standard: because CP/M had made a large library of software portable, Osborne could bundle a whole working office into the box—the CP/M operating system itself, the WordStar word processor, the SuperCalc spreadsheet, two versions of the BASIC language—software that would have cost roughly fifteen hundred dollars bought separately, thrown in essentially for free. Customers did the arithmetic and gasped; the company sold eleven thousand machines in a matter of months against an original business plan that had forecast ten thousand over the product's entire life. None of that would have been possible without CP/M, which turned other people's programs into a commodity Osborne could give away to sell his hardware. It was a vivid demonstration of what a standard makes possible, and a preview of a bundling logic the whole industry would later adopt.

It is easy, knowing how the story ends, to picture Kildall as a naive academic who happened to write a clever program and then fumbled the business, and that too is a misconception worth correcting. By the late 1970s Digital Research was the leading supplier of microcomputer operating systems on earth, a genuinely successful company that had licensed CP/M to a long roster of hardware makers and built a thriving trade around it. Kildall, by all accounts a generous and brilliant programmer more interested in elegant systems than in empire, presided over the most important software standard of the pre-IBM era, and he did so from a position of real strength. That he was more comfortable talking about compilers than about contracts does not mean he was a failure; for years he was, by the measure that mattered, winning.

There was a hardware footnote to CP/M's dominance that would matter enormously, and it involved a name soon to loom over the whole industry. Because so much valuable business software ran under CP/M, and because CP/M ran on the 8080 and Z80 processors rather than on the Apple II's very different 6502 chip, an enterprising firm called Microsoft, then far better known for the BASIC programming language than for anything else, produced a clever add-on board called the SoftCard. Released in the spring of

1980, it was the first piece of hardware Microsoft ever sold. Plugged into an Apple II, the SoftCard added a Z80 processor and allowed the Apple, of all machines, to run CP/M and its enormous library of business programs, including WordStar, which vast numbers of Apple owners had been unable to use before. To the young company's own surprise it became a runaway hit, selling roughly five thousand units within three months at a few hundred dollars apiece, and for a stretch it generated something close to half of Microsoft's entire revenue. It was a vivid measure of how central CP/M had become that even Apple owners were paying to enter the CP/M world, and that Microsoft was happy to sell them the bridge, a small transaction that hinted at the tangled alliances soon to reshape everything.

By the dawn of the 1980s, then, the personal computer had acquired all the pieces of a genuine industry. It had a killer application in the spreadsheet that gave people a reason to buy. It had word processors that transformed the daily work of offices. And it had, in CP/M, a dominant operating system that unified the hardware chaos into a coherent platform on which software could be written once and sold widely. Digital Research sat at the center of that platform, and Gary Kildall, in his Victorian house by the sea, held a position of extraordinary leverage, the proprietor of the standard that the whole business-computing world depended upon. It was the kind of position that fortunes are built on, and for a few years it seemed unassailable.

What almost no one in Pacific Grove could have foreseen was that the largest computer company on earth, a corporation whose blue-suited salesmen had ruled the mainframe world for a generation, was quietly assembling a small team in Florida to build a personal computer of its own, and that when those men went looking for an operating system to run it, the road would lead, inevitably, to Gary Kildall's door, to a meeting whose outcome would rewrite the history of the industry and, in the telling, become one of the most argued-over episodes in the whole story of the personal computer.

The giant was coming, and the choice of whose software would sit inside its machine was about to be decided in a way that would make some men billionaires and leave others forever wondering what might have been.

Chapter 26: An Industry Is Born

On a December day in 1975, in a modest storefront at 1063 West El Camino Real in Mountain View, California, a former electrical engineer named Paul Terrell opened the doors of a shop he called the Byte Shop, and in doing so he helped invent an institution that had not existed before: the retail computer store. Terrell's shop, which opened on the eighth of December, was one of the very first of its kind, selling the strange new machines to walk-in customers who could actually see and touch them before they bought. A few months later, in the summer of 1976, two young men named Steve Jobs and Steve Wozniak walked in with a hand-built circuit board, and Terrell made the decision that changed both their lives and his own. He would order fifty of the machines, he told them, but only if they were delivered as fully assembled boards rather than the bags of loose components that hobbyists were used to soldering together themselves. He agreed to pay five hundred dollars apiece on delivery. It was an enormous order for a company that barely existed, and it forced Apple to become a maker of finished products rather than kits. Jobs, needing to buy the parts, walked into a component distributor called Cramer Electronics and, asked how a penniless twenty-one-year-old proposed to pay, produced his trump card: "I have this purchase order from the Byte Shop chain of computer stores for fifty of my computers, and the payment terms are COD." That single placemat-thin margin of credit, backed by Terrell's order, was very nearly the whole of Apple's founding capital.

Within a few years storefronts like Terrell's were appearing across America; at its height the Byte Shop itself grew to some seventy-three outlets, and a franchise operation called ComputerLand, founded in 1976, spread the model nationwide, its stores becoming the places where ordinary people first laid hands on a personal computer. These stores were more than points of sale. They were showrooms, classrooms, and gathering places, and crucially they were shelves, physical shelves that needed something to hold, and what they increasingly held, alongside the machines, were boxes of software.

For most of the personal computer's short history, software had not been a product at all in the way we now understand the word, and it is worth pausing to correct a common assumption: that a thriving commercial software industry sprang up naturally alongside the first computers. It did not. In the hobbyist era, programs were things you typed in yourself from listings printed in magazines, or swapped on cassette tapes at club meetings, or received bundled free with the hardware you bought. The idea that a program might be a commercial good, manufactured, packaged, priced, advertised, and sold for profit like a book or a record, was genuinely novel, and to many of the early enthusiasts it seemed almost improper, a violation of the free-sharing spirit in which the movement had been born. It was VisiCalc, the electronic spreadsheet, more than anything that proved the idea could work. If a single program could sell hundreds of thousands of copies and drive the sale of the computers needed to run it, then software was not a giveaway to move hardware; software was where the real value lay. That realization, dawning around the turn of the 1980s, gave birth to an entirely new kind of company, the software publisher, whose business was not building machines but creating, duplicating, and selling programs.

These new firms sprang up with startling speed, and many of their origins were as improbable as Apple's. Personal Software, the company that published VisiCalc, was so transformed by that one program's success that it renamed itself VisiCorp, and VisiCalc alone eventually sold on the order of hundreds of thousands of copies at close to a hundred dollars each, a torrent of money from a single idea. MicroPro International turned WordStar into the dominant word processor of the CP/M world and grew into one of the largest software companies on earth. And some of the most enduring names began at kitchen tables. In 1980 a young couple named Ken and Roberta Williams, working out of their home near Los Angeles, wrote an adventure game called Mystery House for the Apple II; Roberta drew the crude on-screen pictures, Ken wrote the code, and they packaged the diskettes in plastic bags and sold them by mail, founding the company that became Sierra On-Line and helped invent the graphic adventure game. The pattern repeated across the industry: a program written by one or two people, a company formed to publish it, and, if the program caught on, a business that could go from a spare bedroom to millions of dollars in revenue within a year or two.

The publishers borrowed their forms from the industries that had come before them. From books and records they took the notion of packaging, and software began to appear in boxes, often handsomely designed, containing a floppy disk or two and a printed manual, sealed for retail sale. The term that came to define the category was shrink-wrap software, referring to the clear plastic film heat-sealed around the box, and shrink-wrap became shorthand for the whole model of mass-market packaged programs sold off a shelf to anyone who walked in. There was more legal cunning in that plastic film than a shopper would ever guess. Publishers began printing a license agreement on the box or just inside it, declaring that by tearing the wrapper the buyer accepted the company's terms, that the software was not sold but merely licensed for use. This shrink-wrap license was a genuine innovation, an attempt to bind a customer to a contract he had never signed, and its distant descendants are the clickwrap agreements you accept every time you install an app or update a phone today, tapping "I Agree" on terms you have not read. A customer could now browse a rack of software the way one browsed record bins, reading the boxes, comparing features, and carrying home a program that would run, thanks to standards like CP/M, on the machine already sitting on the desk.

With value came the anxiety of protecting it, and here the young industry ran headlong into a problem that would haunt it for decades. A floppy disk was trivially easy to copy; the same disk drive that read a program could, with the right software, write a perfect duplicate in seconds, and a program that had cost tens of thousands of dollars to develop could be pirated for the price of a blank disk. Piracy was rampant almost from the beginning, and publishers responded with an escalating arsenal of copy protection schemes. The tricks were ingenious. A publisher might deliberately damage a specific spot on the master disk with a laser or a punch, so that a particular sector was physically unreadable, and then write the program to check, on startup, that this flaw was present. A legitimate original disk had the flaw; an ordinary copy, made by software that faithfully reproduced only the readable data, did not, and so the copy would refuse to run. Others wrote data into the gaps between tracks where standard drives were not supposed to be able to look, or laid down sectors of unusual sizes that normal copying programs could not reproduce. The pirates, often clever hobbyists who regarded cracking protection as a sport, responded with programs of their own designed to defeat the schemes, and an arms race ensued that consumed enormous ingenuity on both sides. Whole underground newsletters circulated, listing the precise steps to "crack" popular titles, and a cracked program often reached more machines than the original ever sold, its protection stripped away and its title screen defaced with the boastful signature of whoever had broken it. Copy protection frustrated legitimate customers, who could not make backup copies of programs they had lawfully bought, as much as it inconvenienced pirates, and the tension between protecting software and respecting the people who paid for it would run through the entire history of the industry, straight down to the online activation and digital rights management of the present day.

The moral argument at the heart of that tension had been made, loudly and early, by a nineteen-year-old. In 1976 Bill Gates, then running his tiny software firm out of Albuquerque, wrote an "Open Letter to Hobbyists" after discovering that his version of the BASIC language was being copied and passed around the clubs faster than anyone was paying for it. "Who can afford to do professional work for nothing?" he demanded, and he laid out the argument that would define the commercial future in a single indignant stroke: "One thing you do is prevent good software from being written. Who can afford to do professional work for nothing? What hobbyist can put three man-years into programming, finding all bugs, documenting his product, and distribute it for free?" To the sharing ethos of the hobbyist clubs it was close to blasphemy, and Gates was denounced for it; but the letter pointed unmistakably toward the world that was coming, a world in which software would be property and programmers would be paid.

The new industry needed channels to reach its customers, and it built them quickly. Magazines proliferated, thick glossy monthlies like Byte and Creative Computing and countless others, their pages fat with advertisements, reviews, program listings, and the breathless coverage of a field reinventing itself every few months. For many buyers, especially those far from a ComputerLand or a Byte Shop, the magazines were the marketplace, and mail order became a major channel, with companies advertising software and hardware in the back pages and shipping it anywhere a check could reach. A reader in a small town could learn about a program from a review, order it by mail from an advertisement, and receive it by post, participating in the revolution without ever entering a store. It was, in embryo, exactly the arrangement that would one day be called electronic commerce; the reader thumbing the back pages of Byte for a mail-order bargain was doing something a modern shopper would recognize instantly, only slower and by post. The magazines also knit the scattered community together, spreading news, standards, and enthusiasm, and their advertising revenue underwrote a torrent of information that helped ordinary people make sense of a bewildering and fast-moving new technology. So thick did the leading titles become, swollen with page after page of advertisements from hardware makers and software publishers and mail-order houses, that a single monthly issue of Byte could arrive in the mailbox with the heft of a small telephone directory, hundreds of pages of it, more advertising than editorial, a physical measure of how much money was suddenly pouring into a business that a few years earlier had scarcely existed. To flip through one of those issues today is to hold the boom in your hands.

Underlying all of it was a single profound shift in where value lived. In the beginning, the personal computer had been sold as hardware, a box of chips and circuits, and whatever software came with it was an afterthought thrown in to help move the metal. By the early 1980s that relationship had inverted. The hardware, increasingly, was becoming a commodity, standardized and interchangeable, while the software was the thing that determined what a computer could actually do and therefore whether anyone would buy it at all. People chose machines based on the programs they could run. The spreadsheet, the word processor, the database, the game: these were the reasons to own a computer, and the companies that made them were capturing a growing share of the industry's wealth and prestige. Software had become the product, and hardware, in a sense, had become the delivery mechanism, a reversal so complete that it would define the economics of computing for the next half century and make the great software fortunes of the coming decades possible.

The whole apparatus the young industry improvised in those years is still recognizably with us, only dematerialized. The shrink-wrapped box on the ComputerLand shelf has become the app in an online store; the license agreement inside the wrapper has become the terms of service you tap past; the mail-order coupon in the back of Byte has become the download button. Even the business model has survived unchanged in its essentials: a small team writes a program, a publisher packages and markets and takes a cut, and a distribution channel puts it in front of millions of buyers. Valve's Steam store for games, Apple's App Store, Google Play—these are the direct institutional descendants of the software publishers and computer stores of 1980, running the same play at planetary scale. What those early entrepreneurs discovered, that a program is a thing that can be manufactured once and sold a million times at almost no additional cost, remains the most seductive economic fact in all of technology, and the foundation of nearly every fortune the digital age has produced.

By the summer of 1980, then, all the elements were in place: the killer applications, the publishers and their shrink-wrapped boxes, the stores and magazines and mail-order channels, the standard operating systems, and the dawning understanding that software was the true heart of the personal computer. The revolution had grown from a hobbyist's pastime into a genuine industry with billions of dollars in prospect, and its explosive growth had begun to attract attention from quarters that had long ignored it. In an office park in Boca Raton, Florida, behind closed doors, a team of engineers from the largest and most formidable computer company in the world was about to enter the game, and nothing about the personal computer, its software, or the men who made it would ever be the same again.

Chapter 27: The Giant Stirs

On a July morning in 1980, in a windowless conference room at the International Business Machines headquarters in Armonk, New York, a lanky executive named William C. Lowe stood before the most powerful men in the computer industry and told them, in effect, that their company was about to be left behind. Lowe ran a modest IBM laboratory in Boca Raton, Florida, a facility that busied itself with small systems well below the notice of the mainframe engineers who ran the company's soul. He had been summoned to Armonk to address the Corporate Management Committee—the small circle of senior officers who governed IBM the way a board of admirals governs a fleet—and his message was blunt. The personal computer was real. Companies with names IBM's leaders had barely heard of, run by men younger than their own children, were selling hundreds of thousands of little machines to ordinary people. And IBM, the undisputed titan of computing, the company whose very name was a synonym for the electronic brain, had nothing to sell them.

To understand how strange that moment was, one has to understand what IBM had become by 1980. It was not merely a large company; it was, by many measures, the most successful enterprise in the history of American capitalism. Its revenues that year approached twenty-six billion dollars, a sum that dwarfed the entire personal-computer industry many times over. It employed well over three hundred thousand people across the globe. Its salesmen, in their dark suits and white shirts, were a legend unto themselves—so relentlessly professional, so reassuringly competent, that a generation of corporate purchasing managers had absorbed a quiet article of faith: nobody ever got fired for buying IBM. The company had dominated the mainframe business so completely that the federal government had spent much of the 1970s prosecuting it under the antitrust laws, an ordeal that had begun with a suit filed in 1969 and would consume nearly a thousand witnesses and tens of thousands of exhibits before the government finally abandoned it as "without merit" in January of 1982. In the world of big computing, IBM was not a competitor. It was the weather.

It would be wrong, though, to imagine that IBM had simply ignored the small machine until 1980, and here a persistent misconception deserves correcting: the IBM PC was not IBM's first personal computer. As far back as September of 1975, the company's General Systems Division had shipped a self-contained desktop machine called the IBM 5100, descended from a portable prototype nicknamed SCAMP that an IBM engineer had built in 1973. The 5100 packed a processor, a keyboard, a five-inch screen, a tape drive, and up to sixty-four kilobytes of memory into a fifty-five-pound box the size of a small suitcase. It was, in every meaningful sense, a personal computer, and IBM had it years before Apple existed. But it carried a price that ran from roughly nine thousand dollars to nearly twenty thousand, and it was aimed at scientists and engineers, not at the man who wanted a machine on his desk at home. It sold poorly, and its lesson within IBM was ambiguous. The company had proven it could build such a machine; it had not proven it understood the market that was now exploding under its nose. The problem in 1980 was not that IBM had never tried. It was that IBM did not know how to try fast, or cheap, or for ordinary people.

That failing was structural, bred into the company by the very habits that had made it great. An IBM product was not designed so much as legislated. A new machine passed through committees and reviews and sign-offs, through market forecasts and quality gates and interdepartmental negotiations, in a process that could consume four or five years before a single unit shipped. The company built nearly everything itself, from the semiconductors to the software to the very screws, because building it all in-house was how you guaranteed the quality and the compatibility that customers paid IBM's premium prices to receive. This methodical, vertically integrated, committee-driven approach had served brilliantly when a computer cost as much as a suburban house and a customer expected it to run without fail for a decade. It was catastrophically wrong for a business in which a scrappy firm in a strip mall could conceive a product in the spring and ship it by Christmas.

And so the giant had watched, with a mixture of condescension and unease, as the microcomputer revolution unfolded outside its walls. The men in Armonk were not fools; they read the trade press, they saw the sales figures, they knew that the Apple II was selling by the tens of thousands and that the humble spreadsheet program called VisiCalc was pulling those machines into offices that had never before contained a computer of any kind. What gnawed at them was not ignorance but a species of pride mixed with fear. Some genuinely doubted that these toys, with their cassette-tape storage and their hobbyist origins, had any place in serious business. Others suspected the opposite—that the toys were the future, and that if IBM did not stake a claim soon, an entire generation of computer users would grow up loyal to some other brand, and would carry that loyalty upward, year by year, until it reached the mainframe accounts that were IBM's very lifeblood. It was said, in a phrase that captured the mood, that IBM was in danger of missing the boat, and that the boat in question was the whole future of computing.

The catalyst, by most accounts, was IBM's chairman, Frank Cary, a man who had risen through the sales ranks and who understood viscerally that a market unaddressed was a market surrendered. Cary had grown impatient with his own company's inability to move; the standing joke inside IBM likened it to teaching an elephant to dance, and Cary wanted the elephant on its feet. When the question of a personal computer came before him, the story goes, he wanted to know why IBM could not simply build one, and he was told that by the time the standard development process had run its course, the opportunity would be gone. It was in this atmosphere of frustration that Lowe made his pitch, and his proposal contained a heresy so complete that it amounted to a repudiation of everything IBM believed about how to make a machine. When he presented his case to the committee, the crude prototype his engineers had cobbled together barely worked at all; what persuaded the room was not the hardware but the plan, and above all the promise of speed. Cary gave Lowe a month to produce a working prototype and roughly a year to put a finished product on the market—a schedule so alien to IBM's culture that veterans could scarcely believe it had been uttered aloud.

There is a revealing detail in how Lowe first framed the choice, one that shows just how far outside its own skin IBM was prepared to step. When he demonstrated the possibility to the committee, the mock-up his people had assembled was based on the guts of an Atari 800, one of the very consumer machines IBM meant to challenge, and Lowe's blunt recommendation was that IBM should not build the computer at all but simply buy Atari, a maker of video games and home computers, "because we can't do this within the culture of IBM." It was an astonishing thing to propose to the lords of Armonk: that the greatest engineering organization in the world was institutionally incapable of building a cheap little computer and had better purchase someone who could. Cary agreed with the diagnosis even as he rejected the cure. By his own reckoning, doing it the normal IBM way would take "four years and three hundred people," and the market would be gone before the paperwork cleared. Lowe's counteroffer—a prototype in thirty days and a product in a year, if only the committee would let a small band of engineers ignore every rule in the building—was accepted precisely because the alternative, acquiring Atari, was even more unthinkable than letting IBM people behave like a startup. The independent group that resulted would be led day to day by an engineer named Bill Sydnes and would soon acquire its nickname, the Dirty Dozen.

It is worth dwelling for a moment on what IBM was risking, because the decision looks obvious only in hindsight. The company had bet the entire firm once before, in the 1960s, on the System/360 family of mainframes, an all-or-nothing gamble on compatibility that had paid off so spectacularly it became the stuff of business-school legend, and the memory of that triumph cut both ways. It bred confidence that IBM could remake a market by force of will, but it also entrenched the slow, meticulous, everything-in-house methods that had made the 360 flawless and now made the company too ponderous to chase a fast-moving toy. Meanwhile the toy makers were no longer quite so small. Apple, the two-year-old company from a California garage, had gone public in December of 1980 in one of the most sensational stock offerings in years, minting several instant millionaires and announcing to Wall Street that there was real money in these machines. To the men in Armonk, that offering was a klaxon. If a company that had not existed when their current mainframes were designed could already command such a valuation, the personal computer was not a fad to be waited out; it was a market to be entered now, or conceded forever.

Lowe told the committee that IBM could indeed build a personal computer, and could do it fast, but only if it were allowed to break every one of the company's sacred rules. It could not build the machine the IBM way, from proprietary parts of its own design, vetted through the usual endless committees. Instead it would have to assemble the computer out of components bought off the shelf from outside suppliers, the same chips and drives and circuit boards that anyone could purchase. It would have to buy its software from outside vendors rather than writing it in-house. It would have to sell the machine through retail stores, alongside the very upstarts it meant to displace, rather than through IBM's own genteel sales force. And above all, it would have to be freed from the corporate apparatus entirely—set up as an independent unit, far from Armonk, answering to no one but the top, with the authority to make its own decisions at the speed the market demanded. What Lowe was describing, in the language of a later era, was a skunkworks: a small, autonomous team, deliberately quarantined from the mother company's antibodies, so that it might create something the mother company could never create on its own. He proposed a target price of around fifteen hundred dollars, a figure that would place IBM not above the market, as it always insisted on being, but squarely inside it.

It was an audacious request, and it ran against the grain of half a century of institutional habit. Yet the committee, prodded by Cary and increasingly persuaded that the alternative was to cede the field, gave its blessing. Lowe was authorized to assemble a team and to prove the concept, and he was granted the one thing IBM almost never granted: permission to be small, to be quick, and to do it his own way. The task he was handed carried a deadline that would have been laughable for any ordinary IBM project—a working, shippable personal computer, ready for the market, in roughly twelve months. To meet it, the men in Boca Raton would have to make a series of choices so radical, and so consequential, that they would not merely determine whether IBM entered the personal-computer business. They would determine who owned its future.

That the giant moved at all owed something to a quieter pressure that historians have often underrated: the long antitrust ordeal. For more than a decade the Justice Department had prosecuted IBM as a monopolist, and while the suit would eventually be dropped, the years of scrutiny had left the company acutely conscious of how it competed. A machine built largely from parts anyone could buy, running software anyone could license, sold through independent stores rather than IBM's own controlled channels, was in one light simply the fastest way to market—but in another light it was a computer conspicuously assembled from an open, competitive marketplace rather than dictated top to bottom by a dominant firm. Openness was good engineering strategy and good legal insulation at once, and the two motives reinforced each other. The company that had spent the 1970s defending itself against the charge of controlling too much would, almost as a reflex, build its personal computer out of things it did not control.

Lowe himself would not see the project through. He was promoted away not long after winning the mandate, and the burden of actually delivering the machine—of turning a thirty-day prototype and a reckless promise into a product on a shelf by the committee's August 1981 deadline—would fall to another man entirely, a warm and driven Floridian who happened to own one of the very machines IBM meant to beat.

The elephant had finally decided to dance, and the choreography was about to be worked out in a low, unremarkable building in the Florida sun by a small band of engineers operating under a code name borrowed from a game of strategy—a group that would come to be known, half in affection and half in awe, as the Dirty Dozen.

Chapter 28: Project Chess

In the late summer of 1980, in a plain low building on the edge of the Everglades in Boca Raton, Florida, a small group of engineers gathered under a code name that captured the strategic gamble they were about to attempt. They called their effort Project Chess, and the machine they meant to build carried the drab internal designation of the Acorn. The team itself acquired a nickname that would outlast the project—the Dirty Dozen—for the roughly twelve engineers first assigned to turn a heretical idea into a shippable product. There was little about the setting to suggest that history was being made. Boca Raton was an outpost of the IBM empire, a warm and pleasant exile far from the gray winters and grayer committees of Armonk and Poughkeepsie, the kind of place to which the corporation dispatched its smaller and less glamorous ventures. That distance was precisely the point. Isolated from the mother company's smothering embrace, the team could work in a way no IBM group had ever worked before, and it had almost exactly one year—the clock had started in the summer of 1980—to place a finished computer on a store shelf.

The man who came to embody Project Chess was not William Lowe, who had won the mandate in Armonk, but a warm, energetic Floridian engineer named Philip Donald

Estridge, known to everyone as Don. Lowe was promoted away early in the effort, and it fell to Estridge to actually deliver the machine. He was, by every account, an inspired choice—a leader who commanded loyalty not through the chilly formality of the IBM manager's playbook but through sheer contagious enthusiasm and a willingness to shield his people from corporate interference. Estridge himself owned an Apple II at home, a fact that told you much about the man; he had felt firsthand what these little machines could do, and he approached the project not as a skeptic sent to check a box but as a believer determined to build something real. He gathered around him a small band of engineers, some of them refugees from earlier, failed IBM attempts at small computers, and he gave them a mission and the freedom to accomplish it. He also gave them permission, almost unheard of at IBM, to work absurd hours in shirtsleeves and to argue with one another as equals, and they repaid him with a devotion that outlasted the project and, in the memories of those who were there, outlasted their careers.

The pace was punishing and the secrecy nearly total. The engineers, led on the technical side by men such as Bill Sydnes and the lead hardware designer Lewis Eggebrecht, had promised Armonk a working prototype in roughly thirty days and a finished, shippable product in a year, timetables that at any other point in IBM's history would have been dismissed as fantasy. To hit them, the team could not wait for the corporation's laboratories to design custom parts, nor for its committees to bless each decision, so it did something IBM almost never did: it trusted a handful of people in a Florida office to make consequential choices on the spot and live with them. They ordered parts from outside vendors under conditions of some secrecy, careful not to reveal that the buttoned-down giant was building a hobbyist's machine, and they worked, by every account, at a fever pitch, driven by the knowledge that the whole experiment would be judged not on elegance but on whether a box could be on a store shelf by the following summer. It was, in the deepest sense, a startup running inside the belly of the largest computer company on earth, and it behaved like one.

The central decision of Project Chess—the one that would define the machine and, in time, doom IBM's control over it—was to abandon the entire IBM philosophy of building everything in-house. There was simply no time. To design proprietary chips, write proprietary software, and manufacture proprietary components in the customary way would have consumed the year several times over. So Estridge's team made the opposite choice at every turn. They would build their computer out of parts that already existed, bought from outside suppliers, the same components any competent engineer could order from a catalog. This was the doctrine of off-the-shelf construction, and it was as alien to IBM as speaking a foreign tongue in the corporate cafeteria. It is worth dispelling a flattering myth here: IBM did not invent the technology inside its own personal computer. The processor was Intel's, the disk drives came from outside vendors, the operating system would be bought from a company in Seattle, and even the machine's built-in BASIC language leaned on outside work. What IBM contributed was not invention but integration, manufacturing muscle, a sales channel, and a name—and, crucially, the judgment to know which existing parts to bolt together.

The heart of the machine would be a microprocessor from Intel, the company that had started the whole revolution with the 4004 a decade before. Here the team made a choice that revealed the shrewd pragmatism running through the entire project. Intel offered a genuinely modern sixteen-bit processor, the 8086, but it also offered a hybrid cousin called the 8088, which was sixteen bits on the inside but spoke to the rest of the computer through an eight-bit pathway. The two chips cost about the same, a few hundred dollars each, so the decision was not really about the price of the processor itself. It was about everything around it. Because the 8088 talked to the world eight bits at a time, the designers could surround it with the abundant, inexpensive eight-bit memory chips, support circuits, and expansion connectors that already filled the supply chain, rather than the scarcer and costlier sixteen-bit parts the 8086 would have demanded. There was, by some accounts, a second motive as well: a genuinely fast personal computer might have embarrassed IBM's own low-end business systems, and the slightly hobbled 8088 kept the newcomer safely in its place. Choosing the 8088 over the 8086 was thus a decision made for cost, for availability, and for corporate politics rather than for raw performance—and it happened to seat, at the center of the IBM personal computer, an Intel architecture whose descendants would dominate computing for the next several decades.

The machine that took shape around that chip was, in its first incarnation, modest to the point of humility. It would ship with as little as sixteen kilobytes of memory—a figure that would seem almost comically small within a few short years—expandable to more. It would store its programs and data on cassette tape or, for those who paid extra, on the newer and far more practical floppy disks. It would display text on a monitor or, through an adapter, on an ordinary television. In its bones it was not a radically more powerful machine than the Apple II it meant to challenge. What made it different was not its specifications but its philosophy, and that philosophy was written most plainly into the machine's very skeleton: it was open.

Openness, in the sense that mattered, meant several things at once, and each was a deliberate choice rather than an accident. First, the team designed the computer around a row of five expansion slots—open connectors into which anyone could plug an add-on card to give the machine new abilities, whether more memory, better graphics, a printer connection, or capabilities no one had yet imagined. This is the single design decision you are most likely to have met in person, because it never went away. The row of slots inside a modern desktop, into which a gamer clicks a graphics card or a hobbyist plugs a sound card, is the direct descendant of Estridge's expansion bus; the technology has changed names many times, from the original IBM bus through ISA and PCI to today's PCI Express, but the idea—that a computer should be a chassis you extend rather than a sealed appliance—was written into the architecture in Boca Raton and has survived every other thing about that first machine.

Second, and more radically, IBM decided to publish the machine's technical specifications for all the world to see. The company released a thick IBM PC Technical Reference Manual that laid bare the computer's inner workings, including the complete source code of its most intimate software, so that outside engineers and programmers could build hardware and write software for the machine without having to beg IBM's permission or guess at its secrets. To grasp how radical this was, picture the alternative that Apple and others practiced, guarding their designs as trade secrets. IBM did the opposite and did it on purpose, for a coldly practical reason: an open machine, its specifications public and its slots inviting, would attract a swarm of outside companies eager to make products for it, and that swarm would give the IBM computer a richness of software and accessories that IBM could never have created alone. Openness was a strategy for building an ecosystem fast, and it worked spectacularly—perhaps too well.

There was one piece of the machine, however, that IBM meant to keep to itself, and the exception would matter enormously. A computer needs a small, foundational program, burned permanently into a memory chip, that wakes the machine when the power comes on and handles the most basic conversations between the software and the hardware. When a program wanted to print a character on the screen or read a keystroke or fetch a sector from a disk, it did not fumble with the raw electronics; it called a routine in this foundational program, which knew the intimate wiring of that particular machine and did the dirty work. This program was called the Basic Input/Output System, universally abbreviated as the BIOS—the very term and the very idea Gary Kildall had pioneered for CP/M a few years earlier. IBM wrote its own BIOS and held the copyright to it, and it was this single proprietary chip that IBM intended to be the machine's lock and key, the one component a competitor could not simply buy off the shelf. In a gesture of its own openness the team printed the BIOS source code in the reference manual, the better to help programmers understand the machine—but printing the code did not surrender the copyright to it. The code remained IBM's legal property, and in an otherwise open machine the BIOS was meant to be the thing that made an IBM personal computer legally, unmistakably IBM's. Whether that single chip would prove a fortress or a flimsy gate was a question no one in Boca Raton had time to ponder.

For all the borrowing, IBM could not quite suppress its own instincts, and in a few places the corporate obsession with quality shows through in ways you can still put your hands on. The clearest is the keyboard. Where competitors gave their machines cheap, mushy keys, IBM insisted on a mechanism of almost absurd solidity, the buckling-spring keyboard—each key sitting atop a tiny coiled spring that physically buckled at the moment of contact, delivering a sharp tactile snap and an audible click that told a touch-typist, without any need to look, that the keystroke had registered. The result, first the Model F keyboard and later the beloved Model M, was so overbuilt that working examples are still in daily use four decades on, and a whole subculture of typists and programmers now pays premium prices for original IBM keyboards or for modern reproductions of that buckling-spring feel. If you have ever heard an enthusiast rhapsodize about "mechanical keyboards" and their satisfying click, you have met, at one remove, a decision made by Don Estridge's team about how a serious business machine ought to feel under the fingers.

The team leaned on the outside world for the machine's built-in software as well. Burned into the computer's read-only memory, alongside the small startup routines, sat a full version of the BASIC programming language, licensed from that same young firm in the Pacific Northwest, so that a buyer who owned nothing but the bare machine and a cassette recorder could still switch it on and begin writing programs. This ROM-resident BASIC, the work of Microsoft, was a second thread quietly binding the fate of the IBM PC to a company most of the corporation had never heard of—one thread being the operating system still to be arranged, the other this language already soldered into the machine. That two of the most fundamental pieces of software in IBM's flagship product would come from the same small outside firm was a fact whose full weight nobody in Boca Raton paused to weigh; the schedule did not permit it.

Every choice the team made bent toward speed, and the sum of those choices was a machine that IBM did not so much invent as assemble. The bet of Project Chess was that IBM's name, wrapped around a fast, open, off-the-shelf design, would be enough to conquer the market. It was a brilliant bet, and it very nearly conquered everything. But the openness that made it possible had planted, in the machine's very architecture, the seeds of IBM's eventual loss of control, because a machine anyone could understand was a machine anyone could copy, and the only thing standing in the way was that one small chip.

Before any of that could unfold, though, Estridge's engineers faced a problem they could not solve with a soldering iron: the machine had no operating system, no fundamental software to breathe life into the hardware, and the search for one would lead IBM to a small office in a Seattle suburb, to a broken meeting in a Victorian house by the California sea, and to one of the most consequential business deals of the century.

Chapter 29: The Deal of the Century

On a summer day in 1980, two IBM emissaries in dark suits arrived at an unassuming office in Bellevue, Washington, to call upon a twenty-four-year-old named William Henry Gates III. The senior of the two, a courtly IBM manager named Jack Sams, had been dispatched to sound out the little software firms of the microcomputer world, and Microsoft was on his list. The company Gates ran was tiny—a few dozen employees writing programming languages for the little computers that IBM's establishment still regarded as toys. Gates and his partner Paul Allen had built their small business on a single flagship product, a version of the BASIC language that ran on nearly every microcomputer of the era, and it was BASIC that the IBM men had come to discuss. But the meeting would spiral outward from that modest purpose into something no one in the room could have foreseen, and by the time it was done it would set in motion a transfer of power that would make Gates, in time, the richest man on earth.

There is a small, human reason IBM's gaze fell on Microsoft in the first place, and it deserves telling because it corrects the impression that the deal was pure meritocratic chance. Bill Gates's mother, Mary Maxwell Gates, was no ordinary parent; she was a formidable civic leader in Seattle who sat on the national board of the United Way, and among her fellow board members on its executive committee was John Opel, a senior IBM executive soon to become the company's chief. Mary Gates, the story goes, mentioned her son's little software company to Opel in the course of their charitable work, and when IBM's managers were casting about for firms that might help with their secret project, Opel is said to have vouched for the outfit "run by Bill Gates, Mary Gates' son." It would be a gross exaggeration to say the mother handed the son his empire; Microsoft still had to deliver, and deliver it did. But at the crucial moment when a giant was deciding which unknown to trust, a connection forged over charity work helped ensure that the giant's representatives got on a plane to Seattle at all.

To appreciate how Microsoft came to hold the keys to the kingdom, one must first follow IBM down a road it did not take. Project Chess needed an operating system—the essential software that manages a computer's memory, its files, its disks, the foundation upon which all other programs run. In 1980 the reigning operating system for serious microcomputers was CP/M, the product of Gary Kildall's Digital Research, and it was the natural choice: it was the standard, it was mature, and it ran the business software IBM's customers would expect. Gates, when the IBM men first raised the question of an operating system, did the honorable thing and pointed them toward Kildall. He even, by most accounts, telephoned Digital Research to smooth the introduction. IBM's representatives drove to Pacific Grove, California, to meet the man whose software could have become the soul of the IBM personal computer.

What happened at that meeting has hardened, over the decades, into one of the enduring legends of the computer age, and it is precisely the kind of tidy, cruel story that ought to make a careful reader suspicious. In the popular telling, IBM's suited emissaries arrived at Digital Research on the appointed day only to find that Gary Kildall was not there. He was, the story goes, off flying his private airplane, indulging a rich man's hobby rather than meeting the most important customer his company would ever have; and IBM, insulted by this cavalier treatment and stymied by his wife and business partner Dorothy McEwen, who balked at signing IBM's stringent nondisclosure agreement, stormed off and took its business elsewhere. Even Bill Gates would later contribute the sticky, dismissive phrase that fixed the myth in place—"Gary went flying"—as if that settled the matter of who deserved the fortune that followed.

It is a marvelous story, freighted with a satisfying moral about the arrogance of the hobbyist and the wages of not taking a giant seriously. It is also almost certainly too neat to be true, and correcting it is one of the small debts history owes to Gary Kildall. Kildall himself insisted for the rest of his life that the tale was a distortion. In his account, the flight that day was not a joyride but a routine business trip; he had another commitment and flew his own small plane to keep it, as he often did, being an experienced pilot rather than a reckless one. He said he was reached, returned, and met with the IBM men, that he signed their nondisclosure agreement once he was in the office, and that the two sides talked through much of the day. He even claimed to have shared a flight to the East Coast with a member of the IBM party and shaken hands on a tentative understanding—though Jack Sams, for his part, denied ever meeting Kildall at all. The accounts of those who were present conflict on nearly every particular, which is itself the point: the legend is far more certain than the evidence.

What can be said with confidence is narrower and less dramatic. Dorothy McEwen, who handled Digital Research's contracts with a caution the business demanded, was genuinely reluctant to sign IBM's sweeping nondisclosure agreement before she even knew what IBM wanted, a hesitation any prudent executive might share. And when terms were eventually discussed, IBM proposed to pay a flat sum—on the order of a quarter of a million dollars—for the right to ship as many copies of CP/M as it liked, while Digital Research, whose whole business model rested on collecting a royalty for every copy sold, wanted its usual per-copy arrangement. The negotiation foundered on that mismatch of culture and money, on the friction between a buttoned-down colossus and a freewheeling small company that saw no reason to sell its crown jewel for a single check. CP/M did not become the operating system of the IBM personal computer, and the image of Kildall soaring obliviously through the California sky while opportunity knocked below is best understood as legend: vivid, widely repeated, and unproven.

Whatever the true reasons, IBM returned to Bellevue with its problem unsolved, and now it laid that problem at the feet of the young men at Microsoft. Would Microsoft, IBM asked, be able to supply an operating system after all? It was a staggering opportunity and an enormous risk, for Microsoft was a languages company and had no operating system of its own to offer. Here Gates and Allen made the decision that would define their fortunes. Rather than turn IBM away a second time, they said yes—and then they set about acquiring, at speed, the very thing they had just promised to deliver. This is the second correction the record demands: Microsoft did not write DOS. It bought it, and only later polished it.

The solution lay a few miles away, at a company called Seattle Computer Products, where a gifted twenty-four-year-old programmer named Tim Paterson had grown tired of waiting for a promised sixteen-bit version of CP/M that never seemed to arrive. Beginning in April of 1980, working with the published CP/M manuals open on his desk, Paterson simply wrote his own operating system to fill the gap. He called it, with an engineer's blunt candor, QDOS—the Quick and Dirty Operating System. The way he built it is the concrete heart of this whole story. Paterson did not copy Kildall's code, which he did not have; instead he copied Kildall's interface, the published list of the roughly three dozen functions a program could ask the operating system to perform—open a file, read a record, write a character—and the exact numbers a program used to request each one. By faithfully mimicking that table of function calls, he ensured that a CP/M program could be converted to run under his system with only mechanical translation rather than a ground-up rewrite. It was a legally grey but technically brilliant piece of imitation, and it produced, in a matter of months, a working sixteen-bit operating system available immediately from a neighbor. Kildall, when he later examined it, was convinced it was a barefaced rip-off of his life's work, and privately he regarded it as plain theft; but the interface Paterson had copied was not, in that era, something the law clearly protected.

Renamed 86-DOS, Paterson's creation was exactly what Microsoft needed. Paul Allen negotiated first for a nonexclusive license, and in December of 1980 Microsoft paid Seattle Computer Products twenty-five thousand dollars for the right to use and sublicense the software—without, under the terms, telling Seattle Computer who the mysterious major customer was. The following July, with the IBM deal secure, Microsoft returned and bought 86-DOS outright for an additional fifty thousand dollars, taking full ownership of what would become the foundation of its empire for a total of seventy-five thousand dollars. Tim Paterson himself left Seattle Computer Products and came to work at Microsoft to adapt his own creation for the IBM machine. Whether Seattle Computer Products understood what it was selling—and whether the price was remotely fair given what IBM was about to do—would become the subject of bitter litigation years later, but at the time it looked to all parties like a sensible trade between neighbors.

The reckoning came in 1986. By then MS-DOS was running on millions of machines and generating a fortune, and Seattle Computer Products, watching the software it had sold for a total of seventy-five thousand dollars underwrite one of the great business fortunes of the century, sued Microsoft, arguing that the deal had never granted Microsoft the sweeping rights it was now exercising. With a jury already deliberating, Microsoft settled, paying Seattle Computer Products roughly nine hundred and twenty-five thousand dollars to make the case go away—a sum that felt enormous against the original price and yet was trivial against what DOS had by then become. Tim Paterson, for his part, spent decades defending his work against the charge that it was merely a copy of CP/M; late in life he even sued an author who had called 86-DOS a "rip-off," and lost, a court finding the characterization a matter of protected opinion. The quarrel over who really deserved the credit, and the money, never entirely died.

Microsoft polished Paterson's work into the product it would deliver, and IBM and Microsoft signed their agreement in the autumn of 1980. On the IBM machine, the operating system would be called PC-DOS. And here, buried in the contract, lay the single clause that would prove the most valuable arrangement of the entire computer revolution—the term on which the future secretly hinged. IBM, accustomed to owning everything it touched, might have insisted on buying the operating system outright, on an exclusive license that would have bound the software to IBM's machine alone. It did not. Instead, whether from inattention, from a settled belief that the true value lay in hardware rather than in software, or from Gates's own quiet insistence, the deal left Microsoft free to license the very same operating system to other manufacturers, under the name MS-DOS. IBM would pay Microsoft only a modest sum for the use of DOS on its own machines, but Microsoft retained the right to sell the identical software to anyone else who cared to build a computer.

At the time this term seemed almost trivial, a minor concession over a piece of plumbing. IBM was the sun around which the industry orbited; who else would even want to build a machine like IBM's? But that clause meant that Microsoft's fortune was not tied to IBM's machine at all. It was tied to the operating system itself—to the standard—and to every computer that would ever run it, from whatever manufacturer, for as long as the architecture endured. Gates had grasped, with a clarity that eluded nearly everyone else in the room, that in a world of interchangeable hardware the real and lasting value would accrue to whoever controlled the software that everything ran upon. He had not merely sold IBM an operating system. He had positioned Microsoft to collect a toll on the entire industry that IBM was about to create, an industry whose sheer size no one yet imagined.

You meet the consequences of that afternoon every time you switch on a Windows computer, for the lineage is unbroken. Microsoft's DOS grew into the foundation on which early Windows ran, Windows grew into the operating system on the overwhelming majority of the world's desktops and laptops, and the licensing model Gates preserved in 1980—sell the software to every hardware maker, collect on every machine—became the mechanism that turned a firm of a few dozen people into one of the most valuable companies on earth. The seventy-five thousand dollars Microsoft paid for a neighbor's quick-and-dirty program may be the most profitable purchase in the history of business. And the arrangement that made it so—licensing the same software to every hardware maker rather than tying it to one—became the template for the entire software industry that followed, the reason that value in computing has flowed, ever since, less to the companies that stamp out the machines than to the ones that control the code those machines must run.

The pieces were now assembled: Estridge's open, off-the-shelf machine, the Intel processor at its heart, and Microsoft's operating system to give it life. All that remained was to introduce the machine to the world—and on a Wednesday in August of 1981, in a hotel ballroom in New York, IBM prepared to do exactly that.

Chapter 30: August 12, 1981

On Wednesday, August 12, 1981, at the Waldorf Astoria hotel in New York City, the International Business Machines Corporation stood before a room of reporters and unveiled a small beige box that it called the IBM Personal Computer. Don Estridge, the man who had driven the machine out of Boca Raton in a single frantic year, was there to present it. Its formal model number was the 5150, a designation as gray and bureaucratic as the company that bore it, but the two words on the front of the machine were the ones that mattered: IBM, and Personal Computer. It is worth correcting a small and common belief here—that IBM coined the phrase "personal computer." It did not. The term had drifted through the hobbyist world and the trade press for years before 1981. But by attaching its own initials to it, IBM did something no upstart in a garage could ever have done. It made the personal computer respectable. It told the corporate world, in effect, that the toy was now a tool, and that the most conservative and trusted name in all of business technology was prepared to stake its reputation on it.

The machine itself was, on paper, unremarkable, and a second misconception is worth retiring at once: the IBM PC did not conquer the market because it was technically superior, because it was not. At its heart sat the Intel 8088 processor, the pragmatic hybrid chip chosen for cost and availability rather than for speed. In its base configuration it carried a mere sixteen kilobytes of memory, a quantity so modest that it could hold only a few pages of text, though it could be expanded far beyond that. It stored programs on cassette tape in its cheapest form, or, more usefully, on one or two floppy-disk drives for those willing to pay. It displayed either crisp green text for the businessman or blocky color graphics for the more adventurous, depending on which adapter card a buyer chose to plug into one of its five open expansion slots. Its operating system was the one Microsoft had assembled and IBM branded as PC-DOS, and the machine arrived with a small stable of programs ready to run, most importantly the spreadsheet VisiCalc and a word processor called Easy-Writer. A basic system could be had for something in the neighborhood of one thousand five hundred and sixty-five dollars, a price that placed it squarely among its competitors rather than below them. There was nothing in this specification sheet to frighten the engineers at Apple or Commodore. A skilled hobbyist could have listed a dozen machines that matched or bettered it feature for feature.

The software the machine shipped with carried its own unlikely story, one that captures how improvised even IBM's grand entrance really was. The word processor bundled with the new computer, EasyWriter, had been written by John Draper, a legendary figure of the computer underground better known by his handle "Captain Crunch"—so named because he had once discovered that a toy whistle packaged in boxes of Cap'n Crunch cereal produced exactly the tone needed to fool the telephone network into granting free long-distance calls, a form of mischief called phone phreaking that had briefly landed him in jail. Draper had, in fact, written the original version of EasyWriter at night while serving time under a work-furlough program, and the program was hurriedly ported to the IBM PC in a matter of days. The haste showed. EasyWriter 1.0 as shipped by IBM was notoriously buggy and awkward, and within months the trade press was reporting that IBM's own customers wished the company had provided something better. That the most respectable corporation on earth launched its flagship machine with word-processing software written by a convicted phone phreak, and shipped it half-broken, is one of the quiet ironies of the whole affair—and a reminder that behind the blue suits and the polished announcement, the IBM PC was assembled in a scramble like everything else in this story.

The base price of one thousand five hundred and sixty-five dollars, moreover, bought remarkably little; that figure was for a machine with the paltry sixteen kilobytes of memory and no disk drive at all, storing programs on cassette tape. A buyer who wanted the computer as it was actually useful—with enough memory to run real software, a floppy-disk drive or two, a monitor, and a printer—could easily spend three or four thousand dollars, a serious sum in 1981. What IBM was selling for that money was not cheapness and not raw capability but permission: permission for a corporation to bring the personal computer through its front door without apology.

And yet the machine's ordinariness was, in a sense, the whole point, and its power lay entirely in the three letters stamped upon it. For fifteen years the corporate purchasing manager had operated by a single unspoken commandment, a rule so reliable that it had passed into proverb: nobody ever got fired for buying IBM. It is worth walking through exactly how that logic played out on the ground, because it explains the entire phenomenon better than any specification could. Imagine a middle manager at an insurance company in 1981, told to equip the accounting department with computers. He could choose a machine from a two-year-old firm founded by long-haired young men in California, cheaper perhaps and even better on paper—but if that company folded, if its machines failed, if the whole thing proved a fad, the failure would have his name on the purchase order, and his career would wear it. Or he could buy IBM. If an IBM machine disappointed, the fault lay with IBM, the most trusted name in the business, and no one could fault the man who had trusted it. The IBM logo was not merely hardware; it was insurance against personal blame. Overnight, the arrival of the 5150 removed the career risk that had kept the microcomputer out of the serious corporate office. A product that had been a curiosity for enthusiasts became, with the affixing of those initials, a legitimate line item in the budget of every corporation in America.

IBM understood the sentiment it was selling and marketed it with unexpected warmth. Rather than trade on the cold authority of the mainframe, the company built its advertising campaign around Charlie Chaplin's beloved silent-film character, the Little Tramp, portrayed by a mime named Billy Scudder, who appeared in print and on television bumbling and then delighting his way to mastery of the friendly new machine, often with a red rose in hand. It was a deliberate and shrewd softening: the most intimidating corporation in the world reintroducing itself to ordinary people through the gentlest figure in the history of the movies, promising that its computer was approachable, humane, nothing to fear. The campaign became one of the most recognized in American business, and it did as much as any specification to carry the IBM PC out of the accounting department and into the popular imagination.

The effect on the market was immediate and overwhelming. IBM had projected cautious sales, guessing it might move a few hundred thousand machines over the life of the product; those forecasts were shattered almost at once. The company sold roughly sixty-five thousand units in the first four months, and by Christmas of 1981 it had taken on the order of a hundred thousand orders, numbers extraordinary for the young microcomputer industry, and the Boca Raton plant strained to build the machines fast enough. Businesses that had watched the personal-computer phenomenon from a wary distance now bought IBM PCs by the thousands, then by the tens of thousands, confident that they were making the safe and sober choice. Software companies, which had hesitated to commit their best efforts to any single microcomputer in a fragmented market, rushed to write programs for the IBM standard, correctly sensing that this was the platform around which the business world would consolidate. The spreadsheet, the word processor, the database—the tools that turned a computer from a novelty into an indispensable instrument of white-collar work—arrived for the IBM PC in a flood, and each new program made the machine more valuable, which drew more buyers, which drew still more software, in a self-reinforcing spiral of the kind that economists would later learn to call a network effect. The elephant had not merely learned to dance; it had cleared the entire floor.

Not everyone was intimidated, and the most memorable reaction to the launch came from the company with the most to lose. Barely two weeks after IBM's announcement, Apple took out a full-page advertisement in The Wall Street Journal that has become one of the most famous in the history of the industry. "Welcome, IBM," the headline read. "Seriously." The copy that followed managed to be gracious and cocky in the same breath, congratulating IBM on its first personal computer and welcoming it "to the most exciting and important marketplace since the computer revolution began 35 years ago." It was a brilliant piece of positioning, the work of Apple's advertising agency, and its real purpose was not courtesy but jujitsu: by publicly greeting the giant as an equal, the two-year-old Apple cast the coming contest as a two-horse race between itself and IBM, the way soft drinks were Coke or Pepsi. In truth the welcome was braver than it was wise. IBM's arrival would validate the whole category, as Apple hoped, but the standard it established would soon belong to neither company outright, and Apple would spend the rest of the decade defending an incompatible island against a rising sea of IBM-compatible machines. Still, the ad captured the drama of the moment perfectly: the scrappy Californian tipping its cap to the descending colossus, and pretending, with a straight face, not to be afraid.

To reach ordinary buyers, IBM had swallowed another of its ancient prejudices and agreed to sell through stores it did not own. The machine went out not only through IBM's own channels but through Sears, Roebuck and Company and the ComputerLand chain, the same retail counters where a customer might already be browsing an Apple or a Commodore. For the company whose dark-suited salesmen had always called on clients in person, handing the product to a shopkeeper was a small revolution in itself, and it put the IBM logo directly in front of the walk-in public for the first time. The stores could scarcely keep the machines in stock. Don Estridge, the once-obscure engineer from Boca Raton, found himself running one of the fastest-growing manufacturing operations in the country, expanding the Florida plant and hiring feverishly to chase a demand that his own company's forecasts had wildly underestimated. Within a couple of years the operation he led would be a multibillion-dollar business in its own right, a startup that had grown, inside the belly of the giant, into one of the largest computer makers in the world.

There was a deeper significance to the triumph, one that reached beyond IBM's own balance sheet. Before August of 1981, the personal-computer industry had been a Babel of incompatible machines. An Apple II could not run a program written for a Commodore PET; a TRS-80 spoke a different tongue from an Atari. Every manufacturer had its own architecture, its own operating system, its own island of software, and a customer who bought into one island was largely stranded there. The IBM PC, by virtue of its instant dominance, began to impose order on this chaos. It became the machine that mattered, the one that software was written for first and hardware was designed to complement. A de facto standard was being born—not decreed by any committee or government, but established by the sheer market gravity of IBM's name. For the first time, the industry had a center, and the shape of that center is still with us: the letters

"PC," which had once been a generic phrase for any small computer, came to mean specifically a machine descended from that August afternoon, so that decades later a shopper distinguishing a "PC" from a "Mac" is unknowingly invoking the standard IBM set at the Waldorf.

It is worth pausing on the irony that would only become visible with time. The very features that made the IBM PC so successful—its open architecture, its off-the-shelf parts, its published specifications, its willingness to let outside companies build hardware and software for it—were the features that would, within a few short years, allow the standard to slip entirely out of IBM's grasp. The openness that Don Estridge's team had chosen in Boca Raton as a strategy for building an ecosystem quickly had made the machine easy to understand, easy to build upon, and, as others would soon discover, easy to copy. The Intel processor could be bought by anyone. The Microsoft operating system could be licensed by anyone, thanks to the fateful clause Gates had preserved. Only the BIOS, that small proprietary program burned into a single chip, stood between the IBM Personal Computer and outright imitation. But in the flush of triumph in the late summer of 1981, none of this was cause for worry. IBM had entered the personal-computer business a year and a half after deciding to, and it had conquered it. The company's stock rose; its salesmen, once so skeptical, now sold the little machines with the same confident authority they brought to million-dollar mainframes.

Within eighteen months, the phenomenon would grow so large, and reshape so much of ordinary life, that the nation's most prominent newsmagazine would break with nearly six decades of tradition to acknowledge it—handing its highest annual honor not to a president or a general or a titan of industry, but to the machine itself.

Chapter 31: The Machine of the Year

The cover of Time magazine dated January 3, 1983, carried no human face. Since 1927, when the magazine had first bestowed the title on the aviator Charles Lindbergh, its year-end "Man of the Year" cover had been reserved for the person, for good or ill, who had most shaped the events of the preceding twelve months—presidents and dictators, peacemakers and generals, the powerful and the notorious. But for the year 1982, Time's editors did something they had never done before. They gave the honor to no one at all. In place of a person, the cover displayed a sculpture commissioned from the American artist George Segal, known for his ghostly white plaster figures: a seated man, chin in hand, contemplating a personal computer that rested on a table before him. The headline read "Machine of the Year," and beneath it a subtitle, "The Computer Moves In." The magazine had judged that the most consequential force of the year was not any individual but an object—the small beige machine that had, in the span of a few years, insinuated itself into the offices and homes and imaginations of the American people.

There is a small irony buried in the making of that issue, the kind history loves. The cover essay, a sweeping meditation on the arrival of the computer age, was written by a Time veteran named Otto Friedrich—who composed it, by his own account, on a fifteen-year-old Royal 440 manual typewriter. The magazine that was crowning the microprocessor the ruler of the age was itself still produced, at the level of the individual writer, by hammering inked keys against paper. It is a reminder that revolutions arrive unevenly, and that the people announcing the future often live, for a while longer, in the past.

The choice was, in its way, a coronation—the moment the personal computer crossed from the trade press and the hobbyist newsletter into the central consciousness of the culture. Time was not a technical journal; it was the magazine that sat on the coffee tables of dentists' waiting rooms and suburban living rooms across the country, the publication through which middle America took the measure of its own moment. For it to declare the computer the story of the year was to announce, to millions of readers who had never touched a keyboard, that something fundamental had shifted. The machine that had been a curiosity of California garages and university laboratories was now, the magazine insisted, a permanent fixture of modern life, as significant to the age as the automobile had been to an earlier one. The essay framed the personal computer not as a gadget but as the leading edge of an information revolution long predicted and now unmistakably arrived, a transformation that would remake work, education, and the home.

The care Time lavished on the presentation signaled how seriously it took the choice. Rather than photograph an off-the-shelf machine, the editors commissioned George Segal, one of the most celebrated American sculptors of the era, famous for his eerie, unpainted plaster figures caught in the ordinary postures of modern life, to create an original tableau for the cover. His seated white figure, contemplating the computer before it with an almost mournful stillness, lent the issue the gravity of art rather than the gloss of a product review—an editorial signal that this was a cultural reckoning, not a gadget of the month. And the audience for that reckoning was vast. Time in 1982 was one of the most widely read publications in America, reaching millions of households every week, the closest thing the sprawling country had to a shared national conversation. When it declared the computer the story of the year, the news reached the sort of readers who had never subscribed to a computer magazine and never intended to: grandparents, schoolteachers, small-town lawyers, the whole broad middle of the country that took its cues from exactly this magazine on exactly this coffee table.

Behind the coronation lay a piece of newsroom drama that the popular version of the story usually gets wrong. It is often said that Time's editors agonized until the last minute over whether to name the computer or to name Steve Jobs, the twenty-seven-year-old co-founder of Apple who had come to personify the whole youthful industry, and that the machine narrowly edged out the man. The truth, as the managing editor Ray Cave would later flatly tell Jobs's biographer, was less romantic: "We never considered Jobs." What actually happened was that Time had assigned its correspondent Michael Moritz to profile Jobs as the human face of the revolution, and Jobs, who had spent long hours with the reporter and had grown convinced the cover would be his, was blindsided. When the issue arrived and he found the plaster sculpture where he had expected his own photograph, and then read the profile, which aired unflattering accounts of his temper and his personal life, he was devastated. By more than one account, the famously imperious young founder wept. It is a strangely human footnote to a story about machines—that the man who did more than almost anyone to put the computer on that cover was reduced to tears by being left off it. The correspondent who wrote that stinging profile, Michael Moritz, would himself go on to an outsized role in the story of Silicon Valley, later abandoning journalism to become one of the most successful venture capitalists of his generation—one more thread binding the people who chronicled the revolution to the people who built and financed it.

There was, in the end, a kind of wisdom in the editors' choice to crown an object rather than a person, even if it broke a fifty-five-year tradition and bruised a famous ego. The personal computer had no single author. It was the accumulated work of hobbyists and engineers and salesmen and programmers scattered across a decade and a continent, and to hand the honor to any one of them—Jobs, or Gates, or Estridge, or Wozniak, or Kildall—would have falsified the truth that no individual had made it happen. By naming the machine, Time acknowledged something profound about the age it was entering: that the forces now reshaping ordinary life were increasingly collective and technological, larger than any hero, and that history was beginning to be made less by great men than by the tools they collectively unleashed.

The numbers behind the coronation were genuinely astonishing, and Time laid them out for its readers. In 1980, personal computers had been a novelty measured in the hundreds of thousands. By the end of 1982, some three million of the machines had been put to use across the country, and the figure was climbing steeply. The magazine reported that a market that had barely existed a few years earlier was now among the fastest-growing corners of the economy, that manufacturers could scarcely build the machines fast enough, and that the personal computer was appearing not only on the desks of accountants and executives but in the bedrooms of children and the dens of hobbyists and the home offices of a new class of the self-employed. The article surveyed the whole strange new landscape: the video games that had hooked a generation of the young, the spreadsheets that had transformed the small business, the word processors that were beginning to make the typewriter obsolete, and the anxious debates about what all this computation would do to jobs, to privacy, to the minds of children raised in its glow.

Much of that swelling total came not from the pinstriped world of the IBM PC at all but from a parallel boom in cheap machines meant for the living room. While IBM conquered the office, companies like Commodore and Atari and Texas Instruments were selling home computers by the millions to families who bought them to play games, to teach the children to program, or simply because the future seemed to demand one on the den table. Commodore's diminutive VIC-20, introduced in 1981 and priced low enough to sell in toy departments and discount stores, became the first computer of any kind to sell more than a million units, and its successor, the Commodore 64, would go on to become the best-selling single computer model in history. These were not the machines that ran corporate payrolls, but they were the machines that put a keyboard and a glowing screen into ordinary households, and it was their combined tide, as much as IBM's triumph, that carried the national count past three million and convinced Time that the computer had genuinely "moved in."

The essay did not flinch from the strangeness of what it was describing. It quoted breathless converts and worried skeptics, and it tried to convey to a mass readership, most of whom had never written a line of code, what it actually felt like to sit before one of these machines and bend it to a task—the spreadsheet that recalculated an entire budget the instant a single number changed, the document that could be revised without retyping, the game that answered back. It was, in its way, an act of translation, rendering a technical revolution into the idiom of the coffee table, and its very existence marked the moment the personal computer stopped being a subculture and became simply part of the American scene.

That the personal computer had earned this recognition was, in no small measure, a consequence of what IBM had accomplished the year before. It was the arrival of the IBM PC in August of 1981 that had transformed the personal computer from a consumer curiosity into a serious instrument of commerce, and it was the flood of business adoption that followed that had driven the numbers Time found so remarkable. Indeed, some accounts hold that it was precisely the runaway success of the IBM machine in the closing months of 1982 that tipped the editors toward crowning the computer as a category rather than any single person or company. The magazine's cover, in a sense, was the culture ratifying what the corporate purchasing managers had already decided: that the machine was here to stay. And yet the story Time told was not IBM's story alone. The essay ranged across the whole ecosystem that had produced this moment—the Apple that had proved a mass market existed, the software makers whose programs gave the machines their purpose, the young entrepreneurs who had built companies from nothing, the great established firms scrambling to catch up. The computer, the magazine understood, was not any one company's triumph. It was a phenomenon larger than any of its makers.

There was a quieter theme woven through the celebration, and Time did not shy from it. The machine that was moving in brought unease as well as wonder. The essay dwelt on the fear that computers might deepen the divide between those who could master them and those who could not, that they might isolate the very individuals they were meant to empower, that a nation of children hypnotized by glowing screens might lose something in the exchange. It raised the specter of surveillance, of data gathered and stored and misused, of a society made legible to whoever controlled the machines. It even worried, with a prescience that reads as almost eerie today, about a coming flood of information so vast that human beings might drown in it, unable to sift the meaningful from the trivial in the torrent the machines would pour out. These were the anxieties of a culture standing at a threshold, uncertain whether the door it was about to walk through led to liberation or to some new kind of confinement. That Time gave them space, even amid the celebration, was a mark of how seriously it took the transformation. Reading those passages today, when the anxieties they named have become the daily texture of life online, one is struck by how early and how clearly the culture saw what was coming, and how little that foresight slowed the machine's advance.

For the men and women who had spent the previous decade building this industry—the hobbyists of Homebrew, the engineers of Intel and MOS Technology, the founders of Apple and the salesmen of Tandy, the young programmers at Microsoft, the team in Boca Raton—the Time cover was a kind of vindication. The revolution they had willed into being, often against the scorn of experts who insisted no ordinary person would ever want a computer, had now been recognized by the nation's paper of record for the middle class. The bicycle for the mind, as one of the industry's evangelists had famously called the personal computer, had found its riders by the millions, and it was carrying them somewhere no one could yet map. What had begun as the private obsession of a few thousand solder-stained enthusiasts had become, in the span of a single decade, a force reshaping the daily life of a civilization. The tradition Time broke that year it never fully restored, either: the year-end honor survives to this day as "Person of the Year," but the door the editors opened in 1982—to naming an idea, a movement, or a machine—was never closed again.

But recognition is not the same as control, and even as the culture crowned the personal computer its machine of the year, the industry that had produced it was undergoing a convulsion invisible to Time's readers. The IBM standard, having conquered the corporate world, was about to escape the very company that had created it. In garages and clean rooms and small offices around the country, engineers were bent over IBM's own published manuals, working out how to build machines that would run every IBM program while bearing no IBM parts at all—and the age of the clone was about to begin.

Chapter 32: The Clones

In the autumn of 1981, in a Houston restaurant called the House of Pies, three engineers who had just left their jobs at Texas Instruments sat over slices of pie and sketched, on a paper placemat, the design of a company. Their names were Rod Canion, Jim Harris, and Bill Murto, and they had money enough for one good idea between them. They toyed, briefly, with other businesses entirely—at one point they seriously considered building and selling a Mexican-style hard disk drive, and, in a detail that has passed into Silicon Valley folklore, even mulled opening a restaurant. What they settled on instead was a computer, and the machine they eventually drew on that placemat was a portable the size and shape of a small sewing machine, meant to be lugged from office to office. But the truly revolutionary idea was not the shape of the box. It was the promise that this box, built by a company that had not existed a year before, would run every piece of software written for the IBM Personal Computer, flawlessly, without IBM's permission and without a single IBM part inside. The company they founded to pursue this idea they called Compaq, and its arrival would help transform IBM's proprietary triumph into an industry standard that IBM could not own.

The dream of building an IBM-compatible machine was obvious enough, and this is the first place a common misconception needs correcting: Compaq was not the first company to build a clone. IBM had, after all, published the specifications of its computer for the world to read, and its processor from Intel and its operating system from Microsoft could both be bought or licensed by anyone with the cash. In principle, any competent engineer could purchase the same chips, license MS-DOS from Microsoft, and assemble a machine that looked and behaved like an IBM PC. In practice, one obstacle stood in the way, and it was precisely the obstacle Don Estridge's team had built for exactly this purpose: the BIOS. That small program, burned into a chip, that woke the machine and mediated between its software and its hardware, was IBM's copyrighted property. A clone maker could buy the Intel chip and license the Microsoft software, but if the machine was to be truly compatible—if it was to run the growing library of programs that assumed they were talking to an IBM PC—it needed a BIOS that behaved exactly like IBM's. And simply copying IBM's BIOS, whose source code IBM had helpfully printed in its technical manual, was a plain violation of copyright that would bring IBM's formidable lawyers down like a hammer.

The first company to ship a clone learned to navigate these waters only partway. Columbia Data Products, a Maryland firm, brought out what is generally regarded as the first IBM-compatible computer around June of 1982, barely ten months after the IBM PC's own debut. It was a genuine achievement and a sign of things to come, but Columbia's compatibility was imperfect—some IBM programs ran, others stumbled—and its business would not endure. The company that solved the problem properly, and in doing so opened the floodgates, was Compaq, and the manner in which it solved it became one of the defining legal and engineering feats of the personal-computer age.

To build a BIOS that worked exactly like IBM's without copying IBM's code, Compaq's engineers employed a technique known as clean-room reverse engineering, a method designed to produce a legally untouchable copy of a functional design. The procedure was elaborate and deliberate, and it is worth following step by step, because it is one of those rare pieces of legal machinery that is also a piece of genuine cleverness. One team of engineers studied IBM's BIOS closely, cataloging everything it did—every input it accepted, every output it produced, every behavior a program might depend upon—and wrote all of this down as a specification of functions, describing precisely what the software accomplished without reference to how IBM's particular code accomplished it. This specification was then handed across a wall, figuratively and almost literally, to a second team, sealed off from the first and composed of programmers who could swear under oath that they had never laid eyes on a single line of IBM's BIOS. This second team wrote a brand-new BIOS from scratch, working only from the description of what the software needed to do, producing original code that reproduced IBM's behavior exactly while sharing not one line with IBM's own. Because these programmers had demonstrably never touched IBM's copyrighted work, the BIOS they created was legally their own, and IBM's copyright, however valid, had nothing to bite on—for copyright protects the expression of a program, the actual lines of code, not the function it performs. Compaq is said to have spent well over a million dollars and the better part of a year, employing something like fifteen programmers, on this painstaking effort, but the result was priceless: a functionally identical, legally clean BIOS.

Armed with it, Compaq shipped the Compaq Portable in March of 1983 for just under three thousand dollars, and the machine made history as the first computer advertised as one hundred percent compatible with the IBM PC—able to run, the company promised, any program IBM's machine could run, unmodified. It was a hefty "luggable," weighing close to twenty-eight pounds and folding up with the keyboard as a lid over a small built-in screen, but that was precisely its charm: a businessman could carry the whole IBM software universe from one office to another in a single sealed case. The claim of total compatibility proved largely true, and the market responded with an enthusiasm that stunned even Compaq's founders. In its first full year the young company sold some fifty-three thousand of the portables and booked more than one hundred and eleven million dollars in revenue, a debut so spectacular that it entered the record books as the fastest any American company had ever reached a hundred million dollars in sales. Compaq had proved that a competitor could match the IBM standard not by offering something incompatible and better, as Apple did, but by offering something identical—and then competing on price, on features, on quality of manufacture, on anything except the standard itself.

None of it would have happened without a shrewd financier who saw the opportunity before almost anyone else. The man who backed the three engineers was Ben Rosen, a former Wall Street technology analyst turned venture capitalist, whose new firm, Sevin Rosen Funds, put up the initial money—around a million and a half dollars—to turn the placemat sketch into a company, incorporated in February of 1982. Rosen became Compaq's chairman and its guiding hand, and his faith was rewarded on a scale that startled even him. Compaq's debut was not merely successful; it set records that still sound implausible. The fifty-three thousand machines and hundred-and-eleven-million-dollar first year made Compaq, by common reckoning, the fastest company in American history to reach a hundred million dollars in annual sales, a benchmark it cleared in its very first full year of operation. A firm that three men had doodled into being over pie in a Houston diner was, within twenty-four months, a corporation with revenues rivaling companies that had existed for generations. The clone was not a cheap knockoff scraping at the edges of IBM's market; it was, from the start, a juggernaut.

What Compaq had accomplished through great expense and effort, another company soon made available to everyone, and this was the true turning point. Phoenix Technologies, along with a handful of rivals such as American Megatrends, applied the same clean-room method to produce a legal, IBM-compatible BIOS not for its own machines but as a product to be sold to anyone who wished to build a clone. For a modest licensing fee—a matter of a few dollars per machine rather than a million dollars up front—any entrepreneur could now buy a legal BIOS off the shelf, order Intel processors and standard parts from suppliers, license MS-DOS from Microsoft, and assemble a fully IBM-compatible computer without spending a fortune or a year in a clean room. Phoenix had, in effect, commoditized the last piece of IBM's proprietary machine. The single chip that Estridge's team had meant to be the lock on the door had been picked, duplicated, and offered for sale to all comers. The barrier to entering the IBM-compatible business collapsed, and through the breach poured a horde of manufacturers, large and small, domestic and foreign, each building machines that ran the same software, plugged into the same accessories, and looked, to the customer, very much like an IBM PC at a fraction of the price.

The consequences arrived swiftly and would prove irreversible. What had been the IBM Personal Computer was becoming, before IBM's eyes, simply the personal computer—a standard architecture, an open platform, a set of specifications that any manufacturer on earth could build to and that no single manufacturer controlled. IBM still sold enormous numbers of machines, still commanded the loyalty of the corporate buyer, still enjoyed the prestige of having created the standard in the first place. But it now competed against a growing army of imitators who could undercut its prices because they carried none of IBM's overhead, none of its vast bureaucracy, none of its costly commitment to doing everything the IBM way. The three most trusted letters in business had built a machine so open, so easy to understand and to copy, that they had inadvertently created a common platform for the whole world to build upon—and the whole world was climbing aboard.

IBM did try, once, to slam the door it had left open, and its failure is the final proof of how thoroughly the standard had escaped. In 1987 the company introduced a new line called the PS/2, built around a proprietary internal design called Micro Channel Architecture that was faster than the old expansion bus but also, not coincidentally, patented and licensed on terms meant to force the clone makers to pay IBM a toll or fall behind. It was a bid to reclaim ownership of the platform IBM had created. But the clone industry was no longer a rabble of imitators; it had become powerful enough to write standards of its own. In 1988 a coalition of nine leading manufacturers—Compaq foremost among them, joined by the likes of Hewlett-Packard, AST, Epson, Tandy, and Zenith, a group the trade press dubbed the "Gang of Nine"—banded together and produced a rival, openly licensed bus called EISA, deliberately built to extend the old standard rather than replace it with IBM's proprietary one. The market largely sided with the Gang of Nine, and Micro Channel withered. The lesson was stark and irreversible: IBM no longer controlled the very architecture it had invented. The industry did, and the industry had decided it liked being open.

Into that opened field poured a new generation of entrepreneurs who owed everything to the breach Compaq and Phoenix had made. Among them was a college freshman in Texas named Michael Dell, who in 1984 began assembling and selling IBM-compatible machines from his University of Texas dormitory room, cutting out the middleman by taking orders directly from customers. Because the standard was open and the parts were commodities, a nineteen-year-old with a screwdriver and a telephone could build computers every bit as capable as IBM's, and sell them for less. The company he founded would one day become the largest personal-computer maker in the world. He was possible only because IBM's machine had ceased to be IBM's.

For the ordinary buyer, the consequence of all this was a gift that has never stopped giving: relentless, grinding competition on price. Because no one owned the standard, no one could charge a monopolist's premium for access to it. Dozens of manufacturers, all building interchangeable machines to the same specification, were forced to compete on cost, on service, on how much memory or speed they could pack into the same dollar, and the savings flowed straight to the customer. A capability that cost thousands of dollars in 1983 could be had for hundreds a few years later and would soon be nearly free. The open architecture turned the personal computer into a commodity, and commodities get cheaper and better with brutal reliability. Every bargain laptop on a back-to-school display, every inexpensive desktop humming in a small office, is a dividend paid by the decision, made in Boca Raton and cracked open in Houston, to build the machine from parts anyone could buy.

You are living inside the outcome of that placemat sketch right now. The entire industry of Windows computers—the Dells and Hewlett-Packards and Lenovos, the endless commodity laptops and desktops on every office and school desk—descends directly from the clone makers who followed Compaq through the breach, all of them building to a standard IBM set and then lost. The final irony is almost too neat: Compaq, the upstart that had cracked IBM's machine open, grew so large that by the late 1990s it was for a time the biggest personal-computer maker in the world; it was later absorbed by Hewlett-Packard, and in 2005 IBM sold its own personal-computer business to Lenovo of China and walked away from the industry it had legitimized altogether. IBM had launched a standard and then watched it slip its leash, and in the scramble that followed, the company would discover that the true and lasting prizes of the revolution it had unleashed would flow not to the maker of the machine but to the two suppliers whose names were stamped on the chip and burned into the software—an arrangement that would come to define computing for a generation.

Chapter 33: The Standard Escapes

In the spring of 1987, in a series of carefully staged announcements, IBM tried to take back the future. The company unveiled a new line of machines it called the Personal System/2, or PS/2, and at the heart of the line lay a redesigned internal architecture bearing the name Micro Channel. To the untrained eye the PS/2 machines looked like a natural next step—faster, sleeker, more capable, with a crisp new graphics standard and a tidy design that hid the ribbon cables and jumpers of the older machines. But to anyone who understood the industry's politics, the Micro Channel was something else entirely: an attempt to slam shut the door that IBM had left open six years earlier. The new bus was genuinely advanced, offering thirty-two-bit data paths, bus mastering, and cards that configured themselves in software rather than by fiddling with tiny switches. But it was also patented and proprietary, deliberately incompatible with the sea of expansion cards and add-ons built for the original standard, and IBM made clear that any company wishing to build compatible machines would have to pay for a license, and pay dearly, including back royalties on the clones it had already sold. IBM was trying to rebuild the fortress it had failed to build the first time. It would fail again, and the failure would teach the industry a lesson it has never forgotten.

To understand why IBM was reduced to this maneuver, one must reckon with what had happened in the years since the clones broke free. IBM had created a standard and then discovered, to its dismay, that a standard is a peculiar kind of asset—immensely valuable, but nearly impossible for its creator to hold. The value of the IBM architecture lay precisely in its ubiquity: software companies wrote for it because everyone used it, and everyone used it because all the software ran on it. But that ubiquity was a shared resource, a commons, and once the clone makers had established their legal right to build compatible machines, the commons belonged to everyone. Buyers, who cared about running their software and not about the badge on the case, increasingly saw little reason to pay IBM's premium when a Compaq or a Dell or a no-name assembler offered a machine that ran the identical programs for hundreds of dollars less. The clones did not merely nibble at IBM's market; they redefined it. IBM's share of the very standard it had invented eroded year after year, until the company that had once been the personal computer was merely the most expensive maker of a commodity anyone could produce.

The legal machinery that made this possible deserves a closer look, because it is one of those quiet technical episodes on which the whole history turns. The one part of the IBM PC that IBM genuinely owned outright was a small program burned into a chip, called the BIOS, the basic input/output system—the bit of code that woke the machine and let the software speak to the hardware. Anyone could buy the identical Intel processor and the identical disk drives on the open market, but copying IBM's BIOS was piracy, and IBM's lawyers stood ready to prove it. Compaq's engineers solved the problem with a technique of almost lawyerly ingenuity called clean-room design. One team studied IBM's BIOS and wrote down, in plain functional language, everything it did, without ever copying a line of the actual code. A second team of programmers, who had never seen IBM's code and were kept deliberately ignorant of it, then wrote a brand-new BIOS that behaved identically, working only from the first team's description. Because no one who touched the new code had ever seen the original, there was nothing to sue over. Compaq spent millions and the better part of a year on this maneuver in 1982; then, in May of 1984, a firm called Phoenix Technologies did the same thing and sold its clean-room BIOS to anyone who wanted one, and the floodgates opened. Any company with a soldering iron and a purchase order could now assemble a machine that ran every program written for the IBM PC. The standard had not merely escaped; it had been handed a key to every door.

The deeper truth, invisible at first but unmistakable in hindsight, was that IBM had given away the two components on which the whole edifice truly rested. When Don Estridge's team chose to build the machine from off-the-shelf parts, it had made IBM dependent on outside suppliers for the two most essential elements of the computer: the processor from Intel and the operating system from Microsoft. Every clone maker, in order to be compatible, had to use an Intel-compatible processor and had to license Microsoft's operating system. This meant that no matter which brand of machine a customer bought—IBM or Compaq or any of the hundreds of others—Intel and Microsoft got paid. The hardware makers competed fiercely with one another, driving prices and profits ever downward in a brutal race that punished everyone who built boxes. But Intel and Microsoft sat above the fray, collecting a toll on nearly every personal computer sold in the world, protected from the price war by the fact that they, and not IBM, owned the pieces that could not be cloned. The processor architecture and the operating system were the true chokepoints, and IBM controlled neither.

This was the arrangement that would, in time, acquire a name that captured the new order of things: Wintel, a fusion of Windows and Intel, the partnership of the software company and the chip company that jointly held the standard IBM had built and lost. It would be some years before Microsoft's Windows fully displaced the plain MS-DOS, and before the term Wintel entered common speech, but the structure was already visible in the mid-1980s to anyone who cared to look. The clause that Bill Gates had preserved in the original 1980 contract—the right to license the operating system to anyone, not IBM alone—had proven to be the most valuable sentence in the history of the computer business. It meant that as the clones multiplied and the standard spread across the earth, Microsoft's fortunes rose with every machine sold, regardless of whose name was on it. Gates had understood, when almost no one else did, that in a world of interchangeable hardware, the money flows to whoever owns the pieces that cannot be swapped out. He owned one of them; Intel owned the other; and IBM, having built the platform for them both, was left holding the one thing that turned out to be worth the least—the machine itself.

It is worth making the economics concrete, because they explain everything that followed. Suppose a family in 1990 bought a personal computer for two thousand dollars. Most of that money went to the maker of the box—for the case, the assembly, the marketing, and the thin margin left after a dozen rivals had competed the price down to the bone. But a slice went to Intel for the processor at the machine's heart, and another slice went to Microsoft for the copy of the operating system on the disk, and those two slices arrived no matter whose logo was stamped on the front. Sell a hundred million machines a year across the whole industry, and Intel and Microsoft collected on a hundred million machines, while the box makers split a shrinking pie a hundred ways and fought one another to exhaustion. The chip and the operating system were the tollbooths on a highway that everyone had to use, and IBM, having built the highway, had somehow neglected to keep either tollbooth for itself.

Against this backdrop, the PS/2 and its Micro Channel were IBM's attempt to reset the game, to force the industry back onto a proprietary track that only IBM could control. The logic was clear enough: if the original architecture had escaped, IBM would create a new one, patent it thoroughly, and license it only on terms favorable to IBM. And the company did not lack for leverage, or so it believed. It was still the largest computer maker on earth, its blue logo still commanded respect in every purchasing department, and it gambled that where IBM led, the industry would once again feel obliged to follow. But the strategy foundered on the very reality it sought to deny. By 1987 the standard no longer belonged to IBM, and the industry felt no obligation to march wherever IBM wished to lead.

The rebellion, when it came, was organized and public. In the autumn of 1988 a group of nine leading manufacturers, with Compaq at its head, banded together and announced that they would not adopt Micro Channel at all. The press promptly christened them the Gang of Nine—Compaq, Hewlett-Packard, NEC, Olivetti, Tandy, Wyse, Zenith Data Systems, Epson, and AST Research—and their collective weight told the story of how thoroughly power had shifted, for together they accounted for more than a third of all personal computers sold, against IBM's roughly one quarter. Rather than pay IBM's tolls, they pooled their engineers and drafted their own thirty-two-bit successor to the original bus, an open specification they named the Extended Industry Standard Architecture, or EISA. It matched most of what Micro Channel offered, but it carried two decisive advantages that Micro Channel could not: it remained backward compatible, so that the millions of ordinary expansion cards already in the world would still slot in and work, and it belonged to no single company that could dictate terms. There is a small, telling anecdote from those weeks. Just before the Gang of Nine went public, IBM approached Compaq privately and dangled an offer—exclusive, favored access to Micro Channel in exchange for abandoning the rival effort. Compaq refused. It had not fought its way to the front of the industry in order to become a licensee of the very company whose grip it had just escaped.

The market, offered a choice between IBM's expensive walled garden and an open standard controlled by no one, chose openness overwhelmingly. Micro Channel withered. It survived for a time inside IBM's own machines and in certain servers, but the broader industry simply routed around it, and the great majority of the personal computers built in the years that followed used the open bus or its descendants. IBM's bid to reclaim the future had been rejected not by any court or regulator but by the industry itself, which had learned that it no longer needed IBM's permission to build a personal computer. The very ecosystem IBM had unleashed in 1981 had grown large enough and confident enough to tell its creator no.

The rebellion also revealed how completely the balance of expertise had shifted. When IBM built the original PC in 1981, it had been the unquestioned authority on computing, and the clone makers were upstarts copying their betters. By 1988 those upstarts employed some of the finest engineers in the industry, held a third of the market, and could design a thirty-two-bit bus as capable as anything IBM produced—and do it as a committee, in the open, for everyone's shared benefit. IBM was no longer the teacher to whom the class looked for answers; it was one voice among many, and no longer even the loudest.

The lesson of these years would echo through the whole subsequent history of technology, and it was as counterintuitive as it was profound. IBM had assumed, as any great company might, that control was the source of value—that owning a technology, guarding it, and forcing customers to come to you was the path to lasting dominance. The personal-computer era taught the opposite. It was openness, not control, that had created the vast market in the first place; the published specifications and off-the-shelf parts had summoned an entire industry of software makers and accessory builders and clone manufacturers whose collective effort made the platform indispensable. And it was the standard itself, not any single company's ownership of it, that generated the value—value that then flowed to whoever held the few pieces that could not be commoditized. The company that tried to own everything, IBM, ended up owning the least. The companies that positioned themselves to profit from an open standard they did not have to defend, Microsoft and Intel, ended up owning the world. Openness plus a standard had beaten proprietary control so decisively that the defeated giant would spend the following decade in retreat, eventually selling its personal-computer business to the Chinese company Lenovo in 2005, its name fading from the machines it had once made respectable.

The pattern IBM stumbled into is one you still live inside every day, though you rarely see it. When you plug a keyboard, a webcam, or a printer into a laptop through a USB port that simply works, no matter who made the cable or the device, you are enjoying the fruit of an open standard that no single company holds hostage. When a graphics card from one manufacturer drops into a slot designed by a consortium and functions without a license negotiation, the ghost of the Gang of Nine is at work. The architecture of the modern computer—its expansion slots, its ports, its buses—is a monument to the discovery IBM made the hard way: that in this industry, the widest road, freely traveled, carries more traffic and generates more wealth than any private toll bridge, however elegantly engineered. IBM built the toll bridge twice, and twice the traffic went around it.

Yet even as this drama of standards and clones and royalties played out in the boardrooms and courtrooms of the industry, a different revolution was gathering—one concerned not with who owned the machine but with how a human being might actually speak to it, and its origins lay in a research center on the West Coast where, years earlier, a band of visionaries had already built a computer you controlled not by typing arcane commands but by pointing at pictures on a screen.

Chapter 34: The Xerox That Saw the Future

On a spring morning in 1970, a slim young physicist named George Pake stood on a scrubby patch of California hillside above Stanford University and imagined a building that did not yet exist. Xerox, the company that had made a fortune turning the humble act of copying onto plain paper into one of the great business franchises of the century, had decided it wanted a laboratory to invent the future. Pake had been hired to build it. He chose the Coyote Hill site in Palo Alto deliberately, far from the corporate headquarters in Rochester, New York, and even farther from the buttoned-down copier salesmen who paid the bills. He wanted distance. He wanted his researchers three thousand miles from anyone who might tell them what was practical. The Palo Alto Research Center opened its doors, and within a few short years the small collection of long-haired computer scientists it gathered there would invent very nearly every element of the machine you are almost certainly using to read these words.

The premise behind PARC was audacious and, in retrospect, prophetic. Xerox's leadership feared that the office of the future would be paperless, and that a company built on ink and toner might be rendered obsolete. So they resolved to invent that future themselves and own it. To run the computing effort, PARC recruited a remarkable concentration of talent, much of it refugees from a defense-funded research world that was contracting as the Vietnam War drained budgets. The most consequential single acquisition came when Xerox scooped up a group of engineers from a Berkeley company called Berkeley Computer Corporation, among them a brilliant, methodical thinker named Butler Lampson and a virtuoso hardware designer named Chuck Thacker. Around them gathered a cast that reads today like a hall of fame: Alan Kay, Bob Taylor, who had once funded the ARPANET from a Pentagon office, and a young Hungarian émigré programmer named Charles Simonyi. They were given money, freedom, and a mandate to dream, and Taylor in particular understood that his job was less to direct these people than to protect them, to keep the copier company's anxieties from reaching into the lab and strangling ideas in the cradle.

The intellectual engine of the place was a weekly ritual that has become part of computing's folklore. Every Tuesday, Taylor gathered his researchers into a room furnished with garish, overstuffed beanbag chairs, and one of them would present a piece of work for the others to dismantle. He called the meeting "Dealer," a nod to the blackjack manual Beat the Dealer, and the sessions were merciless in a way that was somehow collegial rather than cruel—a presenter's cherished theory could be torn to pieces in an afternoon, but the tearing was done in the service of the idea, not against the person. It was in that beanbag room, more than at any drafting table, that the future got argued into shape.

Taylor himself wrote no code and designed no hardware; his genius was for people. A Texan and a trained psychologist, he had run the office at the Pentagon's advanced-research agency that funded the ARPANET, the network that would grow into the internet, and he had learned there how to gather brilliant and difficult individuals and point them at a hard problem without smothering them. At PARC he saw his role as building a wall around his researchers, absorbing the anxieties and demands that flowed west from Xerox headquarters so that the people in the beanbag room never had to feel them. He kept a mental map of who disagreed with whom and used the Tuesday sessions to force those disagreements into the open, on the theory that an argument settled in public was worth a dozen resentments nursed in private. It was an approach closer to running a great university department than a corporate laboratory, and for a decade it produced miracles.

What the lab built, beginning in earnest in 1972 and running for the first time on March 1, 1973, was a machine called the Alto. Its conception can be pinned to a single 1972 memo by Butler Lampson sketching what such a machine ought to be; Chuck Thacker then designed most of the hardware and drove it to reality, work for which he would receive computing's highest honor, the Turing Award, nearly four decades later in 2009. The Alto was not a product and was never sold to the public; it was a research instrument, a proof of concept made real. The first unit cost Xerox roughly twelve thousand dollars in components, and Thacker later estimated that as a commercial product it might have carried a price near forty thousand—a figure that tells you at once why the machine stayed inside the laboratory. Yet the lab built them in quantity anyway, until eventually around two thousand Altos existed, perhaps a thousand humming away inside Xerox facilities and several hundred more placed in universities, so that an entire generation of researchers could live inside the future for a while and get used to it.

By any reasonable definition, the Alto was the first personal computer with a graphical user interface, and it arrived a full decade before the world at large would encounter anything like it. Where the machines of the day spoke in glowing green lines of text, the Alto had a display that stood upright in the orientation of a sheet of paper, and that display was bitmapped, meaning every one of its tens of thousands of pixels could be individually controlled by the computer.

This one decision, championed by Thacker and others despite the expense of the memory it consumed, changed everything. A screen that could turn any dot black or white could draw anything: proportional typefaces, diagrams, crisp black letters on a white field that looked like a page rather than a terminal. It was a small revolution hiding inside an engineering choice, the moment the screen stopped being a teletype with a glow and became, instead, a window onto a simulated page.

To command this new kind of screen, the Alto used a device that had been invented years earlier by Douglas Engelbart down the road at the Stanford Research Institute, a small wooden box on wheels that Engelbart's team had christened the mouse. PARC refined it, eventually replacing the wheels with a rolling ball, and wired it to a screen full of overlapping windows, each a separate rectangle of work that could be stacked and shuffled like papers on a desk. A user could point at something and simply select it. The abstract had become tangible. And because the screen showed text in the very fonts and layout in which it would print, PARC coined a principle that would govern computing for generations: what you see is what you get, mercifully shortened to the acronym WYSIWYG.

It is worth pausing to picture, concretely, how strange and wonderful this was in 1974. Imagine a researcher named, say, Diana, sitting down at an Alto to write a memo. She does not remember a single command. She rolls the mouse until a pointer slides across the white screen, she clicks to place a cursor in a document that already looks like a printed page, and she types. When she wants a word in bold, she does not surround it with cryptic codes; she selects it by dragging the pointer across it, and it thickens on the screen before her eyes, exactly as it will appear on paper. When she finishes, she does not feed a punched deck into a reader or wait for a batch job overnight. She sends the file down a cable to a machine in the hallway that paints her page with a laser, and moments later it slides out, letter-perfect, in the same fonts she saw glowing on the glass. Every part of that experience is ordinary to you now. In 1974 it existed in exactly one place on earth.

The Alto did not stand alone, and that was much of its genius. Thacker, Lampson, and a young engineer named Robert Metcalfe understood that a personal machine gained enormous power when connected to others, and so they invented a way to lash the Altos together over a shared cable, a networking scheme Metcalfe named Ethernet after the luminiferous ether that nineteenth-century physicists had once imagined filled all of space. Down the hall, another team perfected the laser printer, marrying a computer-controlled laser to the guts of a Xerox copier so that the beautiful pages composed on the Alto's screen could emerge, letter-perfect, on paper. By the mid-1970s a researcher at PARC could sit at a personal computer, compose a document in multiple fonts using a mouse and windows, send it across a network to a colleague, and print it on a laser printer. This was, in essence, the office of 1995, assembled and working in a laboratory two decades early.

The particulars of that network are worth recording, because they are the direct ancestors of the wires and signals humming behind every wall today. Metcalfe, working with a colleague named David Boggs—the two called themselves the Boggsy twins—strung a coaxial cable between the Altos and, in 1973, sent data down it at just under three million bits a second, a rate that seemed almost extravagant at the time. His scheme let any machine speak whenever the cable fell silent, and simply wait a random moment and try again if two machines happened to speak at once, an elegantly democratic arrangement with no central controller that could fail and bring the whole system down. That basic idea, refined and sped up many thousandfold, is the Ethernet that still carries much of the world's data. The software kept pace with the hardware: Simonyi's Bravo word processor became fully operational on the fourteenth of September, 1974, which means the first person ever to watch bold and italic text appear on a screen exactly as it would print did so half a century ago, in a lab most of the world had never heard of.

The energy of the place flowed into the software as well. Simonyi, working with Lampson, wrote a program called Bravo that was the first true WYSIWYG word processor, letting a writer see bold and italic and different type sizes on the screen exactly as they would appear on the page. Bravo's descendants would one day conquer the world under a different name, for Simonyi eventually carried its ideas to a young company called Microsoft, where he would oversee the creation of Word. The seeds PARC scattered took root in gardens its parent company would never own—a pattern so consistent across PARC's history that it begins to look less like bad luck than like destiny.

And there lay the tragedy that shadowed the triumph. Xerox, for all its foresight in funding PARC, proved almost comically unable to sell what its researchers invented. The company's culture was built around leasing enormous copiers to corporate purchasing departments, and its executives, three thousand miles away in New York, struggled to grasp what a personal computer even was, let alone how to price and market one. When Xerox finally did bring a commercial version of the Alto's ideas to market in 1981, the machine called the Star, formally the 8010, it was a technical marvel and a commercial afterthought, priced at roughly sixteen thousand dollars per workstation and sold in configurations, with the file servers and printers a real office needed, that cost far more. It was too expensive, too slow, and too late, and it landed with a thud.

Here it is worth correcting a misconception that has hardened into cliché. The historian's shorthand that Xerox simply "fumbled the future" is not entirely fair, and it flatters the tellers of the story more than it illuminates it. Xerox did fund the research, lavishly and for years; it did build the Star and try to sell it; it earned real fortunes from the laser printer, a PARC invention that went on to generate billions.

The company was not blind. The deeper truth is harder and sadder than blindness: an organization optimized to perfection for one business can be constitutionally incapable of recognizing a second, even when it has built the second inside its own walls. Xerox's salesmen knew how to lease a copier to a purchasing manager on a five-year contract. They had no idea how to sell a strange new object to an individual who wanted to point at pictures, and no amount of brilliance in Palo Alto could rewire the instincts of a sales force three thousand miles away.

The numbers tell the story of the mismatch. The Alto had cost twelve thousand dollars to build as a one-off and might have sold, the engineers reckoned, for forty thousand; the Star that finally reached the market in 1981 asked sixteen thousand per workstation and needed file servers and printers besides. Xerox's salesmen, trained to lease copiers by the pallet to purchasing departments, had no framework for an object like that and no commission structure that rewarded selling it. The future sat in the showroom, correctly priced for 1990 and hopelessly priced for 1981, and the men who might have sold it did not recognize what they were looking at.

The engineers at PARC knew what they had. They knew the Alto was not merely a faster calculator but a fundamentally new kind of object, a machine that had crossed some invisible threshold from tool to medium. What they could not do, from inside a copier company, was persuade the world to care. That persuasion would require someone from outside, someone with a salesman's hunger and a designer's eye, someone who could walk into that laboratory, see the future glowing on a screen, and understand in an instant that it was meant not for a handful of researchers but for everyone. But before that visitor arrived, the deepest and strangest dreamer at PARC was already imagining a machine that went further still, a computer not for the office but for a child.

Chapter 35: The Dynabook Dream

Sometime around 1968, before PARC existed and while he was still finding his footing in the research world, Alan Kay began carrying around a mockup made of cardboard and lead ballast, roughly the size and shape of a slim notebook—about eight and a half by eleven inches and half an inch thick, weighted so that it felt in the hand like the real object it pretended to be. He would hold it up over the coming years and describe it to anyone who would listen: a personal computer light enough for a child to carry, weighing less than four pounds, with a crisp flat screen, a keyboard, and enough intelligence to become anything its young owner wished. He called it the Dynabook, and it did not exist. It would not truly exist for decades, until the world caught up to him in the form of the laptop and the tablet. But Kay had a gift rarer than the ability to build such a machine. He had the ability to see it whole, years before the components to make it were even imaginable, and to bend his entire career toward willing it into being.

Kay was an unlikely prophet of computing, a man of restless and omnivorous mind who had been a professional jazz guitarist and had once considered a career in molecular biology. It was biology, in fact, that shaped his deepest idea. He had been struck by the notion that a living organism is built from millions of cells, each a complete and self-contained unit, each capable of communicating with its neighbors, the whole far more robust and adaptable than any single monolithic structure could be. Computers, he came to believe, should be built the same way, not as one vast tangle of instructions but as communities of small, independent objects, each holding its own data and its own behavior, each sending messages to the others. This idea, which he pursued relentlessly through the 1970s at PARC, became the foundation of a programming language and philosophy called Smalltalk, and it gave the world the term and the substance of object-oriented programming, a way of thinking that underlies almost all significant software written today.

To see what Kay meant, imagine trying to draw a circle on a screen. In the older way of thinking, a programmer would write a long recipe of instructions that reached directly into the machine's memory and lit up individual dots, and if anything about the screen changed, the recipe broke. In Kay's way, there simply exists an object called a circle, and it already knows how to draw itself, how big it is, where its center sits, what color it wears. You do not command the machine dot by dot; you send the circle a message—grow, move, change color—and it takes care of the rest, guarding its own inner workings from meddling. Multiply that by a thousand kinds of objects, each a small expert in its own affairs, all conversing by message, and you have not a program so much as a little society. It was a way of taming complexity by dividing it into manageable, living-seeming pieces, and it turned out to be so powerful that the languages most of the world's software is written in today—the ones running the app on your phone and the site in your browser—are its direct descendants.

Two encounters in graduate school had lit the fuse. The first was Ivan Sutherland's Sketchpad, a program from 1963 that let a user draw directly on a screen with a light pen, the very first glimpse of a computer as something you interacted with visually rather than fed with punched cards.

The second was a Norwegian programming language called Simula, built to simulate real-world systems, in which Kay recognized the germ of his cellular idea: little self-contained modules, each modeling one thing in the world, all running at once and passing information among themselves. He fused the two—Sutherland's visual directness and Simula's world of cooperating objects—and out of the fusion came both Smalltalk and the conviction that a computer could be a place a person lived and thought inside, not merely a tool they operated from the outside.

But Smalltalk was never merely a language. For Kay it was the software of the Dynabook, the medium through which a child would learn not just to use a computer but to command it, to reshape it, to think with it. He was profoundly influenced by the developmental psychologists Jean Piaget and Jerome Bruner, and by Seymour Papert, the MIT mathematician who had put children in front of computers and watched them learn geometry by teaching a robotic turtle to draw. Kay came away convinced that the computer was not a business machine or a scientific instrument but something closer to a printing press, a device whose true significance lay in what it would let ordinary people, and especially children, express and discover. In 1972 he set the vision down in a paper with a title that captured everything he believed, "A Personal Computer for Children of All Ages," describing a machine no larger than a notebook, owned by its user, able to hold a small library and display text at the crispness of a printed page. The Alto and the graphical interface that his colleagues were building were, in his eyes, way stations on the road to something grander. He wanted a medium, not a calculator.

Papert's turtle experiments had shown Kay something he never forgot. A child given a little robotic turtle that dragged a pen across paper, and told to make it draw a circle, could not do so by memorizing a formula; instead the child would imagine herself as the turtle, taking a small step and turning a little, again and again, and in discovering that a circle is nothing more than "go a bit, turn a bit, repeat" she learned a piece of real mathematics by inhabiting it from the inside. This was learning by doing, by building, by teaching the machine—and it convinced Kay that a computer's highest use was not to deliver facts to a passive child but to become a kind of clay the child could shape, a material for thinking with. The Dynabook was to be that clay, portable and personal, and Smalltalk was to be the language simple enough that a ten-year-old could mold it and deep enough that she would never reach its bottom.

It was Kay's group at PARC, the Learning Research Group, that pushed the visual interface furthest toward the human. Where other windowing schemes tiled their rectangles neatly side by side, Kay's Smalltalk system allowed windows to overlap, to slide partly beneath one another exactly as sheets of paper overlap on a real desk, a small refinement that made the screen feel less like a machine and more like a workspace. His team experimented with pop-up menus, with icons, with fonts and painting programs, and they let children into the lab to try them, watching how a twelve-year-old's hands and mind engaged with the glowing screen. Some of those children, working under the guidance of researchers like Adele Goldberg, wrote programs of startling sophistication in Smalltalk, animating drawings and composing music and building simple games. The lab's films of children painting and programming on the Alto became quiet evidence for Kay's faith that the computer's destiny lay in the hands of amateurs and creators, not only engineers.

In 1977 Kay and Goldberg set down the fullest statement of the dream in a paper they called "Personal Dynamic Media," arguing that the computer was the first medium capable of simulating every other medium—text, image, sound, animation, even other computers—and of doing so while responding to its user in real time. No book could rewrite itself as you read it; no film could answer a question. A computer could be all of those things and a conversation besides.

They coined a word for such a device, the meta-medium, a medium whose content was other media and whose deepest content was the user's own ideas. Read that description today, with a glass rectangle in your pocket that is at once a library, a cinema, a radio, a sketchpad, a camera, and a telephone, and you are reading a prophecy fulfilled almost to the letter.

He had a way with aphorism that made his ideas travel, and one line in particular, delivered to a gathering of Xerox executives around 1971, would outlive nearly everything else said in that era. The best way to predict the future, he told them, is to invent it. It was at once a boast, a philosophy, and a rebuke. He was telling the men who ran a copier empire that the future was not something to be forecast in a market study but something to be built by people with the nerve and imagination to build it, and that PARC was in the business of building it whether or not the rest of the company understood. The phrase has been quoted so often since, and attributed to so many, that its origin has grown hazy, but it was Kay's, and it distilled the animating spirit of the place.

The line landed with particular sting because Kay meant it as a challenge his audience was failing. Xerox had every ingredient of the future in its own laboratory and could not see it; the men in that room controlled a fortune and a research center without equal, and Kay was telling them, as politely as he could manage, that vision cannot be bought or delegated, only exercised. Whoever was willing to build the future would own it, and Xerox, he feared even then, was not willing.

Here a common misconception deserves correcting, because it flatters the wrong story. The Dynabook is often remembered as a failed product, a tablet that Xerox somehow neglected to build and sell—as though Kay had drawn up blueprints that a bolder company could have manufactured in 1972. That gets the situation exactly backward. The Dynabook was never buildable in its own time, and Kay knew it better than anyone. The flat, high-resolution screen that could run on batteries did not exist; the processor small and cool enough to hold in the hand did not exist; the storage, the price a school could afford, none of it existed. The Alto, wondrous as it was, filled a cabinet, cost as much as a house, and plugged into the wall. The Dynabook was not a product that Xerox fumbled. It was a vision deliberately aimed at hardware a generation away, a fixed star to steer by. Kay's genius was not in engineering a machine ahead of its time but in describing one so precisely that when the components finally arrived, decades later, the world would recognize what to build.

That distance between the dream and the possible weighed on him, and he made a kind of peace with it. He understood that he was working not for the present but for a generation of technology that would arrive after him, and that his task was to keep the vision alive and exact—to hold the cardboard model up, again and again, until enough people could see through it to the real thing waiting on the far side of the decade.

There is a poignancy in Kay's position at PARC, for he was the truest believer in a possibility that his own employer was least equipped to pursue. Xerox wanted, at best, an office machine. Kay wanted to remake human thought. The graphical interface that would eventually change the world was, to him, almost a byproduct, the visible tip of a far deeper reimagining of what a computer was for. He would grow frustrated in later years when the industry adopted the surface of his ideas, the windows and icons and mice, while largely ignoring the substance, the notion of the computer as a dynamic medium for learning and creation rather than a slicker way to type memos and balance ledgers. The revolution that came, he sometimes suggested with a trace of melancholy, was not quite the revolution he had imagined; the world had taken his furniture and left his philosophy behind.

And yet you meet the Dynabook now every single day, and more literally than almost any other prophecy in this book.

When a child pulls a slab of glass from a backpack, taps a drawing app awake, and makes shapes move with a fingertip; when a student carries a laptop weighing barely more than the four pounds Kay specified; when a tablet no thicker than his cardboard mockup holds an entire library and shows type at the sharpness of a printed page—that is the Dynabook, arrived at last and scattered across the planet by the billion. The iPad that a toddler operates before she can read is Kay's paper made real, half a century late. He lived to see it, and to note, with characteristic sharpness, that the machines mostly failed at the part he cared about most: helping their owners think in genuinely new ways rather than merely consume. The furniture had arrived; the philosophy was still waiting.

The influence radiating outward from Kay's beanbag-strewn laboratory was immense, and it was about to find an amplifier no one at PARC had anticipated. For all its brilliance, PARC remained a monastery, its treasures visible only to the initiated and to the occasional privileged guest. The graphical interface, the overlapping windows, the mouse gliding across a bitmapped screen, the whole seductive vision of a computer you could point at rather than command in code, sat waiting behind Xerox's doors for someone reckless and hungry enough to carry it into the world. In the last month of 1979, that someone drove up Coyote Hill Road in a small caravan of Apple engineers, led by a twenty-four-year-old who had already changed the industry once and was looking, restlessly, for the next thing to change.

Chapter 36: The Visit

On a December day in 1979, Steve Jobs and a handful of Apple's most talented engineers were shown into a room at the Palo Alto Research Center and sat down in front of an Alto. Jobs was twenty-four, already rich on paper, already famous within the small world of the microcomputer industry, and consumed by the question that would drive him for the rest of his life: what came next. Apple was preparing for a public stock offering that would make its founders wealthy, and Xerox's venture arm wanted to buy in. Jobs, characteristically, turned the transaction into a bargain of a different kind. In exchange for the privilege of investing in Apple before the offering—Xerox bought a hundred thousand shares at ten dollars and a half apiece, a stake of roughly a million dollars—Xerox would open the doors of PARC and let Jobs and his people see what its researchers had built. It was, on Xerox's part, a spectacular misjudgment of value, though it looked shrewd at the time; the stake would appreciate handsomely, but it was as nothing next to what walked out the door.

The visit had not come out of nowhere. Several of Apple's own engineers, Bill Atkinson among them, had read the papers streaming out of PARC and understood that something extraordinary was taking shape there; it was they, as much as Jobs, who wanted the trip to happen, hoping their restless leader would see with his own eyes what they had only read about. Jef Raskin, an Apple employee who had studied near Stanford and knew the PARC crowd, had been urging the pilgrimage for months. So the caravan that drove up Coyote Hill Road in December 1979 was not a raiding party stumbling upon a hoard it never expected to find; it was a group of unusually well-prepared visitors who already suspected what they would be shown and had bargained, with stock, for the right to see it confirmed.

The first demonstration underwhelmed Jobs, or at least failed to satisfy him, and he pressed for more, sensing that the researchers were holding back their best work. He was right. PARC's scientists were deeply uneasy about showing outsiders the crown jewels, and some of them, led by the Smalltalk pioneer Larry Tesler, had objected to their own management, arguing that the company was about to hand its most precious secrets to a rival. But the order had come from above—Xerox's headquarters wanted the deal—and so on a second visit the engineers relented and gave the Apple contingent the full tour. Tesler ran the demonstration himself, and years later he would describe the strange vertigo of the afternoon. As he showed off the system, Jobs and his engineers asked questions so sharp and so exactly on point that Tesler realized these visitors understood what they were seeing better than most of his own colleagues did. Jobs could not sit still. Tesler remembered him pacing the room, glancing at the screen, taking it all in, and then erupting: "Why aren't you doing anything with this? This is the greatest thing! This is revolutionary!" He came away, Tesler said, convinced that these were the people who would actually build the thing, and rather than feeling robbed he felt, oddly, vindicated—someone had finally grasped what PARC had made.

One moment from that afternoon has passed into legend, and it captures better than any argument what Jobs was really seeing. As the researchers demonstrated Smalltalk, Jobs watched text scroll up the screen a whole line at a time, jerking from one row to the next, and he objected: it should move smoothly, he said, gliding pixel by pixel like paper sliding under the eye. One of the system's chief architects, Dan Ingalls, simply reached into the running program, typed a few lines while everyone watched, and made the scrolling smooth then and there, without stopping or restarting the machine. To Jobs this was almost more astonishing than the interface itself. Smalltalk could be reshaped while it ran, its behavior changed on the fly like wet clay, where every other computer of the age had to be halted, recompiled, and reloaded to accept the smallest alteration. He had asked for something and seen it granted in real time, before his eyes, and the wonder of it stayed with him for the rest of his life.

What they saw was the graphical user interface running in Smalltalk on the bitmapped screen of the Alto. There was a mouse, and it moved a pointer smoothly across the display. There were windows that overlapped like paper on a desk. Text appeared on the screen in the fonts and sizes it would print in. Menus dropped down at the click of a button. To Jobs, watching a machine that could be operated by pointing and clicking rather than by memorizing arcane commands, the effect was less like seeing a new product than like a religious conversion. He would later describe the moment in vivid terms, saying that within ten minutes he knew that every computer would one day work this way. It was, he understood instantly, so obviously right, so plainly the future, that it could not be contained inside a copier company.

To grasp why the effect was so overwhelming, remember what using a computer meant in 1979 for everyone outside that building. To move a file you typed its name and a cryptic command and prayed you had spelled both correctly; a single misplaced character produced an error message and nothing else. To see what a disk held you typed another command and read a terse list of names. The machine gave you a blinking prompt and waited, mute, for you to know the magic words. What the Alto offered instead was a picture of a desk, with the file sitting there as a little icon you could see and point at and drag by hand, no words to memorize, no syntax to get wrong. It was the difference between speaking a foreign language from a phrasebook and simply pointing at what you wanted. Jobs, who cared above all about how a thing felt to an ordinary person, understood in that instant that the phrasebook era of computing was over.

But the legend that grew from that afternoon, the durable story that Steve Jobs walked into PARC and stole the graphical interface from a hapless Xerox, is a distortion, and it is worth setting straight with some care, because it is one of the most repeated falsehoods in the whole history of technology. Xerox was not robbed. It invited Apple in, showed the work voluntarily, and took a stake in Apple as its reward—a stake it had negotiated for, with lawyers, as a condition of the visit. The demonstration violated no law and betrayed no secret that Xerox wished to keep; it was a transaction, and Xerox agreed to the terms with its eyes open. Jobs himself, in a much-quoted later reflection, was fond of paraphrasing a line often attributed to Picasso, that good artists copy while great artists steal, and the mischievous quotation has done much to cement the myth. But the aphorism obscures more than it reveals. What Apple carried away from PARC was not code or blueprints or stolen schematics. It was an idea, and a conviction—and the difference between carrying away an idea you were shown and stealing a design you were denied is the whole difference between inspiration and theft.

More important, in the excitement of the story of what Jobs saw, the world tends to forget what he and his engineers missed. The graphical interface was only the most visible of PARC's inventions, and by some measures the least profound. On the same visit, the Apple engineers were shown Smalltalk, and beneath Smalltalk lay Alan Kay's revolution in how software itself was structured, the object-oriented philosophy that would prove at least as consequential as the mouse. They were shown, or could have seen, the networking that lashed the Altos together, Robert Metcalfe's Ethernet, without which the personal computer would remain an island. Jobs, by his own admission, was so dazzled by the interface that these deeper marvels barely registered. He fixated on the surface, the windows and the pointer, and did not grasp the networking or the programming model. It would take Apple, and the industry, more than a decade to catch up to the parts of PARC that Jobs overlooked on that December afternoon—a curious footnote to a legend that casts him as the man who took everything. He took the one thing his eye could not resist and walked past two others of equal weight.

The oversight was oddly characteristic of the man. Jobs was a genius of the surface, of how a thing looked and felt and made a person feel, and the graphical interface spoke directly to that gift. The networking and the object-oriented philosophy beneath Smalltalk were invisible plumbing, profound but unglamorous, and they did not seize him the way the gliding pointer did. Apple would spend the coming years perfecting a beautiful skin, and only much later, and painfully, teach itself the deeper lessons it had walked past that afternoon.

And what Apple built afterward was not a copy of the Alto but a reimagining of it, and the differences matter as much as the debts. The PARC interface was brilliant but unfinished, a research prototype full of choices that would never have survived contact with an ordinary customer. Its mouse had three buttons, each doing something different, a source of confusion that Apple would ruthlessly simplify down to a single button that anyone could understand—a decision that shaped how hundreds of millions of people would later point at screens without ever having to remember which button did what. In the Alto's windows, clicking often did not do what a novice expected. The PARC system had no consistent notion of pulling menus down from a bar across the top, no clean drag-and-drop, no elegant overlapping that redrew itself instantly and without flicker when a window was moved. Much of what we now think of as the graphical interface, the pieces that made it usable by people who had never touched a computer, was invented not at Xerox but at Apple in the years after the visit, by engineers laboring over problems PARC had left unsolved. The pull-down menu that stays hidden until you reach for it, the single obvious button, the window you can drag and watch repaint cleanly beneath your hand—these were Apple's contributions, not Xerox's, and they were the difference between a laboratory curiosity and a machine your grandmother could use.

The most striking example was that very act of dragging one window in front of another and watching the screen repaint itself smoothly, without flicker, in real time. A young Apple programmer named Bill Atkinson, who had been on the PARC visit, became convinced he had watched the Alto do exactly this, redrawing overlapping regions instantly as windows slid across one another. In fact, as he later learned, the Alto had done no such thing; PARC's system was far clumsier at it than his memory insisted, and the researchers had not solved the problem so cleanly at all. But Atkinson, believing it possible because he thought he had seen it, went home and spent months figuring out how to actually make it work, inventing the mathematics of regions and clipping that made Apple's graphics fast and fluid. In a sense he reinvented, and improved upon, something that had never quite existed, spurred on by a false memory. It is one of the small ironies of the story that a mistaken recollection produced one of the crucial breakthroughs—and a neat rebuttal to the theft legend, for you cannot steal what was never there to take.

There is a final irony that the theft legend usually omits. A decade after the visit, in 1989, Xerox itself went to court against Apple, suing over the graphical interface and seeking a fortune in damages—an implicit admission that Xerox now believed it had given away something precious. The suit went nowhere; a judge dismissed the core of it, in part because Xerox had waited far too long to complain and had, after all, shown the work voluntarily and taken its payment in stock. If the very company whose future was supposedly stolen could not persuade a court that any theft had occurred, the popular story ought to lose some of its melodrama. What happened at PARC in December 1979 was not a heist. It was a transaction whose terms Xerox set, whose value Xerox misjudged, and whose consequences Xerox would spend years trying, and failing, to reverse.

So the truth of the visit is richer and stranger than the myth of the theft. Xerox showed Apple a glimpse of the future it had invented but could not sell, and was paid in stock for the showing. Jobs saw part of it clearly and part of it not at all. And Apple's engineers went home and spent the next several years building something genuinely new out of the inspiration, solving problems Xerox had never solved and simplifying complexities Xerox had never resolved. You can trace the lineage every time you point and click today: the one-button ease, the menu that drops down when you reach for it, the window that glides and repaints beneath your cursor are the surviving grandchildren of that December, and they are Apple's inventions built atop Xerox's vision, neither one sufficient without the other. The graphical interface that would change the world was born in Palo Alto, but it was not born whole at PARC, and it would not reach the public wearing a Xerox label. It would take shape first, expensively and imperfectly, in a machine Apple named after Jobs's own daughter.

Chapter 37: Lisa

In the winter of 1983, a customer walking into a computer dealership and asking to see Apple's newest machine would have been led to a beige rectangle the size of a small suitcase, standing upright with a built-in screen, and told, in a tone appropriate to the occasion, that it cost nearly ten thousand dollars. The machine was called the Lisa, unveiled to the public on the nineteenth of January that year at a list price of nine thousand nine hundred and ninety-five dollars, and it was the most advanced personal computer the world had yet seen. It was also, within a couple of years, one of the most instructive commercial failures in the history of the industry, a machine so far ahead of its market that it fell into the gap between what was possible and what anyone would pay for. Its story is the story of the graphical interface making its first, stumbling contact with the real world of budgets and impatience.

The Lisa project had begun before Jobs's pilgrimage to PARC and had originally been conceived as a fairly conventional business computer, a text-driven machine in the mold of the day. But after the December 1979 visit, the vision changed utterly. The graphical interface Jobs had glimpsed on the Alto became the animating idea of the project, and a team of unusually gifted engineers set out to build the first commercial computer that ordinary office workers could operate by pointing and clicking. The name officially stood for

Local Integrated Software Architecture, a phrase so transparently reverse-engineered that no one took it seriously; everyone understood that Lisa was also the name of Jobs's daughter, born in 1978, whose paternity he had for a time publicly and even legally denied. The machine carried, in its name, a private drama that Jobs would not fully acknowledge for years, and there is a quiet poignancy in the fact that the most personal object he had yet built bore the name of the child he was, at that moment, refusing to claim.

Years later, mellowed and dying, Jobs would finally drop the pretense. Asked by his biographer whether the machine had been named for his daughter, he answered simply, "Obviously it was named for my daughter." Lisa Brennan-Jobs, the child he had once sworn under oath was not his—even as he was building the most advanced computer in the world and giving it her name—eventually reconciled with him and took his surname. The acronym, Local Integrated Software Architecture, had been a fig leaf all along, reverse-engineered by a committee to give the engineers something respectable to say to the press. The truth was that the flagship of Apple's future had quietly carried, from its first day, the name of the daughter its creator was not yet brave enough to acknowledge.

Technically, the Lisa was a triumph, and it introduced to the commercial market nearly everything that would define graphical computing for the next decade. Built around a Motorola 68000 processor running at five megahertz and equipped with a full megabyte of memory—a lavish amount for 1983—it had a mouse, refined by Apple down from Xerox's confusing three buttons to a single one. It had overlapping windows, pull-down menus, icons representing documents and folders, and a metaphor of a desktop on which a user arranged their work. It offered, remarkably for its day, protected memory and the ability to keep several programs running at once and move data between them. It shipped with a suite of seven well-integrated applications for writing, calculating, drawing, and charting.

And it drew its images using a piece of software of extraordinary elegance called QuickDraw, written by Bill Atkinson, the same programmer whose determination to redraw overlapping windows had produced Apple's breakthrough in graphics. QuickDraw made the Lisa's screen fast and fluid where the Xerox Star had been ponderous, and it would become one of the most important pieces of software Apple ever owned.

In several respects the Lisa was not merely ahead of the market but ahead of its own famous successor. It protected each program's slice of memory from the others, so that one misbehaving application could not bring down the whole machine, and it could keep several programs running at once and shuttle information between them—capabilities so advanced that the Macintosh, arriving a year later, would do without them and would not truly regain them for the better part of two decades. The team that built it numbered in the hundreds and labored for years, and they were solving problems no one had ever solved before in a product meant to be sold: how a novice should be shown an error, how a document should be saved, what ought to happen when a user changed his mind. Much of the vocabulary of modern computing—the very idea that you could close a document without saving and be asked, gently, whether you were sure—was worked out by these people, at enormous cost, on a machine almost no one would buy.

To feel what the Lisa was reaching for, picture an office manager in 1983 who has never touched a computer. She sits down and sees not a blinking prompt demanding cryptic incantations but a gray surface with little pictures on it—a sheet of paper, a folder, a small wastebasket. She rolls the mouse and a pointer follows. She points at the folder and presses the button twice, and it opens into a window showing the documents inside. She points at one, drags it onto the wastebasket, and it is gone. She wants to move a paragraph in her letter, so she sweeps the pointer across it to highlight it, chooses "Cut" from a menu that unfurls at the top of the screen, points to a new spot, and chooses "Paste." Nothing she has done required her to memorize a single command or read a single manual. That was the Lisa's astonishing promise: a computer that met the human halfway, that borrowed the furniture of the ordinary desk so that no one had to learn the alien grammar of the machine. In 1983 this was very nearly magic.

Yet for all its brilliance, the Lisa was crippled by the very ambition that made it remarkable. That price of nine thousand nine hundred and ninety-five dollars—the equivalent of more than thirty thousand of today's dollars—placed it far beyond the reach of individuals and made even corporate buyers hesitate. Its sophisticated software demanded a great deal of the hardware of 1983, and the machine, despite its power, often felt sluggish, its elegant animations unfolding with a deliberateness that tried the patience of users accustomed to the instant, if ugly, responsiveness of a text-based computer. Its custom "Twiggy" disk drives, designed in-house, proved so unreliable that Apple was eventually forced to replace them. And it existed in a strange commercial limbo, too expensive to be a personal computer and too unfamiliar, with its radical new way of working, to reassure the conservative corporate purchasing managers who were then busy standardizing on the plainer, cheaper, text-driven IBM PC. The Lisa was a Cadillac in a market that had just discovered it could buy a reliable, boring sedan for a fraction of the price.

To feel the weight of that price, set it beside its rivals. An IBM PC in 1983 could be had, in a serviceable configuration, for a few thousand dollars; an Apple II for well under two. The Lisa asked nearly ten thousand, the price of a new car, for a machine that did tasks a secretary was already performing on cheaper equipment, and it asked corporate buyers to take on faith that pointing at pictures was worth the enormous premium. A purchasing manager whose job depended on not being blamed for a costly mistake looked at the Lisa, looked at the safe and boring IBM on the next table, and chose the IBM nearly every time. The tragedy was that the Lisa was, feature for feature, the better machine by a wide margin. It was simply the better machine at four or five times the price, sold into a market that had just learned to prize thrift above wonder. And the numbers were merciless: Apple poured something on the order of a hundred and fifty million dollars into developing the machine, split roughly between software and hardware, and recouped perhaps a hundred million in sales, a wound of some fifty million dollars against the company's books.

The internal politics of Apple sealed the machine's fate as surely as the market did. Jobs had been the driving force behind reorienting the Lisa around the graphical interface, but he was a difficult and domineering presence, and in 1980 and 1981 the company's management, wary of his temperament, eased him out of the Lisa group and handed leadership to more seasoned executives. Wounded and restless, Jobs did what he would do again and again across his career: he found a smaller, scrappier project and made it his own. He seized control of a modest effort, begun by an engineer named Jef Raskin, to build a cheap and simple computer for ordinary people, a machine Raskin had named after his favorite variety of apple, the Macintosh. Jobs took Raskin's project, pushed Raskin himself aside, and set out to build a graphical computer that would do everything the Lisa did for a fraction of the price. The two projects, Lisa and Macintosh, became rivals within the same company, and Jobs threw himself into making the Macintosh not merely a competitor to the Lisa but its assassin, promising anyone who would listen that his little machine would humiliate the expensive sibling that had cast him out.

There was cruelty in the rivalry, and not only toward machines. Jobs told his Macintosh team, only half joking, that the Lisa people were bozos, and he set out to beat them not merely in the market but in their own company's esteem. The two divisions occupied different buildings and barely spoke. It was a strange way to run a business—two teams inside one firm racing to build overlapping computers, each hoping the other would stumble—and it could only have happened at an Apple young enough, and flush enough, to indulge its founder's appetites.

There was, at least, a family resemblance between the warring siblings, because they shared a common technical inheritance. Bill Atkinson's QuickDraw, the graphics engine that gave the Lisa its fluid screen, was carried over to the Macintosh, and the single-button mouse was common to both. The desktop metaphor, the icons, the pull-down menus, the whole visual grammar that the Lisa team had labored to invent, would reappear on the smaller machine, refined and stripped down and made to run on far cheaper hardware. In this sense the Lisa was not so much a failure as a costly and magnificent prototype, a first draft written in the language of the future, whose vocabulary would be inherited by the machine that finally reached the public. The Lisa team had solved the hard problems; the Macintosh would reap the reward. It is one of the recurring shapes of this whole history, that the pioneer who clears the ground so rarely gets to build the house.

For the Lisa itself, the end came quietly and a little brutally. Sales never approached what Apple had projected; by most accounts the machine sold on the order of ten thousand units over its whole life, a rounding error against the company's hopes. The far cheaper Macintosh, arriving in 1984, cannibalized what little market the Lisa had, and Apple eventually rebranded and repriced the machine as the Macintosh XL in an effort to salvage it, to little effect. The whole product line was discontinued in 1986. And then came the mordant coda that has attached itself to the machine forever. In September of 1989, Apple gathered up roughly twenty-seven hundred unsold Lisa units and, working with a firm called Sun Remarketing, trucked them to a guarded landfill in Logan, Utah, where they were buried—crushed into the earth for a tax write-off, at a cost of about a dollar ninety-five per cubic yard for the space they occupied. It was a quiet mass grave for a machine that had seen the future too clearly and too soon, a landfill in the mountains holding thousands of the most advanced computers of their day.

The Lisa had proven that a graphical computer could be built and sold commercially. It had also proven, painfully, that being right was not enough; the machine also had to be affordable, and fast, and it had to arrive at a moment when the world was ready to embrace it. And here it is worth dispelling the easy verdict that the Lisa was simply a flop and nothing more. Every gesture you make on a modern computer—the double-click that opens a folder, the file you drag to the trash, the menu that pulls down from the top of the screen, the very idea that documents and folders should look like documents and folders—was worked out, for the commercial world, on this expensive, unsellable machine. The Lisa did not fail so much as pay, in full and in advance, for a revolution its younger sibling would collect on. Its ideas did not die in that Utah landfill; they had already escaped, carried into the machine that would make them ordinary.

That moment, Jobs was convinced, was almost at hand, and it would belong not to the Lisa but to its smaller, cheaper, friendlier sibling. He had gathered around the Macintosh a team of young zealots, and he had begun to speak of the little machine in the language of revolution, as a tool that would put the power of computing into the hands not of corporations but of ordinary people. He wanted its arrival to be an event the world could not ignore, and he had found a way to announce it that would air, exactly once, before the largest television audience in America.

Chapter 38: 1984

On the evening of January 22, 1984, tens of millions of Americans settled in to watch the Los Angeles Raiders demolish the Washington Redskins in Super Bowl XVIII, and somewhere in the third quarter they were confronted by sixty seconds of television unlike anything the medium had shown before. The screen filled with rows of gray, shaven-headed drones shuffling in lockstep through a tunnel toward an auditorium, where they sat in ranks before an enormous screen on which a Big Brother figure droned about the anniversary of the Information Purification Directives. Then a young woman in bright orange shorts and a white tank top came sprinting down the aisle, a heavy sledgehammer swinging in her hands, pursued by helmeted riot police in visored black. She spun once to build momentum, like a discus thrower, and hurled the hammer into the giant screen, which exploded in a blast of light and wind that washed over the stunned gray faces. A calm voice and a line of scrolling text delivered the message: on January 24th, Apple Computer would introduce Macintosh, and the audience would see why 1984 would not be like Nineteen Eighty-Four.

The choice of the runner was itself a small telling detail. The woman with the hammer was played by Anya Major, a British athlete and discus thrower cast precisely because she could swing and release the sledgehammer with an athlete's convincing power; the production had tried professional actresses who could not make the throw look real. The gray drones were British extras, some of them genuine skinheads recruited off the streets of London, shaved and costumed to fill the ranks. The whole thing was shot on real film with cinematic ambition by Ridley Scott, who had just made Blade Runner and brought its dystopian grandeur to a sixty-second commercial, on a production budget of roughly nine hundred thousand dollars—an unheard-of sum for an advertisement in that era, more than most feature filmmakers had to work with per minute. The agency was Chiat/Day of Los Angeles, where the concept had come from the copywriter Steve Hayden, the art director Brent Thomas, and the creative director Lee Clow, a team that believed, correctly, that they were making something closer to a short film than a pitch.

And yet the commercial that would become the most celebrated advertisement ever made was very nearly strangled in its crib by the people paying for it. When Chiat/Day screened the finished spot for Apple's board of directors in December 1983, the room went cold. The directors, by several accounts, hated it—one reportedly asked who wanted to fire the agency, and the mood was less admiration than alarm. This did not look like an advertisement; it never showed the product, never named a price, never explained what a Macintosh was or did. The board ordered CEO John Sculley to unload the expensive Super Bowl airtime Apple had already purchased, to get out of the gamble entirely. Sculley, caught between a board that loathed the ad and a young co-founder who adored it, went back to the agency and asked them to sell off the time. And here the story turns on a piece of corporate folklore that has hardened into legend: Chiat/Day, so the telling goes, sold only part of the airtime and quietly reported that it could not find a buyer for the sixty-second slot, so that Apple, having paid for it and unable to unload it, was left with no choice but to let the ad run. Whether the agency genuinely could not find a buyer or simply preferred not to, the result was the same.

The most famous commercial in television history aired because the people who commissioned it failed to cancel it in time.

There is a further wrinkle that corrects a piece of the common memory. It is often said that the ad aired "exactly once," and in the sense that matters—its single national broadcast to the vast Super Bowl audience—that is true. But it had in fact been shown once before, slipped onto a small television station in Twin Falls, Idaho, at one in the morning on December 15, 1983, a technical airing arranged so that the commercial would qualify for that year's advertising awards. The near-secret 1 a.m. showing to the insomniacs of southern Idaho is one of the odd little facts that survive underneath a legend. To the country at large, though, "1984" arrived from nowhere on Super Bowl Sunday, aired in its full length once, and became instantly a piece of pop culture that people discussed for weeks. It never showed the product. It never described what the Macintosh did. It simply promised that a small company was about to strike a blow against the gray conformity of the computing world, against the faceless corporate order that everyone in the audience understood, without being told, to mean IBM. It was less an advertisement than a manifesto, and it set the stage for a machine that Jobs intended to sell not as a tool but as a cause.

The gamble paid off beyond anything Apple's nervous board could have imagined. In the days after the game, all three national television networks and dozens of newspapers replayed and dissected the commercial as though it were news, which in a sense it was; Apple reaped a tidal wave of free coverage worth many times what the airtime had cost. Advertising Age would later crown "1984" the greatest commercial of its era, and it is routinely ranked the finest Super Bowl spot ever made. The advertisement that the directors had wanted to kill, that a chief executive had been ordered to sell off, that reached the air partly because no buyer could be found for the slot, became the founding document of a new idea: that a commercial could be an event, a piece of craft that people actively wanted to see. Apple had spent roughly nine hundred thousand dollars to make it and the price of a single airing to show it, and it received, in return, a permanent place in the culture.

There was a coda that the triumphant retellings tend to leave out. George Orwell's novel Nineteen Eighty-Four was still under copyright, and its trustees were not amused to see their author's nightmare enlisted to sell computers. The Orwell estate, together with the novel's British publisher, sent Apple a stern letter demanding that the commercial be withdrawn. But the ad had already made its single national airing and done its work, and the threat came far too late to matter; the image of the hammer shattering Big Brother was already lodged in the national memory. It is a small irony worthy of Orwell himself that the most famous warning against a future of mass conformity was repurposed, brilliantly, into one of the most effective pieces of mass persuasion ever broadcast.

Two days later, on January 24, 1984, at Apple's annual shareholders' meeting in a packed auditorium at the Flint Center in Cupertino, Steve Jobs walked onstage in a double-breasted jacket and a green bow tie, savored the roar of the crowd, and pulled a small beige computer from a canvas bag. He inserted a floppy disk, and the Macintosh did something no computer had ever done in such a setting: it introduced itself. The screen displayed a parade of fonts and images—a scrolling banner, a hand-drawn portrait, a chessboard—and then, through a speech synthesizer, the machine spoke aloud in a thin, quavering electronic voice, thanking the audience and joking that it was unaccustomed to public speaking, and adding that it would rather trust a computer than a person who had never built one. The crowd came apart with excitement. Jobs had staged not a product announcement but a coronation, and the little machine, glowing and talking on its own, seemed to promise that computing had at last become something warm, approachable, even lovable.

Andy Hertzfeld, watching from the audience, later remembered the ovation going on and on, a wave of noise that would not stop, and members of the Macintosh team weeping openly in their seats. They had worked themselves past exhaustion for this minute, some of them for years, and here at last was the proof that the world felt what they had felt about the little machine. Whatever troubles waited in the sales figures, that afternoon belonged wholly to them.

The Macintosh had been built by a team Jobs had assembled and driven with a ferocity that was by turns inspiring and cruel, a small band of young engineers and designers who came to see themselves, in his phrase, as pirates rather than navy—they even flew a skull-and-crossbones over their building, with the rainbow Apple logo for an eye patch. At the center were a few extraordinary talents. Burrell Smith, a self-taught hardware wizard who had been repairing Apple IIs in the service department before Jobs noticed him, had designed the machine's digital board with an economy that bordered on the miraculous, wringing graphical performance from a spartan and inexpensive set of components. Andy Hertzfeld wrote much of the system software, the invisible code that made the screen and mouse and windows feel alive, working stretches so intense that they became legend within the company. Bill Atkinson brought over QuickDraw, the graphics engine he had perfected on the Lisa, and wrote the drawing program that showed off what the machine could do. And a young artist named Susan Kare designed the icons, the typefaces, and the visual furniture of the Macintosh screen, giving the machine a personality no computer had possessed before.

Kare's contribution is easy to underestimate and impossible to overstate. Working on graph paper, plotting each pixel by hand as if designing a mosaic or a needlepoint pattern, she created the little pictures that told a user, at a glance and without words, what the computer could do: the trash can for discarding files, the pointing hand, the wristwatch that meant wait, the smiling Macintosh that greeted a user at startup, the bomb that announced a crash with a rueful sense of humor. It was painstaking, almost monastic work—each icon a small grid of black and white squares that had to read clearly at the size of a fingernail. She designed the machine's proportionally spaced fonts and named many of them, at first, after the stops on the commuter rail line near Philadelphia where she had grown up: Overbrook, Merion, Ardmore, Rosemont. Jobs objected that the towns were too obscure and insisted the fonts be renamed after world-class cities, and so the world received Chicago, Geneva, and New York instead. These small, human touches were not decoration. They were the difference between a machine that intimidated and one that welcomed, and they translated the abstract idea of the graphical interface into something a first-time user could love on sight.

The machine itself was a deliberate and radical departure from everything the personal computer had been. Where earlier computers sprawled across a desk in a jumble of separate components, the Macintosh was a single sealed box, its screen and its brains and its floppy drive all wrapped in one compact, upright, almost friendly case, small enough to be carried in a padded bag and light enough that a person could lift it easily with one hand. There was no jungle of cables, no arcane setup. A user plugged it in, and there on the screen was the desktop, with its icons and its menu bar and its little arrow, waiting to be pointed at with the single-button mouse that lay beside the keyboard. To open a document you did not type a command; you moved the arrow to a picture and pressed the button. The entire logic of the machine was built on the premise that a computer should adapt to the way people already thought about paper and desks and filing, rather than forcing people to learn the alien grammar of the machine.

Jobs and his pirates had a phrase for what they believed they had made. The Macintosh, they said, was the computer for the rest of us, meaning the vast majority of people who had looked at the blinking command prompts and cryptic manuals of the existing machines and concluded, sensibly, that computers were not for them. The Apple II had been for hobbyists and the IBM PC for corporations, but the Macintosh was meant for everyone else, for teachers and writers and students and small-business owners and curious households, for anyone who wanted the power of a computer without having to become a programmer to unlock it. It was, in aspiration if not yet in price, the closest thing the world had seen to Alan Kay's dream of a personal computer as a medium for ordinary human beings, and its arrival felt, in the electric atmosphere of that January, like the dawn of a new age.

You still live inside the aftershock of that minute of film. When advertisers speak of the "Super Bowl commercial" as an art form worth millions and months of labor, they are chasing the template "1984" set on that single night; the modern spectacle of the game's ads as an event in themselves begins there. And every smiling icon, every trash can you drag a file into, every friendly startup chime carries Susan Kare's fingerprints, her hand-plotted pixels having quietly taught the whole industry that a machine could have warmth. But the electricity of a launch is a fragile thing, and applause does not pay for the machine. As the excitement of January faded and the Macintosh went on sale to a public that had to weigh its charms against its real limitations and its real price, Apple would discover that changing the world and selling enough computers to survive were two very different undertakings, and that the friendly little box had troubles that no advertisement, however brilliant, could hammer away.

Chapter 39: The Machine for the Rest of Us

In the spring of 1984, a few months after the euphoria of the launch, the sales charts inside Apple began telling a story no one wanted to read. The Macintosh had sold briskly in its opening weeks, carried aloft by the spectacle of the Super Bowl commercial and the sheer novelty of a computer that talked and smiled. Seventy thousand machines went out the door in the first hundred days, and Jobs was jubilant, boasting of a pace that seemed to vindicate every gamble. But as the initial wave of enthusiasts and early adopters exhausted itself, the momentum sagged, and by summer and into the fall the beautiful machine was sitting on dealer shelves, gathering dust in the cheerful padded carrying bags Apple had designed for it. The revolution Jobs had promised the world was, for the moment, refusing to sell, and the reasons were not mysterious. They were built into the machine itself.

The Macintosh was hobbled, first and most cruelly, by its memory. In the drive to hit a price the market could bear, and against the pleading of engineers who begged for more, the machine had shipped with just one hundred and twenty-eight kilobytes of memory, a starvation ration for a computer whose graphical interface was, by its nature, ravenous for resources. To put that figure in human scale, it is a few thousandths of what sits inside the cheapest phone today—barely enough to hold a couple of pages of formatted text and the code to draw them. Every window, every font, every icon consumed memory that the little machine could barely spare, and the result was a computer that felt cramped and slow, forever shuffling data to and from its single floppy drive with a grinding patience that wore on the nerves. Copying a disk could require a user to swap floppies in and out a dozen times or more, ejecting and reinserting until the whole exercise felt like a punishment. The elegance that had dazzled the audience in January revealed itself, in daily use, to be running on an engine too small to carry it. Later that year Apple would quietly release a version with half a megabyte, tacitly admitting that the original had been strangled at birth, but the damage to the launch was done.

The second wound was the emptiness of the machine. A computer, however beautiful, is only as useful as the software that runs on it, and in 1984 there was almost nothing to run on the Macintosh. Its radical new graphical design meant that existing programs, written for text-based machines, could not simply be moved over; each application had to be rewritten from scratch to take advantage of the mouse and the windows, a demanding and expensive undertaking that software companies were slow to attempt for a machine whose sales were faltering. It was a vicious circle familiar to anyone who has watched a new platform struggle: buyers stayed away because there was little software, and software makers stayed away because there were few buyers. The Macintosh could do wonderful things in principle, but in practice, in those first many months, there was heartbreakingly little for it to do. Its two flagship programs, MacWrite and MacPaint, were genuine delights that showed off what the machine could become, but a person could exhaust their novelty in an afternoon. And at nearly twenty-five hundred dollars—a price John Sculley had raised from the fifteen-hundred-dollar figure Jobs originally wanted, in order to fund the lavish marketing—it was too expensive to be an impulse and too limited to be an obvious investment.

The software drought was made worse by a decision that had seemed clever at the time. To save precious memory, Apple had baked much of the Macintosh's essential machinery—the routines that drew the windows and menus and handled the mouse—into a chip inside the machine, a library of building blocks called the Toolbox. This was elegant, and it meant every program could share the same polished look without reinventing it, but it also meant that writing Macintosh software required mastering a large and unfamiliar body of these routines, a steep climb that discouraged the very developers Apple most needed. Combined with the machine's cramped memory, which left little room for an ambitious program to stretch out and work, it ensured that good Macintosh software arrived slowly, painfully, and late. Apple's own attempt to sell the machine to corporations as an "office" system, its computers tied together by networking, fell flat, and for a stretch of 1985 it was genuinely unclear whether the Macintosh would survive at all.

As the machine faltered, the tensions at the top of Apple, which had been building for more than a year, broke into open war. Jobs had personally recruited John Sculley, a polished marketing executive from Pepsi, to run the company, famously challenging him with the question of whether he wanted to sell sugar water for the rest of his life or come change the world. But the two men, so alike in ambition and so unlike in temperament, could not share the company for long. Jobs, mercurial and imperious, ran the Macintosh division as a fiefdom and disparaged the rest of Apple, including the Apple II that still earned most of the company's money; Sculley, backed by a board that had grown alarmed at the founder's volatility and at the sinking numbers, moved to contain him. Through the first half of 1985 the conflict escalated into a corporate knife fight, with Jobs at one point attempting to engineer Sculley's ouster while the chief executive was traveling. The gambit failed; word reached Sculley, who forced a confrontation before the board, and the board sided with Sculley. Jobs was stripped of his operational role, left with a grand title and no real power, and in September of 1985, embittered and humiliated, he resigned from the company he had co-founded, sold nearly all his stock, and walked away to start again.

Jobs's exile would last eleven years, and it would prove, in the long run, the making of him. With the money from his Apple stock he founded a new computer company called NeXT and bought a small computer-graphics outfit that would become Pixar, and in the wilderness he learned a patience he had never possessed and lost none of his fire. When he returned to a nearly bankrupt Apple in 1997, he would rebuild it into the most valuable company on earth. But all of that lay unimaginably far ahead in September of 1985, when a humiliated thirty-year-old sold his shares, kept a single one so that he could still attend the annual meetings, and walked out of the company he had built in his parents' garage.

It is one of the great what-ifs of the industry, and it is tempting to imagine that Jobs's departure doomed the machine. It did not. The Macintosh survived, and its survival owed less to any executive than to an unforeseen marriage of technologies that arrived just in time to save it. The very qualities that had made the machine expensive and slow, its high-resolution graphical screen and its fluent handling of fonts and images, turned out to be precisely the qualities needed for a task no one had prioritized during its design. In January of 1985 Apple introduced the LaserWriter, a laser printer descended directly from the technology PARC had pioneered a decade earlier, and though it cost nearly seven thousand dollars, it could print a page at a crispness the office world had never seen from anything short of a professional print shop. Later that year a small Seattle company named Aldus released a program called PageMaker, and when the three pieces came together—the Macintosh, the LaserWriter, and PageMaker, lashed together over Apple's networking—the combination could do something no affordable setup had ever done. It could let an ordinary person lay out a printed page on the screen, exactly as it would appear, with multiple typefaces and images and columns, and then print it, at home or in a small office, at a quality approaching a professional press.

This was desktop publishing, and it rescued the Macintosh. The chain of cause is worth savoring, because it is one of the most elegant accidents in the whole history of the industry. PARC had invented the laser printer and the graphical, font-rich screen and could sell neither to the public. Apple had inherited the graphical screen and built the friendly box and was starving for a reason anyone needed it. Aldus supplied the missing software. And suddenly a school newsletter, a church bulletin, a real-estate flyer, a small magazine—work that had previously demanded a typesetter, a paste-up artist, and a print shop—could be produced by one person at a desk for a few thousand dollars. Small businesses, design studios, newsletters, and eventually whole industries discovered this, and the Macintosh found, in this narrow and unglamorous corner, the killer application it had lacked, a reason to exist that justified its price and forgave its limitations. The machine that had been sold as a computer for everyone found its first durable home among the people who worked with words and images, the writers and designers and small publishers, and that beachhead kept Apple alive and the Macintosh line growing through the difficult years to come. The phrase itself was coined by Aldus's founder, Paul Brainerd, a former newspaperman who had watched the typesetting trade up close and understood exactly which expensive, specialized craft the Macintosh was about to swallow; he called what his program did "desktop publishing," and the name stuck because it told the plain truth—an entire print shop, shrunk to fit on a desk.

Picture the transformation in a single small office. Before, a church secretary who wanted a handsome newsletter had to type her text, send it to a typesetter who would set it in film or metal, take the galleys to a layout artist who cut them with a knife and waxed them onto a board in columns, position the photographs by hand, and carry the finished paste-up to a printer—days of labor and hundreds of dollars, with every last-minute change forcing the whole chain to run again. After, she sat at a Macintosh, typed her text, chose her fonts and dragged her columns and dropped in a scanned photograph, saw the entire page on the screen exactly as it would look on paper, and pressed a button; a minute later a crisp master slid out of the LaserWriter, ready to be copied. A craft that had employed skilled specialists for centuries had been folded into an afternoon at a desk. That was the earthquake, and it began with three Apple-shaped pieces clicking together in 1985.

None of this had been the plan. Apple had not designed the Macintosh to be a publishing machine; the LaserWriter and PageMaker were not steps in any grand strategy conceived in 1982. The rescue was an accident of capability meeting need—the machine happened to be superb at exactly the thing a printing revolution required, and a small software company happened to supply the missing piece at precisely the right moment. It is a useful corrective to the tidy myth of the visionary who foresees every move. The Macintosh survived less because anyone had predicted its salvation than because its very extravagances, the costly graphics and fonts that had nearly sunk it, turned out to be the qualities the world would pay for after all.

You meet the descendants of that rescue constantly, usually without knowing it. Every time you drop a photo into a document and slide it around until the text wraps neatly beside it; every time you choose a typeface from a menu and see it appear on the page exactly as it will print; every flyer, résumé, wedding invitation, or zine laid out on a laptop screen—all of it descends from that 1985 marriage of the friendly box, the laser printer, and PageMaker. Desktop publishing is now simply publishing, so ordinary that the word "desktop" has quietly fallen away, and the craft that once required a shop full of specialized labor is a thing a teenager does on a school assignment.

The larger verdict took longer to render, and when it came, it vindicated the vision even as it had bruised the visionaries. The graphical user interface, born at Xerox, glimpsed by Jobs, and delivered to the public first by the failed Lisa and then by the struggling Macintosh, was simply the right way for human beings and computers to meet, and its triumph, over the following decade, became total. When Microsoft's Windows finally matured into a usable graphical system and spread across the vast installed base of IBM-compatible machines, it carried the ideas of Palo Alto and Cupertino into hundreds of millions of homes and offices, and the command prompt that had defined computing's first decades receded into the tool of specialists. Every smartphone, every tablet, every laptop that a person today touches and points at and swipes descends, in a direct and traceable line, from the Alto in that beanbag-strewn lab and the friendly box that Jobs pulled from a canvas bag. It is worth correcting, here, the tidy story that the Macintosh "won" in 1984; it very nearly died, and what it actually won was the deeper and slower victory of proving that its ideas were correct, ideas that would conquer the world wearing other companies' logos.

Yet while Apple was courting business users and creative professionals with its elegant, expensive graphical machines, and while IBM and its clones were conquering the corporate desk, another battle for the future of computing had been raging on an altogether different front, in the living rooms and rec rooms and children's bedrooms of ordinary families, where cheaper, humbler machines were fighting a ferocious price war for a place next to the television set.

Chapter 40: Jack Tramiel's War

On a winter morning in 1945, a nineteen-year-old prisoner named Idek Tramielski was among the survivors of the Nazi camps liberated as the war in Europe ground toward its end, one of the last of a transport that had begun with his family in the Polish city of Łódź. He had passed through the ghetto there, through Auschwitz, and through a labor camp attached to it. His father had died in the camps; most of the rest of his family was gone. When American troops liberated the camp where he was held, they found a young man who weighed little more than a skeleton and who had learned, in the most literal terms imaginable, that survival was not a metaphor. Two years later he arrived in New York, changed his name to Jack Tramiel, and joined the United States Army that had freed him, where he was trained to repair office equipment and typewriters. That skill would prove the seed of an empire, but the lesson of the camps proved more durable than any technical training. For the rest of his life, when Jack Tramiel wanted to explain how he did business, he reached for the language of combat. "Business," he liked to say, "is war."

By the late 1950s Tramiel was running a typewriter repair shop in the Bronx and then, sensing where the money moved, a company that imported and assembled the machines themselves. He named it Commodore, and the story he told about the name captured the man: casting about for something with martial dignity, he found that Admiral and General were already taken as brand names, so he settled on the naval rank just below. When Japanese competition gutted the typewriter trade, he pivoted to mechanical adding machines; when electronic calculators arrived from Japan and threatened to gut that business too, he nearly went under. It was a hard and humiliating lesson, and Tramiel drew from it a conviction that would shape the personal computer industry for a decade. He would never again let a supplier hold a knife to his throat. If a component was essential, Commodore would own the company that made it. Vertical integration was not a management theory to Tramiel; it was a survival strategy, the corporate equivalent of never again being dependent on someone else for your bread.

The knife, in the calculator business, was the chip. Every calculator maker bought its integrated circuits from a handful of American semiconductor firms, and those firms could raise prices or cut off supply at will—which is exactly what happened when Texas Instruments, one of Commodore's own chip suppliers, decided to enter the calculator market directly and undercut its customers into the ground. Tramiel remembered that betrayal for the rest of his life, and it made his next move inevitable. In 1976 he bought the chipmaker outright. MOS Technology, a scrappy Pennsylvania firm, had recently done something audacious: a team of renegade engineers led by Chuck Peddle, refugees from Motorola, had designed a microprocessor called the 6502 and priced it at twenty-five dollars when competing chips from Intel and Motorola sold for nearly two hundred. The 6502 was the brain inside the Apple II, inside the Atari machines, inside the Nintendo and Commodore consoles that would come later; it was, dollar for dollar, the most important microprocessor of the era. When Commodore acquired MOS, it acquired not just a factory but the beating heart of the coming revolution. Tramiel now owned the silicon, and Chuck Peddle, who came with the deal, promptly pushed his new boss toward a product he insisted was the future. Not calculators. Computers.

The first fruit of that push was the PET, a friendly all-in-one machine with a built-in keyboard and cassette deck, unveiled in 1977 alongside the Apple II and the Radio Shack TRS-80 in what enthusiasts later called the "1977 Trinity" of ready-made personal computers. The PET sold respectably to schools and small businesses, but it was not the machine that made Commodore's name. That machine came in 1981, and it embodied Tramiel's true religion. He had watched Apple and its rivals sell handsome computers to well-off hobbyists and professionals, and he had concluded that they were all fighting over the wrong customers. There were only so many affluent enthusiasts. But there were tens of millions of ordinary families who had never touched a computer and who might buy one if it cost less than a color television. Tramiel condensed this vision into a slogan that became his war cry, and that ought to hang over the whole history of the home computer: "We need to build computers for the masses, not the classes."

The VIC-20 was the answer. Chuck Peddle's engineers built it around a video chip that had been sitting unused in MOS's catalog, and Tramiel priced it with the same brutal logic he had once applied to calculators, aiming for a retail figure below three hundred dollars. He did not sell it through specialized computer dealers who wanted fat margins and hand-holding. He sold it through the same mass-market channels that moved toasters and toys—department stores, discount chains, the aisles where ordinary families already shopped—and he hired William Shatner, fresh from the bridge of the Starship Enterprise, to peer into a television camera and ask why you would buy just a video game when for about the same money you could buy "the wonder computer of the 1980s." The VIC-20 was, by the standards of its more expensive rivals, a modest thing, with a small memory and a screen that showed only twenty-two characters across, so narrow that a line of ordinary text broke awkwardly across it. But it was a real, programmable computer, and it cost what a family could actually afford. In 1982 it became the first computer of any kind to sell more than a million units, and eventually it sold several million. Tramiel had proven his thesis in the only language he trusted, which was volume.

There was method in selling a computer beside the toasters. The specialty computer stores of the day treated a machine as a serious purchase, to be demonstrated and explained by a salesman working on commission, which meant a fat markup and a customer who had already decided, before walking in, that buying a computer was a considered act. Tramiel wanted the opposite. He wanted a parent pushing a cart through a discount store to see a real, programmable computer priced like a toy, grab it on impulse alongside the groceries, and carry it home to the children—no salesman, no ceremony, no markup. To reach that shopper he was willing to accept razor-thin margins on each unit, because he intended to sell not thousands of machines but millions, and because he owned the factory that made the one part his rivals had to buy. Volume was not a consequence of his strategy; it was the strategy.

Owning the chip factory was what made the coming price war winnable, and a price war was precisely what Tramiel wanted. Because Commodore manufactured its own semiconductors, it could absorb price cuts that would bleed a rival dry, and Tramiel understood this with the clarity of a man who calculated advantages for a living. Consider the arithmetic that terrified his competitors. A rival building a home computer had to buy its processor and its custom chips on the open market, perhaps paying the better part of a hundred dollars for the silicon alone before it added a keyboard, a case, a power supply, and a profit. Commodore's silicon cost it only what the raw wafers and the factory time cost, a fraction of the open-market price, because the money a competitor paid to a chip supplier was money Commodore simply paid to itself. So when a competitor dropped its price, Commodore could drop lower, and lower again, and simply keep going long after the other side had run out of margin. Rivals who bought their chips on the open market found themselves in a knife fight against an opponent who owned the knife foundry.

The rival Tramiel most wanted to destroy was the very company that had once betrayed him. Texas Instruments, the chipmaker that had undercut its calculator customers years before, had brought out its own home computer, the TI-99/4A, and it was in some respects a more capable machine than the VIC-20. But TI was a lumbering giant that did not understand the mass market as Tramiel did, and it had made the fatal error of fighting a price war against a man who had been waiting his entire career for exactly this fight. As Commodore slashed prices, TI followed, then followed again, each cut carving into a machine it could not build as cheaply as Commodore could. The war would grow so ferocious that home computers, which had been sold as premium goods, tumbled toward the price of appliances, and one after another the weaker combatants—TI among them—would be driven from the field entirely, bleeding money on every unit they sold. Tramiel did not merely want to win market share. He wanted his enemies gone.

And gone they went. The numbers were staggering. Texas Instruments, a company many times Commodore's size, hemorrhaged money on its home computer as the price war drove the machine below what it cost to build, losing hundreds of millions of dollars before it finally surrendered and abandoned the home-computer business altogether late in 1983. It was not alone. The price war Tramiel had started, and which he alone was truly built to win, turned the home-computer market into a killing field. A swarm of hopeful companies that had rushed in during the boom—makers of machines now half-remembered or wholly forgotten—found they could not sell a computer for what Commodore charged and still survive, and one after another they folded, merged, or fled. Tramiel had wanted a war of attrition, and attrition is exactly what he got, with himself very nearly the last man standing on the field.

Inside Commodore the atmosphere was famously savage. Engineers worked punishing hours; managers were pitted against one another; suppliers were squeezed until they squealed. Tramiel could be charming and paternal one moment and coldly ruthless the next, a man who had seen the worst that human beings could do to one another and had emerged convinced that mercy was a luxury he could not afford. Colleagues told stories of negotiations that felt less like meetings than interrogations, of a boss who would deliberately keep an executive off balance to test how he performed under pressure, of contracts renegotiated at the last possible moment simply to see whether the other party would flinch. He ran the company as a extension of his own will, and the will had been forged somewhere most of his rivals could not imagine.

There is a temptation, in telling the story of a man like Tramiel, to draw a neat moral line from the camps to the boardroom, to say that Auschwitz made him hard and the hardness made him rich. It is a temptation worth resisting, and Tramiel himself resisted it. He rarely spoke of his wartime past in business settings and warned against reducing his life to a tidy parable; the connection between his history and his methods is better understood as something he occasionally acknowledged than something a biographer should overstate. What is beyond dispute is the philosophy he preached and practiced, and the results it produced. By the end of 1981 Commodore had transformed itself from a struggling calculator company into the vanguard of a new market, the home computer, a machine cheap enough to buy on impulse and powerful enough to do real work and play real games.

The war would eventually consume even the warrior. Within a few years Tramiel's relentlessness would collide with Commodore's own chairman, the financier Irving Gould, in a boardroom struggle Tramiel lost; in early 1984, at the very peak of his triumph, he walked out of the company he had built. He did not retire to nurse his wounds. He bought the ailing home-computer division of Atari from Warner Communications and rechristened it Atari Corporation, and from that new perch he turned his guns on Commodore itself, so that the great rivalry of the late 1980s—Commodore's Amiga against Atari's ST—was in truth a war between Jack Tramiel and the ghost of his own former company. For a man who believed that business was combat, it was a fitting third act: to be exiled from his empire and immediately begin another with which to besiege it.

The world Tramiel built has not vanished; it simply changed its address. The logic he pioneered—own the pieces no one else can make, drive the price toward the cost of the raw materials, sell in volumes that stagger the imagination, and let scale crush anyone who has to buy what you make yourself—is the logic that governs the technology industry to this day. When a modern company designs its own processors rather than buying them, so that it can undercut rivals who must pay a supplier, it is running Jack Tramiel's playbook, whether or not it has ever heard his name. The relentless downward march of the price of computing power, the assumption that this year's marvel will be next year's bargain, the idea that a genuinely powerful computer should cost no more than an ordinary household appliance—all of it was proven first in the trenches of the home-computer war that a survivor of the camps waged in the early 1980s. Every cheap, capable device you have ever bought on impulse is a distant descendant of his creed.

By the end of 1981 the VIC-20 had opened the door to the living room, and Tramiel could see through it to the enormous market waiting beyond. What he intended to send through that door next would exploit every advantage he owned—the chip factory, the mass-market channels, the willingness to wage a price war to the death—and it would become the best-selling computer the world had ever seen, the weapon with which he would drive Texas Instruments and his other rivals out of the business entirely.

That machine had a name that would echo through millions of living rooms, and it was called the Commodore 64.

Chapter 41: The Commodore 64

In January 1982, on the crowded floor of the Winter Consumer Electronics Show in Las Vegas, Commodore's engineers unveiled a machine that they had built, in a very real sense, out of the spare parts of ambition. It was a low beige wedge of a computer with a full keyboard, and its name was stamped on the case in the plainest terms the marketing department could devise: the Commodore 64, so called for its sixty-four kilobytes of memory, a figure that in 1982 sounded almost extravagant. The engineers who had produced it, a small team working under punishing deadlines back in California, had done so in a matter of months. They had persuaded management that the leftover chip designs sitting in the lab could be combined into something extraordinary, and they were right. The machine they demonstrated in Las Vegas would go on to sell in numbers that no single computer model has ever matched, and it would eventually take its place in the Guinness World Records as the best-selling single computer model of all time.

The secret of the Commodore 64 lay in two custom chips, both born from the vertical-integration strategy that let Commodore's own MOS Technology division cook up silicon that rivals could only dream of buying. The first was the VIC-II, a video chip that gave the machine sixteen colors and, crucially, hardware sprites, small movable graphic objects that the computer could slide around the screen without laboriously redrawing the entire picture. To grasp why this mattered, imagine a programmer who wants a spaceship to glide across a starfield. Without sprites he would have to erase and repaint every affected pixel, dozens of times a second, a task that would bring an early home computer to its knees. The VIC-II instead let him define the ship once, as a small grid of dots, hand its shape to the chip, and then simply update a pair of numbers, an x-coordinate and a y-coordinate, to move it anywhere on screen. The hardware did the rest. Sprites were what made arcade-style games possible on a home machine, and the VIC-II handed them to programmers almost for free.

The second chip was the true marvel, and it came from Bob Yannes, a young engineer who happened to be an electronic-music hobbyist and who was frustrated that computer sound in 1982 amounted to feeble beeps. Yannes led a tiny group, himself, two technicians, and a computer-aided-design operator, that designed and finished the chip in roughly five months over the latter half of 1981. He built the SID, the Sound Interface Device, not like a toy but like a real synthesizer, with three independent voices, filters, and the ADSR envelope controls, attack, decay, sustain, release, found in professional electronic instruments. Yannes hoped the chip would one day find its way into serious polyphonic synthesizers, and he cared so much about the idea that within a year he had left Commodore to co-found the synthesizer company Ensoniq. He later remarked, with an engineer's mixture of pride and irritation, that most of the people who wrote software for the machine had no real idea what to do with his chip. The best of them, though, understood it perfectly, and the music they coaxed out of that little sliver of silicon became a genre unto itself, the chiptune, whose pulsing melodies still evoke an entire era for those who grew up hearing them.

There is a revealing detail buried in how the machine came

to exist at all, one that overturns the natural assumption that a computer is designed first and its parts chosen afterward. In the case of the Commodore 64 the order was reversed. The VIC-II and the SID were conceived first, as a cutting-edge chipset that Commodore's MOS Technology engineers hoped to sell to other manufacturers for use in games and graphics terminals. It was only after the chips existed that management resolved to build a computer around them, and the team then assembled the entire machine in a frantic sprint of a few months to have a working unit ready for the January 1982 show. The Commodore 64, in other words, was a home for two brilliant chips that had gone looking for a purpose, an object assembled at speed to exploit silicon that already existed. That it worked as well as it did, and sold as it did, owed as much to luck and haste as to any grand plan.

But chips do not sell computers; prices do, and here Jack Tramiel's philosophy did its work with characteristic violence. The Commodore 64 launched at a suggested price around five hundred and ninety-five dollars, already aggressive, and Tramiel drove it down relentlessly from there, until within a couple of years the machine could be had for around two hundred dollars. Because Commodore manufactured its own chips, it could sustain those cuts while competitors bled. Tramiel understood something that the makers of finer, costlier machines refused to accept: that at a low enough price, a computer stopped being a considered purchase and became an impulse, a thing a parent bought because the neighbor's kids had one. So he sold it not only through computer stores but through the aisles of Kmart, through department stores and toy stores, right beside the board games and the bicycles. A family that had come to the store for Christmas presents could walk out with a real computer, and millions of them did.

The man who drove that strategy was among the most improbable figures in the history of technology, and his life explains a great deal about the company he ran. Jack

Tramiel had been born Idek Trzmiel in Poland in 1928, and as a teenager he had survived the Auschwitz concentration camp, where he was examined by the notorious Josef Mengele and selected for a labor party, before being liberated from a satellite camp by American soldiers in 1945. A man who had endured that did not frighten easily in a boardroom, and he ran Commodore with a survivor's flint. It was Tramiel who coined the slogan that became the company's creed and, in a sense, the motto of the whole home-computer age, that the industry should build "computers for the masses, not the classes." He had proven the idea before the Commodore 64 ever existed, with a humbler predecessor called the VIC-20, a cheaper and less capable machine that in 1982 became the first computer of any kind to sell more than a million units. The VIC-20 taught Tramiel that the mass market was real and enormous; the Commodore 64 was his instrument for conquering it.

What they brought home was a machine of genuine capability wrapped in an almost comically humble package. The Commodore 64 booted, as its predecessors had, straight into a version of the BASIC programming language, greeting its owner with a flashing cursor and a readiness to obey typed commands. For a great many children of the early 1980s this blinking cursor was the first thing a computer ever said to them, an open invitation and a small intimidation both. They fed it programs from cassette tapes that loaded with excruciating slowness, or later from the notoriously sluggish 1541 disk drive, a device so slow that programmers wrote whole utilities simply to speed it up. The incantation to load a program from disk, typed exactly, was LOAD "*",8,1, a small piece of arcane knowledge that an entire generation memorized before they had memorized their own phone numbers, and then they waited, watching the screen, while the drive chattered and the game inched into memory. The machine's manual taught BASIC directly, on the assumption that owning a computer meant learning to program it, and for a time that assumption held.

That agonizing slowness became, improbably, a part of the machine's culture. The 1541 disk drive was so sluggish, in part because of a hardware flaw that Commodore had patched over with clumsy software, that loading a single game could take minutes, and an entire cottage industry sprang up to fix it. Programmers wrote "fast loaders," small utilities and cartridges that reorganized the way data moved between disk and computer and could cut a load time by a factor of five or more, and these became prized possessions, traded and admired. The waiting itself entered the folklore, so that a generation of former Commodore owners can still summon, unbidden, the specific rhythm of the drive's chatter and the flashing border that signaled a program creeping into memory. It was in this thrifty, patient, faintly obsessive environment that the machine's users learned to treat their computer not as an appliance but as a puzzle to be understood and outwitted.

Yet what truly made the Commodore 64 immortal was not programming but play. The combination of the VIC-II's sprites and the SID's music made it a formidable games machine, and software houses poured out titles by the thousands. Games arrived on cassette and cartridge and floppy disk, some of them brilliant and many of them shoddy, sold in blister packs and by mail order and, increasingly, copied from friend to friend in a gray economy of duplicated tapes that both cannibalized sales and spread the machine's reach. The library grew to a size no rival could match, thousands upon thousands of titles, and the sheer breadth of software became a self-reinforcing engine. People bought the machine because it had the games; developers made the games because so many people had the machine. This virtuous circle, the same network effect that would later define the software industry, propelled the Commodore 64 far past every competitor.

Around the machine there grew an ecosystem so dense that it became a small economy of its own. Dedicated magazines, thick with type-in program listings, reviews, and letters, arrived monthly and were read cover to cover; the best-known American title devoted to Commodore machines counted its circulation in the hundreds of thousands at its peak. User groups met in libraries and church halls to swap tips and disks. Mail-order houses shipped software in padded envelopes to farmhouses and suburbs alike, and the machine found its way not only into bedrooms but into small businesses, where it kept the books, and into schools, where it taught. This thick surrounding culture of print and community was itself part of the product, a support structure that made the bare machine far more useful and far more beloved than its modest specifications could explain, and it deepened the loyalty that kept owners buying Commodore software long after flashier rivals had appeared.

How far, exactly, has become one of the pleasant arguments of computing history, and it is worth pausing to correct a figure that has been repeated so often it has calcified into fact. Commodore's own executives, never shy about a big number, claimed at various times that the machine sold as many as seventeen million units, and in later years the figure sometimes crept as high as thirty million in casual retellings. Those larger numbers are almost certainly inflated, the product of a company famous for chaotic and self-serving bookkeeping. Researchers who have gone back through what records survive tend to settle on a more sober range, something on the order of twelve and a half to seventeen million machines over the roughly twelve years the model stayed in production. The precise total will never be known. But whichever end of that range is closer to the truth, the conclusion is the same and it is not seriously disputed: the Commodore 64 is the best-selling single computer model of all time, a record that has stood for four decades and shows no sign of falling. No individual model, before or since, has put itself into so many hands.

Part of what those numbers concealed was the strangeness of the achievement. The Commodore 64 was not the best-designed machine of its era. Its BASIC was primitive, its disk drive was a joke, its case was ugly, and its own creators complained that software authors squandered the hardware. It succeeded because Tramiel had understood the market with a clarity that eluded more elegant minds. He had built a good-enough computer, priced it where ordinary people could reach it, sold it where ordinary people already shopped, and then sustained a price war that his rivals could not survive. The machine that resulted was less a triumph of engineering than a triumph of will and manufacturing, a mass-produced marvel that carried computing across the threshold into the homes of the working and middle classes on precisely the terms its maker had promised, computers for the masses and not the classes.

The most enduring legacy of that humble wedge, oddly enough, may be the one its makers valued least. Bob Yannes's SID chip, dismissed by the software authors who misused it, turned out to have a voice so distinctive that it never really died. Decades after the last Commodore 64 rolled off the line, musicians were still writing new compositions for the chip, still gathering at festivals to perform music made on original hardware, still building software emulators and synthesizer plug-ins that reproduce its warm, buzzing, slightly out-of-tune character for use in modern recordings. The chiptune aesthetic that grew up around it now surfaces everywhere, in the soundtracks of independent video games, in the deliberately retro production of pop records, in the ringtones and jingles that borrow its unmistakable timbre. When you hear a piece of new music that sounds gloriously like an old video game, you are very likely hearing the descendants of a chip that three people and a design operator finished in five months, in 1981, because one of them was a frustrated hobby musician who wanted a computer to sing.

Its success, however, was unfolding against a darkening sky, for at the very moment the Commodore 64 was conquering American living rooms, the industry that had first taught those living rooms to love the screen, the home video game business, was hurtling toward a catastrophe that would reshape everything.

Chapter 42: The Great Video Game Crash

In September 1983, a fleet of trucks rolled up to the municipal landfill outside Alamogordo, New Mexico, and began unloading crushed cartridges, circuit boards, and consoles by the tens of thousands. Local reporters watched as the material was dumped into a pit, flattened, and eventually sealed under a layer of concrete and earth. The Atari corporation, headquartered a thousand miles away in California, confirmed only that it was disposing of unsold merchandise from a warehouse in nearby El Paso. In the years that followed, the burial hardened into legend. It was said that Atari had secretly interred millions of copies of a single game, an infamously bad adaptation of the film *E.T. the Extra-Terrestrial*, entombing its greatest failure in the desert where no one would ever find it. For three decades the story was dismissed by many as an urban myth, too tidy and too symbolic to be real. Then, in the spring of 2014, a documentary crew working under a permit from the city, backed by Microsoft's Xbox studio, obtained access to the site and began to dig. On April 26, before a crowd of onlookers, the diggers pulled from the sand exactly what the legend had promised: crushed *E.T.* cartridges, along with copies of *Pac-Man* and dozens of other titles. The myth was true. Atari really had buried its dead in the desert.

Yet even the truth needs correcting, because the popular version exaggerates. Atari did not bury millions of copies of *E.T.* alone. James Heller, the Atari manager who oversaw the 1983 operation and returned to watch the excavation, put the total at around 728,000 cartridges of many different games, of which the *E.T.* copies were only a portion. The burial was never a secret cover-up of a single humiliation; it was a routine act of warehouse clearance, a company dumping dead inventory to reclaim shelf space and write off a loss. What made it legendary was less the deed than the symbolism, for the pit outside Alamogordo happened to be the perfect image for something far larger and far more frightening that was happening to the entire industry. The burial was the picture. The collapse was the story, and it deserves to be understood on its own terms rather than reduced to a single ill-fated cartridge.

Through the late 1970s and into the early 1980s, the home video game console business had grown at a pace that intoxicated everyone touching it. Atari's Video Computer System, later called the 2600, had turned the plastic game cartridge into one of the most profitable products in American retail. Where there is that much money, imitators swarm, and swarm they did. Dozens of companies, some of them serious and many of them opportunistic, flooded the market with cartridges for the 2600 and for a growing thicket of competing consoles. The problem was that almost no one was minding the quality. Atari, in particular, exercised little control over what third parties published for its machine, and the shelves filled with games that ranged from mediocre to unplayable. When the number of titles multiplied faster than the number of players, the market began to choke on its own abundance.

The flood of games had an origin worth understanding, because it began not in cynicism but in a genuine grievance about fairness. In 1979 four of Atari's most talented programmers, David Crane, Alan Miller, Larry Kaplan, and Bob Whitehead, grew furious that the company refused to put their names on the games they created or to pay them in any proportion to how well those games sold; a programmer who had written a title generating tens of millions of dollars earned the same modest salary as one whose game flopped. When management dismissed their complaints, the four walked out and, with a record-industry executive named Jim Levy, founded Activision, the first company in history to make and sell games for a console it did not manufacture. Activision proved that an independent studio could get rich publishing cartridges for someone else's machine, and its success threw the doors open. Where Atari had wanted to keep the game business to itself, it now faced a stampede of third-party publishers, some as gifted as Activision and many merely opportunistic, all racing to pour cartridges onto the same finite shelves. The very act of creative rebellion that had produced some of the era's best games also helped, in time, to drown the market in its worst ones.

Two products came to symbolize the rot, both released by Atari itself in 1982. The first was a home version of the arcade smash *Pac-Man*, rushed to market and so poorly executed that the beloved characters flickered and the gameplay felt broken; Atari nonetheless manufactured cartridges in numbers that exceeded the entire installed base of consoles, betting that the game would sell machines rather than the other way around. In effect the company printed twelve million copies of a game for a world that owned perhaps ten million machines to play it on, a wager that assumed every existing owner would buy it and millions of newcomers would arrive to buy the rest. The second symbol was *E.T.*, for which Atari had paid an enormous licensing fee and then handed a single programmer, Howard Scott Warshaw, roughly five and a half weeks to design and build the entire game before the holiday season, where a normal project of the era might have taken six to nine months. Warshaw was a gifted developer who had made one of Atari's best titles, but no one could have delivered a polished game in that span. The result was a strange, confusing thing in which the alien spent much of his time falling into deep pits and clambering laboriously out of them, an experience that frustrated the children who had loved the film. It too was manufactured in quantities wildly out of proportion to demand. Millions of unsold cartridges piled up in warehouses. Retailers, burned by the glut, slashed prices, and consumers, burned by one bad game after another, began to conclude that home video games were a fad not worth the money. Confidence, the invisible substance on which every consumer market floats, evaporated, and once it was gone no price cut could summon it back, because a shopper who has decided that an entire category of product is junk stops looking at the shelf altogether.

What followed in 1983 was less a slump than a rout, and the numbers are worth stating plainly because they are so extreme they sound exaggerated. Home video game revenue in North America peaked at roughly three and a fifth billion dollars in 1983 and then collapsed to around a hundred million dollars by 1985, a fall of almost ninety-seven percent in two years. An industry had, in effect, evaporated. Some of the giants of the moment collapsed entirely or fled the business. Warner Communications, which owned Atari, watched the division's losses balloon so catastrophically that they dragged down the parent company's stock and forced a humiliating reckoning. Analysts and journalists wrote obituaries for the entire concept of the home video game. In North America, the console business as an industry very nearly ceased to exist, and for a time the very phrase *video game* became commercially toxic, a label that retailers and analysts alike treated as the name of a fad that had died.

The way the console eventually returned is a study in how thoroughly the crash had poisoned the well. When Nintendo brought its Famicom to America, it did not dare call it a game console or sell it through the toy-and-electronics channels that had collapsed. It rebuilt the machine's very identity, renaming it the Nintendo Entertainment System, styling it in gray to resemble a piece of home-stereo equipment rather than a toy, and bundling it at first with a small robot accessory so that skeptical retailers would file it under gadgets rather than the discredited category of video games. Nintendo test-marketed this cautious package in New York late in 1985 before rolling it out across the country in 1986. And it made certain never to repeat Atari's fatal mistake of letting anyone publish anything: it built a lockout chip into the hardware so that unauthorized cartridges simply would not run, stamped approved games with an official "Seal of Quality," and strictly limited how many titles each licensed publisher could release in a year. The tight, top-down control that defines the console business to this day was, in a very direct sense, Nintendo's considered answer to the chaos it had watched consume its predecessors.

But here the story turns, because the crash did not destroy the appetite for interactive entertainment; it merely redirected it. Millions of players who had lost faith in the flimsy single-purpose console looked at the alternative sitting increasingly within reach on department store shelves, and the alternative was the home computer. A machine like the Commodore 64 could play games every bit as good as a console's, thanks to its sprites and its sound chip, and it could do so much more besides. It ran a programming language, wrote school reports, balanced a checkbook, and taught its owner something in the bargain. To a parent who had just watched a hundred dollars of game cartridges become worthless, a real computer that happened to play games looked like the wiser purchase, an investment in the future rather than a toy destined for the closet. The very glut that killed the console handed the home computer its audience, and the Commodore 64, with its unmatched game library, absorbed that audience more completely than any rival.

Jack Tramiel, watching the carnage from Commodore's headquarters, saw not a tragedy but an opportunity, and he pursued it with the ferocity that was his trademark. His chosen target was Texas Instruments, the vast semiconductor conglomerate that had entered the home computer market with a machine called the TI-99/4A. Texas Instruments was in almost every respect a more formidable company than Commodore, larger, richer, and technologically deeper. But it had made a fatal miscalculation. Its machine was expensive to build, it tried to lock third-party software makers out so that it could keep the profitable game business for itself, and its executives had no stomach for the kind of gutter fighting at which Tramiel excelled. Tramiel, owning his own chip foundry, simply drove the price of the Commodore 64 down and down, forcing Texas Instruments to match him or lose the sale. Texas Instruments matched him, and matched him again, until it was selling its computers at a loss on every unit. A company built to profit from making chips found itself losing money on every machine it sold, hemorrhaging cash quarter after quarter in a war of attrition it could not win.

In October 1983, in the depths of the crash, Texas Instruments surrendered. It announced that it was withdrawing entirely from the home computer business, taking a loss of hundreds of millions of dollars and abandoning the field to Commodore. It was exactly the outcome Tramiel had engineered. He had used his ownership of the silicon as a bludgeon, exactly as he had promised himself he would after the calculator wars of the previous decade, and he had driven a company many times Commodore's size out of the market through sheer pricing brutality. For Tramiel it was the fullest vindication of his creed that business was war and that the point of war was to win. The crash that had ruined Atari and terrified the industry had, for Commodore, been a season of conquest.

The man at the center of the legend found his own kind of peace with it. Howard Scott Warshaw, the programmer handed five and a half impossible weeks to build *E.T.*, had also made two of the Atari 2600's most admired games, *Yars' Revenge* and an adaptation of *Raiders of the Lost Ark*, and he never quite deserved the scapegoat's role that history assigned him. After the crash swept him out of the industry,

Warshaw eventually retrained and built an entirely new career as a licensed psychotherapist in Silicon Valley, counseling, among others, the engineers and entrepreneurs of the very technology world that had once chewed him up. That the author of the game blamed for an industry's collapse spent his later life helping technologists manage failure and anxiety is a coda too neat for fiction, and yet it is true. He came, in time, to speak about the whole affair with humor, even titling a memoir around the idea that he had made history by killing an industry.

There is a strange and gentle epilogue to the affair that the men of 1983 could never have foreseen. The cartridges pulled from the New Mexico sand in 2014 did not go back into a pit. They were cleaned, catalogued, and sold to collectors, and a handful were donated to museums, so that a recovered *E.T.* cartridge, dirt still clinging to its casing, now sits in the collection of the Smithsonian's National Museum of American History, and another resides at The Henry Ford museum in Michigan. The single worst-remembered artifact of the whole catastrophe, the game that came to stand for an industry's collective failure of judgment, has become a treasured relic, exhibited as a lesson about hubris and haste. It is a fitting resting place, for the crash it symbolizes was never really about one bad game. It was about what happens when an industry stops caring whether its products are any good, floods the world with them, and assumes that demand will forgive anything. The lesson was expensive, and it was learned.

Yet while the great crash and the price wars played out across North America, an entirely different home computing culture was flowering on the far side of the Atlantic, one that owed almost nothing to Jack Tramiel and produced a generation of machines, and programmers, all its own.

Chapter 43: A Kingdom Across the Sea

In the spring of 1980, a thin, balding, intensely opinionated Englishman named Clive Sinclair unveiled a computer that looked less like a machine than like an afterthought. The ZX80 was scarcely larger than a paperback book, weighed almost nothing, and wore a flat membrane keyboard printed onto its plastic surface rather than proper keys. It had a fraction of the memory of an American home computer, its display flickered and blanked whenever the machine did any real work, and it retailed, in kit form, for under a hundred pounds. To an American accustomed to the solid heft of an Apple II or the growing ubiquity of the Commodore machines, the ZX80 might have seemed a joke. To Clive Sinclair it was a philosophy made manifest. He believed, with the fervor of a true zealot, that the price of a computer was the only thing that truly mattered, and he was willing to sacrifice nearly everything else, comfort, capability, durability, on the altar of cheapness. Where Jack Tramiel wanted computers for the masses at a low price, Sinclair wanted them at an almost impossibly low price, and in doing so he lit the fuse of a home computing boom that unfolded in Britain along lines the American story rarely bothers to record.

The reason the British story diverged is partly a matter of simple economics. American machines, burdened by import duties and shipping and the strength of the dollar, arrived on British shores expensive, often prohibitively so for an ordinary family. Into that gap poured a homegrown industry of cheap, clever, idiosyncratic machines, and Sinclair led the charge. The ZX80 gave way in 1981 to the ZX81, cheaper still and sold in enormous numbers through the post and through the shelves of the high-street chain W. H. Smith, putting a real computer into hundreds of thousands of British homes for the price of a few record albums. Then, in 1982, came the machine that would define a generation. The ZX Spectrum added color and sound, kept the price astonishingly low, and became the beating heart of British home computing, selling in the end more than five million units and outselling in its home market every more expensive rival, the Commodore 64 among them. Its rubber keyboard, mushy and beloved, and its garish clashing colors became as instantly recognizable to a British child of the 1980s as the flashing cursor of the Commodore 64 was to an American one.

Those clashing colors are worth dwelling on, because they illustrate how thoroughly the machine's limitations became its personality. To save precious memory, the Spectrum did not store a color for every individual dot on the screen. Instead it divided the display into a grid of small squares, each eight dots by eight, and allowed only two colors within any one square, one for the foreground and one for the background. When a programmer moved a sprite across the screen, a running man or a swooping alien, its colors would bleed and smear at the edges wherever it overlapped the wrong square, producing a shimmer that British players came to know as "color clash." A lesser culture might have hidden this defect. British programmers instead designed around it, drawing their games in bold single-colored shapes and deliberately arranging the action to keep the clashes graceful, so that an entire visual style, instantly identifiable decades later, grew directly out of a corner cut to save a few kilobytes.

But cheapness was only half of what made Britain different, for the country also produced a machine built on the opposite principle, and it did so with the imprimatur of the state broadcaster itself. In the early 1980s the British Broadcasting Corporation, alarmed that the nation was falling behind in the coming computer age, launched an ambitious project of public education called the Computer Literacy Project, complete with a television series meant to teach ordinary viewers what these machines were and how to command them. The BBC wanted a computer to anchor the series, a machine that would appear on screen and that viewers could buy to follow along, and it set demanding technical specifications. A small Cambridge company called Acorn Computers, founded by Chris Curry and the Austrian-born physicist Hermann Hauser, won the contract in a now-legendary scramble, its engineers reportedly working through the night to lash together a working prototype of their "Proton" design in a matter of days so that it would function when the broadcaster's men arrived to inspect it. The result, renamed the BBC Micro, was a sturdy, expensive, superbly engineered machine that became the computer of British classrooms. A whole generation of British schoolchildren learned their first programming not on a toy but on an Acorn, tied to a national television series, in an educational campaign that had no real equivalent in the United States.

The philosophical gulf between the Sinclair machines and the BBC Micro captured something essential about the texture of British home computing. It was, far more than the American variety, a programming culture. The American home computer, especially in the wake of the Commodore 64 and the video game crash, drifted quickly toward being a games machine that also happened to run BASIC. The British machines, cheaper and often technically constrained, arrived in an environment where software was scarce and expensive, where the state broadcaster was actively urging people to learn to code, and where a thriving ecosystem of magazines treated programming as the whole point. Children who owned a Spectrum or a BBC Micro were far more likely to spend their evenings writing programs rather than merely playing them, and the culture around the machines reflected and reinforced that habit at every turn.

No single artifact captures that programming culture, and the extraordinary things it could wring from feeble hardware, better than a game called *Elite.* Written by two Cambridge students, David Braben and Ian Bell, and released for the BBC Micro in 1984, it was a space-trading adventure of staggering ambition: the player piloted a ship through a galaxy of more than two thousand planets, each with its own economy and politics, buying and selling cargo, fighting pirates, and rising through ranks toward the coveted status of "Elite." What made this miraculous was the machine it ran on. The BBC Micro had just thirty-two kilobytes of memory, less than the size of a short modern email, and there was no conceivable way to store two thousand fully described worlds in so little space. Braben and Bell solved the problem with a technique called procedural generation: instead of storing each planet, they stored a mathematical formula that could conjure a planet's name, position, and character on demand, the same seed number always producing the same world, so that an entire galaxy unfolded from a few lines of arithmetic. On top of this they layered wire-frame three-dimensional graphics, ships that rotated and loomed in convincing perspective, at a moment when most home-computer games were flat and static. *Elite* was ported to nearly every British machine, sold in the hundreds of thousands, and stands as perhaps the purest monument to what the constrained, code-obsessed British scene could achieve: a universe conjured out of almost nothing by two young men who understood their machine completely.

The competition among the British makers was ferocious and occasionally personal. The rivalry between Clive Sinclair and Acorn's Chris Curry, once friends and colleagues, curdled into open animosity, culminating in a famously undignified confrontation in a Cambridge pub, an episode later dramatized in a fondly remembered British television film as a parable of the whole boom. Into this fray, in the mid-1980s, strode a third figure with a temperament closer to Jack Tramiel's than to either Sinclair's or Curry's. Alan Sugar, a blunt, self-made East London entrepreneur who had built his company Amstrad selling cheap hi-fi equipment, brought to computing the same mass-market ruthlessness that had made him rich. Amstrad's home computer, the CPC, was sold as a complete package with its own monitor, sparing the buyer the fiddly business of connecting the machine to a television, and it sold briskly to families who wanted something that simply worked out of the box. Sugar had no romance about technology whatsoever; he wanted to sell boxes to ordinary people at a profit, and he insisted that his job was not to lead the market with clever engineering but to give ordinary buyers what they actually wanted at a price they would actually pay. And he did. In April 1986, in a deal that closed the first great chapter of British home computing, he bought Sinclair's entire computer product range and the Sinclair brand name for five million pounds, absorbing his rival's most famous products into his own empire and leaving Clive Sinclair, the visionary who had started it all, to turn his restless energies toward other, less fortunate inventions. Chief among these was the Sinclair C5, a low-slung, single-seat electric tricycle launched in early 1985 that Sinclair had convinced himself would revolutionize personal transport. It became instead one of the most famous product failures in British history, ridiculed for leaving its driver at exhaust-pipe height in traffic and useless in cold or rain, and it was withdrawn within months, a humiliation that helped push its inventor's computer business into Sugar's waiting arms. That the same restless mind produced both the machine that launched a nation's love affair with computing and one of its most mocked commercial disasters says something true about the era's inventors, who were visionaries and gamblers in equal measure.

The boom was never confined to Britain, and the continental variations on the theme are among the most overlooked chapters of the whole revolution. Alan Sugar's Amstrad machines became runaway successes in France and Spain, markets the American giants had largely neglected, and in Germany they sold under a different badge entirely, as Schneider computers, tailored to local tastes and distribution. A separate standard called MSX, backed by Microsoft and a Japanese partner, tried to do for home computers what the VHS format had done for video recorders, defining a common specification that many manufacturers could build to; it never caught on in Britain or America but became genuinely popular in Japan, the Netherlands, Spain, Brazil, and parts of the Middle East, each country developing its own catalogue of software and its own fond memories. The map of 1980s home computing, in other words, looks nothing like the American-centered story usually told. It is a patchwork of national scenes, each with its favored machine, its own magazines, its own bedroom programmers, and its own games that never crossed a border, a genuinely global phenomenon unfolding in a dozen languages at once.

This British and broader European boom, encompassing not only these machines but a scattering of continental rivals, unfolded on a scale that surprised those who imagined the personal computer as a purely American creation. That image is worth correcting, because for a few intense years the ownership of home computers per household in Britain rivaled or even exceeded that of the United States, and the machines saturated the culture in a way that left a permanent mark. The personal computer revolution was never a story told in a single accent. It was being lived, simultaneously and quite differently, in the terraced houses of Manchester and the tower blocks of Paris and the flats of West Berlin, and the machines that carried it there were homegrown, cheap, and strange.

The most extraordinary consequence of all this was hidden inside the Cambridge company that had built the BBC Micro. Acorn's engineers, wanting a faster and more elegant processor for their next generation of machines and unable to find one they liked, decided to design their own from scratch. They called it the Acorn RISC Machine, and it was built on a philosophy of ruthless simplicity, a chip that did fewer things but did them with astonishing efficiency and sipped so little power that early test units ran correctly even when, by one celebrated account, their power supply was accidentally disconnected and they kept working on the trickle of current leaking through the rest of the circuit. That processor, later renamed simply ARM, went on to become the most widely manufactured computer chip design in the history of the world, and it did so precisely because of the frugality bred into its makers by years of squeezing performance out of cheap British hardware; a chip that sipped power was a chip born of a culture that had never been able to afford waste. Its descendants sit today inside almost every smartphone on the planet, inside tablets and smart televisions and countless small devices, tens of billions of them shipped and counting. The little Cambridge outfit that made the computer of British classrooms had, almost as a side project, designed the brain of the modern mobile age. And the educational mission of the BBC Micro itself never entirely died; decades later, a group of Cambridge engineers, several of them raised on those very machines, would build the Raspberry Pi, a tiny, cheap computer created expressly to teach children to program again, a deliberate and self-conscious heir to the culture this chapter describes.

Yet the very features that made the British scene distinctive, the extreme cheapness, the emphasis on learning to program, the constrained and quirky hardware, also planted seeds whose harvest would prove larger still. The British and European market was fragmented, its hardware was often feeble, and much of the software that ran on it was made not by great companies but by individuals, frequently teenagers, working alone in their bedrooms with a manual, a cassette recorder, and an ocean of time. Out of those bedrooms, in Britain and across Europe and in America too, was rising a generation of self-taught programmers whose obsessions would seed a global industry, and it is to those bedroom coders that the story now turns.

Chapter 44: The Bedroom Coders

On a rainy afternoon somewhere in the north of England, sometime in 1983, a boy of perhaps twelve sat cross-legged on his bedroom floor with a magazine open across his knees and a home computer glowing on the desk above him. The magazine was one of dozens then crowding the newsstands, and its middle pages were given over to something that would baffle a later generation raised on app stores: a program printed in full, line by numbered line, thousands of characters of BASIC code that the reader was expected to type into the computer by hand. The boy typed. He typed for an hour, then two, hunched and squinting, transcribing every semicolon and every cryptic string of numbers, and when at last he ran the program it did not work, because somewhere in those thousands of keystrokes he had made a single error. So he began the maddening work of finding it, comparing his typing against the printed listing character by character, and in the course of that miserable debugging he learned, without ever intending to, how the program actually worked. This was how a generation learned to code. Not in classrooms, though some of them had those too, but on bedroom floors, from magazine listings and manuals, one infuriating bug at a time.

The home computers of the early 1980s were almost

uniquely suited to breed this kind of self-education, because they refused to hide themselves. When a Commodore 64 or a Sinclair Spectrum switched on, it did not present a friendly desktop of icons; it presented a programming language and a blinking cursor, an invitation and a challenge in one. To do anything at all, a child had at minimum to type commands, and the manuals that came in the box taught not merely how to operate the machine but how to program it, on the unquestioned assumption that owning a computer and coding it were the same activity. Software arrived on cassette tape, loaded with a shriek of static and a wait of many minutes during which the screen strobed with hypnotic bars of color, and the tapes could be copied, traded, and pirated with an ease that horrified publishers and delighted children. In this thrifty, hands-on, faintly lawless ecosystem, the line between using software and making it was thin, and countless young people crossed it without quite noticing.

The scale of what resulted was astonishing and is easily underestimated. This was not a handful of prodigies but something closer to a folk movement. By the end of 1983 in Britain, more than four hundred and fifty companies were selling games on cassette, up from around ninety-five only a year earlier, and estimates of the number of young people writing games at home in that period run from ten thousand to fifty thousand, overwhelmingly teenage boys. A great many of them sold their creations for real money, mailing cassettes in plastic bags, advertising in the backs of magazines, and occasionally getting rich. The most famous of them was Matthew Smith, a seventeen-year-old from Wallasey on the Wirral, who in 1983 spent roughly eight weeks writing a platform game called *Manic Miner* for the ZX Spectrum. It was, among other distinctions, the first Spectrum game to play music continuously during the action rather than in silence, a small technical triumph on a machine never built for it, and it made its teenage author unexpectedly wealthy.

Smith's story also supplies a perfect illustration of how raw and unforgiving this craft could be, and it corrects a small legend along the way. His follow-up, *Jet Set Willy,* released in 1984, shipped in a state that made it impossible to complete. The cause was a genuine and fascinating programming error: in one room, called The Attic, an arrow object was set moving along a path that carried its sprite clean past the end of the region of memory the Spectrum used for the screen, so that it began overwriting the very data that described the rest of the game's rooms, corrupting them into instant-death traps and empty voids. When players complained, the publisher, Software Projects, at first tried to brazen it out, insisting that the ruined, deadly rooms were an intentional feature, filled with invisible poison gas. It was not true, and the company soon admitted as much, publishing in the computer magazines a set of POKE commands, short lines that a player typed in to alter specific bytes in memory, that patched the bug by hand and finally let the game be finished. That a beloved commercial product could ship broken, be defended with a fib, and then be repaired by its own customers typing corrections into memory tells you almost everything about the intimacy and informality of the era. As for Smith himself, the strain of that fame seemed to swallow him. He retreated from the industry and, by the end of the decade, from public life altogether, becoming a genuine mystery; for years a website titled "Where is Matthew Smith?" collected rumored sightings, one placing him among tulip fields in the Netherlands, until he resurfaced at last, gently amused by the fuss, on a stage at a games festival in Nottingham in February 2005.

To understand how ordinary this extraordinary education had become, it helps to picture the machinery of the magazine culture that fed it. The newsstands of the early 1980s groaned under specialist titles, and their business model was, in retrospect, astonishing: they printed working software as text, page after page of it, and readers paid to type it in. A single listing might run to several pages of dense code, and to guard against the inevitable typing errors, some magazines printed alongside each line a "checksum," a short code that a companion program would calculate from what the reader had typed so that a mismatch would flag the exact line where a mistake had crept in. Whole afternoons vanished into this ritual. The reward, when it finally ran, might be a crude game or a simple utility that a child could have bought on tape for a pound, but the point was never really the program. The point, though almost no one framed it that way at the time, was the typing and the fixing, the slow forced march through someone else's logic that left the transcriber knowing, at the end, how the thing was built. It was an apprenticeship disguised as a hobby, and it was being served, simultaneously, by tens of thousands of children who thought they were merely playing.

Out of that same restless culture grew one of the strangest and most enduring artifacts of the era, the demoscene, and here too a common assumption needs correcting, for the demoscene did not begin as art. It began in the gray economy of software piracy. The groups who cracked the copy protection on games liked to sign their work, adding a short introductory screen, a "crack intro," before the game itself, boasting of their exploits with scrolling text and flashy graphics. Almost immediately the intros became a competition unto themselves, and then they detached from piracy altogether and became a pursuit in their own right. Young programmers, especially in Europe and above all in the Nordic countries and Germany, began writing "demos," pure showpieces of code whose only purpose was to make the machine do things its makers had never intended, cramming impossible numbers of moving objects onto the screen, coaxing unheard-of music from the SID chip, bending the strict hardware limits of the Commodore 64 and the Amiga until they seemed to break. They gathered at events called demoparties to compete, and they organized themselves into groups with cryptic names and fierce loyalties. The demoscene was, in a sense, computing as sport and as folk art, a subculture devoted to virtuosity for its own sake, and it flourishes still; parties with names like Assembly and Revision draw thousands of coders and artists to this day.

Music, in particular, became an unexpected showcase for this virtuosity, and it produced its own quiet celebrities. On the Commodore 64, composers such as Rob Hubbard and Martin Galway learned to drive Bob Yannes's SID chip so expertly that their soundtracks became reasons to buy games, and the brief tunes that played while a cassette loaded, once mere filler to mask the wait, turned into miniature compositions admired in their own right. A generation could hum these melodies decades later. That a piece of throwaway software written to occupy a child during a two-minute loading delay could become a cherished cultural artifaçt tells you how completely these young people had turned constraint into art, wringing beauty from chips and memory that their designers had considered barely adequate for beeps.

The machines these young people worshipped were themselves advancing, and in 1985 two arrived that redefined what a home computer could be. The first was the Amiga, a machine of startling sophistication conceived by a small team of engineers, championed for a time by Atari's old founder and then, in a twist thick with irony, brought to market by Commodore. Jack Tramiel, having finally lost control of the company he had built, had walked out of Commodore in 1984 and promptly bought Atari's consumer division, so that the two great rivals of American home computing found their leadership scrambled almost overnight. Tramiel's Atari answered the Amiga with the ST, a capable and cheaper machine that became beloved of musicians for its built-in support of the emerging MIDI standard, which let a computer control synthesizers and drum machines. The Amiga, for its part, possessed graphics and sound so far ahead of its rivals that it seemed to belong to a later decade, with custom chips that could juggle color and motion and multiple simultaneous tasks in ways that astonished everyone who saw it. It became the machine of video artists, of animators, of the demoscene's most ambitious wizards, a creative and multimedia instrument at a moment when most computers still thought in text.

What all of this amounted to, taken together, was a hidden apprenticeship for an entire industry that did not yet know it was being trained. The children who had typed in magazine listings and hunted for their own bugs, who had traded cracked tapes and studied demos and pushed cheap machines past their limits, were teaching themselves, informally and joyfully, the exact skills that a coming global business would require. The proof is written across the modern games industry in letters no one can miss. In the Scottish city of Dundee, a young man named David Jones, made redundant from the local Timex factory, spent his severance pay on an Amiga and, with a few friends still in their teens and early twenties, founded a studio called DMA Design in an office he later described as "one step up from bedroom coding." That studio made *Lemmings*, which sold some twenty million copies, and then went on to create *Grand Theft Auto*, and in time was renamed Rockstar North, the maker of one of the best-selling entertainment products of any kind in human history. The line runs unbroken from a bedroom in the 1980s to a global phenomenon: the very same skills, self-taught in the same way, carried across a single career.

DMA Design was not an isolated miracle but one instance of a pattern repeated across Britain. In Warwickshire, two teenage brothers named David and Richard Darling, sons of a games entrepreneur, had grown so prolific at writing games in their bedroom that they founded a company, Codemasters, to sell them, and built it into one of the most successful game publishers in Europe, a firm that endures to this day. Their business model was itself a distillation of the bedroom-coder ethos: cheap games, sold at pocket-money prices, many written by other teenagers recruited from the same scene, including a pair of identical twins, Andrew and Philip Oliver, whose *Dizzy* games sold in the millions. Team17, the studio that made the *Worms* series still played on phones today, likewise grew directly out of the demoscene. Look closely at the founding stories of the British and European games industry and the same shape appears again and again: a teenager, a cheap home computer, a manual, and no formal training whatsoever, followed a few years later by a real company employing dozens and then hundreds of people. An entire industrial sector had been seeded, without design or subsidy, by children teaching themselves in their bedrooms.

There is a bittersweet coda to the era, because the culture that produced the bedroom coder could not survive its own success. As computers grew more powerful and more polished, they also grew more sealed. The machines of the next generation would boot not into a programming language but into a graphical interface, a friendly and forbidding surface that invited the user to consume software rather than write it. Making a competitive game came to require teams and budgets that no lone teenager could muster, and the romance of the bedroom coder faded into nostalgia. Yet the generation it had raised did not vanish. It went to work, carrying into the professional world an intuitive intimacy with the machine that could only have been learned the way they had learned it, from the inside out, through the patient accumulated frustration of code that did not work until, one glorious keystroke at a time, it did.

The home computer had done something profound. It had put a programmable machine into millions of ordinary rooms and, in doing so, had quietly manufactured the human talent on which an entire future economy would depend. But even as those living rooms hummed with cheap computers and cassette games, the center of gravity of the whole revolution was shifting once more, away from the home and back toward the office, where a very different battle was gathering, a battle not over price or games but over the very way human beings would command their machines, fought with pictures and windows and pointing devices, and destined to make a software company in the Pacific Northwest the most powerful force in the industry the world had ever seen.

Chapter 45: Windows Before Windows

On the morning of November 10, 1983, in the ballroom of the Helmsley Palace Hotel in New York, Bill Gates stood before a crowd of reporters and industry analysts and made a promise he would spend the next two years failing to keep. Microsoft, he announced, was building a product called Windows: a graphical interface that would sit atop the plain, character-based world of MS-DOS and give ordinary IBM PCs the pictures, menus, and pointing device that until then had belonged to expensive research machines and a few Californian dreamers. He demonstrated overlapping rectangles on a screen, a mouse skittering across a desk, the promise of running several programs at once. He predicted the software would ship by the spring of 1984 and that it would run on the vast majority of the machines IBM and its imitators were selling. Both predictions were wrong. Windows would not ship for another two years, and when it finally did, almost nobody wanted it. But the announcement itself was the point. Gates had planted a flag on a piece of ground he did not yet control, and he would not abandon it for a decade.

The idea that computers should speak in images rather than in typed commands did not originate in Redmond, and it is worth dispelling at once the popular notion that Windows was where the graphical interface was born. It had been gestating for twenty years, in the work of Douglas Engelbart at the Stanford Research Institute, whose 1968 demonstration first showed a mouse steering a cursor through windows of text, and above all at Xerox's Palo Alto Research Center, where in the 1970s a generation of engineers built the Alto and the Star, machines that displayed a desktop of files and folders and let a user manipulate them by pointing. Xerox never turned these marvels into a commercial success. But in December 1979 a young Steve Jobs, having negotiated a deal that let Apple engineers tour PARC in exchange for a stake in Apple stock, walked out of the building convinced he had seen the future of computing, and he set Apple to work reproducing and refining what he had glimpsed. The result was the Lisa in 1983 and, more consequentially, the Macintosh in January 1984, whose crisp black-and-white desktop, pull-down menus, and single-button mouse made the graphical interface a mass-market product for the first time.

The obstacle that had defeated every graphical machine before the Macintosh was not vision but price, and the numbers from that lineage are startling. When Xerox finally tried to sell its research to the world as the Star office system in 1981, a single workstation cost more than sixteen thousand dollars, and a useful installation of several machines and a printer ran well into six figures; almost no one bought it. Apple's own first attempt, the Lisa of 1983, a beautiful graphical computer that was in many ways the Macintosh's older sibling, carried a price near ten thousand dollars and flopped commercially for the same reason. Douglas Engelbart's original 1968 demonstration in San Francisco, later christened "the Mother of All Demos," had shown the mouse, the on-screen windows, and even video conferencing and hypertext links a full fifteen years before any of it reached a store, and it had required a room full of equipment worth a fortune to accomplish. The graphical interface, in other words, had been technically possible for two decades before it became affordable, and the entire commercial contest of the 1980s was really a race to see who could deliver it on hardware an ordinary person or business could pay for. That framing is essential to understanding why Gates cared so much about the cheap, clone-built IBM PC rather than the elegant machines of Cupertino.

Gates watched all of this closely, and not from a distance. Microsoft was one of the earliest and most important developers of software for the Macintosh; its programmers had early prototypes of the machine in their offices in 1983 and 1984, and Microsoft's Multiplan spreadsheet and its Word processor were among the Mac's launch applications. Gates therefore understood the graphical interface intimately, and he had drawn from it a conviction that would organize the next fifteen years of his company's strategy: that the command line was a temporary condition, that graphics were not a luxury but the inevitable destination of personal computing, and that whoever owned the graphical layer on the IBM-compatible machines would own the industry. The impulse to build Windows had crystallized, by his own account, at the autumn 1982 COMDEX trade show, where he had seen a demonstration of VisiOn, a graphical environment being built by Visicorp, the company behind the pioneering VisiCalc spreadsheet. If someone else could put pictures on an IBM PC, Gates reasoned, then Microsoft had to be the one to do it first and best, for the alternative was to be boxed out of the future by a rival's standard.

The danger was real, because the field was already crowded, and here lies a fact that the triumphant later history of Windows tends to bury: for a while, Microsoft was losing the race. Visicorp shipped VisiOn in 1983. Digital Research, the firm that had lost the operating-system prize to Microsoft when IBM chose MS-DOS, was building a slicker and cheaper alternative called GEM, and Digital Research got GEM into customers' hands in February 1985, beating the still-unfinished Windows to market by the better part of a year. GEM looked so much like the Macintosh, with its overlapping windows and animated flourishes, that Apple's lawyers descended on Digital Research and forced it to tear the offending elements out; the neutered GEM 2.0 that emerged in 1986 had its overlapping windows stripped away, a foreshadowing of a far larger legal storm to come. Quarterdeck had a multitasking environment called DESQview. IBM itself had a text-based windowing product called TopView. The trade press wrote of a "war of the windows," and in that war Microsoft's entry was the one that existed only in press releases and demonstrations.

The delay grew so notorious that Windows became the emblem of a brand-new insult. The word "vaporware," coined to describe software announced with fanfare but never quite delivered, attached itself to the product so firmly that, when Windows 1.0 was finally released, an industry columnist named Stewart Alsop of InfoWorld presented Gates with a mock trophy, a "Golden Vaporware" award, at the launch celebration, with the strains of "The Impossible Dream" playing in the background. The product had arrived roughly eighteen months after its promised date. The joke was affectionate, but it stung, because it was accurate.

When Windows 1.0 finally reached customers in November 1985, it was a disappointment that bordered on embarrassment. Rather than the overlapping windows Gates had shown in New York, the first version arranged its windows in a tiled mosaic, laid side by side like tiles on a floor so that none could cover another, because the underlying hardware and the constraints of memory made true overlapping too difficult and, some believed, because Microsoft wished to avoid provoking Apple. This is the detail most people get wrong when they picture the first Windows: it could not stack its windows the way a modern desktop does, and the signature behavior we now consider the whole point of the thing was simply absent. To understand how the product even functioned, one has to picture it not as an operating system but as a program that ran on top of one. A user still started the machine in MS-DOS, at the familiar C-prompt, and then typed a command to launch Windows, which spread itself across the screen using whatever scraps of memory DOS had left unclaimed. On the slow processors and limited memory of mid-1980s machines it felt sluggish and cramped, and there were almost no applications written to take advantage of it. Reviewers were unkind; buyers were indifferent. Windows 1.0 sold poorly and became, in the folklore of the industry, a byword for a promise made real and found wanting, the punchline to jokes that Gates had to endure for years before the last laugh became his. It is a useful reminder that the eventual titans of the technology world did not stride from triumph to triumph; they stumbled, shipped failures, and were mocked, and the difference between them and the companies that vanished was often nothing grander than a refusal to stop.

It is worth lingering on just how forbidding that first release was to actually buy and run, because it explains the indifference better than any review could. Windows 1.0 demanded, by the standards of 1985, a serious and expensive machine: a couple of floppy drives or a hard disk, a healthy allotment of memory, and a graphics card that many PCs of the day did not have, all to run an environment that offered little the user could not already do faster from the command line. The bundled programs were toys, a clock, a calculator, a simple painting program, a card file, and the small handful of serious applications written to exploit the system could be counted on one hand. A buyer was being asked to spend money and sacrifice speed for the privilege of looking at pictures, and in 1985 the pictures were not yet worth it. The tragedy, from Microsoft's point of view, was that the vision was entirely correct and merely early; the hardware had not yet fallen far enough in price or risen far enough in power to make the graphical dream feel like anything but a burden. Gates's genius, in the end, lay less in seeing the destination, which many saw, than in his willingness to keep marching toward it through two commercial failures and years of ridicule, funding a team that kept losing until, suddenly, the ground shifted beneath it and it won.

Windows 2.0, which arrived in the autumn of 1987, was a meaningful improvement. It brought the overlapping windows Gates had originally promised, allowing one window to sit atop another as papers might overlap on a desk, and it added support for the more capable memory-handling of the newer Intel processors. Microsoft's own applications, Excel and a graphical version of Word, began to give people a reason to run it. Yet even 2.0 remained a minority taste, a thin and often unstable veneer over an operating system that had never been designed to display pictures. The commercial reality of the late 1980s was that the graphical PC was still a promise rather than a fact, and the plain white-on-black C-prompt of DOS remained what most of the tens of millions of PC users saw when they switched on their machines.

The deeper drama of these years, however, was not Windows against GEM or VisiOn. It was Microsoft against IBM. When IBM had chosen MS-DOS in 1980, it had made Microsoft rich; but the two companies had grown into uneasy partners, and by the mid-1980s IBM wanted a next-generation operating system it could control. The result was a joint project called OS/2, announced in 1987 alongside IBM's new line of PS/2 computers, into which Microsoft poured enormous engineering effort. OS/2 was meant to be the serious, powerful successor to DOS, and its graphical shell, called Presentation Manager, was meant to be the future of the interface. The scale of Microsoft's commitment to OS/2 is easy to forget now that the project is a footnote, but at the time it was where the company's best and most numerous engineers were sent, and where its public rhetoric pointed. Gates told developers, in speech after speech, that OS/2 was the operating system of the future and that they should write their programs for it. For a time Gates publicly declared OS/2 the path forward and Windows a stopgap. But he hedged, ferociously. He kept the smaller Windows team alive and funded even as the larger OS/2 effort consumed his best programmers, because he did not trust IBM, and because he suspected that the light, cheap, DOS-compatible Windows might beat the heavy, expensive, hardware-hungry OS/2 in the only court that mattered, the marketplace of ordinary buyers running clone machines they had bought for a few hundred dollars. It was a bet placed against his own stated strategy, and it would prove to be the most valuable bet of his career.

That bet also carried a legal shadow. In 1985, in the midst of Microsoft's dependence on the Macintosh and its scramble to keep its own graphical ambitions alive, Gates had extracted from Apple's chief executive, John Sculley, a licensing agreement covering the visual elements of Windows 1.0. Apple, fearful that Microsoft might withhold its crucial Mac applications, had signed. The precise scope of that agreement, and whether it extended to the later and far more Mac-like Windows 2.0, would soon become the subject of one of the most consequential lawsuits in the history of software, a case that would ask whether the look and feel of a computer screen was something a company could own.

There is a small irony worth carrying forward from these clumsy early years, one that you meet every time you touch a screen today. The overlapping-window desktop that Windows 1.0 could not manage, that GEM was sued for imitating, that VisiOn and TopView and DESQview all reached for and mostly missed, has become so completely the default grammar of computing that it is invisible. The stack of windows on a laptop, the layered cards on a phone, the very metaphor of a "desktop" cluttered with overlapping documents, all of it descends from this crowded, litigious, half-failed moment when a dozen companies raced to be the one that taught the ordinary computer to show instead of tell. The winner of that race was not yet decided in 1987. But the shape of the prize was already clear, and Apple's lawyers were already drafting the complaint that would land in a California courtroom in the spring of 1988.

Chapter 46: Look and Feel

On March 17, 1988, lawyers for Apple Computer walked into the federal courthouse in San Jose, California, and filed a complaint that would occupy the courts for six years and would test a question no one had ever quite been forced to answer: can a company own the way a screen looks? The defendants were Microsoft and the Hewlett-Packard Company, which had shipped a graphical environment called NewWave that ran on top of Windows. But the real target was Windows 2.0, released the previous autumn, which to Apple's eyes had crossed a line the earlier version had not. Where Windows 1.0 had tiled its windows and kept a certain awkward distance from the Macintosh, Windows 2.0 let windows overlap and layer as they did on the Mac, and added the familiar visual furniture of icons and pull-down menus arranged in ways that felt, to Apple's engineers and executives, uncomfortably like a copy of their own creation. It is worth being precise about the accusation, because it is widely misremembered. Apple did not claim that Microsoft had stolen its code; the two programs were written independently and shared no lines of programming, and Apple never alleged otherwise. What Apple claimed was subtler and, in legal terms, far more novel. It claimed ownership of the look and feel, the total visual gestalt, of the Macintosh desktop.

The phrase look and feel had entered the vocabulary of software litigation only a few years earlier, and it carried an intuitive appeal that concealed a genuine legal difficulty. Copyright law protected the expression of an idea but not the idea itself. A novelist could copyright the particular words of a story but could not stop others from writing about star-crossed lovers; a mapmaker could protect a specific map but not the concept of a map. The trouble with a user interface was that it seemed to hover uneasily between expression and idea, between the protectable and the free. Was the image of a document as a rectangular window that could be dragged and resized a creative expression, like a paragraph of prose, or was it a functional idea, like the layout of a dashboard or the arrangement of pedals in an automobile, something that once invented ought to belong to everyone because it was simply the sensible way to solve a problem? Apple insisted on the former. Microsoft, and much of the software industry watching nervously from the sidelines, insisted on the latter, and warned that if Apple prevailed, the ordinary progress of software, in which each generation borrowed and improved upon the conventions of the last, would grind to a halt under a thicket of ownership claims over menus and buttons and windows.

The case turned, in the end, less on grand principle than on a document, and the story of that document is a small tragedy of corporate negotiation. In November 1985, as Microsoft prepared to ship Windows 1.0 and as Apple fretted that Microsoft might withhold the Macintosh versions of Word and Excel on which the young Mac depended, John Sculley, Apple's chief executive, had signed an agreement with Bill Gates. Under its terms Microsoft acknowledged that the visual displays in Windows 1.0 derived from Apple's, and in exchange Apple granted Microsoft a license to use those visual displays. An early draft prepared on Apple's side had tried to nail the limits down tightly, with language providing that the grant would at no time extend to any appearance, look, feel, or visual feature beyond what was already in that first, clumsy version of Windows. But that restrictive language did not survive into the signed agreement. Sculley and his advisers believed, or hoped, they were licensing only the specific and limited elements of Windows 1.0 and preserving Apple's right to object to anything more ambitious. Gates and his lawyers read the final agreement far more expansively, as a broad license to the visual displays as a class, one that would cover future versions of Windows as well. It was, in retrospect, a catastrophic negotiation for Apple, a moment when a company frightened of losing its most important applications had signed away, in ambiguous language of its own drafting, the very claim it would later try to assert. When Windows 2.0 appeared with its overlapping windows, Apple argued the 1985 license did not reach so far. Microsoft argued that it did.

The litigation ground on for years, and in its later and decisive phase it came before Judge Vaughn Walker of the Northern District of California, who subjected the case to a painstaking, almost surreal procedure. Rather than judge the Macintosh interface as a single artistic whole, as Apple wanted, the court broke it apart into its constituent pieces and examined each one on its own. Nearly two hundred individual visual elements were catalogued and interrogated in turn: this style of window, that arrangement of a menu, the way an icon opened, the behavior of a scroll bar. For each, the court asked a sequence of questions. Was this particular element already licensed to Microsoft under the 1985 agreement? If not, was it an unprotectable idea, or the only practical way to express a concept, and therefore beyond the reach of copyright under the doctrine that denies protection where an expression has merged with its function? And if it survived both of those filters, was it in fact similar enough to infringe? Piece by piece, the elements fell away. The great majority, the court found, were either covered by the license or were functional ideas that no one could own. By the time the analytic dissection was finished, Apple's sweeping claim to a total look and feel had been reduced to a small residue of disputed items, and the court held that even taken together they did not amount to infringement, because whatever overlap remained was largely licensed or unprotectable. In 1992 and 1993 Judge Walker issued the rulings that gutted Apple's case. In 1994 the United States Court of Appeals for the Ninth Circuit affirmed, and in 1995 the Supreme Court declined to hear a further appeal. Apple had lost, comprehensively.

There was a delicious irony hovering over the whole proceeding, one that the court did not need to resolve but that everyone in the industry understood. While Apple was insisting that Microsoft had stolen the look and feel of the Macintosh, Xerox, whose Palo Alto laboratory had actually invented most of the elements in dispute, watched from the wings. In 1989, in the midst of the litigation, Xerox filed its own lawsuit against Apple, essentially arguing that if anyone owned the graphical interface it was Xerox, since Apple had drawn so freely from the Star and the Alto during those famous visits to PARC a decade earlier. Xerox's suit was thrown out on technical grounds, largely because too much time had passed, but its very existence exposed the awkward foundation beneath Apple's claim. The company demanding ownership of the desktop metaphor had itself borrowed that metaphor from a research lab it had toured by arrangement. The "look and feel" wars were not a simple story of a thief and a victim; they were a tangle of borrowings stacked upon borrowings, each company having taken from the one before and then cried foul when the next took in turn. The courts, faced with this hall of mirrors, essentially concluded that the fundamental ideas of the interface were too basic and too useful to belong to anyone at all.

The defeat mattered far beyond the two companies. Had Apple won, the shape of the software industry would have been very different, for the ruling would have established that the arrangement of windows and icons and menus could be private property, and every developer of graphical software would have had to invent an interface from scratch or pay for the privilege of the familiar. Instead the courts had drawn a boundary that would prove durable:

the specific artwork of an icon might be protected, the exact code certainly was, but the underlying conventions of the graphical interface, the desktop metaphor and its grammar of pointing and clicking and dragging, belonged to no one. This was a doctrine of considerable consequence for competition. It meant that interfaces could be imitated so long as they were independently built, that users could carry their hard-won habits from one program to another without relearning, and that the graphical style pioneered at Xerox and popularized by Apple would become a common language rather than a walled garden. It was, depending on one's vantage, either the triumph of open innovation or the legal cover under which Microsoft appropriated Apple's finest work.

Apple's case did not unfold in isolation, and to the industry watching, the stakes felt existential because a parallel war was being fought over the same principle on a different front. Lotus, the maker of the dominant spreadsheet, had launched its own aggressive campaign to protect the look and feel of its software, suing smaller companies that had copied the arrangement of its menus and commands so that users could switch without relearning. In one early ruling Lotus won, and for a moment it seemed the courts might indeed decide that the very layout of a program's commands could be owned. That would have been a catastrophe for competition, locking every user into whichever product they had first learned, and the software world held its breath. But the tide turned. In the most important of these cases, an appeals court ultimately held that a menu command structure was an uncopyrightable "method of operation," no more protectable than the arrangement of buttons on a videocassette recorder, and when the dispute reached the Supreme Court the justices split evenly, leaving that pro-competition ruling to stand. Taken together with Apple's defeat, these decisions drew a consistent and durable line through the whole field: the code was yours, the specific art might be yours, but the way a program presented itself to a user, the grammar by which a human operated the machine, was a shared inheritance that the law would not fence off.

For Apple the loss was more than legal. The company had wagered a great deal of executive attention and moral energy on the conviction that it had been robbed, and the courts had told it, in effect, that it had given its work away in a contract of its own signing and that the rest was fair game. The bitterness would linger for years in Cupertino, and it would color the industry's memory of the whole graphical era, in which the question of who deserved credit for the personal computer's most human face would never be cleanly resolved. Steve Jobs himself, who had taken the ideas from Xerox and made them beautiful, took the accusation of theft personally to the end of his life. In one now-legendary confrontation, recounted years later by his biographer, Jobs summoned Gates to Apple and, surrounded by his own staff, shouted that Microsoft was ripping Apple off. Gates, unruffled, delivered a reply that has outlived the lawsuit itself: "I think it's more like we both had this rich neighbor named Xerox and I broke into his house to steal the TV set and found out that you had already stolen it." It was a joke, but it was also, more or less, the argument the courts would go on to accept, and it captured the awkward truth at the center of the whole dispute. Neither man had invented the graphical interface. Both had carried it out of the same unguarded house in Palo Alto.

It is worth remembering, too, what a case like this cost, and not only in money, though the money was considerable, six years of litigation consuming millions of dollars in legal fees on each side and the attention of senior executives who might have been building products. The deeper cost was the uncertainty it imposed on everyone else. For the better part of those six years, no software company could be entirely sure whether imitating a familiar interface, the ordinary way that products had always learned from one another, might now invite a ruinous lawsuit. Programmers second-guessed design choices; lawyers were consulted about the placement of menus. When the courts finally ruled, the relief across the industry was palpable, because the decision restored the freedom that developers had always assumed they possessed and that the litigation had briefly thrown into doubt. Innovation in software had always been cumulative, each product standing on the conventions of the last, and the Apple case, had it gone the other way, would have criminalized the very mechanism by which the field advanced.

The boundary the courts drew in that case has held for decades, and you rely on it constantly without knowing it. Every operating system you have ever used, on every phone and laptop and tablet, presents windows you can drag, icons you can tap, menus that drop down from a bar along the top, and it does so freely, because the Apple v. Microsoft ruling helped establish that these conventions are a shared vocabulary rather than anyone's property. The same fundamental question, where the line runs between a protectable creative expression and an unownable functional idea, would surface again and again as software ate the world, most spectacularly in a battle decades later between Google and Oracle over the reuse of programming interfaces, a fight whose logic traced straight back to the dissection of the Macintosh desktop. The graphical interface became the common tongue of the digital age in part because, in a courtroom in San Jose, one company tried to make it private and failed.

While the lawyers argued over who owned the desktop, Microsoft's engineers were quietly building the version of Windows that would finally make the argument moot by conquering the market outright.

Chapter 47: Windows 3.0

On the evening of May 22, 1990, Microsoft rented the City Center theater in Manhattan, filled six thousand seats, spent a reported three million dollars, and staged the most lavish product launch the software industry had ever seen. The occasion was the release of Windows 3.0, the third major attempt at a graphical interface that Bill Gates had first promised in a hotel ballroom nearly seven years earlier. Simultaneous events were held in cities around the world, linked by satellite, and journalists were handed copies of a program that, for the first time, actually worked well enough to change how people used their computers. The scale of the celebration was itself a statement. After Windows 1.0 had flopped and had earned Gates a mock "vaporware" trophy, and after Windows 2.0 had languished in obscurity, Microsoft was declaring, with money and spectacle, that the graphical PC had at last arrived and that Microsoft owned it. The remarkable thing, in hindsight, is how completely the product justified the noise.

The spectacle that night was deliberately unlike anything software had ever attempted, and it announced a change in the industry's sense of itself. Software had always been sold the way plumbing supplies were sold, in beige boxes to technical buyers, but Microsoft treated the arrival of Windows 3.0 like the premiere of a motion picture, with a theater, a live audience of thousands, satellite feeds to cities on several continents, and a budget that dwarfed anything a mere program had ever commanded. Bill Gates himself took the stage to demonstrate the software, and the message beneath the pageantry was unmistakable: the personal computer had become a consumer product of the first rank, and its interface, the face it showed to ordinary people, was now worth spending millions of dollars to celebrate. Reporters who had grown accustomed to mocking Microsoft's graphical ambitions left the theater having watched a version that, for once, did not stumble. The gap between the promise Gates had made in a hotel ballroom in 1983 and the product on the screen in 1990 had finally closed.

Several things had come together to make Windows 3.0 succeed where its predecessors had failed, and the most important of them was the hardware. The earlier versions had been built for machines that were too slow, with too little memory and processors too primitive to render pictures gracefully. The specific villain was a limit so notorious that it had its own grim reputation among programmers: the 640-kilobyte barrier, a ceiling on usable memory baked into the original design of the IBM PC and the DOS that ran it. No matter how much memory a user installed, DOS and the programs it ran could make direct use of only that first cramped 640 kilobytes, and graphical software, hungry for room to hold its images, was forever bumping its head against the ceiling. By 1990 the Intel 80386 processor had become common, and it offered a way out. Windows 3.0 was written to exploit the 386's advanced abilities, running in what Microsoft called 386 enhanced mode, in which the processor could reach far beyond the old barrier, address many megabytes of memory, and, most cleverly of all, wrap each old DOS program in its own simulated machine so that several of them could run at once, each in its own window on the graphical desktop. For the first time the graphical layer did not feel like a cramped and sluggish costume draped over DOS but like a genuine expansion of what the machine could do.

The cleverness of that memory arrangement is worth unpacking, because it was the engineering heart of the whole triumph. Windows 3.0 could actually start up in one of three different modes depending on the machine it found itself on, gracefully matching its ambitions to the hardware. On a feeble old machine it ran in a limited "real mode" that behaved much like the cramped earlier versions; on a mid-range one it used "standard mode" to reach a few megabytes of memory; and on a powerful 386 it unlocked the full "enhanced mode," commanding many megabytes and juggling several DOS programs at once, each sealed in its own protected compartment so that one crashing program need not drag down the rest. A single product, in other words, could serve the whole sprawling and uneven population of PCs then in the world, offering the cheapskate with an aging machine something usable while rewarding the buyer of a modern one with something genuinely powerful. This adaptability was not glamorous, but it was decisive, because it meant that almost anyone with an IBM-compatible computer could run Windows 3.0 in some form, and the size of that potential audience was exactly what would make the platform irresistible to the people who wrote software.

The interface itself had also matured into something coherent and, crucially, learnable. At its center sat the Program Manager, a window full of icons organized into groups, from which a user launched applications by pointing and double-clicking rather than by memorizing and typing commands. A companion File Manager let people move and copy files by dragging little document icons rather than reciting the cryptic incantations of the DOS command line. The graphics were rendered with a new visual polish, with three-dimensional shading on buttons and a brighter palette on the color monitors that were becoming standard, so that the whole thing looked modern rather than experimental. For a person who had spent years staring at a blank C-prompt, wondering what to type, the effect was liberating.

The computer had finally begun to show, rather than demand, and for millions of people who had quietly believed themselves too stupid to use a computer, that shift was nothing less than a reprieve, an invitation to join a world that had seemed sealed against them.

Bundled with all this seriousness came a small program that would arguably outlast every other part of the release, and its origins are a delightful footnote to the whole grand enterprise. During the summer of 1988 a Microsoft intern named Wes Cherry, working essentially on his own initiative, had written a version of the card game solitaire for Windows. Microsoft chose to include it with Windows 3.0, and did so with a straight-faced justification that happened to be true: the game was a training device in disguise. A generation of office workers had never held a mouse, and the actions the little rodent demanded, pointing precisely, clicking, and above all clicking-and-dragging an object from one place to another, were genuinely unfamiliar and slightly unnerving. Solitaire, in which one drags cards from pile to pile in a low-stakes and quietly addictive loop, turned out to be the gentlest possible way to teach those motions. The cards themselves were drawn by Susan Kare, the same artist who had designed the original Macintosh icons for Steve Jobs, so that a fragment of Apple's visual sensibility rode quietly into millions of Windows machines. Cherry, for his part, never saw a penny of royalties from what became one of the most-played computer games in history; his compensation, by his own cheerful account, was a computer to help him fix the bugs. His creation went on to devour untold millions of office hours for decades to come, and it ships with Windows to this day.

The market responded with a speed that startled even Microsoft. Windows 3.0 sold a million copies within a few months and more than ten million within roughly two years, an unheard-of pace for software of that era, and it kept selling. What made this possible, and what made it so much larger than anything Apple could achieve, was the installed base of cheap hardware. By 1990 the personal-computer market was no longer defined by IBM. It was defined by the clones, the tens of millions of inexpensive IBM-compatible machines built by Compaq and Dell and Gateway and a swarm of anonymous assemblers who bought Intel processors and Microsoft's operating system and undercut one another on price. These machines were everywhere, in offices and homes and schools, and every one of them could run Windows 3.0. Apple's beautiful Macintosh, by contrast, ran only on Apple's own expensive hardware, sold by a single company determined to preserve its margins. Microsoft had no hardware to protect and no margins to defend on machines; it wanted its software on as many computers as possible, at whatever price the market would bear, and the sprawling, competitive, low-cost world of the clones was the perfect vehicle for that ambition. The clone makers, for their part, were locked in a brutal price war with one another, each shaving a few dollars from the cost of a machine to win an order, and this ferocious competition among the hardware builders was itself a gift to Microsoft. The more savagely Compaq and Dell and the anonymous assemblers fought to sell cheap boxes, the more of those boxes went out into the world, and every one of them carried Microsoft's software inside it. The company had, in effect, arranged for its fiercest allies to be dozens of firms that hated one another, all competing to spread the one product they had in common.

This was the pivot on which the whole industry turned, and it is important to be honest about why Microsoft won, because the popular telling gets the reason backward. Windows 3.0 did not conquer the market because it was better than the Macintosh. It plainly was not. The Macintosh remained, in the judgment of nearly everyone who used both, the more graceful, more consistent, more thoughtfully designed machine, and it would stay ahead on sheer polish for years. But grace lost to arithmetic. A business outfitting a hundred desks could buy a hundred Windows PCs for the price of far fewer Macs, and the software written for those PCs, drawing on the enormous and growing pool of Windows users, multiplied faster than anything available for Apple. The graphical interface had been invented at Xerox, perfected and popularized by Apple, and litigated over in the courts, but it was Microsoft that delivered it to the masses, not by making it beautiful but by making it cheap and putting it everywhere. Each new Windows user made the platform more attractive to developers, and each new program made it more attractive to users, in a self-reinforcing spiral that economists call a network effect and that Microsoft rode with ruthless clarity.

If Windows 3.0 opened the door, its successor kicked it off the hinges. In the spring of 1992 Microsoft released Windows 3.1, a refinement rather than a revolution, but one that fixed the rough edges and added a feature of quiet importance: scalable TrueType fonts, which meant that the crisp lettering a user saw on screen would print out on paper looking exactly the same, at any size. This was the missing piece that finally made the Windows PC a serious tool for producing professional-looking documents, and it helped pull the world of desktop publishing, which had been an Apple stronghold, toward the cheaper platform. Windows 3.1 sold even faster than its predecessor, moving millions of copies in its first weeks, and between the two releases Microsoft put its graphical interface onto the great majority of the world's personal computers in the space of about two years. The developers followed the users, as they always do, and a torrent of Windows software, business programs, games, utilities, educational titles, poured onto the shelves, each new program making the platform more indispensable and the alternatives more marginal. The self-reinforcing spiral had become an avalanche.

The success of Windows 3.0 also settled, decisively, the long internal war over Microsoft's own strategy. Through the late 1980s Gates had hedged between Windows and OS/2, the heavier, more ambitious operating system Microsoft was building jointly with IBM. OS/2 was supposed to be the serious future; Windows was supposed to be the stopgap. But OS/2 was expensive, demanded more powerful hardware than most people owned, and never won the affection of the developers who wrote the applications that make a platform worth having. When Windows 3.0 exploded in popularity, the argument was over. Microsoft turned its energy decisively toward Windows and away from the partnership, and the alliance with IBM, already strained by mistrust, began to dissolve into open rivalry. IBM would carry on with OS/2 for years, pouring resources into a technically capable system that a shrinking circle of loyalists admired, but it had lost the platform war before most people realized a war was being fought. Gates's long, hedged, seemingly disloyal bet on the light, cheap, DOS-compatible graphical layer had paid off beyond any reasonable expectation.

By the early 1990s, then, the shape of the personal-computer world had crystallized around a single dominant arrangement: Intel's processors, the clone makers' cheap hardware, and Microsoft's Windows sitting on top of DOS as the interface nearly everyone saw. The combination would come to be called, half admiringly and half resentfully, the Wintel duopoly, and it would define computing for a generation. It is a world you still half-inhabit. The overwhelming majority of the world's desktop and laptop computers still run Windows; the Program Manager and File Manager of 1990 are the direct ancestors of the Start menu and the file explorer on a machine today; and Wes Cherry's solitaire game, drawn by an Apple artist and given away by a Microsoft that never paid its author, was inducted into a video game hall of fame decades later, still installed, still played, on a platform its creator could scarcely have imagined. Microsoft now controlled the ground on which almost all personal-computer software ran, and it possessed something close to a standard, a platform whose ubiquity gave its owner extraordinary power over everyone who wished to write programs for it.

That power was about to be turned, with devastating effect,

on the makers of the applications that ran on Windows.

Chapter 48: The Empire of the Desktop

In the summer of 1990, at the sprawling headquarters of the Lotus Development Corporation in Cambridge, Massachusetts, executives could still afford a certain confidence. Lotus 1-2-3, the spreadsheet that had done for the IBM PC what VisiCalc had done for the Apple II, was the best-selling application in the world, the program that businesses bought a computer in order to run. Down in Utah, the WordPerfect Corporation held a similarly commanding grip on word processing, its software beloved by legal secretaries and offices everywhere for the intricate control it gave over the printed page, a control so precise that devotees spoke of its "reveal codes" feature the way a mechanic speaks of getting under the hood. In Silicon Valley, Borland International, led by the flamboyant French-born entrepreneur Philippe Kahn, was a rising force with fast, cheap programming tools and a spreadsheet of its own called Quattro Pro. These were the giants of the application business, and in 1990 Microsoft was, in that business, a modest player, holding perhaps ten or fifteen percent of the market for the programs people actually used to get work done. Five years later, all of that would be gone.

The instrument of Microsoft's conquest was the very platform it had just won. Windows 3.0 had made the graphical interface the standard, and the applications that had dominated the DOS era, Lotus 1-2-3 and WordPerfect above all, were designed for the character-based world of typed commands and function keys. To thrive on Windows, they would have to be rebuilt from the ground up as graphical programs, and here the incumbents stumbled badly. The reasons were partly psychological, the ordinary difficulty a dominant company has in believing that the source of its wealth is about to become a liability. Lotus, wedded to the enormous success of its DOS product, was slow and hesitant in bringing a strong version of 1-2-3 to Windows, having bet its transitional energies on a different operating system, IBM's OS/2, that never won the market. WordPerfect, insular and headquartered far from the industry's centers in the mountains of Utah, likewise delayed and produced a first Windows version widely judged to be buggy and disappointing. Their customers, migrating to Windows in the millions, arrived on the new platform to find their familiar programs missing or broken, and they went looking for something that worked.

The story of Excel itself shows how long and how patiently Microsoft had prepared for this moment. When the company first released Excel in 1985, it did not put it on the IBM PC at all, where Lotus 1-2-3 reigned unchallengeable, but on the Macintosh, where there was room to grow and where the graphical interface made a modern spreadsheet possible. For several years Excel matured quietly on Apple's machine, learning to be a graphical program while its eventual rival on the PC remained a creature of the text screen. Its very name was a small boast; it was meant to signal a spreadsheet that would excel, that would outdo the incumbent. So when Windows finally gave the IBM-compatible world a proper graphical environment, Microsoft did not have to invent a Windows spreadsheet in a hurry. It already had one, seasoned and elegant, ready to be carried across from the Mac to the vastly larger PC market at the precise instant that market became ready to receive it. Lotus, by contrast, was starting almost from scratch, and by the time it produced a competitive Windows version the game was effectively over. The lesson was one Microsoft would apply again and again: skate to where the puck is going, build the product before the market that needs it exists, and be waiting, fully formed, when the moment arrives.

What worked was Microsoft's own software, and this was no accident of timing. Microsoft had cut its teeth on the Macintosh, where it had learned to write graphical applications years before most of its competitors, and it brought that experience to Windows with lethal effect. Microsoft Excel, the spreadsheet that had grown up on the Mac since the mid-1980s, was already a mature and elegant graphical program by the time Windows became a mass platform, and as Lotus dithered, Excel simply took the market. Microsoft Word, similarly seasoned, advanced against WordPerfect. Between roughly 1990 and 1995, Microsoft's share of the application market climbed from that modest tenth or so to well over sixty percent, an ascent so steep and so complete that it remade the entire economics of software. Excel overtook and then buried Lotus 1-2-3; Word overtook and then buried WordPerfect; and the companies that had seemed unassailable at the start of the decade found themselves, by its middle, reduced to shrinking niches.

The decisive stroke was the bundle. Microsoft began packaging its applications together as a suite called Microsoft Office, first for the Macintosh at the end of the 1980s and then for Windows in 1990, combining Word, Excel, and the presentation program PowerPoint into a single box sold for far less than the programs would have cost individually. PowerPoint itself illustrates how deliberately Microsoft assembled this arsenal. It had not been born at Microsoft at all; it was created by Robert Gaskins and his colleagues Dennis Austin and Thomas Rudkin at a small California company called Forethought, and released in April 1987 for the Macintosh alone. Within three months Microsoft had bought it outright for about fourteen million dollars, the first significant acquisition in the company's history, precisely because

Gates could see that a business suite would one day need a way to make slides. For a company buying software for many desks, the logic of the finished suite was overwhelming: one purchase, one vendor, programs designed to work together and to share the same menus and shortcuts, at a price that made buying a word processor from one company and a spreadsheet from another seem foolish. The suite fed on itself. A company that adopted Word found it natural to adopt Excel, and the documents those programs produced, saved in Microsoft's own file formats, became the currency of business, so that anyone who wished to exchange files with the rest of the world found it increasingly necessary to own the Microsoft programs that could read and write them. Office became, in its own right, a standard nearly as entrenched as Windows itself.

Around this triumph swirled accusations that would eventually harden into legal peril, and one of them deserves careful handling, because it has passed into legend in a form that is almost certainly false. Microsoft's competitors charged that the company enjoyed an unfair and possibly illegal advantage because it controlled both the platform and the applications that ran on it. The company that wrote Windows also wrote Word and Excel, and rivals suspected that Microsoft's application teams received early access to the inner workings of Windows, or that the operating system contained hidden features its own programs could exploit and outsiders could not. A phrase circulated for years, repeated as though it were a documented internal slogan: "DOS ain't done till Lotus won't run," a supposed boast that Microsoft would tune its operating system to sabotage its competitors' software. It makes a wonderful story, and it captured a genuine fear. But investigators who went looking for its origin found no evidence that anyone at Microsoft ever said it, no memo, no witness, and no actual instance of Lotus 1-2-3 being made to fail; the phrase appears to be pure folklore, surfacing in public only in the early 1990s. The truth is both more mundane and more damning. Microsoft did not need to booby-trap its operating system. The structural conflict of interest was enough: the referee of the platform was also its most powerful player, it wrote the rulebook that everyone else had to follow, and it was winning. That was intolerable to its rivals whether or not a single line of Windows was ever rigged against them.

Those suspicions did not stay confined to trade-press gossip; they drew the eye of the government. As early as 1990 the Federal Trade Commission opened an inquiry into Microsoft's conduct, and when its commissioners deadlocked, the Department of Justice took up the matter. The first tangible result came in 1994, in a consent decree that targeted one of Microsoft's most effective and least visible tactics. The company had been selling Windows to computer manufacturers on a "per-processor" basis, charging a royalty for every machine a maker shipped whether or not that machine actually contained Windows, which meant that a manufacturer who wanted to offer a rival operating system on some of its computers would end up paying Microsoft twice and would therefore, quite rationally, offer nothing but Windows at all. It was a quiet, brilliant piece of leverage that used Microsoft's ownership of the standard to smother alternatives before a customer ever saw them, and the government forced the company to abandon it. The 1994 decree was a mild rebuke, easily absorbed, but it was the first formal signal that the state now regarded Microsoft's grip as a matter of law rather than mere commerce, a signal that would swell, later in the decade, into the great antitrust confrontation that nearly broke the company in two.

The human cost of all this fell on some of the proudest names in the industry, and the numbers tell the story with brutal economy. Lotus, having missed the Windows transition and watched Excel devour its franchise, lost its independence in 1995 when the International Business Machines Corporation, the very company whose PC had made Lotus 1-2-3 a phenomenon, bought it for some three and a half billion dollars, chiefly for a groupware product called Notes rather than for the fading spreadsheet. WordPerfect, its market collapsing, was sold to the networking company Novell in 1994 for well over a billion dollars in stock and then sold again, just two years later, to the Canadian firm Corel for a small fraction of that sum, a fire-sale that measured how far and how fast the mighty had fallen. Borland, having bet heavily on its own applications, retreated from the consumer software business altogether, shedding its spreadsheet and reinventing itself as a maker of tools for professional programmers. Within a single half-decade, the diverse and competitive application market of 1990, with its several strong and independent companies, had been consolidated into something close to a Microsoft monopoly, resting on the Microsoft monopoly beneath it.

The file formats deserve a closer look, because they were the quiet mechanism that made the conquest permanent rather than merely temporary. When Word saved a document or Excel saved a spreadsheet, it wrote the data in a private, proprietary arrangement of bytes that Microsoft alone fully understood and could change at will with each new version. This turned an ordinary business document into a subtle instrument of lock-in. A company that had standardized on Word could not easily send its files to a supplier who used a rival word processor, because that rival could not reliably read them, and so the supplier, to do business, bought Word too, and then pressed its own partners to do the same. The documents themselves became evangelists for the software that made them. Every contract, memo, and budget that traveled between organizations in a Microsoft format was a small advertisement and a small coercion, nudging the recipient toward the same purchase. Owning the format was, in the long run, worth more than owning any single feature, because a feature could be copied but a universal standard could not simply be willed into existence by a competitor.

It is worth pausing on how strange and swift this was, because the consolidation of the desktop was not the slow maturing of an industry but something closer to an avalanche. In 1990 a well-informed observer would have named Lotus and WordPerfect as permanent fixtures of business computing, as unlikely to fall as the office buildings they ran in. Their products were entrenched, their brands were synonymous with their categories, their customers were loyal and trained. And yet within five years both were husks, their names surviving mainly as answers to trivia questions, their franchises absorbed or discarded. The lesson was not lost on anyone paying attention: on a platform controlled by a single company, no application franchise, however dominant, was safe if that company decided to compete in your category. The maker of the stage could always choose to become the star.

By 1995 Microsoft stood astride the personal-computer industry in a way no company ever had. It owned the operating system that ran on the overwhelming majority of the world's computers, and it owned the applications that most of those computers ran. Its revenues and its stock price soared; Bill Gates became the richest man in the world; and the company's culture of aggressive, relentless competition, admired by some as brilliance and condemned by others as predation, became the defining temperament of the industry. You are still living inside the result. The document formats that Microsoft's dominance made universal, the descendants of those early Word and Excel files, remain the default currency of offices, governments, and schools across the planet; a résumé, a budget, a set of slides still tends to travel the world in Word, Excel, or PowerPoint, and the suite that swallowed its rivals in the early 1990s still sits, in its cloud-subscription form, on well over a billion devices. The empire of the desktop was complete, or very nearly so. But its very completeness was beginning to attract the attention of forces that measured success against a different yardstick, one written not in market share but in law, and Microsoft's dominance would soon be reframed by government lawyers as something to be feared rather than admired.

Before that reckoning arrived, however, Microsoft would stage the greatest and most triumphant product launch in the history of computing.

Chapter 49: Start Me Up

Just after midnight on August 24, 1995, the doors of a CompUSA store in a suburban shopping center swung open and a line of people who had been waiting in the dark surged inside to buy a piece of software. The scene repeated itself at computer stores across the United States and around the world, in Sydney and London and Tokyo, where the release moved westward with the turning of the earth. People who had never before queued at midnight for anything, let alone for an operating system, stood in parking lots to be among the first to own Windows 95. Some bought copies for machines they did not yet possess. The spectacle was unprecedented, and it was also, in large part, manufactured, the product of a marketing campaign of a scale and audacity the technology industry had never attempted. Microsoft had turned the launch of a computer program into a cultural event, and the world, remarkably, had shown up.

The numbers behind the spectacle were staggering even by the standards of a company that had grown used to excess. Microsoft was reported to be spending some three hundred million dollars to trumpet the arrival of Windows 95, a promotional budget larger than the marketing campaigns of most Hollywood films of the era, and when the spending of computer makers, retailers, and software partners riding the same wave was folded in, industry observers put the total closer to a billion dollars. The campaign's centerpiece was a song. Microsoft had licensed the Rolling Stones' "Start Me Up" for its television advertising, and the choice was pointed, for the new version of Windows introduced a feature called the Start button, a single labeled square in the corner of the screen from which a user could reach everything the computer could do. Here it is worth pausing to correct a piece of folklore that has clung to the launch for thirty years. The figure most often repeated is that Microsoft paid the Stones twelve million dollars for the song, a number so large it became part of the legend of the launch's excess. Microsoft insisted the true figure was far smaller, on the order of three million, and suggested the inflated number had been floated by the band itself to burnish its own market value. The exact sum was never officially confirmed, but the twelve-million-dollar figure so often quoted as fact appears to be closer to myth.

The advertisements, all rolling drums and Mick Jagger's swagger, played the song against images of the new interface, and the phrase start me up became inseparable from the launch. Microsoft blanketed the media in ways that veered from the clever to the surreal. It arranged for an entire day's print run of a British newspaper, more than a million copies, to be given away free with Windows branding. It lit the Empire State Building in the colors of the Windows logo. It planted a three-hundred-foot Windows banner on Toronto's CN Tower. And on the night of the launch it staged an event on a purpose-built outdoor stage at its Redmond campus at which the host of NBC's Tonight Show, Jay Leno, appeared alongside Bill Gates before a crowd of some five thousand employees, journalists, and guests to introduce the product as though it were a summer blockbuster. Leno, surveying the frenzy, joked that the software was so good even he could use it, which was, he added, the whole point. The mixture of technology and celebrity, ordinary and now, was startling in 1995 and would become, in the decades that followed, simply the way the industry behaved when it wanted the world to notice. The press strained to find language for the spectacle. The Washington Post, surveying the frenzy, ran a story headlined "Windows 95's Debut, Microsoft Scales Heights of Hype," capturing the unease many felt watching a company deploy the full machinery of mass celebrity to sell a piece of system software. Skeptics grumbled that the product beneath the noise was an incremental improvement dressed as a revolution, and there was some justice in the complaint; but the grumbling was drowned out, and the queues formed anyway.

Beneath the spectacle was a genuinely important piece of engineering, though here too a common misconception deserves correcting. It is often said that Windows 95 finally freed the personal computer from the old command-line world of DOS, but that is only half true. Windows 95 was not merely a graphical layer sitting atop DOS, as every previous version of Windows had been; it folded the operating system and its graphical interface together into something that felt, to the user, like a single integrated whole. Yet DOS did not vanish. It lingered underneath in a diminished role, still booting the machine and still lurking a menu-click away, so that beneath the friendly new face the old text-driven ancestor kept breathing. What the new system did bring was real: thirty-two-bit computing and, most significantly, preemptive multitasking, a technical advance that let the operating system itself, rather than the programs, decide how to share the processor, so that one misbehaving application was far less likely to freeze the entire machine. It introduced long filenames, freeing users at last from the cramped old limit of eight characters and a three-letter extension that had forced people to name their documents in cryptic abbreviations for a decade and a half. And it promised the plug-and-play installation of new hardware, an often-mocked pledge that a device plugged into the machine would simply work, which frequently it did not but which pointed toward a future in which it would.

The interface itself, though, was what people saw and remembered. The Program Manager of Windows 3.0, with its windows full of icon groups, was gone, replaced by the arrangement that would define the personal computer for the next quarter century. Along the bottom of the screen ran the taskbar, showing every open program as a button so that a user could see at a glance what was running and switch between tasks with a single click. Anchored at the taskbar's left end sat the Start button, and clicking it unfurled a menu that cascaded upward through programs and documents and settings, a single organized doorway into the whole machine. Consider how a first-time buyer met it in practice. She switched on the beige tower, watched clouds drift across a blue sky, and found a nearly empty green desktop with a few icons and, glowing in the corner, a button that said, with almost comic simplicity, Start. Clicking it revealed everything: her programs nested in folders, the documents she had recently opened, a way to find files, a way to change settings, and, at the bottom, the command to shut down. The metaphor was clear and forgiving, and it worked for beginners and experts alike. A desktop scattered with icons, a taskbar tracking one's work, a Start menu holding everything else: this grammar, introduced in August 1995, proved so intuitive and so durable that anyone who sits down today at a Windows 11 machine and clicks the Start button in the taskbar is still, in its essentials, using the interface unveiled that August night.

To teach a bewildered public how to use this new grammar, Microsoft reached, as it had with the Rolling Stones, for celebrity. It commissioned an hour-long promotional training film, billed without irony as "the world's first cyber sitcom," and hosted by Jennifer Aniston and Matthew Perry, two young actors who had just become famous that year on the NBC comedy Friends. For most of an hour the pair wandered a fictionalized Microsoft campus getting the new features explained to them, Aniston at one point confusing the taskbar with a candy bar, in a production so earnest and so dated that it would circulate decades later as a beloved artifact of 1990s kitsch. The gambit captured the strangeness of the moment: an operating system so significant, and so intimidating, that a major software company thought it needed prime-time sitcom stars to coax ordinary people into trying it.

There was irony lurking in the anthem, too, which critics gleefully pointed out. "Start Me Up" contained the word start, echoing the new button, but the very next line of the Rolling Stones song is "you make a grown man cry," a sentiment that struck some observers as an unintentionally apt description of the experience of configuring a mid-1990s PC. And there was a smaller absurdity built into the software itself: to turn the computer off, a user had to click the button marked Start, following a menu named for beginnings all the way down to the command to shut down. The quirk was noticed at once and never entirely lived down.

Windows 95 sold in staggering quantities, more than a million copies in its first four days and some seven million within five weeks, tens of millions within a year, and it carried the graphical personal computer fully into the mainstream of ordinary life. Yet the upgrade was not painless for everyone. The new system was hungrier than its predecessor, running poorly on the four megabytes of memory many existing machines carried and truly comfortable only with eight or more, so that for a great many households the real price of Windows 95 was the price of a new computer to run it on. In this way the launch did double duty, selling not only an operating system but a fresh wave of hardware, and the personal-computer industry as a whole enjoyed one of the great buying booms of its history on the strength of a single software release. It arrived at a moment when the home computer was ceasing to be the preserve of hobbyists and businesses and becoming a common household appliance, and its friendly face helped make that transition possible. For a great many people around the world, Windows 95 was simply what a computer was, the screen they sat down to at work and increasingly at home, and its conventions became the shared assumptions of a computing public now numbering in the hundreds of millions. The launch also marked a subtle shift in how the industry understood its own products. Software had once been sold as a tool, a utility bought grudgingly to accomplish some specific task; Microsoft now sold it as an event, an experience, a thing one might desire for its own sake and line up in the dark to possess. The queues outside the stores were, in a sense, the truest measure of how far the personal computer had traveled since the days of the hobbyist kits soldered in garages, for a machine that had once belonged to engineers and enthusiasts had become an object of mass consumer longing, marketed with the tools of Hollywood and rock and roll. Whether that transformation represented the fulfillment of the personal computer's democratic promise or its capture by a single corporation's marketing machine was a question that would divide observers for years, but no one disputed that something had changed on that August night.

Tucked into the launch, and easy to miss amid the fanfare, was another of Microsoft's bids for the future. Windows 95 shipped with an icon on its desktop for the Microsoft Network, or MSN, the company's own dial-up online service, launched to challenge the reigning giants of the era like America Online and CompuServe. Placing that icon on the desktop of what would become the world's most common operating system was a quiet display of exactly the kind of leverage—using dominance in one market to force a way into another—that would soon draw the scrutiny of regulators. For the moment, though, it registered as merely one more feature of a release that seemed to promise the whole digital world inside a single blue box.

Yet the most consequential thing about Windows 95, in the long run, was something Microsoft had very nearly overlooked. The version that shipped in August 1995 arrived without a web browser, for the company had been slow to grasp the significance of the Internet, which in the mid-1990s was exploding out of the universities and into public consciousness with astonishing speed. A small company called Netscape, formed by veterans of the early graphical web, had released a browser called Navigator that was becoming the way ordinary people experienced the World Wide Web, and Netscape's success suggested a future in which the browser, not the operating system, might become the layer that mattered, the platform on which the next generation of software would run. Gates, who had missed the graphical revolution's first stirrings but never its second, awoke to the danger with characteristic ferocity. On May 26, 1995, mere months before the great launch, he circulated an internal memorandum to his executive staff titled "The Internet Tidal Wave," in which he declared the Internet the most important development since the IBM PC and assigned it, in his words, "the highest level of importance," warning that it would reshape everything. He turned the whole company toward it. Microsoft licensed browser technology from a firm called Spyglass, built its own product called Internet Explorer, and, in an addition that would prove momentous, began bundling that browser directly into Windows itself, first as part of an add-on pack for Windows 95 and then as an integrated and inseparable component of the operating system, given away free to every user of the world's dominant computing platform.

That decision, to fold the browser into Windows and use the monopoly of the operating system to overwhelm a smaller rival in a new market, was a repetition of the strategy that had worked so devastatingly against Lotus and WordPerfect. This time, however, the government was watching, and the tidal wave Gates had summoned would carry Microsoft not only to new heights of power but into the gravest legal battle of its existence.

Chapter 50: The United States v. Microsoft

In late August 1998, in a windowless conference room at Microsoft's headquarters in Redmond, Washington, a government lawyer named David Boies switched on a video camera and began to depose the richest man in the world. Over the better part of three days, Bill Gates sat for hours of questioning, and the man renowned for his ferocious command of detail was, on the tape, evasive and combative and strangely forgetful, quibbling over the meaning of ordinary words, claiming not to recall his own emails, rocking in his chair and staring at the table. When Boies asked him about a message he had plainly written, Gates would parse it into oblivion, demanding to know what the questioner meant by common words like "concerned" or "compete," until the exchanges took on the quality of a hostile philosophy seminar. When portions of the video were later played in open court, the effect was devastating. In one notorious stretch, Boies pressed Gates on an email in which Gates had asked how much Microsoft was getting paid by a partner, and Gates responded by disputing what the word "we" might mean, and whether "ask" meant asking in writing. Reporters in the gallery laughed out loud; the judge was seen shaking his head. The deposition became the most damaging evidence against Microsoft, for it showed the world a company, embodied in its founder, that seemed to hold the law in contempt. It was a turning point in a confrontation that had been building for years, the collision between the most successful company in the industry and a government that had come to see its success as a threat to competition itself.

The roots of the case reached back to 1994, when the Department of Justice, after a long investigation into Microsoft's licensing practices, reached a consent decree with the company. Microsoft agreed to stop certain practices by which it had discouraged computer makers from installing rival operating systems, chiefly the arrangements, known as per-processor licenses, under which manufacturers paid Microsoft a royalty for every machine they shipped whether or not it actually contained Windows, a scheme that made any competing system effectively an extra cost a manufacturer had to pay twice. The consent decree also contained a provision, ambiguous and soon bitterly contested, concerning whether Microsoft could require computer makers to take other Microsoft products as a condition of licensing Windows, while permitting the company to develop "integrated products." It was in the meaning of that single phrase that the browser war would be fought.

That war had begun in earnest with Windows 95 and the rise of Netscape, whose Navigator browser had become the public's window onto the exploding World Wide Web and which threatened, in Gates's own anxious vision, to become a rival platform that might one day make the underlying operating system irrelevant. Microsoft's response was to build Internet Explorer and to bundle it into Windows, free, and then to press the computer makers who depended on Windows to feature Internet Explorer and to marginalize Navigator. The internal rhetoric of the campaign, later exposed in court, was starkly candid. An Intel executive named Steven McGeady testified that a senior Microsoft vice president, Paul Maritz, had spoken of a plan to "cut off

Netscape's air supply" by giving away for free everything Netscape was trying to sell. Maritz denied under oath ever using those words, but the phrase entered the trial and the culture as shorthand for the whole strategy. Netscape, unable to charge for a product its giant competitor gave away and denied the prominent placement on new machines that drove adoption, watched its market share erode.

Nor was the pressure only commercial. On June 21, 1995, two months before Windows 95 shipped, executives from Microsoft met with the leadership of Netscape, and what was said in that room became one of the case's central exhibits. According to notes taken by Netscape's young cofounder Marc Andreessen—who, anticipating trouble, deliberately recorded the meeting in writing as it unfolded—Microsoft proposed, in effect, to divide the browser market between them: Microsoft would own the browser for Windows 95, and Netscape could keep the older operating systems and whatever fell outside Windows, and if Netscape declined to cooperate it could expect to be buried. Microsoft insisted the meeting had been an ordinary business discussion and that Andreessen's account was self-serving. But to prosecutors the notes described a naked attempt by a monopolist to carve up a market with a smaller rival, an illegal collusion offered and, when refused, followed by exactly the campaign of suffocation McGeady had described. To the government, this looked like the Lotus and WordPerfect story repeating on a grander stage: a monopoly in one market, the operating system, being wielded as a weapon to seize dominance in another, the browser. In May 1998 the Department of Justice, joined by twenty states and the District of Columbia, filed suit, alleging that Microsoft had violated the Sherman Antitrust Act, the century-old law under which the great trusts of the industrial age had been broken.

The trial opened in October 1998 in the federal courthouse in Washington, before Judge Thomas Penfield Jackson, and it became a national spectacle. Boies, for the government, proved a devastating cross-examiner, and the evidence he marshaled, above all the trove of internal Microsoft emails in which executives spoke with startling frankness about crushing competitors, painted a portrait of a company that used its power without restraint. One message from a Microsoft executive, describing the company's intentions toward a rival, contained the simple, chilling instruction to "crush" them, and it was precisely this genre of unguarded candor that Boies mined to such effect. Microsoft's defense, that it had merely improved its product by integrating a browser and that consumers benefited from getting one free, was undercut at every turn by its own witnesses' contradictions and by the memory of Gates's evasive deposition. In a famous courtroom moment, Microsoft attempted to demonstrate with a videotape that removing Internet Explorer would degrade Windows, only for Boies to show that the tape had apparently been spliced together from different machines, embarrassing the company before the judge. Jackson made little effort to hide his growing skepticism. In November 1999 he issued findings of fact declaring that Microsoft possessed monopoly power in the market for personal-computer operating systems and had used that power to harm competition and consumers, and in April 2000 he ruled that the company had violated the antitrust laws. In his findings, Jackson wrote in language that left no doubt where he stood, concluding that Microsoft had shown it would use its market power and immense profits to harm any firm that dared pursue initiatives capable of intensifying competition, and that the ultimate casualties were innovation itself and the consumers deprived of the choices a freer market would have offered. The word monopoly, which Microsoft's lawyers had labored to keep out of the courtroom, now sat at the center of a federal judge's official findings, and no appeal would ever dislodge it.

The spectacle transfixed an industry unused to seeing its titans humbled. For two decades Bill Gates had been the boy wonder of American technology, the Harvard dropout who had bet that the world would want a computer on every desk and been proved right beyond all reckoning; now he was cast, in courtroom and cartoon alike, as a robber baron for the digital age, and the transformation in his public image was swift and lasting. Microsoft's rivals, who had spent years complaining privately that the company competed by threat and coercion, testified in the open at last. Gates himself, long afterward, would concede that the episode had been painful and that he had served himself badly in the deposition, learning, as he put it, that being right about technology was no protection against the law. The case unfolded, moreover, against the backdrop of the greatest financial mania the industry had yet seen, the dot-com boom, so that even as the government sought to punish Microsoft for dominating the desktop, a torrent of investment was rushing toward the very Internet companies that would, in time, make the desktop matter less.

The remedy Jackson ordered, in June 2000, was drastic. He directed that Microsoft be broken into two separate companies, one to hold the Windows operating system and the other to hold the applications and everything else, on the theory that a divided Microsoft could no longer leverage its operating-system monopoly to dominate adjacent markets. It was the boldest structural remedy in antitrust since the breakup of the telephone monopoly a generation earlier, and for a moment it seemed that the empire Gates had built might be dismantled by the state. But the breakup never happened. Microsoft appealed, and in the summer of 2001 the United States Court of Appeals for the District of Columbia Circuit, sitting en banc, delivered a mixed verdict that changed the case's course. The appellate court unanimously upheld the core finding that Microsoft had illegally maintained its operating-system monopoly, a significant and lasting condemnation. But it threw out the breakup order, in part on procedural grounds and in part because Judge Jackson had gravely compromised his own standing. During the trial, it emerged, he had given a series of interviews to journalists, speaking scornfully of Microsoft and its executives, comparing the company's leaders at one point to gangland killers and drug dealers who denied their crimes. The appeals court found that these remarks created an appearance of bias so serious that it disqualified him, and the case was sent back to a new judge for the remedy phase to begin again.

By then the political and technological weather had shifted. A new administration in Washington had less appetite for the fight, the Internet stock bubble had burst, and the browser war was effectively over, for Internet Explorer had already won a commanding share of the market and Netscape had been sold to America Online and was fading toward obsolescence. In November 2001 the Department of Justice and Microsoft reached a settlement, approved the following year by the new trial judge, Colleen Kollar-Kotelly, that imposed behavioral restraints rather than structural surgery. Microsoft agreed to share certain technical information with rival software makers so that their programs could work smoothly with Windows, to refrain from retaliating against computer makers who installed competing software, and to submit to oversight by a three-person committee of technical experts with access to its books, records, and source code. But it remained whole, its operating-system monopoly intact, its founder's fortune undiminished. The oversight lingered for years; the last of the settlement's restrictions did not expire until 2011, a full decade after the deal was struck and seventeen years after the government first extracted a consent decree from the company, so that in the end the case shadowed Microsoft for the better part of a generation even as it left the company standing. Nine of the states that had joined the suit initially refused to accept the settlement as too lenient, pressing for harsher terms, and many observers judged the outcome a defeat for the government, a punishment too mild for a violation the courts had unanimously affirmed.

What the long ordeal did and did not accomplish would be debated for decades. It did not break Microsoft, and it did not restore Netscape or resurrect the competitors Microsoft had crushed. Windows remained dominant, and Internet Explorer would hold the browser market for years, at its peak commanding some ninety-five percent of all web browsing. Yet the case was not without effect. The years of investigation, litigation, and public scrutiny consumed the attention of Microsoft's leadership and, in the judgment of many, tempered the company's aggression at a crucial moment, making it more cautious, more inclined to hesitate before crushing a new rival. Some argued that this caution created the opening through which a new generation of companies, building on the open Internet rather than on the Windows desktop, would rise to challenge and eventually surpass Microsoft, companies whose search engines and social networks and mobile devices would define the next era of computing. A small startup called Google was incorporated in September 1998, in the very weeks Gates was giving his deposition, and it is at least plausible that a Microsoft unchastened by antitrust scrutiny would have moved to smother it as it had smothered Netscape. The antitrust reckoning, in this telling, mattered less for the remedy it imposed than for the shadow it cast, a warning that even the mightiest platform monopoly could be called to account.

That shadow reaches into the present. The playbook the government wrote in the Microsoft case, the theory that a company can lawfully hold a monopoly but not lawfully abuse it to seize the next market, became the template for a generation of antitrust actions that followed, including the suits brought decades later against Google, Apple, Amazon, and Meta, and the European regulators who pursued Microsoft on their own account drew directly on the same legal foundations. Europe proved less forgiving than the United States had been: in 2004 the European Commission fined Microsoft some 497 million euros for abusing its dominance, a penalty later followed by others totalling well over a billion, and eventually forced the company to present European users with a "browser ballot" screen offering a menu of rival browsers rather than steering everyone toward Internet Explorer. Anyone who has been prompted by a phone or a computer to pick a default browser rather than simply accept the one the manufacturer preferred is living, in a small way, in the world that United States v. Microsoft made. The desktop empire had been challenged and had survived, but the ground beneath it was already shifting, for the personal computer was about to slip its cords and become something a person could carry.

Chapter 51: The Luggables

In the spring of 1981, at the West Coast Computer Faire in San Francisco, a heavyset Englishman with a booming voice and a genius for provocation set a beige box the size of a small suitcase on a table and popped its lid. Out folded a keyboard. Behind the keyboard, where a briefcase clasp might be, sat a five-inch cathode-ray screen no larger than the display on a modern car's dashboard, and beneath it two slots for floppy disks. Adam Osborne, a former chemical engineer turned computer-book publisher turned gadfly, hoisted the whole contraption by a built-in handle and carried it across the room. It weighed roughly twenty-four and a half pounds—about as much as a full sewing machine, which is very nearly what the thing resembled, right down to the carrying handle and the case that latched shut over its working parts. He called it the Osborne 1, and he had priced it, when it went on sale that April, at $1,795. The figure was so low that the trade paper InfoWorld, reporting the machine on its front page, felt obliged to reassure its readers: "In case you think the price printed above was a mistake, we'll repeat it: $1795." The room understood immediately that something had changed. For the first time, a person could close a computer, pick it up, and walk out the door with it.

Osborne was not an engineer's engineer, and he knew it. His talent was for seeing what other people had built and grasping, faster than they could, what it was actually for. He had made his first fortune writing plain-language manuals for microprocessors when the industry still shrouded its products in unreadable jargon, and he had sold that publishing house to McGraw-Hill. Now he applied the same instinct to the machine itself. The technical heart of the Osborne 1 had been designed largely by Lee Felsenstein, the Berkeley radical and Homebrew Computer Club veteran who had also engineered the earlier Sol-20. Felsenstein built the portable to be rugged and cheap, its tiny screen a deliberate concession to durability and cost. The genius stroke, though, was not the hardware but what Osborne bundled with it.

Osborne cut an unmistakable figure in an industry then full of soft-spoken engineers. Born in Thailand to British parents and raised partly in southern India, he was loud, opinionated, and gleefully rude about products he judged overpriced or overhyped, and he had built his reputation on a book, An Introduction to Microcomputers, that sold in the hundreds of thousands by explaining the new machines in language a layperson could follow. He wrote a widely read and cheerfully abrasive trade column, and he liked to insist that adequate was good enough—that the market did not need the best possible machine, only a genuinely useful one at a price ordinary people could actually pay. The Osborne 1 was that philosophy cast in beige plastic.

At a time when software was sold separately and could easily cost more than the computer, the Osborne 1 arrived with roughly $1,500 worth of programs already included in the price. There was the WordStar word processor, the dominant writing tool of the era; the SuperCalc spreadsheet, a rival to VisiCalc; the CP/M operating system that ran most serious business microcomputers; and the BASIC programming language in two flavors. The buyer paid less for the whole package than the software alone would have cost à la carte. Osborne had inverted the industry's logic. The machine was almost a delivery vehicle for the software, and the whole bundle could be carried onto an airplane and slid under the seat in front of you.

Living with the machine, however, meant living with its compromises, and the most notorious was that five-inch screen. It displayed only fifty-two characters across, but the documents people wrote in WordStar were formatted to the standard width of eighty columns. The consequence was a small daily indignity: to read a full line of your own letter, you had to slide the visible window sideways across the page, scrolling left and right to see text that would have sat whole on any desktop monitor. Users learned to think of the tiny display as a magnifying glass sweeping over a larger sheet they could never see all at once. And yet, squint-inducing as it was, the arrangement worked. Traveling salesmen, journalists, accountants, and lawyers found they could take their work with them in a way that had never before been possible, and they tolerated the porthole of a screen for the freedom it bought.

The market responded with something close to hysteria. Osborne Computer Corporation, founded in 1981, was selling more than ten thousand machines a month by the following year and booking revenues that ran into the tens of millions. It was, by some measures, one of the fastest-growing companies in American history to that point. The little sewing-machine computer had proven that portability was not a novelty but a genuine hunger, and that ordinary buyers would tolerate a compromised display in exchange for untethering their work from a single desk.

Then, with a suddenness that has since become a cautionary parable in every business school, the company collapsed. In 1983 Osborne Computer filed for bankruptcy, and the reasons behind its fall gave rise to a phrase that outlived the company itself: the "Osborne effect." The conventional telling holds that Adam Osborne, ever the showman, spoke too candidly about machines still under development—successors called the Executive, which finally replaced the cramped fifty-two-column screen with a proper eighty-column display, and a portable called the Vixen—and that customers, hearing of the better computers coming, stopped buying the current model and waited. Inventory of the Osborne 1 piled up unsold; cash stopped flowing; the company could not survive the gap. Here the legend outran the history. Business scholars who have examined the wreckage since argue that premature announcement was, at most, one cause among several, and probably not the decisive one; the company was also battered by fierce new competition, by thin margins, by manufacturing and management failures, and above all by the arrival of IBM-compatible rivals that made its CP/M software look suddenly obsolete. The tidy morality tale of a founder talking his own company to death is more satisfying than accurate. But the lesson embedded in the legend was real enough to stick, and to this day executives invoke the Osborne effect as a warning against letting tomorrow's product cannibalize today's sales.

Adam Osborne himself did not vanish with his company. Irrepressible and contrarian to the end, he started over with a software venture called Paperback Software, whose cut-price spreadsheet, a close imitation of the market-leading Lotus 1-2-3, landed him in a landmark copyright suit that Lotus won, a case that helped establish how far the "look and feel" of a program could be protected by law. He wrote and provoked and forecast until his health failed, and he died in 2003, remembered less for any single machine than for one disruptive idea: that a computer could be a finished, affordable, carry-it-home product rather than a kit or a configuration to be assembled by the buyer.

While Osborne's star rose and fell, it had proven the concept, and competitors rushed into the space it had opened. From Solana Beach, on the coast of Southern California, came the Kaypro, built by a company called Non-Linear Systems that had previously made precision electronic instruments. Andrew Kay's machine wore a rugged aluminum case, offered a more generous nine-inch screen that eased the eyestrain of the Osborne's tiny display and, crucially, could show a full eighty columns of text at once, and likewise came loaded with a suite of bundled software. Kaypro buyers, many of them writers and small-business owners, developed a fierce loyalty; the machine became, for a while, one of the best-selling portables in the country and a favorite of novelists, science-fiction authors among them, who prized its readable screen and its indestructible case. A small quirk of its branding still amuses collectors: the first model Kaypro sold to the public was called the Kaypro II, though there had never been a Kaypro I—the "II" was pure marketing, meant to suggest a mature second generation to buyers wary of being anyone's guinea pig.

There was a deeper reason these machines flourished and then, almost overnight, did not, and it had everything to do with the software underneath them. The Osborne, the Kaypro, and their kin all ran CP/M, the operating system that had been the lingua franca of serious business microcomputers through the late 1970s. But when IBM launched its Personal Computer in 1981, it shipped not with CP/M but with a Microsoft product, MS-DOS, and as the IBM PC swept through corporate America the software industry reoriented itself to write for MS-DOS. Within a couple of years the newest and best programs were appearing on the IBM standard, and the CP/M portables, however beloved, found themselves cut off from the mainstream of software, marooned on an operating system the world was leaving behind. This is precisely why Compaq's achievement mattered so much and why Osborne, wedded to CP/M, could not follow: the future belonged to whoever could run the software written for IBM.

The most consequential challenger, though, came out of Houston. In 1982, three former Texas Instruments managers—Rod Canion, Jim Harris, and Bill Murto—sketched their idea for a portable computer on a paper placemat in a Houston pie restaurant. Their company, Compaq, shipped the Compaq Portable in early 1983. It was another luggable in the sewing-machine mold, but it carried a decisive difference: it ran the same software as the IBM Personal Computer. IBM's machine had conquered the business world the year before, and Compaq's engineers had performed a remarkable feat of legal engineering, reverse-engineering IBM's proprietary BIOS chip without copying it. The trick was a discipline called clean-room design: one team studied IBM's chip and wrote a meticulous description of everything it did, and a second team, who had never seen IBM's code and could swear so in court, wrote fresh software to match that description. The undertaking was neither quick nor cheap—Compaq is said to have devoted many months, a team of engineers, and something on the order of a million dollars to reproducing a chip that fit in the palm of a hand—but the result behaved exactly like IBM's BIOS while infringing none of IBM's copyrights. This made the Compaq Portable the first fully compatible IBM clone, and it made Compaq itself the fastest company in American history to reach a hundred million dollars in sales in its first year, booking some $111 million in 1983. Compaq would ride that head start to become, within a few years, one of the largest personal-computer makers in the world, and in doing so it lit the fuse on the entire clone industry that would eventually reduce IBM's own hardware to one option among many.

For a few frantic years in the early 1980s the luggable was one of the hottest categories in computing, and the competition was ferocious. Prices fell, features multiplied, and the machines grew heavier as makers crammed in larger screens and even hard disks, some tipping the scales at close to thirty pounds. Travelers developed a rueful vocabulary for them—"transportable" and "schleppable" among the gentler terms—and learned the hard geometry of wedging a suitcase-sized computer into an airplane's overhead bin or beneath a seat while carrying an actual suitcase besides. The category burned bright and brief. Almost as quickly as it had arisen it was overtaken, first by the IBM-compatible standard that stranded the CP/M pioneers, and then by a wholly new idea of portability, one that promised not merely to move the computer but to fold it, lighten it, and free it from the wall.

The luggables were, in truth, a transitional species. Nobody would mistake a twenty-four-pound box with a five-inch screen for the sleek notebooks that lay a decade ahead. They had to be plugged into the wall; there was no battery to speak of. They were "portable" only in the sense that a suitcase is portable—you could move them, but you would not want to hold one for long, and the people who lugged them through airports coined a wry name for the strain they put on the arm and shoulder. And yet they accomplished the essential imaginative leap. They severed the assumption, unquestioned since the mainframe era and largely intact through the first years of the desktop microcomputer, that a computer belonged to a place. The Osborne 1 and its imitators taught an entire generation of workers that the machine could belong to a person instead, that it could travel from office to home to hotel room, that the document you were writing was yours to carry rather than the building's to keep. Once people had tasted that freedom, they wanted more of it: a lighter machine, a bigger screen, and above all a way to cut the cord to the wall socket.

The luggables themselves have long since vanished from desks and gone to museums, but their ghost is everywhere. The impulse Osborne bottled—that a person should be able to close the machine, lift it, and carry their whole working life out the door—is the same impulse that puts a laptop in a backpack and a computer in a pocket today, and every business-school seminar that still warns against the Osborne effect is paying tribute to a beige sewing-machine of a computer that most of its students have never seen. That final ambition—to fold the computer flat, run it on a battery, and truly hold it in the lap—would be realized not in a garage or a pie shop but in the studio of an industrial designer thinking about how objects meet the human hand.

Chapter 52: The Clamshell

In 1982, aboard the Space Shuttle, an astronaut opened a slim magnesium box the color of gunmetal, tilted up a glowing amber screen, and began to type. The computer was called the GRiD Compass, and it had flown into orbit because it could do something no other machine of its era could: fold shut into a flat slab a person could tuck under one arm and carry through a hatch. On the ground, a Compass cost $8,150, far beyond the reach of ordinary buyers, and so its market was narrow—NASA, the military, a handful of executives who valued its ruggedness and its glamour. But in the design of that closed and reopened box lay the shape of nearly every laptop computer that would follow for the next forty years.

The Compass had been designed by Bill Moggridge, a British industrial designer who would later help found the discipline that came to be called interaction design—and the story of how he founded it is bound up with this very machine. Moggridge had shaped a handsome object, but when he finally took a working prototype home and sat down to use it, he had a small epiphany that changed his career. The elegance of the hardware, he realized, evaporated the moment a person had to wrestle with the confusing software glowing on its screen; the physical object and the experience of using it could not be designed as separate problems. That insight—that the designer's job extended past the shape of the box to the whole encounter between the user, the object, and the software running inside it—was the seed of what became interaction design. His practical insight about the hardware was equally consequential and deceptively simple. The luggables of the previous chapter—the Osborne, the Kaypro, the Compaq Portable—had treated the screen and the keyboard as fixed parts of a rigid box. Moggridge instead hinged the screen so that it lay flat against the keyboard when closed, protecting both, and swung up to meet the eyes when open. This clamshell arrangement, in which the display folds down over the keys like the two halves of a shell closing on a hinge, solved the twin problems of portability and protection in one elegant gesture. It also happened to look like the future. The Compass used a bright electroluminescent flat-panel display rather than a bulky cathode-ray tube, and it ran on a design so far ahead of its market that most people never saw one. But Moggridge had drawn the template, and the industry spent the following decade filling it in.

The Compass was as advanced inside as it was out. In place of a spinning disk it used bubble memory, an exotic solid-state storage that held its data even without power and could survive shocks that would have destroyed a conventional hard drive—precisely the quality wanted in a machine meant for cockpits and command posts. And it was to cockpits and command posts that much of it went. The GRiD found its customers in the United States military and intelligence agencies, was reportedly carried by special forces into the field, and flew aboard the Space Shuttle, where NASA nicknamed its onboard unit the Shuttle Portable Onboard Computer, or SPOC—an affectionate nod to Star Trek's Mr. Spock. Only a few thousand were ever built, and at more than eight thousand dollars apiece they were objects most people glimpsed only in magazines, but every one of them was, unmistakably, a laptop, years before the word was in common use.

Curiously, the machine that first brought the folding portable to a mass audience did not fully adopt the clamshell at all. In 1983, Radio Shack introduced the TRS-80 Model 100, a flat, book-sized computer with a keyboard and a small liquid-crystal display fixed in the same plane rather than folded over one another. It weighed under four pounds, ran for hours on ordinary AA batteries, and switched on instantly. For journalists it was a revelation. Consider how it worked in the field: a reporter could bang out a story in a stadium press box or a hotel lobby, then transmit it home not by any network but through the telephone itself. The Model 100 had a built-in modem, and a writer on the road who lacked a direct line would cradle an ordinary telephone handset into the rubber cups of an acoustic coupler, dial the newsroom's number, and let the machine sing its data down the line as a stream of warbling tones that a matching modem at the far end translated back into text. For most of a decade the Model 100 was a fixture of the working press, and many of the writers who used it remembered it with a devotion they never felt for the faster machines that replaced it. Its software had reportedly been written in part by a young Bill Gates, and Microsoft's founder is said to have called it one of the few programs he personally coded that he was truly proud of, describing it as among the last software he wrote himself. It is a lovely story, and largely true, but it has hardened into a tidier legend than the facts support: the compact code crammed into that read-only memory was a collaboration involving Microsoft programmers and the Japanese manufacturer Kyocera, and the precise division of authorship on the ROM has been debated ever since. Whatever the split of credit, the machine was a genuine hit; by some accounts the Model 100 and its variants sold well into the hundreds of thousands and beyond, a remarkable success for a device that never fully committed to the folding shape its rivals were already racing to adopt, and proof that battery life and instant readiness could matter to buyers as much as raw power.

Through the middle 1980s, the Japanese electronics giants

brought the pieces together. Toshiba, in particular, pushed the folding, battery-powered, disk-equipped portable toward something a business traveler could genuinely rely on, shipping a series of laptops that ran IBM-compatible software and steadily shrank in weight while the screens grew sharper. The screens told their own story of progress. The cheaper early laptops used passive-matrix displays, dim and sluggish, in which the pointer could disappear entirely while you moved it—"submarining," users called it, as the cursor dived beneath the surface—and colors smeared behind anything that scrolled. The costlier active-matrix screens, which gave each individual pixel its own tiny transistor, were brighter, faster, and vastly more legible, and for years the display remained the single most expensive component in a laptop, so that the quality of the screen, more than the speed of the processor, marked the real distance between a cheap portable and a good one. The liquid-crystal display, still imperfect, improved year by year; hard drives shrank; batteries lasted a little longer. The word "laptop" entered common speech to describe a machine you could actually balance on your knees, and by the end of the decade it had become an ordinary sight in airports and conference rooms. Toshiba's persistence paid off handsomely; by the early 1990s it had become the largest maker of laptop computers in the world, and the portable had graduated from a specialist's curiosity into a genuine industry. The transformation in daily working life was profound: a lawyer could carry a case file into court, a salesman could turn a laptop around on a client's desk, a scientist could take a laboratory's worth of calculation into the field, and a writer could work on a train. What had begun as an eight-thousand-dollar object for astronauts and generals was becoming, model by model and year by year, an ordinary tool of the traveling professional. The template Moggridge had drawn was filled in by a scrum of competitors through the mid-1980s. Toshiba's T1100 of 1985 is often called the first mass-market laptop, a battery-powered, IBM-compatible clamshell a business could buy by the dozen; Zenith won large government contracts to put folding portables on the desks of soldiers and tax collectors; and a parade of machines from other makers jostled to be lighter, cheaper, and longer-lived than the last. None was a household name, and most are forgotten now, but collectively they carried the folding computer from a glamorous rarity to a dependable tool, so that by the time Apple and IBM arrived to perfect its layout, the clamshell itself was already settled fact. Yet these early laptops shared an awkward habit inherited from the desktop: the keyboard sat at the front edge of the machine, leaving no place to rest the heels of the hands, and the pointing device, if there was one at all, was an afterthought clipped to the side.

The layout that would finally feel natural—the one still under nearly every set of hands today—arrived at the start of the 1990s from two rival camps. In 1991, Apple introduced the PowerBook, and its designers made a choice that now seems obvious but was then a small revolution: they pushed the keyboard toward the back of the machine and left a broad, flat expanse of palmrest in front of it, with a trackball centered where the thumbs naturally fell. Suddenly the wrists had somewhere to rest, and the pointer could be moved without lifting a hand from the deck. Apple did not introduce one PowerBook but three at once, in October 1991—the entry-level 100, the mid-range 140, and the top-of-the-line 170—and the family sold so briskly that it brought Apple a reported billion dollars in revenue in its first year on the market. There was a quiet irony in the smallest of them: the PowerBook 100, the lightest and most portable of the trio, was not built by Apple at all but by Sony, whose mastery of miniaturization packed the design into a case slimmer than Apple's own engineers had been able to achieve. The line rescued the company's reputation for portable computing after an earlier misstep had nearly poisoned the well. That misstep was the Macintosh Portable of 1989, a lead-heavy slab weighing some sixteen pounds that critics mocked as a machine you could carry only in the sense that you could carry a bowling ball, and it had left Apple's engineers determined to build something a human being would actually want to hold.

The following year, in 1992, IBM answered with a machine that became an icon in its own right: the ThinkPad. Where the PowerBook was rounded and friendly, the ThinkPad was a severe black rectangle inspired, its designer Richard Sapper said, by the traditional Japanese bento lunchbox—plain and unremarkable on the outside, holding something carefully arranged within. The name itself came from deep within IBM's own culture: for decades the company had handed its employees small pocket notebooks embossed with its one-word corporate motto, THINK, and the new portable was conceived as a thinking person's notepad, a ThinkPad. Its designer, Richard Sapper, was an industrial designer of international standing who had earlier created the celebrated Tizio desk lamp, and he brought to the machine an austere, almost severe sense of restraint. At the center of its keyboard, nestled between the G, H, and B keys, IBM placed a small red pointing nub called the TrackPoint, which let a typist move the cursor without ever moving the fingers from the home row. A few years later, in 1995, IBM pushed the same design intelligence to a small marvel of engineering with the ThinkPad 701C, whose full-sized keyboard was too wide for the compact case and so unfolded, as the lid opened, from two interlocking halves that spread outward like the wings of a butterfly—a mechanism so elegant that it was later added to the design collection of the Museum of Modern Art in New York. The black case, the red dot, and the reassuring solidity made the ThinkPad the machine of choice for engineers, executives, and eventually astronauts of a later generation, and ThinkPads flew aboard the Space Shuttle and took up long residence on the International Space Station, closing a loop that had opened with the GRiD Compass a decade before.

Between them, the PowerBook and the ThinkPad settled the argument about what a laptop should look like. The palmrest, the keyboard set back from the front edge, an integrated pointing device the hands could reach without wandering—these became the grammar of the portable computer. The trackball gave way within a few years to the flat touchpad—which Apple's PowerBook 500 series helped popularize in 1994, replacing the rolling ball with a smooth pad that read the movement of a fingertip—and the TrackPoint survived as a beloved minority preference, still found on ThinkPads today and defended by its loyalists with something close to religious fervor, but the fundamental arrangement held. Open the lid of almost any laptop sold in the present day and the layout will be instantly familiar: a keyboard pushed toward the hinge, a wide palmrest beneath it, and a pointing surface set into the deck where the thumbs fall. A person could now open a machine, rest both wrists on it, type a document, move the cursor, and close it again, all without a mouse, a wall socket, or a desk. The computer had at last become something that lived in the space between a lap and a pair of hands.

What that untethered machine still could not do gracefully was produce a finished page. A laptop could compose the words, but the crisp, typeset document—the kind that had once required a print shop, a typesetter, and a small fortune—remained the province of professionals. That, too, was about to change, and the revolution would come not from a portable computer but from an unlikely marriage of a beige desktop, a heavy laser printer, and a piece of software that let anyone lay out a page.

Chapter 53: The Page and the Laser

On a January afternoon in 1985, at Apple's annual shareholders' meeting in California, Steve Jobs stood beside a machine that weighed nearly eighty pounds and cost as much as a good used car, and he told the crowd that it would change how the world put words on paper. The machine was the Apple LaserWriter, a printer priced at $6,995, and to the untrained eye it looked like an oversized office copier. But when a Macintosh sent a document to it, the page that emerged was not the ragged, dot-matrix scrawl that home computers produced. It was clean, black, and sharp—text and images rendered at three hundred dots to the inch, indistinguishable at a glance from the output of a professional typesetting shop that might charge a small business hundreds of dollars for a single page. The LaserWriter did it for pennies, in seconds, on a desk. Jobs, characteristically, presented it not as a mere printer but as the missing piece of a revolution, the final link that would let the Macintosh do something no other computer could.

The magic inside that heavy box was not, as most people assumed, the laser printing mechanism. That part was borrowed: the printing engine came from Canon, essentially the same photocopier hardware the Japanese company sold to the office market, and on its own it was no more revolutionary than a Xerox machine. What made the LaserWriter extraordinary was the software brain Apple had installed inside it—a language called PostScript—and the story of PostScript begins not at Apple but at Xerox's fabled Palo Alto Research Center, where two researchers named John Warnock and Charles Geschke had been trying to solve the problem of describing a page to a machine. A printed page is not a grid of dots to a human designer; it is a set of shapes, curves, and letterforms that must scale cleanly to any size and print at any resolution. Warnock and Geschke had devised a way to describe those shapes mathematically, as instructions a printer could interpret. When Xerox showed no urgency about turning their work into a product, the two men did what a growing number of PARC alumni were doing in those years: they left, in 1982, and founded their own company. They called it Adobe, after Adobe Creek, which ran behind Warnock's house in Los Altos.

There was a bitter familiarity to the pattern. Xerox's Palo Alto Research Center had, in those very years, invented or refined an astonishing share of modern computing—the graphical user interface, the mouse, the laser printer, Ethernet networking—and had watched, again and again, as the commercial fortune in its ideas walked out the door in the persons of the researchers who created them. Warnock and Geschke leaving to found Adobe was one more chapter in that long, rueful story, and PostScript one more billion-dollar industry that Xerox had held in its hands and let slip through its fingers. The lesson, often drawn since, is that invention and the will to sell are two different gifts, and that the second is somehow the rarer of the two.

The breakthrough that Adobe's small team—Warnock and Geschke joined by Doug Brotz, Ed Taft, and Bill Paxton—brought to fruition was that PostScript was device-independent, and it is worth pausing on exactly what that meant, because it is the whole point. In PostScript, the letter "a" is not a fixed pattern of dark and light dots but a set of mathematical curves, a recipe for a shape. Because it is a recipe rather than a picture, the same description can be handed to a modest desktop laser printer, which renders it out of three hundred dots per inch, or to a professional imagesetter costing tens of thousands of dollars, which renders the identical shape at more than two thousand dots per inch—the same layout, the same letterforms, produced at ever finer quality with no change to the file. A designer could proof a newsletter on the cheap printer beside the desk and then send the very same document to a commercial shop to be printed at magazine quality. Steve Jobs recognized what he was looking at, invested in Adobe, and licensed PostScript for the LaserWriter. The terms of that deal became legend in Silicon Valley: Jobs paid a $1.5 million advance against future royalties and bought roughly a fifth of the young company for another $2.5 million, a stake that would grow to be worth vastly more. To interpret PostScript, the printer needed a more powerful processor and more memory than the Macintosh it served: inside the LaserWriter sat a Motorola 68000 chip running at twelve megahertz with half a megabyte of memory, more raw computing power than the Mac feeding it the document. That was precisely the point. The intelligence lived in the printer, and Apple linked the two over its AppleTalk network, so that a whole office of Macintoshes could share a single costly LaserWriter, each one sending a richly designed page and trusting the machine to render it perfectly.

This device-independence gave rise to a small new industry of its own, the service bureau, a shop equipped with a high-resolution imagesetter such as the Linotronic, where a designer who had proofed a document on a humble desk printer could bring the very same file to be output at typeset quality on film or photographic paper, ready for the printing press. The designer supplied the disk; the bureau supplied the resolution of two thousand dots and more to the inch; and the old wax-and-knife paste-up trade withered a little further with each job that passed through.

But a beautiful printer and a clever page-description language still left a gap. Someone using a Macintosh in 1985 could type a memo, but arranging text and images into the multi-column, professionally composed layout of a newsletter, a brochure, or a magazine required tools that did not yet exist on a personal computer. That final piece arrived from Seattle, from a former newspaperman named Paul Brainerd. Brainerd had worked at a company that made typesetting systems for newspapers, and when it closed its Seattle operation he took several of its engineers and founded a company he named Aldus, after Aldus Manutius, the Venetian printer of the Renaissance who had helped invent the modern book. In 1985 Aldus shipped a program called PageMaker, and it did for layout what a word processor had done for writing. On the Macintosh screen, a person could draw columns, pour text into them, place photographs and headlines, adjust margins, and see on the display very nearly what would emerge from the printer—the principle the industry called "what you see is what you get."

To describe what his software made possible, Brainerd reached for a phrase that would name an entire new industry: desktop publishing. The words captured the audacity of the idea. Publishing—the setting of type, the composition of pages, the production of printed matter for distribution—had for five centuries been the work of skilled craftsmen using expensive and specialized equipment. The phrase declared that it could now be done on a desk, by an ordinary person, with a computer and a printer.

To grasp how radical that was, one has to picture the world it replaced. Producing a printed page in 1980 was a manual craft performed in stages by specialists. A typesetter keyed the text into a phototypesetting machine that exposed the letters onto photographic paper, which was developed into long strips called galleys. A paste-up artist then cut those galleys apart with a blade, coated the backs with hot wax, and pressed the pieces down onto a board by hand, aligning columns and headlines with a ruler and a practiced eye until a finished "mechanical" was ready to be photographed for the printing press. A single correction meant resetting a line, waxing it, and slicing it into place. The work was skilled, slow, and expensive, and it stood between an ordinary person and a professional-looking page like a locked door. Desktop publishing handed that person the key.

The revolution required all three pieces at once, and this is the crucial point that the individual histories of each product tend to obscure. The Macintosh supplied the graphical screen on which a layout could be seen and manipulated. PageMaker supplied the tools to compose that layout. PostScript and the LaserWriter supplied the means to turn it into a flawless printed page. No one of the three would have started an industry alone. A Mac without a laser printer produced beautiful layouts that could only be printed crudely; a LaserWriter without PageMaker was a very expensive way to print memos; PostScript without a graphical computer to feed it had nowhere to live. Together, arriving within months of one another in 1985, they formed a complete chain from idea to printed page, and the chain was affordable enough for a small design studio, a church, a school, or a person working at a kitchen table.

The consequences reached in two directions. In the wider world, desktop publishing democratized design. Church bulletins, community newsletters, restaurant menus, wedding invitations, small-press books, fan magazines, and startup marketing materials suddenly bore the crisp typography that had once signaled professional production. A generation of designers who could not afford a traditional typesetting house set up shop with a Mac and a LaserWriter and undercut the old print trade. The economics were startling. A church that had once paid a print shop hundreds of dollars to typeset and produce a weekly bulletin could now buy the equipment, learn PageMaker in an afternoon, and produce the same bulletin in-house for the cost of paper and toner; a small business that could never have hired a professional designer could lay out its own brochure over a weekend. Zines and fanzines, the homemade magazines of subcultures and enthusiasts, blossomed into a golden age, their makers freed at last from the ransom-note look of the typewriter and the photocopier. The change was not entirely gentle—many established typesetters and paste-up artists watched their crafts evaporate, and purists complained, not always wrongly, that easy tools produced a flood of ugly, over-decorated pages by people who had never studied type and could not resist packing a single flyer with a dozen clashing fonts. But the gate had been opened, and it never closed again.

The second consequence was narrower and, for one company, existential. The Macintosh had launched in 1984 to dazzled reviews and, after the first burst of curiosity, disappointing sales; its friendly graphics and limited software library left many businesses cold, and by 1985 Apple was in genuine trouble, its founder Jobs pushed out of the company that summer. Desktop publishing rescued it. Because the Mac's graphical foundation made it uniquely suited to visual layout work, and because PageMaker and PostScript appeared first and worked best on the Macintosh, the machine found a professional constituency that no competitor could serve as well. Designers, publishers, ad agencies, and print shops bought Macs not because they were cheaper or more powerful than the IBM-compatible machines that dominated the office, but because they alone could do this one thing supremely well. For years, desktop publishing was the reason a serious business bought a Macintosh, and the loyalty of the creative professions became the bedrock on which Apple survived its lean years and eventually rebuilt.

The tools themselves kept evolving, and not always in PageMaker's favor. By the early 1990s a rival program called QuarkXPress, prized by professional designers for its precision and control, had overtaken PageMaker in the high-end market, and in 1994 Aldus itself was absorbed by Adobe, uniting the layout program and the page-description language under one corporate roof. Adobe would eventually retire PageMaker altogether in favor of a more powerful successor called InDesign, but by then the revolution Brainerd had named was long since won; the argument was no longer whether ordinary people could set type, only which program they would use to do it.

The page had been conquered, and its conquest has outlasted almost every machine that took part in it. Type itself became a battleground along the way. Adobe kept the inner workings of its high-quality Type 1 fonts closely held, licensing them for a fee, and the two other giants of the industry, Apple and Microsoft, resented paying tribute for something so fundamental as the shapes of letters. Together they developed a rival font technology called TrueType and built it directly into their operating systems, giving away for free what Adobe had sold. The "font wars" of the late 1980s and early 1990s were fought over precisely this—who would own the letterforms that appeared on every screen and every page—and their eventual truce, which folded the strengths of both approaches into shared standards, is the reason a computer today can display thousands of typefaces without anyone thinking twice about where they came from.

Adobe went on to build an empire on the descendants of that first insight: the Portable Document Format, the PDF, which every office and government and school now uses to send a page that looks the same on every screen and every printer, is PostScript's direct heir, the same idea of describing a page as a recipe rather than a picture. Every time a document arrives as a PDF that prints identically whether it lands on a cheap inkjet or a commercial press, the ghost of the LaserWriter is at work. But the machine that could set a beautiful page was still, at heart, a device for text and static pictures. It could not yet sing, speak, or show a moving image, and the next expansion of what a personal computer could hold would come not through the printer but through a silver disc and a card that gave the machine a voice.

Chapter 54: Sight and Sound

In 1993, a player sat down at a home computer, slid a silver disc into a tray, and found himself standing on the dock of a deserted island. Waves lapped. A gull cried somewhere overhead. Ahead lay a marble stairway, a ruined library, the humming machinery of some vanished civilization, all rendered in still images so richly detailed that they looked less like a computer game than a series of paintings. There were no monsters, no scores, no timers—only silence, atmosphere, and a growing sense of mystery. The game was called Myst, and it would go on to sell some six million copies and reign for most of the decade as the best-selling computer game in the world, unseated only when The Sims arrived years later. It could not have existed a few years earlier, because the images and sounds that filled it would not have fit on any storage a home computer possessed. Myst arrived on a compact disc, and the compact disc was rewriting what a personal computer could be.

The game itself was the work of two brothers, Rand and Robyn Miller, working in a small studio called Cyan in rural Washington State, and the way they built it says much about how new all of this was. There was no dedicated game engine, no polished toolkit for constructing three-dimensional worlds. The Millers assembled Myst largely inside Hyper-

Card, a gentle Macintosh program meant for organizing stacks of virtual index cards, treating each painted view of their island as a "card" the player could click to move to the next. The images were rendered one frame at a time on Macintosh computers, a process so slow that a single scene could take hours to compute. The Millers labored over the project for the better part of two years, and to lend their still world flickers of life they leaned on a young Apple technology called QuickTime, which let short clips of video play inside a window on the screen—a fuse burning down, a book's pages turning, a trapped man's face delivering a warning. Published by Broderbund, Myst became a fixture of the very CD-ROM computers it had helped to sell. The result felt like magic precisely because the medium was so humble; two brothers had painted an entire world and pressed it onto a disc.

For its first fifteen years, the personal computer had been a machine of text and numbers. It processed words, calculated spreadsheets, and printed pages, and even its games were mostly built from crude blocks of color and beeps from a tiny internal speaker. The reason was arithmetic. A floppy disk held a little over a megabyte of data—enough for a document, a spreadsheet, or a simple program, but nowhere near enough for a photograph-quality image, a recording of a human voice, or a passage of music. Rich media are enormous compared to text, and the personal computer of the 1980s simply had no place to put them. The barrier was not imagination but capacity.

The compact disc broke that barrier. Invented for music and introduced to consumers in the early 1980s, the CD stored data as microscopic pits pressed into the disc and read by a laser as it spun, and a single disc held around 650 megabytes—roughly the equivalent of four hundred and fifty floppies. Adapted for computers as the CD-ROM, it offered, for the first time, storage measured not in the low millions of bytes but in the hundreds of millions, and it offered that storage cheaply, because a disc could be pressed for pennies once the master was made. Suddenly there was room. There was room for thousands of photographs, for hours of sound, for full-motion video, for the sprawling painted worlds of a game like Myst. The question was no longer whether a computer could hold rich media, but what one would do with all that space.

The drives that read these discs became a specification buyers learned to compare. The first CD-ROM drives spun at the same rate as an ordinary audio CD player, delivering data at about a hundred and fifty kilobytes a second; manufacturers then doubled that speed, and doubled it again, advertising drives as "2X," "4X," and onward to speeds many dozens of times faster, each multiple measured against that original audio baseline. A faster drive meant video that stuttered less and games that paused less often to load, and the "X" number stamped on the box became, for a few years, a badge of how modern a machine was, a number shoppers recited the way a later generation would recite megapixels or gigahertz.

The answer that captured the public imagination most vividly was the encyclopedia. In 1993, Microsoft released Encarta, a complete encyclopedia on a single CD-ROM. Where a printed encyclopedia filled a shelf, cost hundreds of dollars, weighed as much as a child, and went out of date the moment it was bound, Encarta fit in a shirt pocket. And it did what no printed book could: it played recordings of birdsong beside the articles on birds, let a reader hear a snippet of a Beethoven symphony, showed animations of how a volcano erupted or how the heart pumped blood, and let a curious mind leap from one entry to another by clicking a highlighted word. Yet Encarta's origins puncture a common assumption, for Microsoft did not sit down and write a great encyclopedia from scratch. The company had first approached the most prestigious name in the field, Encyclopædia Britannica, and been rebuffed; Britannica, proud of its leather-bound sets and its army of door-to-door salesmen, saw little future in a cheap plastic disc and declined to license its content. Microsoft turned instead to a humbler and less costly source, the Funk & Wagnalls encyclopedia, whose text formed the foundation of Encarta's first edition, dressed up with sound, animation, and Microsoft's software. The upstart medium had been built, in part, on a reference work that the aristocrat of the trade had disdained—a decision that would help doom the printed encyclopedia, Britannica included, within a generation. For millions of families, a CD-ROM encyclopedia was the reason they finally bought a computer, and it hastened the slow death of the door-to-door encyclopedia salesman and, eventually, of the printed set itself. The disruption cut both ways in the end. Encarta's cheap, singing disc helped drive the printed encyclopedia toward extinction—Encyclopædia Britannica ceased printing its famous multi-volume set in 2012, after more than two centuries—but Encarta itself did not live to enjoy the victory. A free, collaboratively written encyclopedia on the open web, Wikipedia, would in its turn make even a CD-ROM encyclopedia look quaint, and Microsoft shut Encarta down in 2009. The reference book had been overthrown twice in a single generation, first by a silver disc and then by the web.

The disc did not stop at games and encyclopedias. A whole genre of children's software bloomed, "living books" that read a story aloud and let a child click any object on the page to make it wiggle or honk, and there were CD-ROM atlases that zoomed from continent to city street, movie guides that played film clips beside their reviews, cookbooks that showed a technique in motion. Not all of it was good. The era produced a torrent of hastily assembled "shovelware," discs padded with clip art and low-grade video for no better reason than to justify the coveted multimedia label. But the best of it genuinely reimagined what a reference work or a storybook could be, and it planted in a generation of children the expectation that information should move, speak, and answer to a click.

But storage alone was not enough to make a computer a machine of sight and sound. A disc full of music is useless if the computer cannot play it, and here the standard PC of the late 1980s was nearly mute. Its only sound-making device was a small internal speaker capable of little more than beeps and buzzes, a relic of the machine's origins as a business tool, designed to chirp a warning rather than to make music. Into that silence stepped a company founded in Singapore called Creative Technology and its expansion card, the Sound Blaster. Its founder, Sim Wong Hoo, had started out trying to build a computer that could sing and speak in the languages of Asia, and out of that ambition came a card that, slotted inside an ordinary PC, gave the machine a proper voice: it could synthesize music, play back recorded speech and sound effects, and drive a pair of speakers with something approaching the fidelity of a stereo. It arrived at the turn of the 1990s and quickly became so dominant that "Sound Blaster compatible" turned into the informal standard that game makers designed for, a label printed on software boxes as a promise that the program would actually be heard. A PC with a Sound Blaster and a CD-ROM drive could, for the first time, deliver a game with a real musical score and spoken dialogue rather than bleeps. The card went on to become one of the best-selling PC expansion products ever made, and Sim's venture grew from modest beginnings in Singapore into a global electronics concern.

"Multimedia" became the defining buzzword of the era, splashed across advertisements and magazine covers until it seemed to mean everything and nothing at once. Games rushed to show off what the new capacity allowed. The 7th Guest, released the same year as Myst, filled two whole discs with grainy full-motion video of live actors haunting a Victorian mansion, and however crude such footage looks now, at the time the sight of filmed human beings moving inside a computer game struck players as something close to sorcery. The novelty of the moment is hard to recover: people would gather around a screen simply to watch a postage-stamp-sized video clip play in one corner and marvel that the machine could manage it at all.

The visuals advanced in step. Early PCs had displayed a handful of garish colors on coarse grids, but a graphics standard called VGA, introduced by IBM in 1987, gave the machine the ability to show a screen of six hundred and forty by four hundred and eighty pixels in a palette of hundreds of thousands of possible colors, rich enough to render photographs and lifelike scenes. VGA and its successors turned the screen from a grid of blocky characters into a canvas, and it was on that canvas that the painted worlds of Myst and its contemporaries could appear.

By the early 1990s the pieces existed but did not always fit together, and a buyer had no easy way to know whether a given computer could actually run the new wave of software. A game or an encyclopedia might demand a CD-ROM drive, a Sound Blaster-compatible sound card, VGA graphics, and a certain amount of memory, and a customer staring at a shelf of nearly identical beige boxes could not tell which machines qualified. To cut through the confusion, a group of manufacturers formed the Multimedia PC Marketing Council and agreed on a badge called the Multimedia PC, or MPC, standard. A computer bearing the MPC logo promised a defined minimum—a CD-ROM drive, a sound card, sufficient memory and processing power—so that a shopper could trust that software marked "multimedia" would run on any machine that carried the same mark. The standard was crude and quickly outgrown, revised upward more than once as hardware improved, but it did its job. It told ordinary buyers that "multimedia" was a thing a computer could be, and it told manufacturers what to build.

The cumulative effect of these developments—the CD-ROM's vast cheap storage, the Sound Blaster's voice, VGA's richer eye, and the MPC badge that tied them together—was to change the fundamental character of the personal computer. The machine that had begun as a calculator and a typewriter became, over the course of a few years, a device for images, music, and games. Families gathered around it not only to write letters and balance checkbooks but to explore an island of mysteries, to hear an encyclopedia sing, to watch a grainy video clip play in a small window on the screen. The computer moved out of the home office and into the living room and the child's bedroom. It became entertainment, education, and play, and in doing so it broadened its audience from professionals and hobbyists to nearly everyone. The very word for the household machine began to change: where a computer had once been a tool one used, it was becoming a place one went, a thing a family gathered around in the evening much as an earlier generation had gathered around a radio or a television set. The silver disc has since gone the way of the floppy, its role assumed by the invisible torrents of streaming that pour music and film through the internet, but the expectation it created—that a computer is naturally a machine of sight and sound, that of course it will play, sing, and show—is the direct inheritance of that first generation of multimedia PCs, and every phone that answers a spoken question or plays a film in the palm of a hand is their descendant, tracing its lineage back to a beige box, a silver disc, and a card that first taught the computer to speak.

There remained, however, one great obstacle standing between the computer and the ordinary household that now wanted one. Assembling that machine of sight and sound—getting the CD-ROM drive, the sound card, and the graphics all to work together without conflict—could reduce a grown adult to tears, and the long, maddening struggle to make the personal computer as simple to set up as a toaster was a battle the industry had barely begun to win.

Chapter 55: Plug and Pray

Somewhere in a suburban home in the early 1990s, a father sat on the carpet at two in the morning surrounded by the disemboweled parts of a personal computer, a screwdriver in one hand and a photocopied manual in the other, trying to persuade a newly purchased sound card to make a sound. He had installed it in the correct slot. He had run the setup program from the floppy disk that came in the box. And still the machine sat mute, or worse, refused to start at all, because the sound card and the modem he had installed the week before were now fighting invisibly over the same scrap of the computer's attention. The manual spoke of jumpers and interrupts in a language he did not understand. He was not incompetent. He was an ordinary person colliding with a machine that had never been designed to be set up by ordinary people, and his midnight ordeal was so common in that era that it earned a bitter nickname. The industry called its official solution Plug and Play. Everyone who lived through the reality called it plug and pray.

The trouble was rooted in the way the IBM PC had been designed at the start of the 1980s, in an age when a computer might contain one or two add-in cards and the person installing them was presumed to be an engineer. Every device that needed the processor's attention—a sound card, a network card, a modem, a scanner—had to be assigned an interrupt request line, universally abbreviated as an IRQ. An IRQ was, in essence, a numbered doorbell the device could ring to say it needed servicing, and the original PC offered only sixteen of them, of which a good half were already spoken for by the keyboard, the disk drives, the system clock, and other essential machinery. There were also finite ranges of memory addresses and a small set of data channels, called DMA channels, to be divided up. To make this concrete: the popular Sound Blaster card typically wanted interrupt line five, DMA channel one, and a range of addresses beginning at the hexadecimal number 220, and if any other device in the machine had already claimed line five, the two would ring the same doorbell, the computer could not tell which was calling, and one or both would simply fail. Resolving the conflict often meant physically opening the case and moving tiny plastic connectors called jumpers over rows of metal pins, according to charts buried in a manual, by trial and error, in the dark, until each card had a doorbell of its own.

Even when the hardware was seated correctly, the computer had to be told, in software, that the new device existed and how to talk to it. This was the domain of the driver, a small program that translated between the operating system and a specific piece of hardware, and drivers came on floppy disks that were easily lost, quickly outdated, and specific to a single model. Beyond the drivers lay two text files that governed how the whole machine woke up: config.sys and autoexec.bat, cryptic lists of commands that loaded drivers and reserved memory in a precise order. A single mistyped line in one of these files—a misplaced character, a driver loaded before the memory it needed—could leave the computer unable to start, or able to start but unable to run the very game the child had been promised. Families kept boot floppies as insurance and learned, through hard experience, never to change a working configuration without writing down exactly what it had been. An entire cottage industry of thick paperback guides and paid technicians grew up around the single task of making a personal computer work at all.

Lurking beneath all of this was an even more fundamental constraint, and it produced one of computing's most durable myths. The original IBM PC's design reserved the first 640 kilobytes of memory for running programs, an amount that seemed lavish in 1981 but grew cramped as software swelled, and wringing a demanding game into that "conventional memory" became a black art. Users learned to juggle a whole bestiary of memory managers—himem.sys, emm386, and third-party tools like QEMM—that shuffled drivers into obscure regions called upper memory blocks to free up precious space below the 640K line, editing config.sys line by patient line until a game finally reported just enough room to run. The barrier was so notorious that a quotation attached itself to Bill Gates, endlessly repeated, in which he supposedly declared that "640K ought to be enough for anybody." It is almost certainly apocryphal. No one has ever produced a reliable source, and Gates himself has flatly and repeatedly denied saying it, once writing that the line "floats like a rumor, repeated again and again" with never a citation to be found. The myth endured anyway, because it captured a real and maddening truth: the machine's foundations had been laid in an age that never imagined how much would one day be asked of them.

In many households the person who mastered these dark arts was, improbably, a child. A teenager who wanted to play the latest game learned, out of sheer necessity, to read the cryptic error messages, to edit config.sys and autoexec.bat by hand, to build a special "boot disk" that loaded only the drivers a particular game required and nothing else, and in doing so became the family's resident expert, summoned to the rescue whenever a parent's spreadsheet refused to print. It was an education by ordeal, and a whole generation of future engineers and technicians got their first real understanding of how a computer worked because they were forced, at the age of twelve, to negotiate a truce between a sound card and a modem.

The industry knew this could not last if the computer was ever to become a household appliance, and the answer took shape as a set of standards under the banner of Plug and Play. It is worth correcting a common belief here, for Plug and Play is often remembered as something Microsoft simply invented and bolted onto Windows. In truth it was an industry-wide effort, requiring the operating system, the computer's underlying firmware, and the add-in devices themselves all to cooperate, and it built on ideas that had been circulating for years. The principle was straightforward and the execution fiendish: a card, when installed, would announce what it was and what resources it needed; the operating system would survey all the devices, assign each a non-conflicting set of interrupts and addresses, load the correct driver, and do it all without the user ever opening the manual or touching a jumper. Plug and Play arrived in earnest with Windows 95 in the summer of 1995, and it was a genuine advance. When it worked, a person could slide in a card, restart the machine, and watch the operating system recognize the new hardware and welcome it. When it did not work—and in the early years it often did not, defeated by older "legacy" cards that predated the standard and could not announce themselves, or by drivers that misreported what they needed—the users who had once said "plug and pray" now muttered it with a knowing smile, for the promise and the reality had not yet met.

Even Windows 95's own tools bore witness to how often the dream failed. Buried in the system was a screen called the Device Manager, a list of everything installed, and beside any device that had not been configured correctly sat a small yellow exclamation mark—a warning icon that became, for a generation of users, an object of quiet dread. A new sound card or modem might trigger a "New Hardware Found" wizard that then installed the wrong driver, or demanded a floppy disk the owner did not have, or produced a resource conflict the system cheerfully announced but could not itself resolve, leaving the hopeful user staring at that yellow mark and reaching, once again, for the manual. The gap between the friendly wizard and the sullen reality was precisely the gap between plug and play and plug and pray.

Part of the eventual cure came from replacing the aging expansion slots themselves. The original PC's slots, a design known as ISA, had no built-in way for a card to declare its identity or its needs, which is why the early jumpers and conflicts had been so intractable. A newer slot standard called PCI, introduced by Intel in the early 1990s, was built from the ground up to let the machine interrogate each card and negotiate its resources in software, and as PCI steadily replaced ISA through the middle of the decade, the invisible cooperation that Plug and Play had promised began, at last, to work as advertised. The revolution was as much in these unglamorous slots and buses as in any feature a marketer could put on a box.

The deeper problem, though, lay not only in the invisible assignment of interrupts but in the visible chaos at the back of the machine. The rear panel of a mid-1990s PC was a jungle of incompatible ports, each shaped differently and each dedicated to one kind of device. There was a serial port for the modem, a parallel port for the printer, a round port for the keyboard and another, confusingly similar, for the mouse, a game port for the joystick, and specialized connectors for whatever expansion cards had been added. Each port used its own connector and its own electrical standard; none could substitute for another; and most could not be unplugged and replugged while the computer was running without risking a crash or worse. Adding a device often meant there was simply no appropriate socket left, which meant opening the case again and installing another card, which meant another round of the interrupt struggle.

The solution to the jungle of ports was a single, humble connector that would, over the following decade, quietly conquer the world. It was called the Universal Serial Bus, or USB, and its specification, Revision 1.0, was released on January 15, 1996, the work of a consortium of seven companies including Intel, Microsoft, Compaq, IBM, and others who had grown tired of the mess. The effort had been driven inside Intel by an engineer named Ajay Bhatt, who liked to tell interviewers that his motivation was thoroughly ordinary: he had come home one day and found himself unable to get a printer working for his family, and the sheer wrongness of a task so simple being so hard set him on the road to a universal connector. USB's ambition was announced in its name: one universal port, one connector shape, that any device could use—keyboard, mouse, printer, scanner, camera, storage drive, and countless things not yet invented. A single USB port could, through inexpensive hubs, be split to serve many devices at once, so a computer no longer needed a different socket for every gadget. Better still, USB devices could be connected and disconnected while the computer ran, recognized on the spot without a restart, and in many cases powered directly through the same cable that carried their data, dispensing with a separate power adapter. USB improved in generations of its own. A refined version 1.1 in 1998 smoothed out the early rough edges, and USB 2.0, arriving in 2000, multiplied the speed some fortyfold to around 480 megabits per second, fast enough for external hard drives and video. A rival standard called FireWire, developed largely by Apple, was faster still in its early days and became the favorite for connecting digital camcorders, but USB's sheer ubiquity and lower cost eventually carried the field. The technology was slow to take hold at first—the earliest USB devices were scarce and the earliest ports sat unused, and it took the arrival of machines built entirely around it, most famously Apple's original iMac in 1998, which threw out every legacy port and offered nothing but USB, to force the industry's hand—but by the end of the 1990s and into the 2000s it swept the old ports away one by one, until a new computer might have nothing on its back panel but a row of identical rectangular slots.

Taken together, Plug and Play and USB accomplished something as important as any faster processor or richer display:

they made the personal computer, at long last, into an appliance. The father on the carpet at two in the morning gave way, over a decade, to a person who unpacked a machine, plugged a cable into any available port, and simply began to work. The interrupt conflict, the jumper chart, the hand-edited config.sys, the lost driver disk—these receded into the folklore of a rougher age, remembered by those who had suffered them and unknown to the millions who came after. And the victory proved so complete that its evidence is now in nearly every pocket and on nearly every desk: the same rectangular connector, in its later and smaller forms, still charges the phone, links the keyboard, and carries the files, and the simple expectation that a cable plugged into a port will just work, with no manual and no prayer, is the quiet monument to a battle most people never knew was fought. The machine had shed the last of its demand that its owner be an initiate. It could be bought, opened, and used by anyone, and the anguished midnight rituals of interrupts and jumpers survived only as war stories told by those who had once endured them.

And now that anyone could set one up and make it sing, the personal computer stood ready for the transformation that would matter most of all—the moment it stopped being an island on a desk and reached out, through a telephone line, to join every other computer in the world.

Chapter 56: The Modem Hums

In a suburban bedroom sometime around 1985, a teenager sat in the dark and listened to his computer sing. It was a strange, unlovely song: a dial tone, then a rapid clatter of touch-tones as the modem punched out a phone number, then a high whistle answered by a second whistle, and finally a burst of hissing static that rose and fell like surf before settling into silence. To an adult passing in the hallway it sounded like a machine malfunctioning. To the boy hunched over the keyboard it was the sound of a door opening. Somewhere across town, or across the country, another computer had picked up the line, and for the price of a local phone call the two machines were now talking to each other. On his screen, glowing green characters began to scroll: a welcome message, a menu, the handle of the stranger who ran this particular electronic outpost from his own bedroom, a person the boy would likely never meet in the flesh yet already, in some new and undefined way, knew. The personal computer, conceived as a solitary tool for calculation and word processing, had just become something its inventors had scarcely imagined. It had become a way to reach other people.

The device responsible for the transformation was the modem, a squat box whose name compressed the two things it did: it modulated the digital ones and zeros of a computer into the warbling audible tones that could travel down an ordinary telephone line, and it demodulated the tones arriving from the other end back into data. The telephone network had been built to carry the human voice, and the modem's ingenuity lay in disguising computer data as a kind of voice the network would agree to carry. The screech that so annoyed parents and siblings was not noise but conversation: it was the handshake, the ritual by which two modems, before exchanging any real data, whistled test tones back and forth to discover the fastest speed the particular quality of that particular phone line would bear, then agreed on it and settled into work. The modem that set the pattern came from a company called Hayes, whose Smartmodem of 1981 could be controlled entirely by the computer through a simple vocabulary of typed commands, each beginning with the letters AT, for "attention"—AT followed by a telephone number told the modem to dial it. This "AT command set" became so universal that "Hayes compatible" turned into a standard every rival had to meet, and the little AT prefix survives, buried and unseen, inside the cellular modems of smartphones to this day. Early modems crawled at three hundred bits per second, slow enough that a patient reader could follow the text as it painted itself across the screen one character at a time, faster than a person could read but only just. By the late 1980s they had reached twelve hundred and then twenty-four hundred bits per second, and through the 1990s they would climb to fourteen thousand four hundred, then twenty-eight thousand eight hundred, and finally to fifty-six thousand, near the theoretical limit of what a voice line could carry, and each leap felt like a small miracle of acceleration.

What these modems connected to, in the beginning, was a sprawling and largely hidden archipelago of hobbyist systems known as bulletin board systems, or BBSes. The concept had been born in Chicago in the winter of 1978, when two members of a local computer club, Ward Christensen and Randy Suess, found themselves snowed in during the

Great Blizzard that buried the city that January. With time on their hands, they built a system that let people dial in with a modem, leave messages, and read the messages others had left, exactly as one might pin notes to a corkboard in a community center. They called it the Computerized Bulletin Board System, and, in the generous spirit of the era, they did not patent it or hoard it; they wrote up exactly how they had done it and published the design in Byte magazine so that anyone could copy it. Within a few years the idea had propagated into the tens of thousands. A BBS was typically one person's obsession, run out of a spare bedroom on a single spare phone line, which meant that only one caller could connect at a time and that dialing a popular board could mean hearing a busy signal for hours before finally getting through. Each board had its own personality, dictated by the tastes of its sysop, the system operator who ran it: some traded software, some hosted freewheeling debates, some catered to games or gossip or the exchange of files that skirted the edges of legality. To dial long distance was expensive, so the culture stayed intensely local, a lattice of small towns in cyberspace, each with its own regulars who might live a few miles apart and never meet.

The BBS world was not entirely disconnected from itself, either. In 1984 a sysop named Tom Jennings devised FidoNet, a volunteer scheme by which bulletin boards would quietly dial one another in the dead of night, when long-distance rates fell to their lowest, to pass along bundles of messages, so that a note posted on a board in one city could ripple across the continent over a few nights of relayed phone calls. And the whole subculture had been dragged into public view a year earlier by a Hollywood film. The 1983 thriller WarGames, in which a teenager's modem accidentally dials into a military computer and nearly triggers a nuclear war, taught a mass audience both the allure and the menace of a machine that could reach out over the telephone—and it inspired a wave of young "war-dialers," so named for the movie, who set their modems to ring through thousands of numbers in sequence, listening for the answering whistle of another computer.

Above this grassroots world floated the commercial services, larger and glossier and far more expensive. CompuServe, which had begun in the late 1960s selling spare time on its mainframes to businesses, opened its computers to consumers in 1979 and grew through the 1980s into the establishment favorite, charging by the hour for access to news, weather, stock quotes, discussion forums, and the pioneering electronic mail that let one member send a message to another. Its addresses betrayed the service's mainframe origins: a CompuServe member was identified not by a name but by a string of digits divided by a comma, something like 71234,567, which people patiently read aloud to one another over the telephone. The hourly meter bred its own anxieties; families learned to compose their messages offline and connect only long enough to fire them off, watching the clock because every minute added to the bill. Its rival Prodigy, a joint venture backed by the deep pockets of IBM and Sears, launched nationally in 1990 with a very different bet: a graphical, colorful interface, a flat monthly fee rather than hourly charges, and a strip of paid advertising along the bottom of every screen, on the theory that online life should resemble a shopping mall more than a computer terminal. Both services were walled gardens, self-contained kingdoms whose members could talk to one another but not easily to the wider world, and both assumed that what people wanted online was information delivered from above, like a newspaper piped through a wire.

They were half right. People did want information, but what they craved even more, it turned out, was each other. Nowhere was this clearer than on Usenet, a decentralized web of discussion groups that had grown up around 1980 among university computers linked by the academic networks that would eventually merge into the internet. Usenet had no owner and no center. Messages, called posts, were passed from machine to machine across the network until they had propagated everywhere, organized into a great branching tree of topics, or newsgroups, on every conceivable subject, from programming languages to science fiction to recipes to arguments about politics that could smolder for years. It was here that much of the vocabulary and folklore of online life was minted, the flame wars and the frequently asked questions, the etiquette and the feuds, the sense of a community that existed nowhere and everywhere at once. For those with access to it, chiefly students and academics and engineers, Usenet was a revelation: proof that a conversation could scale beyond a single bedroom board to encompass the whole networked world.

The company that would carry this promise to the masses began as an obscure gaming service and nearly died several times before it found its footing. America Online, led by a young and relentless executive named Steve Case, understood something the older services had missed. Ordinary people were intimidated by computers, and the way to win them was to make going online feel warm, simple, and human. AOL's software installed itself easily, and it greeted the user with a friendly human voice announcing "Welcome," and, most memorably, "You've got mail." That voice belonged to a man named Elwood Edwards, and the story of how it came to be is a small parable of the era's informality: in 1989 Edwards's wife worked at the company, mentioned that they were looking to add a voice to the software, and Edwards recorded four short phrases at home on a cassette for a fee of two hundred dollars. Those few seconds of audio would go on to be heard billions of times and to lend their name to a Hollywood romantic comedy, all for a flat two hundred dollars and no royalties. AOL pushed to the foreground the two things people actually enjoyed: sending messages to friends and gathering in chat rooms with strangers. To acquire those people, it embarked on one of the most relentless marketing campaigns in the history of American business, blanketing the country in free trial discs. The strategy was the brainchild of the company's marketing chief, Jan Brandt, and it worked at a scale that beggars belief. The discs arrived in the mail, fell out of magazines, sat in baskets at checkout counters, came bundled with frozen dinners and airline meals, until it seemed there was no household in America that did not have a small stack of them accumulating in a drawer. AOL spent something on the order of thirty-five dollars to acquire each new subscriber this way, and at the campaign's peak the company was reportedly consuming a large fraction of the world's entire manufacturing capacity for compact discs and registering a new member roughly every six seconds. Each disc offered a month of free hours, and enough of the people who tried it stayed that AOL's membership swelled from hundreds of thousands into the millions, and then into the tens of millions. Inside AOL the whole sprawling internet-to-come was tamed into a tidy grid of "channels" reached by "keywords"—type a keyword and you were whisked directly to a company's area—and for a great many newcomers in the mid-1990s, AOL simply was the online world, so complete and self-contained that they never suspected there was anything beyond its walls. The company's ascent reached its giddy peak in January 2000, when the upstart online service announced it would acquire the venerable media giant Time Warner in a deal valued at some one hundred and sixty-five billion dollars, one of the largest mergers in history and, as it turned out, one of the most disastrous, a monument to the hubris of the dial-up boom raised at the very moment the boom was about to break.

For the household, the new connection came with a peculiar cost: it commandeered the telephone. A family with a single phone line faced a nightly negotiation, for while the modem was online the line was busy, and a teenager lost in a chat room could block every incoming call for hours, prompting the era's characteristic cry—"get off the internet, I need the phone!"—and driving exasperated parents to order a second line dedicated to the computer. Picking up an extension while the modem was working produced a burst of shriek and static that could sever the connection outright, dumping the user without ceremony back to a dial tone. The always-on, everywhere connection of later years, which asks nothing and interrupts nothing, would have seemed an impossible luxury to anyone who ever had to choose between a phone call and the internet.

By the early 1990s, then, the personal computer had quietly acquired a second identity. It was still a machine for spreadsheets and letters and games, but increasingly it was also a telephone of a new kind, a way to reach out across distance to correspond, to argue, to flirt, to belong. The habits and rituals born in that age still surround us: the little chime that announces a new message, the chat room reincarnated as the group thread, the flame war migrated to the comment section, even the nostalgic scree of a dial-up handshake now preserved in museums and sampled in songs as the sound of a lost frontier. Millions of people had discovered that the box on their desk could connect them to other minds, and they had done so through a patchwork of private boards and proprietary services, each a separate island with its own currency and customs, none of them able to speak fluently to any other. The online world was real, and growing fast, but it was fragmented, a Babel of incompatible systems waiting for a common tongue.

What none of these islands could offer was a way to speak to all the others at once, a single language every machine and every service could share. That tongue was already being invented, quietly, by a soft-spoken English physicist at a laboratory beneath the mountains near Geneva.

Chapter 57: The Web Arrives

In March 1989, a thirty-three-year-old English software engineer named Tim Berners-Lee handed his supervisor at the European laboratory for particle physics a document with an oddly tentative title. It was called "Information Management: A Proposal," and across the top, in the handwriting of the boss who received it, was scrawled a phrase that would become the most famous faint praise in the history of computing: "Vague but exciting." The laboratory, known by its French acronym CERN, sprawled across the border of Switzerland and France near Geneva, a warren of buildings and underground tunnels housing thousands of physicists from dozens of countries who came and went on short contracts, each bringing their own computers, their own data, their own incompatible ways of storing what they knew. Berners-Lee's frustration was mundane and universal: information was everywhere at CERN and impossible to find, locked in the heads of departing scientists and the disks of mismatched machines. His proposal was an attempt to solve that problem, and its ambition, buried in the dry prose, was to weave all the world's scattered documents into a single connected fabric.

The key idea was not new, and Berners-Lee never claimed it was. The dream of linking documents so that a reader could jump instantly from one to another had been articulated by Vannevar Bush in 1945 and given a name, hypertext, by the visionary Ted Nelson in the 1960s, and demonstrated in fragments by Douglas Engelbart. What Berners-Lee brought was not the concept but the engineering discipline to make it work across the messy reality of a global network of dissimilar machines. Over 1990, working on a sleek black NeXT computer, the very machine Steve Jobs had built after his exile from Apple, he assembled the pieces with astonishing economy. He devised a language for writing documents that could contain links, called HyperText Markup Language, or HTML. He devised a set of rules by which a computer could request such a document from another computer, the HyperText Transfer Protocol, or HTTP. And he devised a scheme of addresses so that every document anywhere could be named uniquely, the Uniform Resource Locator, or URL, the string beginning with "http" that would soon be printed on billboards and business cards around the planet. By the end of 1990 he had also written the first browser, a program to read these documents, which he called WorldWideWeb, and the first server, a program to serve them, and he had given his whole creation a name that stuck: the World Wide Web.

Here it is worth pausing to correct a confusion that persists to this day, one that even careful people repeat: Berners-Lee did not invent the internet. The internet, the underlying network of cables and routing rules that lets computers exchange packets of data, had been growing since the 1970s out of the American research project called ARPANET. What Berners-Lee invented was the Web, a system that runs on top of the internet the way a postal service runs on top of roads. The roads already existed; he built a way to address, wrap, and deliver documents along them so that an ordinary person could follow them without knowing a thing about the machinery underneath. The distinction matters because it explains why the Web arrived so suddenly. The hard work of connecting the world's computers had already been done. Berners-Lee supplied the missing layer that turned a network of specialists into a library for everyone.

The physical evidence of that first year is almost comically modest. The world's first web server was that single NeXT machine sitting in Berners-Lee's office, and because losing it would have meant losing the entire Web, someone stuck a strip of tape to its case and wrote in red ink a plea that reads now like a relic from the dawn of a religion: "This machine is a server. DO NOT POWER IT DOWN!!" The first website, hosted at the address info.cern.ch, went live to the internet on the twentieth of December 1990, and its subject was the Web itself: what the project was, how to make your own page, how the whole strange contraption worked. Because Berners-Lee's browser ran only on the rare and expensive NeXT computers, a mathematics student on placement at CERN named Nicola Pellow wrote a stripped-down alternative that could run on nearly any terminal, the so-called line-mode browser, which showed no pictures and no fonts, only numbered links a reader could select by typing a digit. It was ugly and it was universal, and it let the Web escape the handful of machines that could run the fancy version. That first website carried, among its plain paragraphs, a running list of every other web server in existence, a directory a single person could maintain by hand because there were, at first, only a few to list. Within a couple of years there would be too many to count, and the little hand-kept list would give way to the search engines that became the Web's new front door, but for a brief window one could hold the entire World Wide Web in a single scrollable page.

For its first year the Web existed almost entirely inside CERN, a private convenience for physicists. Then, in August 1991, Berners-Lee posted a short message to an internet newsgroup, inviting anyone who was interested to try the software and build their own pages, and with that quiet act he loosed the Web upon the world. The decision that gave it its power was one he and CERN made deliberately in 1993: to place the whole thing in the public domain, to charge no royalties and demand no license, so that anyone anywhere could run a server or write a browser without asking permission or paying a fee. Had the Web been patented and sold, it might have become one more walled garden like the commercial online services, another island in the archipelago. Instead it was a commons, open to all, and that openness was the oxygen that let it burn. Berners-Lee has said many times that he does not regret giving it away, and he never grew rich from it in the way the entrepreneurs who followed him did, a fact he regards not as a loss but as the point.

Yet in those early years the Web remained a spare and text-heavy thing, appreciated mostly by scientists and programmers who did not mind typing commands and reading plain gray pages. The browsers of the moment could show links and text but struggled to display images inline, mixing pictures and words on the same page the way a magazine did. The transformation that turned an academic curiosity into a mass phenomenon came from an unlikely place, a government-funded supercomputing center in the flat farmland of central Illinois. At the National Center for Supercomputing Applications, attached to the University of Illinois, a twenty-one-year-old undergraduate named Marc Andreessen was working a menial part-time job that paid a few dollars an hour writing software when he discovered the Web and grew convinced that it needed to be beautiful, easy, and visual before ordinary people would ever use it. In the winter of 1992 and into 1993, together with a talented staff programmer named Eric Bina, he wrote a browser that displayed images and text together on the same page, that could be installed with a few clicks, and that ran not only on expensive workstations but on the Windows and Macintosh computers sitting on millions of ordinary desks. They called it Mosaic, and they gave it away free.

To understand why Mosaic felt like magic, imagine the difference in concrete terms. Under the old line-mode browser, a page about a museum was a column of gray text with a list of numbered links at the bottom, and to follow one you typed its number and waited for the next wall of text to scroll up. Under Mosaic, that same page could show the museum's photograph at the top, its name in bold, and its links as blue underlined words embedded in ordinary sentences, so that reading and navigating became the same fluid motion. You did not learn commands; you moved a mouse and clicked, and the page changed. That single design choice, putting the image on the page with the words rather than in a separate window, is the reason a schoolteacher or a shopkeeper could sit down and use the Web with no training at all, and it is the ancestor of every web page you have ever seen.

Mosaic, released in 1993, hit the small world of the early Web like a thunderclap. Suddenly a Web page could be a thing of color and pictures, a poster rather than a telegram, and suddenly using it required no expertise at all: one simply pointed and clicked, following the underlined links from page to page in the wandering, hyperlinked motion that would soon be called surfing. The number of Web servers on the planet, a few dozen at the start of 1993, exploded into the thousands and then the tens of thousands within a year. Journalists began to write about this new thing, and the writing itself drew more people in, a self-reinforcing spiral of attention and growth. Mosaic did not invent the Web, but it made the Web visible, and in doing so it revealed the scale of the audience that had been waiting.

Part of what made the Web spread so quickly was a feature so humble it is easy to overlook, one that flowed directly from Berners-Lee's decision to make the whole system open. Every page carried its own instructions with it, written in plain HTML, and any browser could reveal them: a menu command called "View Source" let a curious visitor peer behind any page and read exactly how it had been built, the tags and links laid bare like the studs behind a wall. This meant that no one needed a manual or a course to learn how to make a web page. They needed only to find a page they admired, look at its source, copy the parts they liked, and change the words to their own. The Web taught itself to a generation, hobbyist to hobbyist, page by borrowed page, and the result was an explosion of amateur creativity unlike anything the tightly licensed software industry had ever produced. Personal home pages bloomed by the millions, most of them clumsy and some of them beautiful, and every one of them was a small act of publishing that would once have required a printing press and a distributor. The commons Berners-Lee had built rewarded imitation rather than punishing it, and that generosity, engineered into the very format of a page, was as responsible for the Web's growth as any browser.

Andreessen, restless and ambitious, did not stay in Illinois to enjoy his creation. In 1994 he moved to Silicon Valley and fell in with Jim Clark, a seasoned entrepreneur who had founded the workstation maker Silicon Graphics and who was looking for his next act. Together they founded a company, initially called Mosaic Communications and soon renamed Netscape, and they recruited many of the original Mosaic programmers away from the university with the promise of stock and freedom. Their goal was to build a browser so much better than the original that it would sweep the field, and in late 1994 they released it: Netscape Navigator, faster than Mosaic, more capable, and, in a stroke of strategy that would define the era, free to download for individuals even as the company planned to make its money selling server software to the businesses rushing to put themselves online. Within months Navigator commanded the overwhelming majority of a market that had barely existed a year before.

Then came the day that lit the fuse of an entire decade. On August 9, 1995, Netscape offered its stock to the public. The company was barely sixteen months old and had never turned a profit, a fact that would once have made a public offering unthinkable. The bankers had originally planned to price the shares at fourteen dollars; sensing the frenzy building, they doubled that figure the night before to twenty-eight. When trading finally opened, nearly two hours late because the demand was too great for the exchange to match buyers and sellers, the first trade printed at seventy-one dollars. The stock touched nearly seventy-five before the day was out and closed around fifty-eight, valuing a company that gave away its main product at close to three billion dollars. Marc Andreessen, then twenty-four, held a stake worth some fifty-eight million on paper. Asked later how he had experienced the biggest day of his young life, he offered a line of studied cool that became part of the legend: he had woken up around nine, logged on to see how the stock had done, and gone back to sleep.

The following winter, on February 19, 1996, Andreessen appeared on the cover of Time magazine, seated barefoot on a gilded throne beneath the headline "The Golden Geeks," and that image, the boy wonder crowned before he had shaved off his youth, became the founding icon of a new gold rush. The Netscape offering did not merely make its founders rich. It sent a signal, heard in every venture capital office and business school and garage in America, that the Web was not a hobby but the next great frontier of commerce, and that fortunes on a scale not seen in a generation were there for the taking by anyone bold enough and quick enough to build for it. You still live inside that signal. Every address you type that begins with "http," every page assembled from HTML, every link you tap without a thought, descends directly from a black computer in a Geneva office with a strip of red-inked tape begging the world not to switch it off.

In a suburban campus north of Seattle, the most powerful software company on earth had noticed the same thing, rather later than it should have, and its founder was about to turn the whole firm on a dime.

Chapter 58: The Browser on Every Desk

On May 26, 1995, three months before the Netscape offering set the world on fire, Bill Gates sat down to write a memorandum to the senior staff of Microsoft and gave it a title borrowed from the language of natural disaster. "The Internet Tidal Wave," he called it, and over the pages that followed he confessed, with the bluntness he reserved for internal audiences, that his company had been looking the wrong way. Microsoft had spent years and fortunes preparing for a networked future it had expected to control, an online service of its own and proprietary standards it would own. But the future had arrived from an unexpected quarter, built on the open protocols of the internet and made visible by a browser from a company that had not existed two years earlier. "The Internet is the most important single development to come along since the IBM PC was introduced in 1981," Gates wrote, and he assigned it the highest level of importance, above every other priority at the firm. He named the enemy without flinching. A new competitor born on the internet, he warned, was Netscape, whose browser was dominant with something like seventy percent of usage, a position that let it decide which extensions to the Web would catch on and which would wither. Whoever controlled the software people used to reach the internet, Gates understood, controlled the most important piece of ground in computing, and at that moment the company holding that ground was not his own.

The danger Gates perceived was not merely that Microsoft might miss a lucrative market. It was that the browser might make the operating system irrelevant. If people spent their days inside a browser, running programs delivered over the Web, then it would no longer matter much whether the machine underneath ran Windows or anything else, and the great engine of Microsoft's wealth, the near-monopoly of Windows on the world's PCs, might quietly lose its grip. Netscape's own leaders said as much, boasting that they would reduce Windows to a set of poorly debugged device drivers, a mere layer of plumbing beneath the browser that truly mattered. Gates heard the threat plainly, and the memorandum was his declaration that Microsoft would meet it with the full weight of the company. Within weeks the firm was reorganizing itself around the internet, and its programmers were racing to turn a small, licensed browser project into a weapon.

That browser was Internet Explorer. Here it is worth correcting a common belief, for Microsoft did not build Explorer from scratch and never pretended otherwise. The first version, shipped in the summer of 1995 bundled with an add-on package for Windows, was based on code licensed from a company called Spyglass, which had itself descended from the original Mosaic, the same academic browser that had spawned Netscape. In a bitter twist that would later become the stuff of business-school lectures, Spyglass had agreed to a licensing deal that paid it a share of the revenue Microsoft earned from the browser, and since Microsoft chose to give Explorer away for nothing, that share amounted to almost nothing at all. Early versions were crude and far behind Navigator in speed and features, and for a time it seemed that Microsoft's late start might prove fatal. But the company possessed two advantages Netscape could not match, and it wielded both without mercy. The first was money. Microsoft poured more than a thousand engineers and upward of a hundred million dollars a year into a product it did not sell, releasing new versions in rapid succession until, by the third and fourth iterations in 1996 and 1997, Explorer had drawn even with and in some respects surpassed its rival.

The second advantage was more decisive, and it would land the company in the gravest legal trouble of its history. Microsoft simply gave Internet Explorer away, not merely free to download but built directly into Windows itself, so that every new PC arrived with the browser already installed, woven into the operating system so deeply that it could not easily be removed. Against a competitor whose entire business rested on selling browser-related software, this was a strategy of devastating simplicity. Netscape had been giving Navigator to individuals while charging companies for the servers and the corporate versions, but it could not indefinitely outgive an opponent who bundled its browser with the operating system that ran on nine of every ten computers sold on earth. Microsoft leaned on the manufacturers who installed Windows, using the leverage of its essential product to discourage them from favoring Netscape, and it tuned Windows so that Explorer felt like a native part of the machine rather than an add-on. What the strategy amounted to was captured, years later, in a phrase that surfaced during courtroom testimony and never left the public memory. An Intel executive named Steven McGeady told a federal court that a senior Microsoft man had described the plan to him as a campaign to cut off Netscape's air supply, to give the browser away and smother a company that lived on selling it. The Microsoft executive denied ever using those words, but the phrase fit the facts so well that it stuck to the whole episode like a label.

The bitterness of the fight showed itself in ways more childish than any memo. When Microsoft launched the fourth version of Internet Explorer in the autumn of 1997, its engineers threw a party and, in the small hours afterward, hauled a giant illuminated Explorer logo, a stage prop the size of a small car, onto the front lawn of Netscape's headquarters in Silicon Valley as a taunt. Netscape's employees arrived the next morning to find the enemy's emblem planted on their grass. Rather than remove it, they turned it into a trophy: they tipped the logo onto its back, and atop it they stood their own seven-foot mascot, a grinning green dinosaur named Mozilla, propped in a posture of triumph. Beside it they set a hand-lettered sign giving the current score of the war in market share, Netscape leading Microsoft by a wide margin. It was a fine joke, and it was also a snapshot of a battle already turning, because the numbers on that sign would invert within two years.

The share of people using Navigator, which had approached ninety percent in 1995 and stood near eighty-six at its 1996 peak, began to erode and then to collapse, and by the end of the decade Internet Explorer had captured the overwhelming majority of the market. Netscape, the company that had lit the fuse of the entire boom, was sold in 1998 to America Online in a deal valued at some four billion dollars, a sum that seemed enormous but marked the end of its independence. Its free browser survived chiefly by being handed, in its final act, to a nonprofit foundation, which released its source code to the world so that anyone could build on it. From that gift grew an open-source descendant that would one day rise again and challenge Microsoft all over again under the name Firefox, its logo still a stylized nod to the dinosaur that once stood on the lawn.

The victory came at a price. The tactics Microsoft used to win the browser war, the bundling and the pressure on manufacturers and the welding of Explorer into Windows, drew the attention of the United States Department of Justice, which in 1998 brought a landmark antitrust suit accusing the company of abusing its operating-system monopoly to crush competition in browsers. The trial that followed would consume years, produce a ruling that Microsoft had indeed broken the law and even, briefly, an order that the company be split in two, and though that breakup was ultimately overturned on appeal and the case settled, the ordeal marked the moment the government treated the software giant as the dominant industrial power it had become. The browser war, in other words, was won and lost twice: once in the marketplace, where Microsoft prevailed, and once in the courtroom, where the manner of its winning was judged an offense.

The courtroom drama produced its own indelible images, none more damaging to Microsoft than the spectacle of its own founder on videotape. Bill Gates gave a deposition that was played in court, and his performance, evasive and combative, quibbling over the meaning of ordinary words like "concerned" and "compete," turned public opinion against the company more effectively than any lawyer's argument. The presiding judge, Thomas Penfield Jackson, would later remark that he found Gates's testimony inconsistent with the plain evidence of the company's own internal emails, the very messages, the "Tidal Wave" memo among them, in which executives had described their intentions in language far blunter than anything they were willing to admit under oath. It was a lesson the whole industry absorbed: in the age of electronic mail, the candid memo written in the heat of competition could return years later as testimony, and the paper trail of a strategy could become the evidence of a crime. Microsoft survived the ordeal, paid its settlements, and emerged intact, but the swaggering invincibility of its first two decades was gone, and the company spent the years that followed looking over its shoulder at regulators on two continents.

Yet the deeper consequence of these years had nothing to do with which company's logo sat in the corner of the screen. It was that the browser, whoever made it, had become the single most important program on the personal computer, the lens through which more and more of the world was seen.

The machine that had been sold in the 1980s as a tool for balancing budgets and writing memos was now sold, above all, as a way onto the internet. In advertisements and store displays, the reasons to own a computer shifted decisively. People bought machines to send electronic mail to their children and grandchildren, to read the news, to look up facts, to shop, to visit the growing profusion of Web sites that businesses and enthusiasts and eventually everyone was rushing to create. Electronic mail, which had lived for decades as a niche convenience of engineers and executives, became within a few years an utterly ordinary fact of daily life, a thing that grandparents and schoolchildren used without a second thought, and the address beginning with a name and an at-sign joined the telephone number as a basic coordinate of a person's existence.

For the ordinary person, the drama in the boardrooms and the courtroom was invisible; what they experienced was a set of new rituals that would come to feel eternal. A household got online by way of a screeching modem that dialed the telephone and negotiated its connection in a burst of electronic hiss, tying up the family phone line so that a teenager surfing the Web meant a busy signal for anyone trying to call. Millions reached the internet not directly but through America Online, whose compact discs arrived unbidden in every mailbox in the country and whose cheerful recorded voice, announcing "You've got mail," so saturated the culture that Hollywood built a hit romance around the phrase in 1998. To these users the browser and the internet were simply the same thing; few could have said where one ended and the other began, and fewer still cared. What they knew was that a window had opened in the corner of the living room onto a world that had not been reachable the year before, and that reaching it had become as casual as turning on the television. The war over which company's browser framed that window mattered enormously to the combatants and hardly at all to the people looking through it, which was, in the end, the surest sign of how thoroughly the Web had won. And it was AOL, having bought the defeated Netscape, that owned that framing for millions, bundling the browser into the walled garden through which so many Americans first typed a web address, so that the losing side of the war quietly kept a foothold in tens of millions of homes even in defeat. The victor took the market; the vanquished kept the memories, and the phrase in the recorded voice, and a place in the story of how a nation first went online, its dinosaur mascot outliving the company that had raised it.

The habits formed in those years are the ones you still keep. Every time you open a tab and expect the whole of human activity to be a search box away, every time a company prints a web address rather than a phone number, every argument about whether a company has too much power over the software on your devices, is an inheritance of the browser war. Even the antitrust questions that swirl around today's technology giants are argued in the vocabulary the Microsoft case established, the language of bundling and default settings and the quiet power of what comes preinstalled. By the last years of the 1990s, the transformation was complete. The personal computer had been conceived as an instrument of individual empowerment, a bicycle for the mind, and it remained that. But it had also become something its earliest champions had only dimly foreseen: a universal on-ramp, a device whose chief purpose for hundreds of millions of ordinary people was to connect them to a network that now spanned the globe. The box on the desk was no longer an island. It was a window, and through it flowed a world.

Behind that window, running nearly all of those machines, sat a partnership of two companies whose grip on the industry had become so total that people had coined a single word to name it.

Chapter 59: Wintel

In the electronics stores of the early 1990s, a customer wandering the aisles of beige computer towers would have noticed, stuck to the corner of nearly every machine, a small square sticker in swirling blue letters. It read "Intel Inside," and it was accompanied, on the screen when the machine powered on, by a short synthesized chime and, in the software, by a version of Microsoft Windows. Two logos, two companies, two products that between them defined what a personal computer was. The customer had likely never heard of either firm when the decade began; by its end their names had become as familiar as the appliances they inhabited. The industry had a nickname for the pairing, a portmanteau stamped together from Windows and Intel, and it captured a truth about the age. This was the era of Wintel, when two companies that made neither the finished machines nor sold them to the public nonetheless dictated the terms on which the entire personal-computer industry lived, and captured the lion's share of the money it generated.

The arrangement had crystallized out of the accident of 1981, when IBM, hurrying to build a personal computer, had chosen an Intel processor to run it and a Microsoft operating system to command it, and then, fatefully, had allowed both suppliers to sell the same essential ingredients to anyone else who wished to build a compatible machine. As the clone makers multiplied through the 1980s, competing one another's prices and profits into the ground, the two indispensable suppliers sat above the fray, selling the two components no clone could do without. Every machine that ran the standard software needed an Intel-compatible processor, and by the 1990s nearly every one of them needed Windows, and so while dozens of manufacturers fought over the thin margins of assembling boxes, the fat margins pooled upstream, in Santa Clara where Intel made its chips and in Redmond where Microsoft wrote its code. By the middle of the decade Intel held roughly nine-tenths of the market for the microprocessors at the heart of the personal computer, and Windows an even firmer grip on the software that ran on them, a pair of near-monopolies bolted together.

It is tempting to picture the two firms as harmonious allies, and this is the first misconception worth dispelling, for the marriage was often loveless and occasionally hostile. The companies needed each other, but each resented the other's power and schemed to reduce it. Bill Gates, summarizing a 1995 meeting with Intel's chairman for his own executives, wrote with the frankness of private correspondence that he had kept pushing one point on the Intel side, that Microsoft was the software company here and would not have any kind of equal relationship with Intel when it came to software. Intel, for its part, poured money into research on software and networking that trespassed on Microsoft's turf, and Gates was known to lean hard on Intel to abandon such projects. The word Wintel implied a single organism; the reality was two giants chained back to back, each keeping a wary eye on the other even as they marched in the same direction and grew rich on the same customers.

Intel's half of the empire rested on a lineage of processors that grew more powerful with a regularity that had come to seem like a law of nature. The 8088 chip inside the first IBM PC had given way to the 286, and then, in 1985, to the 386, the first of Intel's processors capable of the true multitasking and expansive memory that graphical software would demand. The 486 followed at the end of the decade, faster still and with a mathematics coprocessor built in. Then, in 1993, Intel broke with its own numbering and christened its new flagship with a name rather than a number, partly because a federal court had ruled that numbers could not be trademarked and rivals were free to sell chips called 386 and 486 of their own. The new chip was the Pentium, and its arrival announced Intel's ambition to be not a faceless supplier of components but a consumer brand in its own right. That ambition had already found its purest expression two years earlier, in 1991, when Intel launched the "Intel Inside" campaign, paying the manufacturers who used its chips to display the logo, and later adding the four-note chime that would sound from millions of machines. In doing so it persuaded ordinary buyers who understood nothing of microprocessors to demand a particular brand of a part they would never see or touch. It was one of the most successful marketing strategies in the history of technology, transforming a hidden component into a household name and cementing the perception that a computer without Intel inside was somehow suspect. The strategy so raised Intel's profile that in 1997 its chief executive, Andy Grove, a Hungarian refugee who had joined the company as its third employee, was named Time magazine's Man of the Year.

Yet the Pentium's debut also delivered the sharpest humiliation of Intel's rise, and it is a story worth telling in full because it reveals how a single arithmetic error can become a corporate crisis. In 1994 a mathematics professor named Thomas Nicely, working at a small college in Virginia on a problem in number theory, noticed that his brand-new Pentium was returning wrong answers when it divided certain large numbers. The flaw lived in a lookup table buried in the chip's division circuitry, from which a handful of entries had been mistakenly omitted, so that for a rare few combinations of numbers the processor produced a result that was subtly, quietly wrong. Divide one particular pair of numbers and the Pentium gave an answer off in the fifth decimal place, an error tiny in isolation but catastrophic for anyone whose work depended on exactness. Intel had known of the defect for months and judged it too obscure to matter, offering replacements only to customers who could prove they needed the precision. The public disagreed. The story spread from academic mailing lists to the newspapers to the nightly news, and the image of a computer that could not be trusted to do long division became a national joke. When a major computer maker halted its Pentium shipments in protest, Intel finally surrendered, announcing in December 1994 that it would replace any affected chip for anyone who asked, no questions and no proof required. The reversal cost the company a pretax charge of four hundred and seventy-five million dollars, the first full recall of a computer chip in history, and it taught Intel a lesson its marketing had ironically made unavoidable: once you have persuaded the public to care about the brand inside the box, the public expects that brand to be perfect.

There is a small piece of that campaign lodged in the memory of nearly everyone who lived through the era, and it is worth knowing who put it there. The Intel chime, the four rising notes that sounded whenever the logo flashed at the end of a commercial, was not assembled by a committee or generated by a machine but composed in 1994 by an Austrian musician named Walter Werzowa, who built the three-second signature from more than forty layered sounds, drawing on a rack of synthesizers, and shaped its rhythm to echo the very syllables of the slogan, In-tel In-si-de. Those few notes went on to play, by some estimates, somewhere in the world every few minutes for decades, one of the most heard pieces of music ever written, and almost no one who could hum it could name the man who wrote it or the company whose chip it advertised. It was branding of the purest kind, a jingle for a component buried so deep inside the machine that its owner would never lay eyes on it, and it worked precisely because it asked nothing of the listener but recognition. The genius of "Intel Inside," sound and sticker together, was to make ordinary people loyal to a part they could not see, would never touch, and did not understand.

Microsoft's half rested on Windows, which after years of false starts had finally triumphed. Windows 3.0 in 1990 and 3.1 in 1992 had at last made the graphical interface fast enough and stable enough to matter, selling tens of millions of copies and putting pictures and a mouse on the ordinary office desk. Then, in August 1995, came Windows 95, launched with a marketing campaign of unprecedented scale and hysteria, complete with a rolling advertising anthem licensed from a famous rock band, midnight store openings, and lines of customers waiting to buy an operating system as though it were a concert ticket. Windows 95 hid the old DOS underpinnings behind a polished new interface, introduced the Start button and the taskbar that would define the look of the PC for a generation, and sealed Microsoft's dominance of the desktop so thoroughly that the question was no longer whether a PC ran Windows but merely which version.

Together the two companies powered a machine that had become, for its buyers, a treadmill. Each new generation of Intel processor ran faster than the last, but each new version of Windows and of the applications that ran atop it demanded more speed and more memory than the last, so that the extra power delivered by the hardware was consumed almost entirely by the extra appetite of the software. A machine that had felt swift when purchased would feel sluggish within a few years, not because it had slowed but because the software it was now expected to run had grown heavier. The phenomenon was captured in a wry saying that circulated through the industry, a pairing of the two men who ran the two companies: what Andy giveth, Bill taketh away, meaning that the performance gains delivered by Intel's Andy Grove were promptly absorbed by the ever-expanding software shipped by Bill Gates. The result was an endless cycle of upgrades that kept both companies' revenues climbing, as customers replaced perfectly functional machines simply to keep pace with software that would no longer run comfortably on the old ones.

The treadmill of upgrades ran on a single number that shoppers were taught to worship: the clock speed of the processor, measured in megahertz and then, as the years passed, in gigahertz. Manufacturers advertised it like horsepower, and buyers who understood nothing else about a machine learned to ask how many megahertz it had, so that the megahertz race became the central drama of the hardware trade. The rivalry reached a symbolic peak in the spring of 2000, when Intel's smaller competitor AMD beat it to the milestone of a processor running at a full gigahertz, a billion cycles a second, crossing the line a few days ahead of the giant and forcing Intel into an unseemly scramble to match it. The victory was fleeting and, as engineers well knew, the number was a poor measure of how fast a computer truly felt, since a chip's real performance depended on far more than the speed of its clock. But the megahertz myth suited both companies, for it gave the public a simple reason to believe that this year's machine was meaningfully better than last year's, and a simple reason to buy again. Only years later, when clock speeds stopped climbing and chipmakers turned instead to packing multiple processing cores onto a single sliver of silicon, did the marketing quietly abandon the number it had spent a decade teaching everyone to chase.

The duopoly was not entirely unchallenged. On the hardware side, a scrappy competitor named Advanced Micro Devices, or AMD, had begun life as a licensed second source for Intel's designs, a hedge IBM had insisted upon so as not to depend on a single supplier, and over the years AMD had grown from imitator into genuine rival, building its own processors that ran the same software as Intel's but sold for less. The two companies waged a long and bitter war over speed and price and the right to make Intel-compatible chips, a war fought as much in courtrooms over the licensing of designs as in the marketplace, and while AMD never dethroned its larger opponent, it kept prices honest and gave the box makers a second door to knock on. On the software side, the challengers were fewer and fared worse; IBM's OS/2 and, later, the free operating systems of the open-source movement each carved out territory, but none came close to loosening Windows's hold on the ordinary desktop.

What the two companies had achieved, in the end, was a kind of invisible sovereignty. They did not make the computers that people bought, nor sell them, nor service them. Dozens of manufacturers did all of that, competing furiously and earning little for their trouble. Yet Intel and Microsoft, by owning the two ingredients that every one of those machines required, extracted the bulk of the industry's profits year after year while bearing almost none of the risk of the brutal business of building and selling the finished product. It was among the most lucrative positions any pair of companies had ever occupied, a toll booth astride the road that all personal computing had to travel. Traces of that sovereignty are still all around you: the descendant of the Pentium hums inside a majority of the world's laptops and the vast server farms that run the internet, and Windows still commands most of the desktops in the world's offices, even as the phone in your pocket, built on entirely different chips and software, has quietly grown into the machine that finally broke the spell.

The men who assembled the actual machines, meanwhile, were locked in a very different kind of contest, one measured not in profit margins but in their steady disappearance, and its most ruthless innovator had started his company in a college dormitory with a thousand dollars.

Chapter 60: Direct

In a dormitory room at the University of Texas at Austin in 1984, a nineteen-year-old freshman named Michael Dell was running a business his parents did not know about and would not have approved of. He was supposed to be studying to become a doctor. Instead, from Room 2713 of the Dobie Center, he was buying components, assembling personal computers, and selling them by mail to customers who called a phone number they had found in the back pages of trade magazines. He had noticed something that the established makers had missed, something so simple it seemed almost too obvious to build a company on. The machines sold in computer stores were marked up enormously, sometimes doubling in price as they passed from manufacturer to distributor to retailer to buyer, and much of that markup paid for a chain of middlemen who added little the customer valued. Dell reasoned that if he built the machines himself and sold them directly to the people who would use them, cutting out every link in that chain, he could offer a better computer at a lower price and still make a healthy profit on each one.

He had begun even more modestly than the legend usually allows, and the detail is worth pausing on because it shows how the great idea arrived by degrees rather than as a flash. Before he assembled anything, Dell bought up unsold IBM PCs that dealers were desperate to move, upgraded them in his room with extra memory and larger disk drives, and resold them by mail at prices ten to fifteen percent below retail, pocketing the difference. Only once that trade was thriving did he graduate to building complete machines of his own from parts. He had started with a thousand dollars and a name that has been almost entirely forgotten: the company was first registered not as Dell Computer but as PC's Limited. Within months the little enterprise was taking in tens of thousands of dollars a month, his grades were suffering, his roommate had grown exasperated, and before the school year was out he had left his studies to run the business full time. In May 1984 he reincorporated it under his own name, Dell Computer Corporation, and moved it out of the dormitory and into the world.

The insight that started as a dormitory hustle grew into one of the most influential business models in the history of manufacturing, and its power lay in a set of ideas that reinforced one another. The first was selling direct, bypassing the retailer so that the company spoke straight to its customer, took the order straight from that customer, and kept the margin the middleman would otherwise have pocketed. Here a misconception is worth correcting, for Dell is often credited with inventing the mail-order computer, and he did not. Others sold machines by mail before him and beside him. What Dell invented, or at least perfected until no rival could match it, was the marriage of direct selling to a manufacturing discipline that turned the ordinary logic of business inside out. That was the second idea, building to order. Because Dell was not stocking store shelves with machines built in advance, it did not have to guess what customers would want and gamble on inventory. Instead, it waited until a customer placed an order and specified exactly the configuration desired, the size of the disk, the amount of memory, the speed of the processor, and only then assembled that particular machine for that particular person.

The third idea was the one that made the whole system

spin, and it borrowed from the lean manufacturing philosophies then transforming the automobile industry: just-in-time production, in which parts arrived at the factory only shortly before they were needed, so that Dell held almost no inventory of its own. To grasp why this mattered, consider the peculiar economics of computer parts. In an industry where the value of components fell relentlessly month after month, a warehouse full of processors and memory chips was like a warehouse full of melting ice, worth less every day it sat unsold. Dell's competitors, building machines in advance and shipping them to stores, often owned parts that had lost a slice of their value before the finished computer was ever bought, and every price cut in the components they already held was a loss they simply had to swallow. Dell, by contrast, drove the parts through its factories so fast that it held only days of inventory where rivals held weeks or months, buying components almost at the last possible moment and therefore always at the latest, lowest price. The arrangement did something stranger still with money. Because customers frequently paid Dell by credit card at the moment they ordered, while Dell paid its own suppliers weeks later, the company collected cash from buyers before it owed cash to vendors. Growth, which starves most young manufacturers of capital, actually generated cash for Dell, a self-funding machine that could expand without borrowing.

It is worth picturing how an order actually moved through Dell's machine, because the elegance of the system lay in the choreography. A customer, having dialed a toll-free number or, later, filled in a form on Dell's website, chose the exact ingredients of the machine, so much memory, so large a disk, this processor rather than that one, and paid on the spot. That order flashed to a factory floor where nothing had yet been built. Only then were the parts pulled from bins, most of them delivered by suppliers who kept their own inventory in warehouses minutes away and were paid only as Dell consumed their goods, and a team assembled that one specific computer, tested it, boxed it, and handed it to a shipper, often within a day or two. At no point did Dell own a finished computer waiting for a buyer, and at no point did it own many parts waiting for an order. The company famously drove its inventory down to a handful of days' worth of components, where rivals building machines in advance carried weeks or months, and because those components lost a fraction of their value every week they sat, Dell's near-empty warehouses were not a sign of caution but the very engine of its advantage. In a business where the raw materials were quietly rotting, the firm that touched them last and held them shortest won.

This model thrived precisely because of what the personal computer had become. In the earliest years, a computer had been a marvel, a distinctive creation, and buyers had cared deeply about which company made it and what special virtues it possessed. But the triumph of the IBM standard and the flood of clones had drained that distinctiveness away. By the 1990s, one Windows machine with an Intel processor was very much like another, built from the same interchangeable parts sourced from the same handful of suppliers, running the same software and doing the same things. The personal computer had become a commodity, a standardized product distinguished chiefly by price, the way a gallon of gasoline or a bag of sugar was distinguished chiefly by price. And when a product becomes a commodity, the advantage flows to whoever can make and deliver it most cheaply, which was exactly the contest Dell's model was built to win.

The consequence was a long, grinding collapse in both prices and profits, a phenomenon the industry came to call, with grim humor, the box wars. Through the 1990s the price of a capable personal computer fell year after year, from many thousands of dollars toward one thousand and eventually below it, until a machine of astonishing power could be had for the price of a decent television. For consumers this was a triumph, the democratization the pioneers had dreamed of, computing power spreading into ordinary homes because it had finally grown cheap enough to buy on a whim. For the manufacturers it was a war of attrition fought over margins so thin they were measured in single percentage points, a business in which fortunes could be made only on staggering volume and lost on the smallest misstep in cost or timing.

The combatants in this war were the great names of the box-making trade, and they fought by different strategies. Gateway, founded on a cattle ranch in Iowa by a young entrepreneur named Ted Waitt, adopted a direct-sales model much like Dell's and wrapped it in folksy branding, shipping its machines in boxes printed with the black-and-white spots of a Holstein cow, a gimmick that made a virtue of its rural origins and lodged the brand in buyers' minds. Compaq, which had risen in the early 1980s as the first company to build a fully legal IBM clone and had grown into the largest maker of PCs in the world, sold through stores and dealers and struggled to match the ruthless efficiency of the direct sellers. Hewlett-Packard, an elder statesman of Silicon Valley with a distinguished history in instruments and printers, threw its weight into the personal-computer business and competed on the breadth of its product line and the strength of its brand. The competition among them was merciless, and it produced one of the largest mergers in the industry's history when Hewlett-Packard, in a deal announced in 2001 and completed the following year amid bitter opposition from members of the founding family, absorbed Compaq in an effort to gain the scale it believed necessary to survive.

Through it all, Dell rose and rose. The company's relentless efficiency, its command of the direct model, and its refusal to hold inventory it did not need let it undercut competitors while remaining profitable, and by the late 1990s and into the new century Dell had climbed to become one of the largest makers of personal computers on the planet, at times the very largest. Michael Dell, who had started with a thousand dollars and a stack of components in a dorm room, had become one of the wealthiest people in the country before he was forty. His company's success was a testament to a hard truth about the industry it dominated: that the great money in personal computers, at least in the making of them, was to be found not in genius or novelty but in logistics, in the unglamorous mastery of supply chains and cash flow and the shaving of pennies from a product that had become as standardized as a household staple.

The model proved so contagious that it long outlived the box wars, and you meet its descendants every time you order almost anything made to your specification and shipped straight to your door. The build-to-order configurator, the promise that nothing is made until you ask for it, the supply chain tuned so tightly that inventory barely exists, these ideas migrated out of the computer trade and into the way modern commerce works, from custom sneakers to bespoke automobiles to the vast just-in-time logistics of online retail. Dell had shown that the winning move in a commodity business was not to build a better product but to build a better system for making and delivering it.

Yet the very perfection of Dell's model contained the seed of its later humbling, and the reversal is instructive. The direct approach had been forged in an age when a personal computer was a fairly uniform desktop box that a buyer could specify from a list of options, and it depended on customers who knew enough to configure their own machine and were content to wait a few days for it to arrive. As the market shifted toward laptops, whose intricate designs left little to configure, and toward casual shoppers who wanted to hold a machine in their hands before buying it, the advantages of selling straight from the factory began to fade. Rivals, meanwhile, had studied Dell's supply-chain discipline and narrowed the gap, so that its once-insurmountable edge in cost thinned to almost nothing. By the middle of the 2000s Dell had slipped from its perch as the world's largest PC maker, and in 2007 Michael Dell, who had stepped back from running the company he founded, returned as chief executive to steer it through a decline he could slow but not reverse. Eventually the firm would retreat from the public stock market altogether in order to remake itself away from the glare of quarterly scrutiny. The lesson was the oldest one in business, and the box wars taught it again: a model perfectly tuned to the conditions of one era can become a liability when the conditions change, and no efficiency is permanent in an industry that reinvents its products every few years.

And that was the paradox at the heart of the box wars. The personal computer, born of revolutionary dreams and countercultural fervor and the conviction that it would liberate the human mind, had matured into an appliance, a cheap and interchangeable commodity bought on price and replaced without sentiment, its magic so thoroughly absorbed into daily life that people no longer thought of it as magic at all. The revolution had succeeded so completely that it had become ordinary.

The deeper meaning of Dell's rise, and of the box wars generally, is that the personal computer had completed a journey the automobile had made decades before, from an object of wonder and craftsmanship into a mass-produced good whose maker competed chiefly on cost and delivery. The romance had drained out of the manufacturing, and the profit with it, and what remained was a contest of spreadsheets. It was not a story of villains, for the customers were the plain winners, but it was a story with a melancholy edge for anyone who remembered when a new computer had seemed like a small miracle rather than a commodity ordered like a pizza.

But one company had refused to play the commodity game, and by the middle of the 1990s that refusal had brought it to the edge of extinction, weeks, some said, from running out of cash.

Chapter 61: The Return of the King

In the winter of 1996, the company that had once promised to change the world was, by the reckoning of most who watched it, dying. Apple Computer, the firm two young men had founded in a Cupertino garage two decades earlier and had grown into the emblem of the personal-computer age, was hemorrhaging money and market share with a speed that alarmed even its most loyal admirers. Its share of the personal-computer market had dwindled to a sliver. Its product line had metastasized into a bewildering thicket of nearly identical machines with confusing names that no customer could keep straight. It had spent years and a fortune trying and failing to build a modern operating system to replace the aging software at the heart of the Macintosh, a project that had collapsed under its own ambitions. Its chief executive changed, and then changed again, and the business press wrote its obituaries in advance, debating not whether Apple would be bought or broken up but merely when. The contempt was public and casual. In October 1997, asked at a conference of technology executives what he would do if he were running the ailing Apple, Michael Dell, whose direct-sales juggernaut was then ascendant, answered without hesitation that he would shut it down and give the money back to the shareholders. It was the sort of thing one said about a company already in the ground.

The rescue arrived from an unlikely direction, and it turned on the company's failure to build that operating system on its own. Needing a modern foundation for the Macintosh and unable to create one, Apple's leadership went shopping for one, and after considering several candidates they settled, late in 1996, on a small and elegant company called NeXT. NeXT had been founded eleven years earlier by Steve Jobs, the co-founder whom Apple had pushed out in 1985 after a bruising power struggle, and it made sleek black computers running an advanced operating system that had never found a mass market but was admired by engineers as among the most sophisticated software of its kind. When Apple bought NeXT, for a sum in the hundreds of millions of dollars, it was buying that operating system to serve as the new brain of the Macintosh. But it was also, whether it fully understood this or not, buying back its exiled founder, for the deal brought Steve Jobs home to the company he had started and been cast out of, at first as an adviser, then, within months and after the ouster of the chief executive who had brought him back, as the leader in all but title.

The manner of his ascent is worth recalling, because it was neither instant nor inevitable. Jobs came back at first only as an informal adviser to Gil Amelio, the chief executive who had engineered the NeXT purchase, and for several months he kept a deliberately low profile while quietly consolidating influence, placing allies in key positions and studying the wreckage. When Apple's losses mounted and the board lost faith in Amelio, they pushed him out in the summer of 1997 and turned to the founder, who accepted the top job only provisionally, styling himself the interim chief executive, a title he wore for more than two years and abbreviated, with characteristic wit, to iCEO. He took a salary of one dollar a year, a gesture that was part theater and part genuine signal that his stake in Apple's revival was to be measured in its stock and its survival rather than a paycheck. And survival was the honest word for the stakes. By some internal reckonings the company was perhaps ninety days from insolvency when he took the reins, not because it lacked cash but because it was burning through what it had while its sales collapsed and its dealers lost confidence. Into that emergency Jobs brought a clarity that bordered on brutality, and the first thing he did was to stop the bleeding by killing most of what the company was doing.

Jobs returned to a company in chaos, and he set about saving it with a series of decisions that ranged from the ruthless to the astonishing. The most surprising came in the summer of 1997, on the sixth of August, at a trade show in Boston, when Jobs appeared on stage to announce a truce with the company Apple loyalists regarded as the great enemy. Microsoft, he told the stunned and partly hostile audience, would invest one hundred and fifty million dollars in Apple, would commit to continuing its essential Office software for the Macintosh for five years, would make its browser the Mac's default, and would settle the long-simmering legal disputes between the two firms by cross-licensing their patents. When the enormous image of Bill Gates appeared on a screen above the stage to elaborate, looming over the hall like a colossus, the crowd booed. Jobs rebuked them with a line that has outlived almost everything else said that day. "We have to let go of the notion that for Apple to win, Microsoft needs to lose," he told them, and he pressed the point that the destructive, tribal thinking of the enemies-forever school was exactly what had brought the company low.

Here a durable misconception deserves puncturing, because the episode is so often described as the day Microsoft saved Apple from bankruptcy. It did no such thing. Apple, for all its troubles, still held well over a billion dollars in cash, and a hundred and fifty million, while not nothing, would not by itself have kept the lights on for long or turned the company around. What mattered about the deal was not the money but the message and the software. The message was a public vote of confidence from the most powerful firm in the industry, delivered at the very moment the world had concluded Apple was finished. The software was the guarantee that Microsoft Office, the suite of programs that businesses could not live without, would keep running on the Macintosh, removing the single most common reason a wavering customer might abandon the platform. Jobs, ever the showman, had turned a humiliating dependence into a moment of theater, and he had bought not a lifeline of cash but a lifeline of credibility.

Then he set about the harder work of remaking what Apple was. He slashed the tangled product line to a handful of machines, killed projects that scattered the company's energy, and launched, in the autumn of 1997, an advertising campaign built around two words, "Think Different," and a gallery of portraits of Einstein, Gandhi, Picasso, and other rebels and geniuses, a campaign that sold no product at all and instead sold the idea of Apple itself as the brand of the misfit and the visionary. Above all he reasserted the conviction that had always separated Apple from the commodity box makers: that a computer should be an object of design, a thing of beauty and delight, not an interchangeable beige appliance sold on price. In this he found a collaborator whose talent matched his own, a young British designer named Jony Ive who had been quietly toiling in Apple's design studio, on the verge of quitting, and whom Jobs elevated into one of the most important figures in the company. Together they produced, in 1998, the machine that announced Apple's return to the world.

It was called the iMac, and it looked like nothing else on any desk in any office or home. Where every other computer was a rectangular box in shades of beige or gray, the iMac was a single curved shape of translucent blue-green plastic, a shade the company named Bondi blue after the color of the sea at a famous Australian beach, its internal workings faintly visible through the tinted shell, its whole personality friendly and rounded and unafraid. It combined the monitor and the computer into one unit, so that a buyer had only to lift it from the box, plug it in, and connect the telephone line to be online, and its very name, with that lowercase i, proclaimed its purpose: the internet, arriving just as the Web was drawing millions of new users, and the iMac was built to be the simplest possible way onto it. Jobs made a point of what the machine lacked as much as what it had. It shipped without a floppy disk drive, the storage device that had been standard on personal computers since the beginning, a deletion that critics called reckless and that Jobs defended as a clear-eyed reading of a future in which files would move over the network rather than on scraps of magnetic plastic.

The gamble worked spectacularly. The iMac sold hundreds of thousands of units in its first months and millions before it was done, drawing throngs of buyers, many of them purchasing their first computer or their first Apple, back into stores that had all but stopped stocking the brand. It restored Apple to profitability within a year and reintroduced the company to a public that had nearly written it off, proving that design and simplicity could still command a premium in a business that had convinced itself only price mattered. The following year Apple offered the machine in a row of fruit-toned colors, grape and tangerine and lime, an idea so alien to the gray computer trade that it turned the choosing of a computer into something closer to choosing a car or a pair of shoes.

The two campaigns that bracketed the revival reveal how completely Jobs understood that he was selling a feeling as much as a machine. The "Think Different" advertisement, which first aired in the autumn of 1997, showed no computer at all. Over a minute of black-and-white footage of Einstein and Gandhi, Martin Luther King and Amelia Earhart, Picasso and John Lennon, the actor Richard Dreyfuss read a prose poem that began, "Here's to the crazy ones. The misfits. The rebels. The troublemakers. The round pegs in the square holes." It ended with the claim that the people crazy enough to think they could change the world were the ones who did, and it never once mentioned a product. It was an advertisement for a state of mind, and it dared a demoralized company and a doubting public to see Apple as the home of that spirit. The iMac's own commercials, by contrast, sold the machine on a single concrete promise: simplicity. One famous spot walked through the steps of getting the computer onto the internet, plug in the machine, connect the phone line, and then, deadpan, announced that there was no step three. Against rivals whose setup could involve a thicket of cables, cards, and cryptic software, that joke was a competitive weapon, and it made the iMac's rounded, cheerful shell the outward sign of an inner ease that ordinary buyers had long been told they did not deserve.

The foundation Jobs had bought with NeXT finally bore fruit in 2001, when Apple released Mac OS X, a wholly new operating system built upon the rock-solid engineering of the NeXT software, marrying its industrial strength to a luminous new interface of soft colors and glassy translucence. It was the modern foundation Apple had spent years failing to build and had at last acquired, and it would underpin every Macintosh for decades and, in time, the far more numerous devices Apple had not yet imagined. The revival was real and it was gathering force, and it rested on a philosophy Jobs had held since the beginning and now imposed on the whole company: that the point of a computer was not its specifications but the experience of using it, and that the way to win was not to make the cheapest machine but the one people loved.

As for Michael Dell's suggestion that Apple be shut down and liquidated, Jobs never forgot it, and history handed him the reply. Years later, in early 2006, when the market's valuation of Apple climbed past that of Dell's own company, Jobs sent a note to his staff that leaked, as he surely intended, to the world. It observed, with theatrical restraint, that it had turned out Michael Dell was not so good at predicting the future, and that Apple was now, by the market's reckoning, worth more than Dell. In the years that followed the gap only widened, until Apple became by some measures the most valuable company on earth, and the lowercase i that Jobs had stamped on a friendly blue computer in 1998 would migrate onto a music player and then a telephone and reshape not just one company but the whole of modern life.

That conviction was steering Apple away from the ground on which the box wars were fought, toward something the industry had not yet named. If a computer could be a consumer object, an appliance of pleasure and design rather than a commodity of specifications and price, then perhaps the most important computers of the future would not sit on desks at all, and Apple, alone among the survivors of the personal-computer wars, was beginning to think about what those devices might be.

The turnaround would become the most studied comeback in the history of business, taught in classrooms as proof that a great company written off for dead can be revived by focus, taste, and nerve. But at its heart lay something simpler than any case study could capture, a stubborn refusal to accept the industry's verdict that computers were interchangeable commodities to be sold on price alone. Jobs had bet the company's survival on the opposite proposition, that people would pay more, and love a machine more, when someone had cared about every curve of its shell and every step of its setup. In a business that had spent a decade insisting design was a luxury it could not afford, that bet looked reckless. It turned out to be the most valuable idea anyone in the industry had.

Yet even as Apple charted its return, a very different and far more radical challenge to the whole industry was gathering, built not by a company at all but by a loose confederation of programmers scattered across the world, working for free and giving their work away.

Chapter 62: The Other Road

In September 1983, a programmer at the Massachusetts Institute of Technology named Richard Stallman posted a message to an internet newsgroup announcing that he was about to give away the work of the rest of his life. He intended, he wrote, to build a complete operating system, free for anyone to use, and he called the project GNU, a self-referential and slightly mischievous acronym that stood for "GNU's Not Unix," meaning that it would work like the widely admired Unix system but would owe that system nothing and belong to no one. Stallman was a figure of fierce and singular conviction, a brilliant hacker of the old MIT tradition who had watched with mounting dismay as the software he loved was locked away behind corporate walls, its inner workings hidden, its users forbidden by law and license from studying it, improving it, or sharing it with a friend. His radicalization had a famously petty origin: a new laser printer in his lab kept jamming, and Stallman wanted to modify its software so it would alert users when it did, only to discover that the manufacturer had refused to release the code and made him sign an agreement never to share it even if he could. To most people this would have been an annoyance. To Stallman it was a revelation of a moral wrong, a betrayal of the spirit of open inquiry and mutual aid that had defined the early hacker culture, and he resolved to fight it not with protest but with code, by building a body of software so complete and so free that no one would ever need to accept the shackles again.

The philosophy Stallman constructed around this crusade was as important as the software, and it turned on a distinction he insisted upon endlessly: that "free" meant free as in freedom, not free as in price. What mattered was not that the software cost nothing but that its users possessed four liberties: to run it for any purpose, to study how it worked by reading its underlying source code, to change it to suit their needs, and to share their changes with others. To protect these freedoms he devised a legal instrument of ingenious cunning, the General Public License, which used the machinery of copyright against itself. Software released under this license could be freely copied and modified, but anyone who distributed a modified version was obliged to release their changes under the same terms, so that the software and all its descendants would remain forever free and could never be captured and enclosed by anyone. He called the mechanism copyleft, a pun that captured its inverting spirit, and it would prove one of the most consequential legal innovations in the history of computing. The concrete effect is easy to state: a corporation could take Stallman's code and build a product on it, but the moment it shipped that product to customers, it was bound to hand over its own additions for the world to use in turn, a trap door through which private effort fell back into the commons.

Through the 1980s Stallman and the volunteers who rallied to his Free Software Foundation built piece after piece of the promised system, a powerful text editor, a superb compiler to turn programs into runnable code, and a host of the essential tools that a Unix-like system required. By the start of the 1990s they had assembled nearly all of it. But at the heart of the machine, the kernel, the core program that manages the processor and the memory and speaks directly to the hardware, the GNU project's own effort had bogged down in difficulty, and the free operating system remained tantalizingly incomplete, a body without a beating heart.

The heart arrived from a quarter no one had anticipated, from a twenty-one-year-old computer science student in Helsinki. On the twenty-fifth of August 1991, a young Finn named Linus Torvalds posted his own message to an internet newsgroup devoted to a small teaching operating system called Minix, under the modest heading "What would you like to see most in minix?" He was doing a free operating system, he wrote, but it was just a hobby, and it would not be big and professional like GNU. What he had begun was a kernel, written for the inexpensive Intel processors that sat inside ordinary personal computers, and he had done it partly out of curiosity and partly out of frustration at the cost and restrictions of the commercial alternatives available to a student. He released his early code over the internet and invited anyone who wished to examine it, improve it, and send back their improvements, and he placed it, before long, under Stallman's General Public License.

Even the name was an accident, and correcting the record here dispels a small myth, for Torvalds did not proudly christen the system after himself. He thought that egotistical and wanted to call it Freax, a mash of "free" and "freak" and the letter x that hung over so many Unix systems. When he uploaded the code to a Finnish university server so others could download it, the administrator who ran the site, a man named Ari Lemmke, disliked the name Freax and, without much ceremony, filed the software away in a directory he labeled "linux," a blend of Linus and Unix. The label stuck, and so one of the most widely used pieces of software ever written owes its name not to its creator's vanity but to a stranger's editorial whim.

What happened next was something genuinely new in the making of complex things. Torvalds's kernel, combined with the vast collection of tools the GNU project had already built, formed a complete and free operating system, and around it there gathered, over the internet, a global community of volunteer programmers who developed it together in a manner that no company could have organized and few would have believed possible. Thousands of people scattered across the world, most of whom never met, contributed code, found and fixed errors, and traded improvements, coordinating through mailing lists and later through ever more sophisticated tools, with Torvalds at the center as the trusted arbiter of what went into the official version. An early chronicler of the movement, the programmer Eric Raymond, contrasted this open, churning method with the closed, top-down way companies built software, calling one the bazaar and the other the cathedral, and he distilled the bazaar's secret strength into a maxim he named in Torvalds's honor: given enough eyeballs, all bugs are shallow. The claim was that a problem baffling to any one programmer would be obvious to someone, somewhere, among the multitude reading the code, and that the sheer number of eyes trained on open software would catch flaws that a small secret team would miss. Critics insisted the bazaar could never produce software robust enough for serious work. They were wrong. Refined by the relentless scrutiny of everyone who cared to look, Linux grew steadily more capable and more reliable, and the manner of its making became a model that would later be given a friendlier, more businesslike name: open source.

The movement even acquired its familiar modern name almost by accident, in a single week early in 1998. When Netscape, reeling from the browser war, made the startling decision to release the source code of its browser to the public and let volunteers carry it forward, a small group of advocates gathered in California to figure out how to sell this alien idea to corporations who heard the word "free" and thought only of shoddiness and communism. One of them, a nanotechnology researcher named Christine Peterson, proposed dropping Stallman's morally freighted phrase "free software" in favor of a cooler, more businesslike term she had turned over between meetings: open source. The name stuck, an industry group formed around it within days, and Netscape released its browser's code on the last day of March that year, seeding the project that would become Firefox. The rebranding was more than cosmetic. "Free software" had asked companies to embrace a philosophy; "open source" asked them only to appreciate a superior method of building reliable code, and under that friendlier banner corporations that would never have signed Stallman's manifesto poured money and engineers into the commons. Already one such project, a web server called Apache, built and maintained by scattered volunteers, ran a larger share of the world's websites than all its commercial competitors combined, quiet proof that software written by a leaderless crowd and given away could beat anything money alone could buy.

The world Linux conquered was not the one its makers might first have expected. On the ordinary desktop, where Microsoft's Windows ruled through its command of the manufacturers and the sheer inertia of the software people already knew, Linux made little headway, remaining a taste of enthusiasts and technicians who did not mind its rougher edges. But in the machine rooms where the internet itself lived, on the servers that stored the world's Web pages and routed its electronic mail and performed the heavy computation behind the scenes, Linux triumphed almost completely. It was free, so it cost nothing to deploy across thousands of machines. It was open, so the engineers who ran it could inspect it, tune it, and fix it themselves rather than waiting on a vendor. And it was reliable enough to run for years without failing. As the Web exploded through the late 1990s and into the new century, the unglamorous computers that powered it ran, more and more, on this operating system built by volunteers and given away, until an enormous share of the internet's infrastructure rested quietly upon it, invisible to the billions who used it every day without ever knowing its name.

The business world, which had regarded free software as a curiosity or a threat, soon learned to embrace it, and the moment of conversion can be dated with some precision.

In the summer of 1999 a company called Red Hat, which made its money not by selling Linux, which was free, but by packaging it neatly and supporting it for corporations that wanted a throat to choke when something went wrong, sold its shares to the public. The offering was one of the most spectacular of the entire dot-com era, its stock soaring on the first day, and it proved that a fortune could be built atop software that anyone was free to copy. The proof drew the giants in. Within a year the mighty IBM, the very company whose choices had created the Wintel order, announced that it would pour a billion dollars into Linux, betting that the operating system built by volunteers was more reliable and more flexible than anything it could write in-house. When the largest and oldest computer company on earth staked that kind of money on software given away by a global crowd, the argument was effectively settled. Open source was no longer a rebellion against the industry; it had become part of the industry's foundation, a way of building things so evidently superior for certain purposes that resisting it came to seem like sentiment rather than strategy.

Beneath the technical victory lay a philosophical one, and it was the deepest theme of the whole story. From the beginning, the personal-computer revolution had been an argument about power, about who should control the machine and the knowledge it embodied, and the free-software movement pressed that argument to its logical conclusion. The commercial model, embodied above all by Microsoft, held that software was property, its inner workings a trade secret, its use governed by a license that granted the user permission but never ownership or understanding. Stallman and Torvalds and the movement they inspired held the opposite: that software, like scientific knowledge, belonged to everyone, that its source should be open for all to read and improve, and that the users of a machine, not the corporation that sold them its software, should be its true masters. It was a return, in a way, to the oldest ideals of the hacker culture from which the whole revolution had sprung, the conviction that information wanted to be free and that the computer was an instrument of liberation, now armored in law and proven at planetary scale.

The remarkable thing is how completely this other road came to carry the traffic of the modern world, even if you have never heard the names of the people who built it. The phone in your pocket, if it runs Android, runs atop the very Linux kernel that a Finnish student began as a hobby. The overwhelming majority of the servers that deliver your email, your video, your searches, and your social feeds run Linux; so does every one of the world's fastest supercomputers; so do the devices humming inside televisions, cars, thermostats, and routers in nearly every home. The free-software argument that once sounded utopian, that code should be open and shared, became simply the way much of the digital world is built, so ordinary that the companies most associated with proprietary software now count themselves among the largest contributors to open-source projects. The road not taken by the ordinary desktop turned out to be the road that most of computing quietly traveled.

The personal computer had traveled an extraordinary distance, from a hobbyist's kit assembled from a magazine advertisement to a commodity appliance on a billion desks, from a solitary calculator to the universal gateway of a networked world, and along the way it had spun off rival philosophies of design and ownership and freedom that would shape everything that came after. But the machine on the desk, for all its triumph, was about to be eclipsed, for the same relentless miniaturization that had shrunk a room of vacuum tubes into a chip was preparing to shrink the whole computer once more, down to a slab of glass and metal that would slip into a pocket and change the world again.

Chapter 63: The Computer in Your Pocket

On the morning of January 9, 2007, in a darkened auditorium at the Moscone Center in San Francisco, a man in a black turtleneck and faded jeans stood before a crowd of the faithful and told them he had been looking forward to this day for two and a half years. Steve Jobs paced the stage of the Macworld conference with the practiced ease of a preacher who knows the sermon by heart, and he told them that every so often a revolutionary product came along that changed everything. Then he made a promise that sounded, at first, like a joke. Today, he said, Apple would introduce three revolutionary products: a widescreen iPod with touch controls, a mobile phone, and a breakthrough internet communications device. He repeated the list. He repeated it again, faster, until the audience began to understand. These were not three products. They were one. "And we are calling it iPhone." Today, he added, Apple was going to reinvent the phone. The applause that followed was the sound of an industry's center of gravity shifting, though almost no one in the room, and few outside it, yet grasped how far.

Behind that polished morning lay years of secrecy and no small amount of doubt within Apple itself. The project had been developed under the code name Purple, in a locked building whose doors bore a sign borrowed from a film about a Las Vegas casino, and Jobs had wrestled for months over whether to build a tablet or a phone first, and whether to entrust the phone's brain to the iPod team or the Macintosh team. The two internal groups had competed to design it, and the version that won was, in essence, a tiny Macintosh. It is worth dispelling here a common belief, for the iPhone was not the first smartphone, nor the first phone with a touchscreen. Devices that merged a phone with a pocket computer had existed since IBM's Simon in the mid-1990s, and the market in 2007 was full of them, made by BlackBerry and Palm and Nokia and others. What Jobs claimed, and delivered, was not the invention of the category but its reinvention, a wholesale rethinking of how a person and a pocket computer should touch each other.

What Jobs held up that morning was, beneath its glass and aluminum, a computer. It ran a stripped-down version of the same Unix-derived operating system, OS X, that powered the Macintosh sitting on desks around the world. It had a processor, memory, storage, and a graphical interface, only the interface was not driven by a mouse or a keyboard but by the human finger, pressed directly against a capacitive touchscreen. The distinction was more than cosmetic. The resistive screens on earlier devices worked by physical pressure, registering the poke of a hard stylus against two flexible layers, which is why those phones came with plastic sticks tucked into their frames. Apple's screen instead sensed the faint electrical charge of living skin, a technology called capacitive sensing, and because it watched the whole surface at once it could track several fingers simultaneously. That single capability, multitouch, made possible the gestures that would become second nature to billions: the flick that scrolls a list with lifelike momentum, the two-finger pinch that shrinks a photograph or a map, the spread that zooms it back. Jobs mocked the physical keyboards and plastic styluses of the smartphones then on the market and asked who wanted a stylus. "Nobody wants a stylus," he said, and answered his own question by declaring that we were all born with the ultimate pointing device, our fingers. The machine in his hand dispensed with the fixed buttons that constrained every rival, replacing them with software that could rearrange itself into whatever the moment required, a numeric keypad for dialing, a typewriter for messaging, a blank canvas for a photograph.

Not everyone was impressed, and the reactions of the men who ran the incumbent giants have aged into cautionary tales. Steve Ballmer, then chief executive of Microsoft, laughed the device off in an interview that year, marveling that Apple wanted five hundred dollars, fully subsidized with a plan, for what he called the most expensive phone in the world, one that would not appeal to business customers because it lacked a keyboard. There was, he insisted, no chance that the iPhone would get any significant market share, no chance at all; he would rather have Microsoft's software in seventy or eighty percent of the world's phones than the two or three percent Apple might manage. It was a reasonable-sounding judgment from the standpoint of 2007, and it was catastrophically wrong, a monument to the difficulty of seeing a new thing clearly while standing inside the old one.

It is easy, from the vantage of the present, to forget how much the first iPhone could not do. Priced at four hundred and ninety-nine dollars for the smaller model and available at first only in the United States, locked to a single carrier under a two-year contract, it ran only on the slower cellular networks of its day; it had no app store, no copy and paste, no video recording. Third-party developers were, at launch, told to write web pages rather than native programs. And yet the thing that mattered was already fully present in that first device: the recognition that a phone was no longer primarily a phone. It was a pocket-sized general-purpose computer that happened, among its many talents, to make calls. When Apple reversed course and opened the App Store in the summer of 2008, letting outside programmers write software that ran directly on the device, the true scale of what had been built became clear. Within a few years, a single slab of glass could serve as a camera, a map, a music library, a games console, a bank, a newspaper, a flashlight, a level, a compass, and a portal to the entire accumulated text of the World Wide Web. The bicycle for the mind had learned to fit in a trouser pocket.

Apple did not have the new world to itself for long, and the shape of the contest that followed rhymed with the one that had defined the personal computer a generation earlier. Google, the search company, had quietly bought a small startup called Android in 2005, and after the iPhone's debut it hurried that project toward a rival vision: not a single beautiful device sold at a premium by one company, but a free operating system that Google would give to any manufacturer willing to build a phone around it. The first Android handset reached buyers in the autumn of 2008, and the strategy was, in its essentials, the one Microsoft had used to conquer the desktop, spread the software everywhere across many makers rather than bind it to a single expensive machine. It worked again. Within a few years Android ran on the majority of the world's smartphones, most of them cheaper than an iPhone, while Apple kept the largest share of the industry's profits, a division of spoils that echoed the old split between the box makers and the owners of the standard. The incumbents of the old mobile world, meanwhile, were swept away with astonishing speed. Nokia, which had sold more phones than any company on earth, and BlackBerry, whose keyboard-clad devices had been the badge of every executive, both misjudged how completely the rules had changed and collapsed from dominance to irrelevance within half a decade, a warning of how little the past protects a company when the ground beneath an industry shifts.

The numbers that made this possible were staggering, and they were the direct inheritance of a law first sketched by Gordon Moore four decades earlier. The transistor count on a chip had gone on doubling, roughly every couple of years, with the metronomic patience that Moore had predicted, and by the late 2000s that relentless doubling had delivered something once unthinkable: a smartphone whose processor, memory, and graphics outstripped the desktop personal computers over which families had marveled in the 1990s. The device that a teenager carried to school in 2010 was, by any honest measure of raw computation, more powerful than the beige tower that had run the household a decade before, and vastly more powerful than the machines that had guided astronauts or run corporations a generation earlier. The revolution that had begun with a hobbyist squinting at the flashing lights of an Altair had arrived, by way of sand and lightning and Moore's stubborn curve, at a computer small enough to lose down the back of a sofa.

The App Store did more than add features to a phone; it conjured an economy that had not existed the day before. By opening the device to any programmer willing to abide by its rules and take a share of the proceeds, Apple turned millions of independent developers into a labor force building, in effect, the phone's true value, and the sheer variety of what they made became a marketing slogan in itself. Apple began advertising that whatever a person might wish to do, there was an app for that, a phrase so central to the pitch that the company took the unusual step of trademarking it. Small teams and lone coders wrote programs that were downloaded tens of millions of times, and a few grew into companies worth billions, so that the store became a gold rush reminiscent of the one the Netscape offering had touched off a decade earlier, only now the frontier was a screen the size of a playing card. This was the deepest sense in which the iPhone was a computer rather than a phone: like the personal computers before it, its worth lay less in what its maker had built than in the open-ended universe of things that other people could build to run on it. A telephone did one thing; a platform did whatever the world could imagine for it.

Jobs himself had seen where this was heading, and he had a phrase for it. Speaking at a technology conference in the spring of 2007, months before the iPhone shipped, he described a coming "post-PC" era, an age in which the personal computer would no longer sit at the center of a person's digital life but would become one device among many, sharing the stage with phones and other portable machines. Some accounts trace the underlying idea further back, to the researchers at Xerox and MIT who had long imagined computing dissolving into the environment, but it was Jobs who gave the notion its popular name and its commercial proof. In 2010 he made the argument physical. Standing on another stage, he lowered himself into a leather armchair, picked up a thin slab larger than a phone but smaller than a laptop, and used it to browse the web, read email, and flip through photographs while reclining like a man in his living room. The iPad, he said, was not a big phone and not a small laptop; it was a new category, a machine for the way people actually consumed information when they were not sitting at a desk. Critics scoffed at the name and dismissed it as a toy. It went on to sell by the tens of millions and to define a category that had failed, for decades, every company that had tried it.

The evidence that an era was ending soon showed up in the ledgers of the companies that had built the old one. For thirty years, the story of computing had been a story of ever-rising personal-computer sales, more desktops, more laptops, more Windows machines pouring out of factories in Texas and Taiwan every year. Then, around the start of the 2010s, the line bent and began to fall. The market researchers at IDC, who counted these things for a living, reported that shipments of personal computers in the first quarter of 2013 had fallen by roughly fourteen percent from the same period a year earlier, the steepest quarterly decline the firm had ever recorded. Analysts reached for explanations, and the clearest one was sitting in everyone's hand: people who once would have bought a new PC were spending their money, and their attention, on smartphones and tablets instead. The machine that had liberated the individual from the mainframe was itself being displaced by a machine still smaller and still more personal.

It would be a mistake, though, to read that falling line as an obituary. The smartphone did not kill the personal computer; it inherited from it. Everything that had made the PC revolutionary, the idea that computation belonged to the individual rather than the institution, the graphical interface born at Xerox and popularized by the Macintosh, the notion that a person's documents and music and correspondence were theirs to carry, passed intact into the device in the pocket. The phone was the personal computer's heir, not its assassin, the next turn of a wheel that had been rolling since a room-sized ENIAC filled a hall with vacuum tubes and a technical priesthood guarded the switches. The genealogy ran unbroken from the mainframe to the microprocessor to the desktop to the laptop to the glass rectangle now consulted, on average, dozens of times a day by more human beings than have ever lived at once. You are almost certainly holding one, or sitting an arm's length from it, as you read these words, and every tap and swipe you make on its surface is a gesture Steve Jobs demonstrated to a skeptical world on a January morning, over the laughter of men who were certain it would never catch on.

And so the machine that a generation of dreamers had fought to pry loose from the institutions completed its long migration outward, from the raised floors of corporate data centers into the palms of billions, which raised, at last, the deeper question of what it meant that the computer had won so completely it was about to disappear.

Chapter 64: The Revolution That Won by Disappearing

In September 1991, a computer scientist named Mark Weiser published an essay in Scientific American that opened with a sentence at odds with everything the industry then believed about itself. "The most profound technologies are those that disappear," he wrote. "They weave themselves into the fabric of everyday life until they are indistinguishable from it." Weiser was the chief technologist at Xerox PARC, the same California laboratory that had invented the graphical interface a generation earlier and watched others grow rich on it, and from that vantage he had come to a heretical conclusion. The personal computer, the glowing box that the whole world was busy putting on every desk, was not the destination. It was a way station. The real future of computing, he argued, lay in machines so small, so numerous, and so thoroughly embedded in ordinary objects that people would cease to perceive them as computers at all. He had a name for this vision, coined a few years earlier: ubiquitous computing. And he drew a deliberate contrast with the era's other prophecy, virtual reality, which sought to pull human beings inside an artificial world behind a screen. His idea ran the opposite way. He wanted to push the computer out of its box and scatter it invisibly through the real world, so that it would serve people without ever demanding that they stop and pay attention to it. He called the result, in a later phrase, calm technology, that which informs but does not shout for our focus.

Weiser did not live to see how completely he had been right. He died in 1999, at the age of forty-six, when the World Wide Web was still young and the smartphone had not been imagined, before almost any of the invisible machines he predicted had arrived in ordinary homes. But within two decades of his death his prophecy had come true past the point of metaphor. Sometime in the second decade of the new century, in a kitchen that could have been anywhere, a person spoke a question aloud and a device answered, drawing on machines humming in warehouses a thousand miles away. There was no keyboard, no blinking cursor of the kind that had once defined what it meant to use a computer. Behind that unremarkable moment stood more computing power than had existed in all the world at the instant ENIAC was first switched on, marshaled through networks that circled the planet. The computer had not gone away. It had done exactly what Weiser said the most profound technologies do. It had vanished into everything, and in doing so had become so ordinary that people stopped noticing it was there at all.

This was the revolution's final and most complete victory: not conquest but disappearance. Here it is worth correcting the obituaries that were written when personal-computer sales began to fall in the early 2010s, for the headlines announcing the death of the PC had the story exactly backward. The personal computer did not die. It reproduced. The object that this book has traced from the flashing panel of an Altair to the glass slab of an iPhone dissolved into the fabric of ordinary life until it was no longer a thing one used but a condition one lived inside. There were computers in the cars that braked before their drivers could, computers in the watches that counted heartbeats, computers in the thermostats and doorbells and refrigerators, computers in the pacemakers tucked beside human hearts. There were computers one never saw at all, banked in the vast anonymous buildings that the industry had taken to calling the cloud, holding the photographs and letters and half-finished thoughts of billions of people who trusted them without ever learning where they physically were. The machine that a hobbyist had once soldered together at a kitchen table had multiplied past counting and slipped below the threshold of attention, the way a technology does only when it has truly won.

Consider what actually happens in that ordinary kitchen moment, because tracing it makes the disappearance concrete. A spoken question is captured by a microphone and converted into a stream of digital data, which travels over a home network to a router, out through a cable or a strand of glass fiber, across the switching centers of an internet built on the open protocols of the 1970s, and into one of those warehouse-sized data centers, where thousands of processors, most of them running the free operating system a Finnish student began as a hobby, turn the sound into words, search vast stores of information for an answer, and send it racing back along the same path, all in less time than it takes to draw a breath. Every layer of the revolution this book has told is present in that single second: the microprocessor born at Intel, the networks born at the research agencies, the graphical and voice interfaces born at Xerox and refined at Apple, the open-source software born of Stallman's stubbornness and Torvalds's hobby, the commodity economics that made the whole apparatus cheap enough to give away. The user perceives none of it. That perceiving nothing is the measure of the triumph.

The comparison that the pioneers themselves reached for, again and again, was electricity, and Weiser had used it too. In the nineteenth century, electric power had been a marvel, a thing of exhibitions and demonstrations, tended by specialists and installed at great expense. Within a few generations it had retreated into the walls. No one, flipping a switch, thinks of the generators and transformers and the century of accumulated genius that make the light come on; the miracle has become infrastructure, invisible precisely because it is everywhere. Computing followed the same arc, only faster. What had begun in the 1940s as a room-sized wonder tended by a priesthood in white coats became, in the span of a single human lifetime, as unremarkable and as indispensable as the current in the wires. To be without it was no longer to be old-fashioned; it was to be cut off from the ordinary machinery of modern existence.

Weiser had not merely theorized about this future; he had tried to build it. At Xerox PARC in the late 1980s and early 1990s his team constructed experimental devices in three sizes, which they called tabs, pads, and boards, inch-scale, foot-scale, and yard-scale computers meant to be as plentiful and unremarkable as sticky notes, sheets of paper, and whiteboards. The idea was that a person might be surrounded by dozens or hundreds of such machines without thinking of any of them as a computer, the way a room full of books and pens and windows is not experienced as a room full of technology. His prototypes were clumsy and the wireless networks of his day too feeble to sustain them, and he died before the pieces fell into place. Yet the shape of what he imagined arrived almost exactly on schedule. The smartphone was his pad; the smartwatch was his tab; the wall-sized display in the conference room was his board. And the numbers vindicated him utterly: by the 2010s the average new car contained scores of small processors, an ordinary household held dozens more, and the world was manufacturing billions of microchips a year, the overwhelming majority of them destined not for anything anyone would call a computer but for objects that merely happened to think a little. The visible machine on the desk had always been the smallest part of the story. The rest was dissolving into the walls, exactly as the man from Xerox had promised, informing without demanding, present without being seen.

What the revolution delivered, measured against the dreams of the idealists who had preached it in the head shops and hobbyist clubs of the 1970s, was in many ways more than they had dared imagine. It handed the tools of creation to anyone who wanted them: the writer who no longer needed a publisher's press, the musician who recorded an album in a bedroom, the filmmaker with a camera in a phone, the small merchant who reached customers on the far side of the world. It built a marketplace of a scale no economist had modeled, in which commerce flowed at the speed of light and a shop in one country served a buyer in another before either had finished breakfast. And it connected people, reunited the scattered, gave voice to the silenced, let a grandparent watch a grandchild's first steps across an ocean of distance. The power over information that had once belonged to governments and corporations passed, as the dreamers had demanded, into the hands of individuals. On that count, the People's Computer Company and Ted Nelson and the young radicals of Homebrew had been vindicated beyond their wildest slogans.

But the same power that liberated could also be turned, and the revolution's costs came due alongside its gifts. Weiser had hoped for calm technology, machines that would recede politely into the background and leave human attention free. What arrived was often the opposite. The machines that knew so much about their users came to watch them, logging every search and purchase and midnight worry, until surveillance became not the exception but the business model, the quiet price of things that seemed to be free. The devices designed to command attention learned to hold it against the will of the people holding them, engineered to be difficult to set down, so that the bicycle for the mind sometimes pedaled its rider in circles. And the openness that had once defined the revolution, the ragged, competitive, anyone-can-play openness of the clone wars and the hobbyist clubs, narrowed over time into a landscape dominated by a handful of enormous platforms, a few companies through whose gates nearly all of digital life now passed. The technology that had been meant to break up concentrations of power had, in its maturity, built new ones of a size the world had never seen. It was possible to celebrate what the revolution had achieved and to grieve what it had cost, and honesty required doing both at once.

There is an irony in this that the pioneers would have savored and lamented in equal measure. The whole revolution had been launched, in the head shops and hobbyist basements of the 1970s, as a rebellion against the very idea of a computing priesthood, against the institutions that hoarded machines behind locked doors and told ordinary people what they were permitted to compute. The rebels had won that fight so completely that a child now carried more power in a pocket than those guarded mainframes had ever mustered. And yet in winning they had built, without quite meaning to, a new dependence deeper than the one they overthrew. The person who spoke a question into the air and received an answer owned neither the machines that answered nor the data they drew upon nor the software that ran them; those lived in distant buildings belonging to a handful of corporations, as remote and as unaccountable, in their way, as the old computer rooms had ever been. The mainframe had not been abolished. It had been moved offstage, multiplied a millionfold, and rented back to everyone by the sip. Power over computing had been handed to the individual and, at the same time, quietly gathered again into a few enormous hands, and both things were true, and the tension between them is the unfinished business the revolution bequeathed to the century that followed.

Still, it is worth pausing on the sheer improbability of the thing. The men and women in this book did not set out to remake civilization. They set out to build a computer small enough and cheap enough that a single person could own one, a bounded, almost modest ambition, pursued in garages and hotel ballrooms and corporate labs by people who were, for the most part, ignored or dismissed by the institutions of their day. The smart money, for a long time, was against them. The president of a great computer corporation had reportedly seen no reason anyone would want a computer in their home; the men who ran the software and telephone giants had laughed at the browser and the pocket phone that would humble them. That the outsiders succeeded at all is remarkable; that they succeeded so completely that their invention became invisible is the kind of victory that history rarely grants. The revolution won not when the personal computer sat on every desk, but when it left the desk entirely and disappeared into the world, precisely as a quiet man at Xerox had foretold.

And so we return, at the end, to the image with which so much of this began: the bicycle. Steve Jobs, borrowing a fact about the efficiency of locomotion, had called the computer a bicycle for the mind, not a replacement for human thought but an amplifier of it, a simple tool that let an ordinary person travel intellectual distances impossible on foot. The metaphor has aged into something richer than he perhaps intended. A bicycle, after all, is a humble machine, cheap and personal and democratic, owned by the rider rather than the state, requiring the rider's own effort to go anywhere at all. It carries you farther than your legs alone could manage, but only if you pedal; it extends the human, it does not replace the human. That was always the promise, and the peril, of the thing these people built. The computer amplifies whatever is fed into it, curiosity or distraction, connection or control, the best of us or the worst.

The revolution is over, in the sense that its central battle has been won so thoroughly that we no longer think to fight it. But the next one has already begun, in machines that no longer merely amplify human thought but appear, in their fashion, to think for themselves, raising once more the oldest question of this whole long story: whether the tool will remain a bicycle for the mind, pedaled by the person who owns it, or become something the person no longer steers. The people who first pried the computer loose from the institutions could not have foreseen where their bounded ambition would lead. But they left us the essential inheritance and the essential warning, folded into the same small machine: that computing power is a form of power, and that the deepest question is never what the machine can do, but whose hands it rests in, and what, with it, we choose to become.

Epilogue: A Bicycle for Everyone

Begin with a single machine and end with a number no one can quite hold in the mind. In the middle of the twentieth century, a computer was a room. It filled a hall with vacuum tubes and cabinets and the low roar of cooling fans, it cost more than most people would earn in a lifetime, and it was tended by a priesthood of specialists in white coats who fed it punched cards and carried away its answers on reels of tape. To use such a machine, an ordinary person did not walk up and type. An ordinary person filed a request, waited a day, and received a printout from a functionary who stood between the human and the machine like a temple guard. Computing was power, and power, as it always does, gathered itself into institutions—the government, the corporation, the university—that could afford the room and the priesthood and the reels of tape.

The story told in this book is the story of how that arrangement came apart. Over the span of a single human life, the room shrank to a chip, the chip fell in price until a hobbyist could afford it, and the machine walked out of the institution and into the home, the pocket, the wristwatch, the air of the kitchen. By the end of the story there were more personal computers than there were human beings, and computation itself had become as ordinary as running water.

Power over information—over calculation, communication, creation, and memory—drained out of the institutions that had hoarded it and spread into the hands of billions. Whatever else one wishes to call that, it was a transfer of power on a scale the world had rarely seen, accomplished not by revolution in the streets but by engineers with soldering irons and dreamers with slogans.

Look closely at how it happened, though, and a pattern repeats so often it begins to feel like a law. The hobbyists invented; the corporations legitimized; the inventors, more often than not, lost control of what they had made. It was hobbyists and misfits who built the first personal computers—Wozniak at a Homebrew meeting, Roberts in an Albuquerque strip mall—working for love and obsession rather than any credible market. It was corporations that made those inventions respectable and universal: IBM, arriving late, gave the personal computer a coat and tie and put it on the world's desks. And again and again the people who saw the future first were not the ones who profited from it. Xerox invented the graphical interface, the mouse, and the networked office, and then watched Apple and Microsoft carry those ideas to the bank. Gary Kildall wrote the operating system that ran the first serious microcomputers, and it was Microsoft's imitation that conquered the world. The inventor's tragedy and the industry's engine turn out to be the same mechanism.

There is a second lesson buried in the wreckage, and it may be the most useful thing this history has to teach. Openness beat "best," and standards beat brilliance. The most elegant machine did not win; the most open one did. IBM's Personal Computer was not the finest design of its era, but its architecture was published and imitable, and that openness spawned an army of clones that made its standard universal and, in the end, reduced IBM itself to one vendor among many. The Macintosh was a more beautiful machine than any PC, and it lost the market for a generation because it was closed. The internet triumphed over slicker proprietary networks because its protocols belonged to no one. Time after time, the thing that everyone could build on defeated the thing that one company controlled, however superior the latter might have been on the day it shipped. A standard shared is a standard that spreads; a marvel locked away is a marvel that dies with its maker's market share.

None of this was inevitable, and that is worth insisting upon, because hindsight flattens the past into a smooth ramp of progress. It was not smooth. Fortunes were made by luck as often as by genius, and lost the same way. Brilliant companies died of a single bad decision, and mediocre ones survived because they held the right standard at the right moment. The people living through it did not know they were making history; they thought they were making payroll, or a deadline, or a point. The revolution looks orderly only because we know how it ended.

And it has not ended. The old battle—to pry the computer loose from the institution and place it in the individual's hands—has been won so completely that we no longer think to fight it. But the questions it raised have not been settled; they have merely been handed forward, larger than before. Who owns the computing power now? For the machine did not stay in the individual's hands so much as pass through them into the cloud, into a handful of enormous platforms that hold the world's data in buildings most people will never see. The hobbyist's dream of a computer you could throw out a window has given way to a computer you can never quite locate, run by companies you cannot quite escape. And a new kind of machine has arrived, one that does not merely amplify human thought but seems to generate its own, reopening every old question about control and dependence in a sharper key. Who will own the intelligence in the machine? Who will steer it? Whose ends will it serve?

These are the unfinished questions of the next era, and this book cannot answer them, because they are not yet history. What it can offer is the pattern that the last era left behind, and a single stubborn image to carry into the next one. The pioneers of the personal computer reached, over and over, for the same humble metaphor: the machine as a bicycle for the mind, a simple tool that carried an ordinary person farther than they could travel alone, owned by the rider and powered by the rider's own effort. The dream was never a machine that would do our thinking for us. It was a machine that would extend the reach of every mind willing to pedal. Whether the next generation of machines honors that dream or betrays it will depend, as it always has, not on what the technology can do, but on whose hands it rests in—and on whether we remember, this time, to demand a bicycle for everyone.

Timeline of the Personal Computer

This chronology follows the personal computer from the invention of the transistor to the dawn of the post-PC world. Dates mark first public demonstration, announcement, or shipment as noted; where sources disagree, the most widely accepted date is given.

1945 — Vannevar Bush publishes "As We May Think" in *The Atlantic*, imagining the Memex, a desk-sized machine for linking and retrieving all human knowledge.

1947 — In December, physicists John Bardeen, Walter Brattain, and William Shockley demonstrate the first working transistor at Bell Labs, the switch that would eventually replace the vacuum tube.

1947 — On September 9, Grace Hopper's team at Harvard tapes a dead moth into the Mark II logbook as the "first actual case of bug being found," a joke on engineering slang for a fault that already dated back to Edison.

1948 — Claude Shannon publishes "A Mathematical Theory of Communication," founding information theory and giving the world the "bit."

1950 — Alan Turing publishes "Computing Machinery and Intelligence," proposing the imitation game now known as the Turing Test.

1951 — The UNIVAC I, the first commercial computer in the United States, is delivered to the U.S. Census Bureau.

1954 — Texas Instruments produces the first commercial silicon transistor, developed by Gordon Teal.

1956 — William Shockley founds Shockley Semiconductor Laboratory in Mountain View, seeding what will become Silicon Valley; Bardeen, Brattain, and Shockley share the Nobel Prize in Physics for the transistor.

1957 — In September, the "traitorous eight," including Robert Noyce and Gordon Moore, leave Shockley to found Fairchild Semiconductor; in October, the Soviet launch of Sputnik spurs the United States to create ARPA.

1958 — On September 12, Jack Kilby demonstrates the first working integrated circuit at Texas Instruments.

1959 — Robert Noyce at Fairchild develops the practical silicon planar integrated circuit; he and Kilby are later recognized as its co-inventors.

1960 — The first commercial planar integrated circuits ship; at Bell Labs, Mohamed Atalla and Dawon Kahng invent the MOSFET, the transistor that will populate future chips.

1962 — At MIT, Steve Russell and friends write *Spacewar!*, one of the first video games, on a DEC PDP-1.

1963 — Douglas Engelbart invents the computer mouse at the Stanford Research Institute.

1964 — IBM announces the System/360 mainframe family; John Kemeny and Thomas Kurtz create the BASIC programming language at Dartmouth.

1965 — In the April 19 issue of *Electronics*, Gordon Moore observes that the number of components on a chip is doubling at a steady pace, a prediction later dubbed Moore's Law; Ted Nelson coins the word "hypertext."

1968 — In July, Robert Noyce and Gordon Moore found Intel; on December 9, Engelbart gives the "Mother of All Demos" in San Francisco, unveiling the mouse, hypertext, video conferencing, and windows.

1969 — On October 29, the first message is sent over the ARPANET; work begins on the Unix operating system at Bell Labs.

1970 — Xerox founds its Palo Alto Research Center (PARC); Intel introduces the 1103 dynamic RAM chip.

1971 — On November 15, Intel ships the 4004, the first commercial microprocessor, packing 2,300 transistors—a full computer's brain on a single chip; Ray Tomlinson sends the first network email.

1972 — Intel releases the 8008, an early 8-bit microprocessor; Nolan Bushnell and Ted Dabney found Atari and release *Pong*; Dennis Ritchie creates the C programming language.

1973 — Xerox PARC completes the Alto, the first computer with a graphical interface, mouse, and networking; Robert Metcalfe invents Ethernet; France's Micral N becomes one of the first non-kit commercial microcomputers.

1974 — In April, Intel releases the 8080, the microprocessor that will power the first personal computers; Gary Kildall writes CP/M; Ted Nelson publishes *Computer Lib / Dream Machines*.

1975 — In January, the Altair 8800 appears on the cover of *Popular Electronics*, igniting the hobbyist movement; sold as a kit for roughly $400.

1975 — On March 5, the Homebrew Computer Club holds its first meeting in Menlo Park; in April, Bill Gates and Paul Allen found Microsoft to write BASIC for the Altair.

1975 — MOS Technology introduces the 6502 microprocessor for about $25, undercutting rivals and enabling a wave of affordable machines; *Byte* magazine begins publishing.

1976 — On April 1, Steve Jobs, Steve Wozniak, and Ronald Wayne found Apple Computer; the hand-built Apple I goes on sale as a bare board.

1976 — In February, Bill Gates publishes his "Open Letter to Hobbyists," denouncing the copying of software; Zilog releases the Z80, a popular 8080-compatible chip.

1977 — The "Trinity" arrives: the Commodore PET (shown in January), the Apple II (introduced in April at the West Coast Computer Faire), and the Tandy TRS-80 (August)—the first mass-market, ready-to-use personal computers.

1977 — Atari releases the Video Computer System (later the 2600), bringing programmable cartridge gaming into the home.

1978 — Intel introduces the 16-bit 8086 processor; Wozniak designs the Apple Disk II floppy drive; MicroPro's WordStar helps define word processing.

1979 — In October, VisiCalc, the first spreadsheet program, ships for the Apple II and becomes the software businesses buy computers to run; Intel releases the 8088 and Motorola the 68000.

1979 — In December, Steve Jobs and a team from Apple visit Xerox PARC and see the graphical interface that will shape the Lisa and the Macintosh.

1980 — IBM's Boca Raton skunkworks begins "Project Chess" to build a personal computer; Seagate ships the ST-506, an early 5-megabyte hard disk; Sinclair's ZX80 brings computing to British hobbyists; Commodore releases the VIC-20.

1981 — On August 12, IBM introduces the IBM PC (model 5150), running PC DOS from Microsoft; Adam Osborne ships the Osborne 1, the first commercial portable; Xerox releases the Star, the first commercial machine with a graphical desktop.

1981 — Sinclair's ZX81 and the Hayes Smartmodem both

appear, expanding home computing and dial-up communication.

1982 — The Commodore 64 debuts and goes on to become the best-selling computer model of all time; Compaq is founded in February; Columbia Data Products ships the first IBM PC clone; Intel releases the 80286.

1982 — Sun Microsystems and Lotus Development are founded; Sinclair's ZX Spectrum launches in Britain; the GRiD Compass, the first clamshell laptop, reaches NASA and the military.

1983 — Apple releases the Lisa, the first commercial machine with a graphical interface; Lotus 1-2-3 arrives and dominates the IBM PC; *Time* names the computer its "Machine of the Year" for 1982.

1983 — The Compaq Portable ships in March as the first fully IBM-compatible clone, built on a legally reverse-engineered BIOS; IBM releases the PC XT with a built-in hard disk; the North American video-game market collapses in the Great Crash.

1984 — On January 24, Apple launches the Macintosh, heralded by the "1984" Super Bowl commercial directed by Ridley Scott; IBM releases the PC AT; Michael Dell founds the company that becomes Dell.

1985 — In November, Microsoft ships Windows 1.0; Aldus PageMaker and Apple's LaserWriter together launch desktop publishing; Commodore releases the Amiga; Intel introduces the 32-bit 80386.

1985 — In September, Steve Jobs resigns from Apple after losing a boardroom struggle and founds NeXT.

1986 — Compaq beats IBM to market with the Deskpro 386, the first PC built on Intel's 386—a sign the clone makers now set the pace.

1987 — IBM launches the PS/2 line with its proprietary Micro Channel Architecture and, with Microsoft, the OS/2 operating system; Apple ships HyperCard, Bill Atkinson's hypermedia toolkit.

1988 — In November, the Morris Worm disrupts the early internet; Apple sues Microsoft over the "look and feel" of Windows; a consortium of clone makers answers IBM's Micro Channel with the open EISA bus.

1989 — Intel releases the 486 processor; in March, Tim Berners-Lee proposes the World Wide Web at CERN; Nintendo launches the Game Boy.

1990 — On May 22, Microsoft releases Windows 3.0, the version that makes the graphical interface a mass-market success on the PC; Berners-Lee writes the first web browser and server at CERN; the ARPANET is decommissioned.

1991 — In August, Linus Torvalds releases the first Linux kernel and Berners-Lee posts the Web software publicly; Apple introduces the PowerBook and, with IBM and Motorola, forms the alliance that will produce the PowerPC chip.

1992 — Microsoft ships Windows 3.1; IBM introduces the ThinkPad laptop.

1993 — The Mosaic web browser, written largely by Marc Andreessen at NCSA, brings the Web to a general audience; Intel launches the Pentium processor; Microsoft ships Windows NT; id Software releases *Doom*.

1994 — Netscape (founded as Mosaic Communications) is created and ships Navigator, which rapidly becomes the dominant browser; Amazon and Yahoo are founded; the World Wide Web Consortium forms.

1995 — On August 24, Microsoft launches Windows 95 amid a global marketing frenzy, bundling Internet Explorer and cementing its hold on the desktop; Sun releases Java; JavaScript and the first DVD specification appear; Pixar's *Toy Story*, backed by Jobs, becomes the first fully computer-animated feature.

1996 — Deep Blue wins a game against world chess champion Garry Kasparov but loses the match; the U.S. Robotics PalmPilot launches the handheld market; the browser wars escalate.

1997 — On May 11, IBM's Deep Blue defeats Kasparov in a full match; Steve Jobs returns to a near-bankrupt Apple as interim chief executive, having sold NeXT to Apple months earlier; Microsoft invests $150 million in its old rival; Apple launches "Think Different."

1998 — In August, Apple introduces the iMac; in May, the U.S. Department of Justice files its landmark antitrust suit against Microsoft; Windows 98 ships; Google is founded.

1999 — Wi-Fi (802.11b) arrives; Apple ships the iBook; Napster launches, upending the music industry; the dot-com boom peaks.

2000 — A federal judge rules against Microsoft and orders it broken up (later overturned on appeal); the dot-com bubble bursts; Windows 2000 and Windows Me ship; USB flash drives appear.

2001 — Microsoft ships Windows XP in October; Apple releases Mac OS X in March, the iPod in October, and opens its first retail stores; Wikipedia launches; a settlement ends the breakup threat against Microsoft.

2003 — Apple opens the iTunes Store, legitimizing digital music downloads; AMD ships the Opteron, bringing 64-bit computing to the x86 world.

2004 — Mozilla releases Firefox 1.0, reviving competition in browsers; Facebook is founded; Ubuntu makes desktop Linux friendlier.

2005 — YouTube is founded; Apple announces it will switch its Macs to Intel processors.

2006 — Apple ships its first Intel-based Macs; Amazon launches its Web Services cloud platform; Nintendo releases the Wii; Twitter debuts.

2007 — On January 9, Apple unveils the iPhone (released June 29); Steve Jobs popularizes the phrase "post-PC" for the coming era; Amazon launches the Kindle; Google reveals Android.

2008 — The global installed base of personal computers passes one billion, according to Gartner; Apple opens the App Store and ships the MacBook Air; Google releases the Chrome browser; the first Android phone goes on sale.

2009 — Microsoft ships Windows 7 to strong reviews; low-cost netbooks surge in popularity.

2010 — On January 27, Apple introduces the iPad (released April 3), defining the modern tablet category; Jobs frames tablets and phones as "post-PC devices."

2011 — In August, Steve Jobs resigns as Apple's chief executive; he dies on October 5; for the first time, smartphones outsell personal computers worldwide.

2012 — Microsoft ships the touch-oriented Windows 8 and its own Surface tablet; the Raspberry Pi, a $35 computer, launches and revives hobbyist computing.

2013 — Global personal-computer shipments fall by roughly 13.9 percent in the first quarter, the steepest quarterly decline on record, confirming the arrival of the post-PC age.

Who's Who

The personal computer had no single inventor. It was built, imagined, financed, and marketed by hundreds of people; this gallery introduces the ones whose choices shaped the story most, listed alphabetically by surname.

Paul Allen — Co-founder of Microsoft with his boyhood friend Bill Gates. He spotted the Altair on the cover of *Popular Electronics* and helped write the BASIC that launched the company. Ill health and disagreements led him to leave day-to-day work in 1983, but his early stake made him one of the wealthiest people in the world.

Marc Andreessen — Lead author of the Mosaic web browser as a student at the University of Illinois and co-founder of Netscape, whose Navigator brought the World Wide Web to millions. His browser turned the internet from an academic tool into a mass medium, and he became a defining figure of the dot-com era and, later, a prominent venture capitalist.

Bill Atkinson — Apple software wizard who wrote much of the Lisa and Macintosh graphics software, including QuickDraw, and invented HyperCard, an early hypermedia tool that anticipated the Web. His code made the Macintosh's overlapping windows and smooth graphics possible, and he was among the small band who defined how the first popular graphical computer looked and felt.

Steve Ballmer — Microsoft's first business manager, hired by Bill Gates in 1980, and the company's chief executive from 2000 to 2014. A famously energetic salesman, he presided over Windows XP and enormous profits but also over Microsoft's slow response to search, mobile, and the post-PC shift.

Tim Berners-Lee — British computer scientist who invented the World Wide Web at CERN between 1989 and 1991, creating the HTTP protocol, URLs, and HTML. Crucially, he and CERN gave the technology to the world for free, ensuring the Web belonged to no single company.

Dan Bricklin — Co-inventor of VisiCalc, the first electronic spreadsheet, conceived while he was a business student watching a professor erase and recalculate a blackboard grid. VisiCalc became the "killer app" that gave ordinary businesses a reason to buy an Apple II.

Vannevar Bush — American engineer and wartime science administrator who, in his 1945 essay "As We May Think," imagined the Memex, a desk-sized machine for linking and retrieving all of human knowledge. His vision of associative trails through information inspired generations of pioneers, from Engelbart to the creators of hypertext.

Nolan Bushnell — Founder of Atari and a father of the video-game industry, whose *Pong* and Video Computer System put computing power into living rooms as entertainment. He also, briefly, employed a young Steve Jobs and declined a chance to invest in Apple.

Rod Canion — Co-founder and chief executive of Compaq, whose legally reverse-engineered clone made the IBM standard portable and helped break IBM's grip on its own machine. Under his leadership Compaq grew from a sketch on a placemat into one of the fastest-growing companies in American history.

Michael Dell — Founder of Dell, who began assembling and selling computers from his university dormitory. His model of building machines to order and selling them directly to customers, cutting out the retailer, eventually made Dell the largest PC maker in the world.

Larry Ellison — Not central to the desktop story but a defining Silicon Valley figure, founder of Oracle and a close friend of Steve Jobs. His database software ran on the servers behind the businesses the personal computer transformed.

Don Estridge — The IBM engineer who led "Project Chess," the skunkworks team that built the IBM PC quickly using off-the-shelf parts and an open architecture. His decisions to use an outside processor and operating system made the PC a standard and, unintentionally, handed the industry's future to Intel and Microsoft. He died in a plane crash in 1985.

Federico Faggin — Physicist and engineer who led the design of the Intel 4004, the first commercial microprocessor, and pioneered the silicon-gate technology that made it possible. He later co-founded Zilog to build the Z80, one of the most popular chips of the era.

Bob Frankston — Co-inventor of VisiCalc with Dan Bricklin, the programmer who turned the spreadsheet concept into working software squeezed into the tiny memory of the Apple II. His engineering made Bricklin's idea fast enough to be useful.

Bill Gates — Co-founder and longtime leader of Microsoft, who licensed the operating system that ran the IBM PC and built the software company that came to dominate the personal-computer era. A ferocious competitor and strategist, he understood before almost anyone that the money would be in software, not hardware, and became the world's richest person.

Adele Goldberg — Xerox PARC computer scientist who helped develop the Smalltalk programming language and its graphical environment, and who managed the demonstrations given to Apple's visitors in 1979. She reportedly objected to showing Apple so much, sensing what would follow.

Andy Grove — Hungarian refugee who became Intel's third employee and, as chief executive, its driving force. His disciplined management and famous motto, "Only the paranoid survive," steered Intel's pivot from memory chips to microprocessors and made it the engine of the PC industry.

Andy Hertzfeld — One of the principal software authors of the original Macintosh, responsible for much of its operating system and its playful character. His later memoir preserved many of the stories of the small, intense team that built the machine.

Ted Hoff — Intel engineer who conceived the architecture of the 4004, proposing a single general-purpose chip in place of many specialized ones. His insight that one programmable processor could replace a drawer full of custom circuits pointed the way to the microprocessor.

Grace Hopper — U.S. Navy officer and computing pioneer who championed machine-independent programming languages, helping create COBOL, and who popularized the term "debugging" after a moth was found in a relay. Her insistence that computers should speak something closer to human language shaped how software would be written.

Jony Ive — British industrial designer at Apple whose work defined the look of the iMac, iPod, iPhone, and iPad. His partnership with Steve Jobs produced the clean, tactile aesthetic that became the visual signature of the post-PC age.

Steve Jobs — Co-founder of Apple and the charismatic force behind the Apple II, Macintosh, iPod, iPhone, and iPad. Not an engineer himself, he was a visionary of products and marketing, obsessed with design and simplicity, who was pushed out of Apple in 1985 and returned in 1997 to save it. He popularized both the "bicycle for the mind" and "post-PC" ideas.

Mitch Kapor — Founder of Lotus Development and designer of Lotus 1-2-3, the spreadsheet that became the killer app of the IBM PC and made Lotus, for a time, the largest software company in the world. He later co-founded the Electronic Frontier Foundation to defend civil liberties online.

Alan Kay — Xerox PARC researcher who imagined the Dynabook, a portable personal computer for children, and helped pioneer the graphical interface and object-oriented programming. His conviction that computers should be personal, creative tools for everyone shaped the philosophy behind the Macintosh and much that followed.

Jack Kilby — Texas Instruments engineer who, in 1958, built the first working integrated circuit, sharing credit for the invention with Robert Noyce. His breakthrough, for which he later won the Nobel Prize, made it possible to shrink whole electronic systems onto a sliver of silicon.

Gary Kildall — Creator of CP/M, the first widely used microcomputer operating system, and founder of Digital Research. His company famously lost the IBM contract to Microsoft in a much-mythologized episode; a gifted programmer, he also pioneered ideas later taken up by others but never received the fortune his work enabled.

Butler Lampson — Brilliant Xerox PARC computer scientist who contributed to the Alto, laser printing, networking, and much else, and who wrote an early memo predicting the personal computer. A later Turing Award winner, he was one of the intellectual pillars of the lab that invented the modern interface.

J.C.R. Licklider — Psychologist and computer scientist whose essays on "man-computer symbiosis" and the "Intergalactic Computer Network" imagined interactive, networked computing decades early. As a funding director at ARPA, he bankrolled the research, including Engelbart's, that led to the mouse, the interface, and the internet.

Mike Markkula — Former Intel marketing manager and early investor who provided Apple with funding, a business plan, and adult credibility in its crucial early years. He wrote the company's founding marketing philosophy and served for a time as its chief executive and chairman.

Regis McKenna — Influential Silicon Valley marketing strategist whose firm shaped the public images of Intel, Apple, and many others. He helped turn the Apple II and its founders into a story the press and the public wanted to believe.

Gordon Moore — Co-founder of Intel and author of "Moore's Law," the 1965 observation that chip density doubles at a steady rate. That prediction became the metronome of the industry, a self-fulfilling roadmap that engineers spent half a century racing to keep.

Ted Nelson — Self-taught visionary who coined the term "hypertext," dreamed of the universal library Project Xanadu, and wrote the countercultural manifesto *Computer Lib / Dream Machines*. His idea that everyone should command computing power helped inspire the hobbyists who built the first personal machines.

Robert Noyce — Co-inventor of the integrated circuit and co-founder of both Fairchild Semiconductor and Intel, and a founding father of Silicon Valley. Nicknamed "the Mayor of Silicon Valley," his easy leadership style and open-plan, egalitarian companies set the region's culture.

Adam Osborne — British-American writer and entrepreneur who launched the Osborne 1, the first commercially successful portable computer, bundled with free software. His company's collapse gave rise to the "Osborne effect," the cautionary tale of announcing a future product before the current one has sold.

Tim Paterson — Programmer who wrote QDOS ("Quick and Dirty Operating System") at Seattle Computer Products. Microsoft bought it and adapted it into MS-DOS for the IBM PC, the foundation of its later dominance.

Chuck Peddle — Engineer who designed the inexpensive MOS Technology 6502 microprocessor and the Commodore PET. The 6502, priced at a fraction of its rivals, powered the Apple II, the Commodore machines, the Atari home computers, and the Nintendo console, bringing computing within reach of the masses.

Jef Raskin — Apple employee who conceived the Macintosh project and named it after his favorite apple, envisioning a simple, low-cost appliance for ordinary people. Steve Jobs took over the project and reshaped it, and the two clashed, but Raskin's ideal of an easy-to-use computer endured in the finished machine.

Ed Roberts — Founder of MITS, whose Altair 8800 launched the personal-computer industry and gave Microsoft its first customer. Having started the revolution, he sold his company in 1977 and later became a country doctor.

John Sculley — Former PepsiCo executive whom Steve Jobs famously recruited to Apple by asking whether he wanted to sell sugar water or change the world. As chief executive he presided over the boardroom fight that pushed Jobs out in 1985 and led the company through both success and the missteps of the early 1990s.

William Shockley — Co-inventor of the transistor and the man who brought silicon to the valley by founding Shockley Semiconductor in Mountain View. His abrasive management drove away the "traitorous eight" who founded Fairchild, indirectly seeding the entire semiconductor industry, even as his later years were marred by discredited views on race.

Charles Simonyi — Hungarian-born programmer who worked at Xerox PARC on one of the first WYSIWYG word processors, then joined Microsoft, where he oversaw the development of Word and Excel. He carried PARC's ideas about how software should look directly into the products that would run on every desk.

Clive Sinclair — British inventor and entrepreneur whose cheap ZX80, ZX81, and ZX Spectrum computers brought home computing to millions in the United Kingdom. A brilliant miniaturizer with a taste for the audacious, he was knighted for his contribution before later ventures faltered.

Richard Stallman — Programmer who founded the free software movement and the GNU Project, championing software that users are free to run, study, share, and modify. His licenses and philosophy laid the ethical and legal groundwork for the open-source software that would later run much of the internet.

Alan Sugar — British entrepreneur whose company Amstrad sold affordable all-in-one computers and word processors that put the technology into ordinary British homes and offices. A blunt, self-made businessman, he prized value over sophistication and reached buyers the fancier brands missed.

Bob Taylor — Research manager who funded the ARPANET while at ARPA and then, at Xerox PARC, assembled and led the team that invented the Alto, the graphical interface, and Ethernet. He built no circuits himself but had an extraordinary gift for gathering brilliant people and pointing them at the future.

Linus Torvalds — Finnish student who created the Linux kernel in 1991 and released it freely, seeding the open-source operating system that now runs much of the world's computing, from web servers to Android phones. His pragmatic, collaborative style made global volunteer software development work.

Jack Tramiel — Holocaust survivor and founder of Commodore, whose price-slashing "war" and the Commodore 64 brought the home computer to the mass market. His motto, "business is war," and his ruthless pursuit of low prices reshaped the industry and, some say, helped trigger its shakeouts.

Ronald Wayne — The third co-founder of Apple, who drew the first logo and drafted the partnership agreement before selling his stake within weeks for a few hundred dollars. His caution cost him a fortune but spared him the risks he feared.

Steve Wozniak — Co-founder of Apple and the engineering genius who single-handedly designed the Apple I and the Apple II, the machine that ignited the industry. A pure hobbyist at heart who loved elegant, economical designs, he cared more for the joy of engineering than for business, and left Apple's daily work in the mid-1980s.

Glossary

A field guide to the machines, programs, and jargon of the personal-computer revolution, arranged alphabetically. Definitions aim for the general reader; terms in **bold** elsewhere in the list have their own entries.

Altair 8800 — The 1975 kit computer, built around the Intel 8080 and sold by MITS, whose *Popular Electronics* cover launched the personal-computer industry.

Amiga — Commodore's 1985 multimedia computer, prized for advanced graphics and sound well ahead of its rivals.

Apple I — Steve Wozniak's 1976 single-board computer, Apple's first product, sold as a bare board to hobbyists.

Apple II — Wozniak's 1977 machine, a fully assembled color computer with expansion slots that became one of the first great commercial successes.

Apple Lisa — Apple's 1983 business computer, the first commercial machine with a graphical interface; expensive and commercially unsuccessful, but a forerunner of the Macintosh.

ARPANET — The U.S. Defense Department research network, first switched on in 1969, that pioneered packet switching and grew into the internet.

Assembly language — A low-level programming language

in which each instruction corresponds closely to a single operation the processor performs, translated into machine code by an assembler.

BASIC — Beginner's All-purpose Symbolic Instruction Code, an easy-to-learn programming language that shipped with most early personal computers; Microsoft's first product.

BBS — Bulletin Board System, a computer a hobbyist ran so others could dial in by modem to trade messages, files, and software before the public internet.

BIOS — Basic Input/Output System, the low-level firmware that starts a PC and connects the operating system to the hardware; IBM's was famously reverse-engineered by clone makers.

Bit — The smallest unit of digital information, a single 1 or 0; short for "binary digit."

Bitmapped display — A screen in which every pixel is individually controlled by memory, allowing arbitrary graphics and fonts rather than only fixed characters.

Booting — The process by which a computer starts itself and loads its operating system, from the phrase "pulling oneself up by the bootstraps."

Browser — Software for viewing pages on the World Wide Web, such as Mosaic, Netscape Navigator, and Internet Explorer.

Bus — The set of shared electrical pathways that carry data among a computer's processor, memory, and peripherals; a wider or faster bus moves more information at once.

Byte — A group of eight bits, enough to represent a single character; memory and storage are measured in kilobytes, megabytes, gigabytes, and beyond.

CD-ROM — Compact Disc Read-Only Memory, an optical

disc holding hundreds of megabytes, which brought multimedia software to personal computers in the early 1990s.

Clock speed — The rate, measured in megahertz or gigahertz, at which a processor steps through its operations; long used as a rough shorthand for a computer's speed.

Clone / compatible — A computer built by another maker to run the same software as the IBM PC by imitating its architecture; the clones turned the PC into a universal standard.

Command line — A text interface in which the user types commands, the dominant way of controlling computers before the graphical interface.

Commodore 64 — Commodore's 1982 home computer, aggressively priced and the best-selling single model of all time.

Commodore PET — Commodore's 1977 all-in-one computer, one of the "Trinity" of the first ready-made personal computers.

Compaq Portable — Compaq's 1983 luggable, the first fully IBM-compatible clone, built on a legally reverse-engineered BIOS.

Compiler — A program that translates software written in a human-readable language into the machine code a processor can execute directly.

Computer Lib — Ted Nelson's self-published 1974 manifesto (bound back-to-back with *Dream Machines*) urging ordinary people to seize control of computing.

CP/M — Control Program for Microcomputers, Gary Kildall's operating system that became the first widely adopted standard for business microcomputers.

CPU — The central processing unit, the part of a computer that carries out instructions; on a personal computer, the CPU is a single microprocessor chip.

Desktop metaphor — The interface idea of representing files and programs as documents, folders, and a desktop, borrowed from the office and popularized by the Macintosh.

Desktop publishing — The use of a personal computer, page-layout software, and a laser printer to produce printed pages, launched by PageMaker and the LaserWriter in 1985.

DRAM — Dynamic Random Access Memory, the inexpensive, high-capacity working memory used in most computers; it must be refreshed constantly and loses its contents when powered off.

Dynabook — Alan Kay's early-1970s vision of a portable, book-sized personal computer for children and creativity, an idea that anticipated the laptop and tablet.

Ethernet — The networking technology invented at Xerox PARC in 1973 for connecting nearby computers, still the dominant standard for wired local networks.

Expansion slot — A connector inside a computer that accepts add-in cards for extra memory, graphics, sound, or other functions.

Floppy disk — A flexible magnetic storage disk in a protective sleeve, the standard removable medium of the personal-computer era.

GRiD Compass — A 1982 clamshell laptop with a flat display, an early ancestor of the modern notebook, used by NASA and the military.

GUI — Graphical User Interface, a way of controlling a computer with windows, icons, and a pointer rather than typed commands.

Hard disk — A sealed, high-capacity magnetic storage device that holds data on spinning rigid platters, far larger and faster than a floppy.

Homebrew Computer Club — The influential Silicon Valley

hobbyist group, founded in 1975, where Steve Wozniak first showed the Apple I.

HTML — HyperText Markup Language, the simple set of tags Tim Berners-Lee devised to describe the structure of a web page and its links.

HTTP — HyperText Transfer Protocol, the rules by which web browsers and servers exchange pages over the internet.

IBM PC 5150 — IBM's 1981 personal computer, whose open architecture made it the business standard and spawned the clone industry.

IC (integrated circuit) — A "chip" combining many electronic components on a single piece of silicon, invented in 1958–1959 by Kilby and Noyce.

Intel 4004 — Intel's 1971 chip, the first commercial microprocessor, containing about 2,300 transistors.

Intel 8080 — Intel's 1974 microprocessor that powered the Altair and many early machines.

Intel 8088 — The Intel processor chosen for the IBM PC, a lower-cost variant of the 8086.

Internet — The global network of interconnected computer networks, descended from the ARPANET, on which the World Wide Web and email run.

Kernel — The core of an operating system that manages the processor, memory, and hardware; the part Linus Torvalds wrote in 1991 was a kernel.

Killer app — A program so useful that people buy the computer specifically to run it, as VisiCalc did for the Apple II and Lotus 1-2-3 for the IBM PC.

Macintosh — Apple's 1984 computer, the first commercially successful machine with a graphical interface and mouse, marketed as "the computer for the rest of us."

Mainframe — A large, powerful computer serving many users at once, the dominant form of computing before minicomputers and personal machines; IBM's specialty.

Microprocessor — A complete central processing unit on a single chip, the invention that made the personal computer possible.

Minicomputer — A refrigerator-sized computer, smaller and cheaper than a mainframe, popular in the 1960s and 1970s and typified by Digital Equipment's PDP line.

Modem — A device that converts digital data into audio tones for transmission over telephone lines, connecting home computers to bulletin boards and the internet; short for "modulator-demodulator."

Moore's Law — Gordon Moore's 1965 observation that the number of transistors on a chip doubles at a steady rate, driving computing's exponential progress.

Motherboard — The main circuit board of a computer, holding the processor, memory, and expansion slots.

Mouse — The hand-held pointing device invented by Douglas Engelbart, central to the graphical interface.

MS-DOS — Microsoft's disk operating system, adapted from QDOS and licensed to IBM, which became the foundation of the company's dominance.

Open architecture — A hardware design whose specifications are published so that others can build compatible add-ons and machines, as with the IBM PC.

Open source — Software released with its source code freely available to be used, studied, modified, and shared, as with Linux.

Operating system — The master program that manages a computer's hardware and runs other software, from CP/M and MS-DOS to Windows, macOS, and Linux.

Osborne 1 — Adam Osborne's 1981 portable, the first commercially successful luggable, sold with a bundle of software.

Osborne effect — The business phenomenon, named for Osborne Computer, in which announcing a future product too early kills sales of the current one.

PageMaker — Aldus's 1985 page-layout program that, with the LaserWriter, launched desktop publishing.

Peripheral — Any device attached to a computer beyond its core electronics, such as a printer, keyboard, mouse, monitor, or external disk drive.

Pixel — A single dot of a screen image; short for "picture element." The more pixels, the sharper the display.

Plug and play — The goal, largely achieved by the mid-1990s, of hardware that a computer recognizes and configures automatically, sparing users the ordeal of setting it up by hand.

Post-PC era — The age, named by Steve Jobs in 2007, in which smartphones and tablets displace the personal computer as the center of digital life.

RAM — Random Access Memory, the fast, temporary working memory a computer uses while running programs; its contents vanish when power is lost.

Reality Distortion Field — A phrase coined by Apple staff for Steve Jobs's ability to convince himself and others that the impossible was achievable.

ROM — Read-Only Memory, permanent memory holding firmware such as the BIOS that survives when the computer is switched off.

S-100 bus — The expansion bus introduced with the Altair 8800 that became an early industry standard for connecting add-in cards.

Semiconductor — A material, usually silicon, that conducts electricity under some conditions but not others, the basis of transistors and every computer chip.

Shareware — Software distributed free for trial, with users asked to pay if they keep using it, a distribution model that flourished on BBSes.

Silicon — The abundant element, refined from sand, from which most chips are made, and the namesake of Silicon Valley.

Sound card — An expansion card that adds high-quality audio to a personal computer, important for games and multimedia.

Spreadsheet — A program of rows and columns that automatically recalculates figures, pioneered by VisiCalc; the personal computer's first killer app.

Transistor — The tiny electronic switch invented at Bell Labs in 1947 that replaced the vacuum tube and made modern computing possible.

TRS-80 — Tandy/Radio Shack's 1977 computer, sold through its national chain of stores, one of the "Trinity."

Vaporware — Software or hardware announced, sometimes with great fanfare, but long delayed or never actually shipped; a frequent tactic and hazard of the industry.

VisiCalc — The 1979 spreadsheet program that first made businesses buy personal computers; see also spreadsheet.

WIMP — Windows, Icons, Menus, and Pointer, the shorthand for the elements of a graphical user interface.

Windows — Microsoft's graphical operating environment, and later operating system, first shipped in 1985 and made dominant by version 3.0 in 1990 and Windows 95.

Wintel — The dominant 1990s alliance of Microsoft Windows software running on Intel processors.

Word processor — Software for writing, editing, and formatting text, such as WordStar and later Microsoft Word, one of the personal computer's core uses.

World Wide Web — Tim Berners-Lee's system of linked hypertext documents, made public in 1991, that made the internet accessible to ordinary people.

WYSIWYG — "What You See Is What You Get," the principle that a document appears on screen exactly as it will print.

Xerox Alto — Xerox PARC's 1973 research computer, the first with a graphical interface, mouse, and networking.

Xerox Star — Xerox's 1981 commercial workstation, the first product to bring the graphical desktop to market, though it sold poorly.

Z80 — Zilog's popular 8-bit microprocessor, compatible with the Intel 8080, that ran many CP/M machines and home computers.

6502 — The inexpensive MOS Technology microprocessor designed by Chuck Peddle that powered the Apple II, Commodore PET, and many others.

Appendix I: The Personal Computer Revolution in Numbers

Numbers can lie, but the numbers in this story mostly tell the truth, and the truth is staggering. Over roughly four decades, the machine on the desk became millions of times more powerful, thousands of times cheaper for what it did, and common enough that there came to be one for nearly every family on Earth. What follows is a tour of the most striking figures in the revolution—verified where they can be, and flagged as estimates where the record is murky. Read them slowly. Each one is a small window onto how completely the world changed.

2,300 transistors. That is how many microscopic switches Intel packed onto the 4004, the first commercial microprocessor, in 1971. The whole "computer on a chip" was smaller than a fingernail and ran at a clock speed of roughly 740 kilohertz—less than a millionth the speed of a modern processor. It was a marvel, and by today's standards it was almost unimaginably feeble.

From thousands to billions. Follow the transistor count forward and the curve becomes vertiginous. The Intel 8080 that powered the Altair held about 6,000 transistors. The 8088 inside the first IBM PC held roughly 29,000. The 386 of 1985 reached about 275,000; the Pentium of 1993 crossed 3 million. By the 2020s, a single high-end processor could contain more than a hundred billion transistors. In other words, a chip you can hold between two fingers came to hold tens of millions of times more components than the one that started it all.

A doubling every two years, for fifty years. This relentless growth was not an accident but a target. Gordon Moore's 1965 observation—that the number of components on a chip was doubling at a steady pace—hardened into Moore's Law, the industry's self-imposed metronome. A doubling every two years means a thousandfold increase every twenty years, and a millionfold every forty. From the 4004 in 1971 to the chips of the 2010s, engineers achieved roughly that: about twenty doublings, a factor of a million or more, sustained longer than almost anyone in 1971 believed possible.

Roughly $400 for a box of parts. The Altair 8800 that launched the hobbyist movement in January 1975 sold as a kit for about $397 (assembled versions cost more, and prices soon rose to $439 and beyond). For that sum a buyer received a box, some chips, and the privilege of soldering it together—with no keyboard, no screen, and no software but the ones and zeros entered by flipping switches. It was less a product than an invitation.

$1,298 for the Apple II. When Apple's breakthrough machine went on sale in 1977, the base model with 4 kilobytes of memory cost $1,298; a well-equipped version with 48 kilobytes ran to more than $2,600. That was serious money—well over $6,000 in today's dollars for the top configuration—but for it you got a finished, colorful computer you could take home and switch on. The price of admission to computing had fallen from a corporation's budget to a family's.

$1,565 for the machine that set the standard. IBM's Personal Computer, introduced in August 1981, started at $1,565 for a bare configuration. A genuinely useful setup, with more memory, a monitor, and disk drives, could easily reach $3,000 or more. Yet because IBM's name reassured cautious businesses, that price was one companies were willing to pay by the millions—and the clones that followed would drive it steadily down.

$595 for the people's computer. Commodore launched the Commodore 64 in 1982 at $595 and then, true to founder Jack Tramiel's philosophy of price war, kept cutting until it sold for well under $200 in some markets. Low prices, sold through department stores and toy shops rather than computer dealers, are what turned the home computer from a hobbyist's indulgence into a mass-market appliance.

About $350 per megabyte of storage. In 1980, a 10-megabyte hard disk for a personal computer cost roughly $3,500—around $350 for each megabyte, a figure that should be read as an illustrative estimate, since prices varied widely. A single megabyte is about the size of one modern digital photo compressed, or a few seconds of music. Today, storage costs a small fraction of a cent per gigabyte—a thousand megabytes—so the price of storing information has fallen by a factor of many millions. That collapse, as much as any chip, is what made photos, music, and video part of everyday computing.

Kilobytes to gigabytes. Early personal computers measured their memory in the smallest of units. The Altair shipped with just 256 bytes of memory—not kilobytes, bytes—enough to hold this sentence and little more. Typical machines of the late 1970s had 4 to 64 kilobytes. A modern laptop routinely carries 8 or 16 gigabytes, roughly a million times as much working memory as those first home computers. Programs grew to fill the space, but the sheer expansion of room to think is one of the revolution's quiet miracles.

The best-selling machine of its age: about 12.5 million. The Commodore 64 is widely regarded as the best-selling single computer model in history, but exactly how many sold is genuinely disputed. Commodore's own figures suggested around 17 million; the founder once claimed 22 to 30 million; careful modern analysis of surviving records points to roughly 12.5 million. The honest answer is that the true total lies somewhere in that range and will probably never be known precisely—a reminder that even famous numbers deserve a raised eyebrow.

Millions of Apple IIs, and a machine that would not die. The Apple II and its variants sold in the millions over a production run that stretched from 1977 to 1993—an extraordinarily long life for any computer. It was the machine that made Apple a real company and, thanks to VisiCalc, the machine that first proved a personal computer could earn its keep in business.

One billion personal computers, around 2008. In the middle of 2008, according to the research firm Gartner, the number of personal computers in use worldwide crossed one billion for the first time. The firm projected the second billion would arrive by around 2014, driven not by the wealthy countries that had bought the first billion but by China, India, and other fast-growing markets. In roughly a single human generation, a device that had not existed commercially in 1974 had become common enough for one to exist for every seven people alive.

Tens of millions of copies of Windows. When Microsoft launched Windows 95 in August 1995, it sold on a scale the software business had never seen—millions of copies in the first weeks and tens of millions within the first year. In the decades that followed, Windows would come to run on well over a billion devices at a time, the near-universal software layer of the PC world and the foundation of Microsoft's fortune.

The peak, and the turn. Global personal-computer shipments climbed for decades and are generally reckoned to have peaked around 2011, at roughly 360 to 365 million machines shipped in a year. Then came the turn: in the first quarter of 2013, worldwide PC shipments fell by about 13.9 percent compared with a year earlier—the steepest quarterly decline the industry had ever recorded. Nothing had broken. People were simply reaching, more and more, for the small glowing rectangles in their pockets instead.

A supercomputer in every pocket. The final number is the one that closes the circle. A modern smartphone contains a processor with billions of transistors, running at gigahertz speeds, with more memory and storage than a room full of 1980s computers—and it costs, in real terms, a fraction of what the Apple II did. The bicycle for the mind that Steve Jobs described in 1980 became something he could not have fully imagined: a machine so cheap, so powerful, and so personal that billions of people now carry one everywhere they go. The revolution did not end. It went in our pockets.

Appendix II: How the Machines Worked

You do not need to understand how a car engine works to drive to the shops, and you have read this whole book without once being asked to understand what a transistor actually does. But the personal computer is one of the most remarkable machines humanity has ever built, and a little knowledge of what happens inside the beige box turns it from magic into something better: something comprehensible, and all the more astonishing for being so. This appendix explains, in plain language and without leaving any jargon unexplained, how these machines actually work.

A transistor is a switch with no moving parts. Everything begins here. A transistor is a tiny device, made mostly from silicon, that can either let electricity flow or block it, depending on whether a small control voltage is applied. Think of it as a light switch, except that instead of a finger flipping it, a second wire flips it—so one part of the circuit can switch another on and off. That is the whole trick. A switch that is "on" can stand for the number 1, and "off" for the number 0, and from those two symbols, arranged in the millions, a computer builds everything it knows. The transistor's ancestor was the vacuum tube, a glass bulb the size of a thumb that did the same job but ran hot, burned out, and guzzled power. Replacing tubes with transistors is what let computers shrink from room-sized to desk-sized.

An integrated circuit is many switches on a single sliver of silicon. At first, transistors were made one at a time and wired together by hand—slow, costly, and prone to failure. The great leap of 1958 and 1959 was to build many transistors, and the wires connecting them, onto a single flat chip of silicon all at once, like printing a whole page instead of writing each letter. This is the integrated circuit, or "chip." Because the components are microscopic and made together in one process, they can be produced by the billion, cheaply and reliably. The entire history of computing getting faster and cheaper is, at bottom, the story of engineers learning to print ever more transistors onto ever smaller chips.

A microprocessor is a whole computer's brain on one chip. By 1971, engineers could fit enough transistors on a single chip to build the central part of a computer—the part that does the actual calculating and decision-making. That chip is the microprocessor, and its arrival is what made the personal computer possible, because now the "brain" that once filled a cabinet cost a few dollars and fit on a fingertip. Everything else in the computer exists to feed the microprocessor, store its results, or show them to you.

How the brain thinks: fetch, decode, execute. A microprocessor does not really "think" at all. It does something much simpler, over and over, billions of times a second. A program is just a long list of extremely basic instructions—add these two numbers, put the result here, compare that to this, if it is bigger jump to another part of the list. The processor works through them in a relentless three-step loop. First it fetches the next instruction from memory. Then it decodes it, working out what the instruction is asking for. Then it executes it, actually doing the addition or comparison or move. Then it fetches the next one, and the next, without ever tiring or getting bored. Each step is almost laughably simple. The power comes entirely from doing them so fast, and in such vast numbers, that the blur of tiny operations becomes a spreadsheet recalculating, a game animating, or a letter appearing on the screen as you type.

Bits and bytes: the alphabet of the machine. Because a transistor is either on or off, computers count in twos, not tens. A single on-or-off value is a bit. Bits are grouped into bytes of eight, and a byte can represent one character—a letter, a digit, a punctuation mark. From there the units climb by roughly a thousand at each step: a kilobyte is about a thousand bytes, a megabyte about a million, a gigabyte about a billion. When you hear that an early computer had 64 kilobytes of memory and a modern one has 16 gigabytes, that is the difference between holding a short book and holding a large library—about a million to one.

Three kinds of memory: working, permanent, and stored. People often muddle the different kinds of memory, so here is the distinction. RAM, or random-access memory, is the computer's workspace—fast, roomy, and temporary. It holds whatever the machine is working on right now, and it forgets everything the instant the power goes off, the way a whiteboard is wiped clean at the end of a meeting. ROM, or read-only memory, is permanent and unchangeable, holding the basic instructions the computer needs the moment it switches on—including the start-up program that wakes the rest of the machine. And then there is storage, such as a disk, which keeps your files safely even when the power is off, the way a filing cabinet keeps documents overnight. When you "save" a document, you are copying it from the temporary whiteboard of RAM to the permanent filing cabinet of storage; when you "open" it again, you copy it back.

How a floppy disk stores data. A floppy disk is a thin, flexible circle of plastic coated with a magnetic material, sealed in a protective sleeve. Data is written by magnetizing tiny spots on the surface in one direction or the other—one direction for a 1, the other for a 0. A little head, rather like the needle on a record player but never quite touching, sweeps across the spinning disk to magnetize those spots when writing and to sense them when reading. Because the pattern is magnetic, it stays put when you remove the disk and carry it to another machine, which is exactly what made floppies the currency of the early software world: programs could finally be handed from person to person.

How a hard disk stores much more, much faster. A hard disk works on the same magnetic principle but takes it to extremes. Instead of a floppy sheet of plastic, it uses rigid metal platters, coated and polished to a mirror finish, spinning thousands of times a minute inside a sealed case. The read-write heads float a hair's breadth above the surface on a cushion of air, moving in and out to reach any spot almost instantly. Because the platters are rigid and spin so fast, and because the heads can be positioned so precisely, a hard disk holds vastly more data than a floppy and reaches it far more quickly. That combination of huge capacity and speed is what let computers hold not just a document or two but everything—the operating system, the programs, and years of a person's files, all at once.

What an operating system actually does. Underneath every program you use sits a master program called the operating system—CP/M, then MS-DOS, then Windows and macOS and Linux. Its job is to manage the machine so that individual programs, and you, do not have to. It keeps track of which files are where on the disk, so a word processor can simply ask for "my letter" instead of knowing the physical spot it occupies. It shares the processor and memory among competing programs. It talks to the keyboard, screen, and printer so that each program need not know the details of every device. An operating system is, in short, the government of the computer: mostly invisible, occasionally infuriating, and impossible to do without.

Why the graphical interface beat the command line. For its first decades, controlling a computer meant typing exact commands in a language it understood, and remembering that language yourself—the command line. Get a single character wrong and nothing happened. The graphical user interface, born at Xerox PARC and carried to the world by the Macintosh and then Windows, replaced that with something you could see. Files became little pictures called icons. Programs opened in rectangles called windows that you could move and stack like papers on a desk. A mouse let you point at what you wanted and click, instead of describing it in words. The reason this won so completely is simple: recognition is easier than recall. You do not have to remember the name of a command if you can see the thing you want and point at it. The graphical interface did not make computers more powerful; it made their power reachable by everyone, and that turned out to matter more.

How a modem turns bits into sound, and back. Finally, how did these machines first talk to one another, long before broadband and Wi-Fi? Over the ordinary telephone line, which was built to carry sound, not data. A modem solves this by translating. To send information, it turns the computer's ones and zeros into different audio tones—the screeches and hisses that anyone who used the early internet remembers—and pushes them down the phone line as if they were speech. A modem at the other end listens to those tones and translates them back into ones and zeros for the receiving computer. The name captures the round trip: modem is short for modulator-demodulator, the device that turns data into sound and sound back into data. It was slow, and it tied up the family phone, but through that thin thread of noise the isolated machines of the world first reached out and found each other—and the revolution became a network.

Appendix III: Myths and Misconceptions Corrected

Every great story attracts legends, and the birth of the personal computer has attracted more than most. Some of these tales are simplifications that hardened into "facts"; others are outright inventions repeated so often they feel true. The real history is usually more interesting than the myth, because it is more human—full of ambiguity, luck, and people who were neither pure heroes nor pure villains. Here are the misconceptions worth correcting.

Myth: Apple simply stole the graphical interface from Xerox. This is the most durable legend of all, and it is only a quarter true. Apple did not sneak into Xerox PARC; it was invited. In late 1979, in exchange for allowing Xerox's venture arm to buy a block of Apple shares before Apple went public, Steve Jobs and a team were given two demonstrations of the lab's work, including the graphical interface. What Jobs saw electrified him, and Apple unquestionably drew inspiration from it. But the Xerox interface was not the Macintosh. Apple's engineers added overlapping windows that could sit on top of one another, pull-down menus, drag-and-drop, the trash can, and a simple one-button mouse—Xerox's cost hundreds of dollars and had three buttons. They spent years and enormous effort turning a research prototype into something an ordinary person could afford and use. Xerox got Apple stock and a place in history; Apple got inspiration and did the hard work of making it real. "Borrowed and transformed" is fairer than "stole."

Myth: Gary Kildall lost the IBM deal because he blew it off to go flying. The story is delicious and endlessly repeated: IBM's suits arrived to license Kildall's operating system, found him joyriding in his private plane, and left in a huff to strike a deal with Microsoft instead. The reality is murkier and less flattering to the legend. Kildall was indeed a pilot and was flying that day—but on business, not for fun. The meeting at his company, Digital Research, went ahead with others present, and it foundered not on his absence but on a disagreement over IBM's demanding non-disclosure agreement and terms. Kildall's own account, and those of others present, dispute the caricature of a careless hobbyist who couldn't be bothered. He lost the deal of the century, but he lost it to a tangle of legal caution, hard bargaining, and bad luck, not to an afternoon of aimless flying.

Myth: Bill Gates wrote MS-DOS. He did not. When IBM needed an operating system for its new PC and Microsoft agreed to supply one, Microsoft did not yet have such a system to sell. Instead it acquired an existing operating system—called QDOS, for "Quick and Dirty Operating System," later 86-DOS—written by a programmer named Tim Paterson at a small firm called Seattle Computer Products. Microsoft bought the rights for a modest sum, adapted the software, and delivered it to IBM as PC DOS and MS-DOS. Gates's genius was not in writing the code but in the deal: he kept the right to license the operating system to other manufacturers, which is precisely what made Microsoft, rather than IBM, the true winner of the PC era.

Myth: the first computer "bug" was a real moth. There really was a moth. On September 9, 1947, technicians working on the Harvard Mark II found a dead moth caught in a relay, taped it into the logbook, and wrote beside it, "First actual case of bug being found." But the word "bug," meaning a fault in a machine, was already old slang—Thomas Edison used it that way in the 1870s. The joke in the logbook works precisely because everyone already called faults "bugs"; finding a literal insect was funny for that reason. So the moth did not give us the term. It was a witty nod to a word engineers had been using for seventy years, and the preserved page now sits in the Smithsonian as a charming footnote, not an origin.

Myth: the Altair 8800 was the first personal computer. The Altair launched the personal-computer industry, which is not the same as being the first personal computer. Several earlier machines have a claim. The Kenbak-1, sold in 1971, was a small computer intended for individual use, though it had no microprocessor. The French Micral N of 1973 was a commercial microcomputer built around Intel's 8008. Depending on how you define "personal computer"—Does it need a microprocessor? Must it be sold assembled? Must ordinary people actually buy it?—the honor shifts among several contenders. What makes the Altair special is not that it was first, but that it was the first to catch fire: it inspired the hobbyists, the software, and the companies that turned a curiosity into an industry.

Myth: IBM invented the personal computer. IBM's 1981 machine was enormously important—it made the personal computer respectable to business and set the standard the whole industry would follow—but it arrived years after Apple, Commodore, Tandy, and a swarm of others were already selling personal computers by the hundreds of thousands. IBM's own team, working in a Florida skunkworks, knew they were latecomers, which is exactly why they broke company tradition and built their machine quickly out of off-the-shelf parts. IBM did not invent the PC; it legitimized it, and in doing so accidentally handed control of the future to Microsoft and Intel.

Myth: Steve Jobs was the engineer who designed the Ap-

ple computers. Jobs was a visionary, a marketer, and a relentless perfectionist, but he was not the engineer behind Apple's first machines. The Apple I and the Apple II were designed almost single-handedly by Steve Wozniak, an engineer of rare brilliance whose elegant, economical circuits made those computers possible and affordable. Jobs's contributions were real and crucial—he pushed to sell the machines, insisted on a friendly case and design, and understood what the product could become—but the actual engineering was Wozniak's. The two men were a partnership of complementary gifts, and flattening that into a single genius does both a disservice.

Myth: Moore's Law is a law of physics. It sounds like one—the steady, inexorable doubling of transistors—but Moore's Law is nothing of the kind. It began in 1965 as an observation by Gordon Moore about a trend he noticed in the young chip industry, and it became a kind of shared goal, a roadmap the entire industry chose to chase. Engineers kept it alive not because nature demanded it but because they spent billions of dollars and untold ingenuity making each doubling happen roughly on schedule. It is a self-fulfilling prophecy, sustained by human effort and money, and like all such trends it eventually began to slow as the transistors approached the size of atoms.

Myth: Xerox was too foolish to see what it had. People love to say that Xerox "fumbled the future," blind to the treasures in its own lab. The truth is more poignant. Xerox did build and even sell a graphical computer, the Star, in 1981—it simply cost too much and came too early. The company's leadership, a world away in New York and built around the photocopier business, struggled to grasp how to turn brilliant research into products, and its most visionary people grew frustrated and left. It was not that no one at Xerox saw the future; it was that a large, successful company found it agonizingly hard to bet against its own profitable present. That is a failure of organizations, not of eyesight, and it has been repeated many times since.

Myth: the IBM PC succeeded because it was the best machine. It was not, by most technical measures, the best personal computer of 1981. Others were faster, cheaper, or more elegant. The IBM PC won for reasons that had little to do with engineering: the reassurance of the IBM name to nervous corporate buyers, an open design that invited other companies to make add-ons and software, and the availability of the spreadsheets and word processors that businesses needed. "Nobody ever got fired for buying IBM," the saying went, and that sentiment, more than any circuit, made the PC the standard.

Myth: the "1984" Macintosh commercial ran again and again. Apple's famous Super Bowl advertisement, directed by Ridley Scott, is remembered as one of the greatest commercials ever made—so it surprises people to learn it was broadcast nationally during the game essentially once. Its legend was built by the enormous news coverage it generated and by its endless replaying since, not by saturation at the time. A single airing, and the conversation around it, was enough to make it immortal.

Myth: Bill Gates founded Microsoft to build the operating system for the IBM PC. Microsoft existed for six years before the IBM deal. Gates and Paul Allen founded it in 1975 to write a version of the BASIC programming language for the Altair, and for years the company's business was programming languages, not operating systems. The IBM contract in 1980 was a pivot, not a beginning—a piece of extraordinary luck and shrewd dealing layered on top of an existing company, not the reason that company was born.

Myth: the personal computer sprang from garages and hobbyists alone. The garage is a cherished image—Jobs and Wozniak in the Jobs family garage, the plucky amateurs who changed the world—and there is truth in it. But the components they used came from decades of work in corporate and government laboratories: the transistor from Bell Labs, the integrated circuit from Texas Instruments and Fairchild, the microprocessor from Intel, the interface and networking from Xerox, and much of the early funding and vision from the U.S. military's research agencies. The revolution was made by hobbyists standing on the shoulders of vast institutions. Both halves of that sentence are true, and the story is richer for holding them together.

Appendix IV: Questions & Answers

A history can answer the question "what happened?" without ever quite answering "why?" This appendix takes up the questions a thoughtful reader is left holding at the end of the story—the ones about causes, patterns, and meaning. The answers are necessarily arguable; historians and veterans of the industry still debate them. But each represents the best sense this book can make of the evidence.

Why did the open, IBM-compatible machine beat technically superior closed computers? Because a computer is only as valuable as the software and add-ons available for it, and openness is what summons those in abundance. When IBM published the specifications of its PC and let anyone build compatible hardware and software, it created a vast, competitive marketplace: dozens of companies making cheaper machines, thousands making programs and peripherals, all of them reinforcing one another. A closed machine like the Macintosh or the Amiga might be more elegant, but a buyer choosing it was betting on a single company's ability to supply everything. The open standard offered more choices, lower prices, and the comfort of a crowd. In technology, a good-enough product with a thriving ecosystem almost always defeats a superior product that stands alone—a lesson the industry has relearned many times since.

Why did the inventors so often lose control of their creations? The pattern is haunting: Ed Roberts sold MITS; Gary Kildall lost the operating-system fortune to Microsoft; Xerox let the interface walk out the door; even Steve Jobs was thrown out of the company he founded. Part of the reason is that the skills required to invent something are not the skills required to build a durable business around it. Vision and engineering brilliance are one gift; manufacturing, marketing, distribution, financing, and ruthless competition are quite another. Pioneers also tend to fall in love with the thing itself, while the fortunes were made by those who understood the thing's leverage—Gates saw that software licensed to many makers would outlast any single machine. And there was simple bad luck and bad timing. The people who first see the future are rarely the ones positioned to own it.

What actually was the "killer app," and why did it matter so much? A killer application is a program so useful that people buy an entire computer just to run it. The first and most important was VisiCalc, the electronic spreadsheet released in 1979 for the Apple II. Before VisiCalc, a personal computer was a fascinating toy that a spouse or an accountant could reasonably call a waste of money. After it, an accountant, a manager, or a small-business owner could do in an afternoon what had taken a week of erasing and recalculating by hand—and suddenly the machine paid for itself. The killer app mattered because it answered the only question that turns curiosity into a purchase: not "what can this machine do?" but "what will it do for me?" Lotus 1-2-3 played the same role for the IBM PC, and the pattern repeated for word processing, desktop publishing, and eventually the web browser.

Why did Apple survive when Commodore and Atari did not? All three rode the home-computer boom of the early 1980s; only Apple lived to see the next century. Several things set Apple apart. It cultivated a loyal following and a premium brand rather than competing purely on price, which spared it the margin-destroying wars that Jack Tramiel's Commodore both waged and ultimately fell victim to. It established a real foothold in business and education, giving it steadier revenue than the toy-store trade. And it was fortunate, at the crucial moment, to have leaders—first the discipline of the early team, and later the returning Steve Jobs—who could reinvent the company around new products. Commodore and Atari, brilliant at building cheap machines, never made that leap; when the price war exhausted itself and the market shifted, they had no second act. Apple, more than once, did.

What made Windows win the graphical-interface wars? Windows was, for years, clearly inferior to the Macintosh interface it imitated, and yet it triumphed. The reason is the same open-standard logic that made the PC dominant in the first place. Windows ran on the cheap, abundant IBM-compatible hardware that businesses already owned by the tens of millions, so adopting it required no new machine. Microsoft's control of MS-DOS, on which early Windows sat, gave it enormous leverage with computer makers, who bundled Windows on nearly every PC they shipped. And once most computers ran Windows, software companies wrote for Windows first, which drew still more users, which drew still more software—a self-reinforcing spiral. The Macintosh had the better interface; Windows had the numbers, the prices, and the momentum, and in a network-driven market those win.

Was Microsoft's dominance earned or unfair? Both, and that is why it ended in an antitrust courtroom. Microsoft earned its position through genuine shrewdness: the foresight to license its operating system widely, the discipline to keep improving its products, and an understanding of the software business sharper than any rival's. But once dominant, it also used that dominance in ways courts on two continents judged illegal—leaning on computer makers, bundling its web browser to crush Netscape, and wielding its control of Windows as a weapon. The honest verdict is that Microsoft won fairly and then defended its winnings unfairly, which is a very common shape for the story of monopolies.

Why did the graphical interface take so long to reach ordinary people? Xerox had a working graphical computer in 1973, yet most people did not use one until Windows became common in the 1990s—a gap of two decades. The delay came down to cost and computing power. A graphical interface demands far more memory and processing muscle than a text one, and in the 1970s the chips and memory to deliver it smoothly were ruinously expensive. The Xerox Star that finally sold the idea in 1981 cost as much as a car. Only as Moore's Law drove the price of memory and processing down through the 1980s did it become affordable to give every user the graphics that had once required a research budget. The idea was ready long before the economics were.

Did the countercultural, idealistic roots of the revolution actually matter? They mattered enormously, though it is easy to be cynical about it. Many of the people who built the personal computer genuinely believed they were putting power into the hands of individuals and loosening the grip of governments and large corporations that had monopolized computing. That conviction—expressed in the Homebrew Computer Club's sharing of designs, in Ted Nelson's manifestos, in the very phrase "computer for the rest of us"—shaped what got built and why. It is also true that the same revolution produced some of the largest corporations in history. Both things are real. The idealism was sincere, it drove real invention, and it was, in time, partly swallowed by the commercial giants it helped create.

Why was Silicon Valley the place it all happened? No single reason, but a rare convergence. Stanford University supplied talent and encouraged its professors and students to start companies. William Shockley brought the transistor to the area, and the engineers who fled his difficult management founded Fairchild, which in turn spun off dozens of firms, including Intel—a chain reaction of talent. A culture of job-hopping, easy funding from a growing venture-capital industry, good weather, and a frontier willingness to try and fail all reinforced one another. Once a critical mass of chip makers, programmers, and investors gathered in one valley, the concentration became self-sustaining, and every later wave built on the last.

Why did IBM, the giant that legitimized the PC, end up losing it? IBM made the personal computer respectable and then watched others get rich from it. By choosing an open design built on Intel's chip and Microsoft's operating system, IBM invited competitors to build cheaper, compatible machines—and they did, by the millions, steadily eroding IBM's share of a market it had defined. When IBM tried to reassert control with proprietary designs later in the 1980s, customers and clone makers simply declined to follow. The lesson is bitter and instructive: IBM held the brand and the initial standard but not the two pieces that mattered most, the processor and the operating system, and whoever controls the essential standard controls the profits. In 2005, IBM sold its personal-computer business altogether.

Was the personal computer revolution good or bad for society? It was profoundly both, and any honest answer has to hold the two together. The personal computer and its descendants democratized creativity and information on a scale without precedent: anyone could write, calculate, design, publish, learn, and eventually connect with anyone else on Earth. It created immense wealth and whole new kinds of work. It also concentrated staggering power in a handful of companies, displaced countless jobs, eroded privacy, and—especially once the machines went online and into our pockets—brought new forms of distraction, isolation, and manipulation. The same tool that put a library in every home also put a slot machine in every palm. The technology itself is neutral; what it did to us depended, and still depends, on how we chose to use it.

Where does the revolution go from here? The story in this book ends around 2013, at the moment the personal computer stopped being the center of digital life and the smartphone took its place. But the revolution did not end—it dispersed. Its DNA is in every phone, every tablet, every watch and speaker and car that now carries a processor descended from the 4004. The dream that animated the whole enterprise, of a "bicycle for the mind" that amplifies human ability, has been realized more completely than its pioneers imagined, and it continues to unfold in artificial intelligence, in ubiquitous connectivity, and in machines yet to be built. The personal computer as a beige box on a desk may be fading. The personal computer as an idea has never been more alive.

Appendix V: Seeing the Revolution Today

The wonderful thing about this history is that so much of it survives, and much of it you can touch, or at least switch on. The machines in this book were made by the thousands or the millions, and enough have been preserved—in museums, in collectors' basements, and in the amber of software emulation—that the revolution is not only readable but visitable. This closing appendix is a guide for the curious reader who wants to go and see it, whether that means booking a flight or simply opening a browser tab.

The Computer History Museum, Mountain View, California. If you make only one pilgrimage, make it here, in the heart of Silicon Valley where much of the story happened. The Computer History Museum holds the deepest collection of computing artifacts in the world, from ancient calculating machines to a working reconstruction of Charles Babbage's Difference Engine to the actual hardware of the personal-computer age—Altairs, an Apple I, early Macintoshes, and much more. Its permanent exhibition, "Revolution," traces two thousand years of computing, and the museum has recorded hundreds of oral-history interviews with the pioneers, many freely available online. Even if you never visit in person, its website is one of the richest and most reliable resources on everything in this book.

The Smithsonian, Washington, D.C. The Smithsonian Institution's National Museum of American History preserves the artifacts where computing meets the broader American story. Here you can find the logbook page with the famous 1947 moth taped inside it, early transistors and integrated circuits, and machines that shaped the era. The Smithsonian's collections, much of them documented online, treat the computer not as a gadget but as a force that reshaped work, culture, and daily life—the same lens this book has tried to use.

The Science Museum, London. For readers in Britain or Europe, the Science Museum in London offers a magnificent view of computing's longer arc. Its collection includes portions of Babbage's nineteenth-century engines—the ancestors of the whole idea of a programmable machine—alongside galleries tracing electronic computing into the personal era. The museum's "Information Age" gallery sets the personal computer within the larger history of communication, from the telegraph to the mobile phone, a reminder that the machine on the desk was one chapter in a much older human effort to compute and connect.

The National Museum of Computing, Bletchley Park. On the grounds of Bletchley Park, where British codebreakers cracked German ciphers in the Second World War, sits The National Museum of Computing, a treasure for anyone who wants to see history running rather than resting. It houses a working rebuild of Colossus, the pioneering wartime codebreaking machine, and the restored WITCH, one of the oldest working digital computers in the world, its relays and lamps clicking and glowing as they did in the 1950s. The museum also keeps a hands-on gallery of home and personal computers from the 1970s and 1980s—the very British machines, Sinclairs and Acorns and Amstrads, that filled the bedrooms of a generation. To watch these machines actually operate is to feel the distance the revolution traveled.

The legacy of Living Computers, Seattle. For a decade, Microsoft co-founder Paul Allen's Living Computers: Museum + Labs in Seattle offered something almost no other institution did: a chance not merely to look at historic computers but to sit down and use them, from room-filling mainframes to the home machines of the 1980s, many restored to full working order and connected for visitors to try. The museum closed to the public during the pandemic and, after Allen's death, did not reopen; its remarkable collection was slated for dispersal. Its spirit—that old computers are best understood by touching them—lives on in the growing movement of "retrocomputing," and in the many enthusiasts who keep these machines alive.

The Internet Archive and the miracle of emulation. You do not, however, need a plane ticket to run a piece of history, because the most transformative museum of all is a website. The Internet Archive, at archive.org, has assembled an astonishing free collection of vintage software that runs directly in your web browser through the magic of emulation—programs that mimic old hardware faithfully enough that the original software believes it is running on a 1981 machine. Its Software Library includes thousands of classic MS-DOS programs and games, early Macintosh and Apple II titles, and the operating systems and applications this book has described. Click one, and a moment later WordStar or an early spreadsheet or a beloved game boots up in your browser exactly as it did decades ago, no vintage hardware required. It is the closest thing to a time machine that this history offers.

Running an Apple II or a DOS PC in your browser. For the specific machines at the center of this story, the experience is remarkably easy. Thanks to projects that recreate the Apple II entirely in web-browser code, you can visit a site, watch the familiar boot prompt appear, and type in BASIC just as a hobbyist did in 1978. The Internet Archive's MS-DOS collection does the same for the IBM PC world: choose a program, and an in-browser emulator loads it in seconds, letting you experience the command line, the early graphics, and the sound of software from the era. These emulators are not merely nostalgic toys; they are serious tools of preservation, ensuring that software written for machines that no longer exist can still be studied, played, and understood.

MAME and the preservationists. Behind much of this stands a decades-long volunteer effort to save computing's past from oblivion. MAME, which began as an arcade-game emulator and grew into a broad preservation project, painstakingly documents and recreates old hardware in software so that programs are not lost when the last physical machine finally dies. Alongside it, communities of hobbyists dump the contents of aging chips and disks, restore rotting hardware, and write the emulators that let the rest of us experience the results. Preservation of software is genuinely hard—magnetic disks decay, formats are forgotten, companies vanish—and we owe the survival of much of this heritage to unpaid enthusiasts who simply refused to let it disappear.

Reading the story in its own words. Beyond artifacts and emulators, the revolution left a vast written and filmed record you can explore from an armchair. The oral-history archives of the Computer History Museum let you hear the pioneers tell their own stories. Documentaries capture the personalities and the moments; contemporary magazines, many now scanned and searchable online, preserve the breathless excitement and the wild claims of the time. The "Further Reading" section of this book points to the finest narrative histories and memoirs. To read the participants' own accounts, with their disagreements and self-justifications intact, is to appreciate how uncertain and contingent it all felt while it was happening—how little anyone knew they were living through a revolution.

The revolution in your pocket. In the end, the most complete museum of the personal-computer revolution is the device you almost certainly have within arm's reach right now. Every smartphone is the direct descendant of the machines in this book, and it contains, in miniature and multiplied a millionfold, everything they pioneered: a microprocessor tracing its lineage to the Intel 4004; memory and storage that dwarf a warehouse of 1980s computers; a graphical interface born at Xerox PARC and perfected across decades; a network connection that fulfills the dreams of Licklider and Berners-Lee; and software built on ideas first worked out on Altairs and Apples and PCs. When you unlock your phone, you are holding the revolution's culmination, and using it exactly as its idealists once hoped ordinary people someday would. The bicycle for the mind is no longer a rare and expensive machine in a study. It is in a billion pockets, and the ride is only beginning.

Further Reading

- **Paul Freiberger and Michael Swaine,** *Fire in the Valley: The Making of the Personal Computer* — The foundational narrative history of the industry's birth, from the Altair through the early Apple and IBM years.
- **Steven Levy,** *Hackers: Heroes of the Computer Revolution* — The classic account of the hacker ethic, tracing the culture from MIT's labs to the Homebrew hobbyists and early game makers.
- **Walter Isaacson,** *The Innovators* — A sweeping group biography of the people who built the digital age, from Ada Lovelace to the founders of the internet.
- **Walter Isaacson,** *Steve Jobs* — The authorized biography, drawing on extensive interviews, of Apple's co-founder and his role across the personal-computer and post-PC eras.
- **Michael Hiltzik,** *Dealers of Lightning: Xerox PARC and the Dawn of the Computer Age* — The definitive history of the lab that invented the graphical interface and watched others profit from it.
- **Robert X. Cringely,** *Accidental Empires* — A witty, insider's account of how the personal-computer industry's fortunes were made, often by luck as much as genius.
- **Steve Wozniak with Gina Smith,** *iWoz* — Apple's en-

gineering genius tells, in his own voice, the story of designing the Apple I and Apple II.

- **James Wallace and Jim Erickson,** ***Hard Drive: Bill Gates and the Making of the Microsoft Empire*** — An early, thorough biography of Gates and the rise of Microsoft.
- **Jon Gertner,** ***The Idea Factory: Bell Labs and the Great Age of American Innovation*** — The story of the laboratory that produced the transistor and much of the science underlying modern computing.
- **Leslie Berlin,** ***Troublemakers: Silicon Valley's Coming of Age*** — A history of the people and companies that shaped Silicon Valley in the crucial 1970s and 1980s.
- **Katie Hafner and Matthew Lyon,** ***Where Wizards Stay Up Late: The Origins of the Internet*** — The authoritative account of how the ARPANET, ancestor of the internet, was built.
- **Computer History Museum (Mountain View, California)** — Extensive exhibits and oral-history interviews with the pioneers, a primary institutional source for this book.
- **Smithsonian Institution** — Its collections and the National Museum of American History document the machines and their inventors.
- **Encyclopaedia Britannica** — A reliable reference for dates, definitions, and biographical detail throughout the period.
- **Robert X. Cringely,** ***Triumph of the Nerds*** **(PBS documentary, 1996)** — A three-part film, rich with firsthand interviews, that dramatizes the rise of the personal computer.

A Note on Sources and Method

This is a work of popular history, and it makes no claim to be anything else. It does not rest on new archival discoveries or on interviews conducted by its author; it rests on the public record of the personal-computer age and on the labor of the reporters, historians, and participants who documented that age as it unfolded and in the decades since. Its ambition is synthesis rather than revelation: to gather a story that has been told in fragments—across corporate histories, engineering memoirs, magazine features, museum exhibits, and courtroom transcripts—and to braid those fragments into a single continuous narrative that an ordinary reader can follow from the vacuum tube to the smartphone. Where this book is good, the credit belongs to the writers and witnesses named in the Further Reading and drawn upon throughout; where it errs, the fault is its own.

The bedrock sources are of several kinds. First are the secondary histories written by people who covered the industry directly—Freiberger and Swaine, Levy, Hiltzik, Cringely, Wallace and Erickson, Berlin, Gertner, Hafner and Lyon—and the biographies, notably Isaacson's, that grew out of long access to the principals. Second are the machines and the magazines themselves: the actual computers, now preserved in museums, and the period press that announced them, above all *Popular Electronics*, whose January 1975 Altair cover began the story, along with *Byte*, the hobbyist and industry bible of the era, and the general-interest coverage in *Time* and elsewhere that marked the moments when computing broke into public consciousness. Third are the institutional archives, chief among them the Computer History Museum, whose oral-history program has recorded the pioneers speaking for themselves, and the Smithsonian, whose collections preserve the objects. Standard references such as *Encyclopaedia Britannica* were used to confirm dates, spellings, and definitions.

A history of this kind must reckon honestly with legend, because the personal computer has generated more than its share. Its founding stories have been told so often, and so fondly, that several have hardened into myth, and myths tend to smooth away exactly the accidents and rival claims that make history interesting. This book has tried to handle the famous ones with care rather than repeat them uncritically. The garage in which Apple was supposedly born, for instance, was a real place and a real workshop, but the tidy image of two young men conjuring a company from nothing in a suburban garage compresses and romanticizes a messier reality involving bedrooms, borrowed money, a third founder who left within weeks, and the crucial adult backing of Mike Markkula; where the record complicates the legend, the text says so. The story of Gary Kildall and CP/M—the tale that IBM came calling and Kildall was out flying his airplane, so the contract fell to Microsoft—has been repeated for decades as a parable of the deal that made Bill Gates rich and ruined Digital Research, and it is almost certainly too neat; the surviving accounts conflict, the participants remembered it differently, and this book presents it as a contested episode rather than settled fact. So too with the claim that "Jobs stole the GUI from Xerox": Apple's engineers did see the graphical interface at PARC in 1979, and it profoundly shaped the Lisa and Macintosh, but the reality involved a stock arrangement between the two companies, a great deal of independent Apple engineering, and a longer lineage running back to Engelbart—so the loaded verb "stole" is set aside in favor of the more accurate and more interesting truth.

A word is owed about numbers, because this book gives many and trusts few of them completely. Much of the story is well documented: machines were reviewed, lawsuits produced sworn testimony, and public companies filed audited accounts. But some of the most tempting figures are the least reliable. Early firms rose and collapsed too fast for careful bookkeeping; unit-sales claims were frequently marketing rather than measurement; and the private fortunes made and lost in the boom were often simply guessed at by outsiders. Where this book cites such quantities—the units a company sold in a month, the worth of a bundle of software, the speed at which a fortune was made—they are the best available estimates, and the text names them as estimates rather than dressing them as certainties. The same caution applies to precise dates for events that unfolded gradually, and to the attribution of inventions that, on close inspection, had many parents.

Finally, a note on scope and proportion. The narrative slows down where the drama and the documentation are richest—the hobbyist years, the founding of the great companies, the interface wars of the 1980s—and speeds up as it approaches the present. This is deliberate. The recent era, from the rise of the Web through the smartphone and the post-PC turn, is enormous, fast-moving, and not yet fully historical; it is summarized here in broad strokes rather than covered exhaustively, because the perspective that turns current events into settled history has not yet arrived, and because the deeper purpose of these closing chapters is to trace an arc rather than to catalog every device. Countless people, companies, and machines that deserve their own chapters appear here only briefly or not at all. That is the price of telling one coherent story instead of an encyclopedia, and readers who want more are urged toward the fuller accounts listed in the Further Reading, whose authors did the primary work on which this synthesis stands.

www.ingramcontent.com/pod-product-compliance
Lightning Source LLC
La Vergne TN
LVHW100132061126
851857LV00010B/60
* 9 7 9 8 2 3 5 3 4 9 2 4 7 *